DATE DUE

Childho   in

Also by Carolyn Steedman and published by
Rutgers University Press

Landscape for a Good Woman (1986)

Childhood, Culture and Class in Britain: Margaret McMillan, 1860–1931

CAROLYN STEEDMAN

Rutgers University Press
New Brunswick, New Jersey

States of America in cloth and
University Press, 1990

First published in the United Kingdom in paperback by
Virago Press, 1990

Library of Congress Cataloging-in-Publication Data

Steedman, Carolyn.
    Childhood, culture, and class in Britain : Margaret McMillan,
1860–1931 / Carolyn Steedman.
        p.   cm.
    Includes bibliographical references.
    ISBN 0-8135-1539-4 (cloth)   ISBN 0-8135-1540-8 (pbk.)
    1. McMillan, Margaret, 1860–1931.   2. Early childhood educators—
Great Britain—Biography.   3. Early childhood education—Great
Britain—History.   4. Educational sociology—Great Britain—History.
I. Title.
LB775.M3172S74   1990
372.41—dc20   89-29176
                                                             CIP

Manufactured in the United States of America

Contents

List of Plates

Acknowledgements

I would like to thank all the librarians and archivists in whose collections I have pursued Margaret McMillan over the last ten years. Special thanks are owed to David James, Archivist of the Bradford Record Office, for his continued interest in this project, and to Sheila Meredith, formerly Archivist of the former McMillan Collection at the Rachel McMillan College Library in Deptford – the only archive I know where they give you a cup of tea. For the tea, and continued sympathy, support and insight, my warmest thanks. Much of the research for this book was funded by a Nuffield Foundation Small Grant in the Social Sciences. I would like to express my gratitude to the Foundation for this support, and to Patricia Thomas, its Deputy Director, for her continuing belief that the work would be done, and this book finally written. The History Twenty One Foundation made me a grant for travelling expenses involved in archive research: I am extremely grateful for its help. As is the case for most of the work I have produced in the last five years, my time as a Fellow in the Sociological Research Unit of the University of London Institute of Education during 1984 was invaluable – for the time it gave me and, more important, for the confidence in this, and other projects, that the Fellowship embodied. I would like to express my gratitude to the Sociology Department of the Institute, and in particular to Basil Bernstein. Barbara Bloomfield was the best of research assistants, and wrote very funny letters from the front. For her work, and the letters, my thanks. It seems to me that writers do not come into possession of their own ideas, their own words, until those words have been read, and a reader can tell them what it is they have been saying. Raphael Samuel was my reader for this book: I am very grateful for his help.

Abbreviations

ILP	Independent Labour Party
NAC	National Administrative Council (of the ILP)
NSA	Nursery School Association
SDF	Social Democratic Federation
SLP	Socialist Labour Party
SSS	Socialist Sunday School
TUC	Trades Union Congress
WEA	Workers' Educational Association

In order to distinguish the two McMillan sisters I have occasionally had to refer to Rachel by her Christian name, whilst Margaret always retains the dignity of the appellation 'McMillan'. This has the unfortunate effect of infantalising and trivialising Rachel McMillan (this is within a well-established narrative tradition, as the reader will discover); but sometimes, sentences simply wouldn't have worked without this usage.

Merrie England: A Series of Letters to John Smith of Oldham – A Practical Working Man, 1894 . . .
Dear Mr Smith, I am sorry to hear that you look upon Socialism as a vile and senseless thing . . . Nevertheless, as you have good metal in you, and are very numerous, I mean to argue the point . . . Is human nature sweet and holy, and fruitful of good things? Yes. When it gets light and air and culture . . . The people need more than wages . . . They need culture . . . (Robert Blatchford, *Merrie England*, 1894, pp. 115, 149)

Nothing stands against *real* culture, because real culture gives not only strength but the highest form of it. And this supreme gift is the condition, not the *reward* of victory. The people have to get it *before they win*, not afterwards. (Margaret McMillan, 'How I Became a Socialist', *Labour Leader*, 11 July 1912)

'But how are you to give this culture,' asks Mrs Smith. (Margaret McMillan, *Early Childhood*, 1900, p. 59)

Childhood, Culture and Class in Britain

PART ONE

Introduction

IF Margaret McMillan (1860–1931) is remembered today, it is through a body of educational writing that celebrates her work in early childhood education, during and after the First World War. In this celebration, her time on the Bradford School Board between 1894 and 1902 is referred back to, and two central concerns, the feeding of schoolchildren and their medical inspection, are highlighted in a prefigurative way, so that these aspects of her work can be established as biographical items that explain later developments. It is the years after 1910, when she founded an open-air treatment centre and school in the slums of Deptford, that allow a series of biographies to present her as a prophet of childhood, pioneer of nursery education, and a modern Santa Barbara.

In this way, her first fifty years – her membership of the Independent Labour Party (ILP), her time as a socialist journalist and propagandist – are all neatly severed from her last twenty, the time she spent as prophetess, seer and saint. It is this division that has given a hagiographical shape to many retellings of McMillan's life story. Two influences on such retellings have been first, popular histories of childhood (in which, throughout the nineteenth century, kind people are seen to rescue children from factory, mine and physical deterioration, and events march towards the enlightened present of the schooled child); and second, conventional histories of education, which in the middle years of this century – the time when McMillan was established as a heroine of childhood rescue – frequently eschewed analysis of political and social structure as one of their central organising devices.[1]

The way therefore seems clear for the historian, and for the progress of this book. Any historical account of Margaret McMillan must restore to her a background that is rooted in culture and class. It must, for instance, make something of her birth in Westchester County, New York, the second daughter of a Scottish *émigré* family; of her father's death in 1865; of the return of a mother and two small daughters to Inverness, to a house of cold, lower-middle-class restriction – an expulsion from a garden of paradise and from a garden of childhood, and also a prefiguring of the garden in the slum that was the Deptford Centre, half a century later.

A new biographical account must find a proper place for the Highland Clearances, their reverberation and consolidation in both myth and political organisation in the Highland capital during the 1860s and 1870s. It must place the working life of two lower-middle-class young women – Margaret and her sister Rachel – in some perspective; must acknowledge that McMillan was unusually well educated for a girl from her background, having been sent to Germany and Switzerland to train as a finishing governess. It must speculate reasonably on the years she spent governessing in the English shires – speculation that will involve arguing that the fiction she produced for the labour press in the 1890s constitutes some evidence of this period, which is otherwise quite lost to historical view. It must place McMillan's 'conversion' to socialism within the trajectory of British ethical socialism in this period, in a way that both confirms existing analyses of it as a politics, and at the same time provides new insight into the uses made of it by individuals.

It must say what being recruited to the ILP in 1893, moving to Bradford to teach a course of adult education in the Labour Institute there, and being elected to three School Boards in that city all suggest about the possibilities for women's economic and political activity in the 1890s. Using McMillan's involvement in municipal affairs and the national ILP, it must present an argument about the possible relationships of women to political structures at the end of the nineteenth century, and about the disenfranchisement of women at the municipal level by the 1902 Education Act, which removed the administration of elementary schools from the School Boards, to which women could be elected, to the county and district councils, to which they could not. It can present McMillan's move back to London in 1903 as a removal from the kind of direct political support and political structure that Bradford had provided, and suggest that a mapping of her socialism might locate a first deviation here.

The historian may then look at the female figure on the socialist platform, at the woman who possesses a charisma and calls forth an adulation that even Keir Hardie cannot command; the historian may speculate on the public lecture and the political speech as highly popular forms in the nineteenth century, and suggest that they may have provided a setting for a female rhetoric which an audience could interpret and understand in a manner quite lost to historical view.[2]

Such a biographical account must certainly discuss McMillan's role as the intellectual of the ILP, as translator of a wide range of physiological and psychological ideas into a coherent theory of childhood and socialism, with a redeemed and regenerated working-class childhood proclaimed the path to a new world of social relations. It can show how, through much of her fiction and her other journalism,

4

McMillan rewrote and reconstructed her own childhood, and found new places for it within her autobiography; so we might see that significant legacy of British Romanticism – the Wordsworthian child, the figure that represents a marriage between immanence and mortality and provides an aetiology of the self and a means of self-understanding – being used by one woman, in one particular historical context – and for a political purpose, to boot. As an interesting perspective on the history of ideas, this particular account can note that McMillan's theory of childhood formed the basis of ILP policy on the family and education, but that neither the ILP executive nor the membership knew, or cared to know, very much about the sources of their policy.

So, this book may ask: what do we understand of the status of a theory when those who hold to it do not know its provenance? And this account can be honest about the ideas that McMillan translated, formulated and transmitted to the ILP (and later to the Labour Party), can suggest that what changes people's minds, influences daily practice and even the inconsidered, half-understood theoretical framework of particular pieces of legislation are not the grand bodies of thought, the named philosophies, but the little and inconsistent theories of those who are considered mere ideologues: men like Henry George and Joseph Fels; women like Margaret McMillan. So the reader may finally view this book as a drama of contradiction, of ironic proportions, where what is used to frame social thought and social policy cannot be included in a history of it; and where what is rescued remains marginal unto the last.

All this can be done; but there is a problem of sources involved in doing it, for Margaret McMillan has controlled the production of biographies concerning her from beyond the grave. The official one, written by Albert Mansbridge in 1932 a year after her death, set the dominant narrative theme of later accounts. In *Margaret McMillan, Prophet and Pioneer* she was established as a pioneer of early childhood education, and Mansbridge dealt with what she did in the late 1880s and 1890s, her time as a socialist propagandist, under the heading of general work for progressive causes.[3]

Both D'Arcy Cresswell, in *Margaret McMillan, A Memoir* (1948), and George Lowndes, in *Margaret McMillan, The Children's Champion* (1960), followed Mansbridge's account, sometimes supplementing it with oral history or the written memories of those who had known her, and with McMillan's own published work.[4] Life stories must always be retold in response to the political and social climate in which biographers find themselves, and in the light of the new interpretations that the altered climate permits them to make, so there are important differences of emphasis in these three accounts (and in Elizabeth Bradburn's *Margaret McMillan: Framework and Expansion of Nursery Education* [1976]).[5] However, their consistent organising principle is a particular conception of childhood. In all three studies the child is understood as both a spiritual *and* a social being, adult attitudes towards children are seen as the measure of a society's progress in civilisation and spirituality, and an unusual, or extraordinary, and perhaps saintly woman is presented as their prophet and their saviour.

These four accounts, written between 1932 and 1976, all make constant reference back to Margaret McMillan's own *Life of Rachel McMillan*, published in 1927, four years before her death.[6] If biography is a peculiarly difficult form to objectify and analyse (difficult partly because of the ingenuousness with which it appears to follow the trajectory of a life), then *Life of Rachel McMillan* ought to be a case-study in its examination. Here, Margaret McMillan tells the story of her own life as she purports to tell that of her sister. Rachel McMillan, who was born in 1858 and died in 1917 after a professional but not a public life, became the focus of her sister's political work and spiritual life in the 1920s, though they appear not to have been at all close during their first forty years. The *Life* says remarkably little about Rachel (indeed, there turns out to be not much more to discover of her than what McMillan presented in 1927), and apart from the opening chapter, which offers a classic late-nineteenth-century 'childhood', it presents itself far more as a memoir of socialism and social movements at the turn of the century than as a biography.[7] It is still used as a historical account of late-nineteenth-century socialism, of the early days of the ILP, and of the tremulous excitement that the party's vision of the new life brought to its adherents.[8] This is an appropriate use, for although there are some major omissions in both the overt and the covert biographies the book contains, the political history that is presented in *Life of Rachel McMillan* is generally verifiable from other sources. However, so thorough has been the confusion between the two sisters (a confusion that seems to have been planned by Margaret McMillan) that they are mistaken for each other in a wide range of educational and other writing.[9]

There is no major collection of McMillan papers, and the archive sources that do exist serve only to highlight isolated episodes in her life.[10] Mansbridge borrowed a good deal of material from her contemporaries in 1931–32, when he worked on the official biography. He transcribed letters, returned the originals, and perhaps ignored or even suppressed some of the information he was given.[11] Thus was the core of the McMillan Collection in the Rachel McMillan College Library in Deptford formed, as any archive collection is, by the presuppositions, interests and courtesies of its collector. Its silences, and the gaps within it that are repeated in Mansbridge's *Prophet and*

Pioneer, serve to return the reader and the researcher again and again to McMillan's own *Life of Rachel McMillan*.

Just as the McMillan Collection started by Mansbridge is no transparent repository of historical information, so the *Life of Rachel McMillan* is not an innocent secondary source. It was written ten years after Rachel's death, when its author was sixty-seven, and many contemporaries and later commentators would argue that she had lost the socialist conviction of her youth and middle years. Throughout the 1920s McMillan was immersed in the nursery school movement, which sought to unite diverse political opinion in the pursuit of the social good that early childhood education, especially the education of young working-class children, seemed to promise.[12] One of the most important factors in McMillan's life at the time of writing was her friendship with the Conservative MP Lady Astor, by whose beauty, glamour and political clout she was entranced – McMillan had always had a penchant for duchesses, a point which will be discussed below.[13] Nancy Astor, in her turn, relied to a considerable extent on McMillan's expertise and theoretical stance on childhood education in formulating her own nursery school campaign. The *Life* was completed two years before its author, veteran ILP-er and socialist agitator was to appear on Conservative platforms in Astor's Plymouth constituency during a by-election in 1929. Indeed, McMillan dedicates the ostensible biography of her sister's life to Lady Astor, with the aphorism that echoes through McMillan's many letters to her: '*Party* is not enough'.[14]

There was this grand apostasy of 1929; there were also smaller shifts in political perception during the war years and the 1920s. A condemnation of the behaviour of working-class mothers, especially in their linguistic interaction with their children, is noted throughout the following pages as an element in McMillan's writing after about 1910. In the 1920s she started to discuss drink as a factor contributing to working-class poverty, whilst in the 1890s she had been scathing about those who produced 'good old drink' as the explanation for working-class degradation.[15] (But as she expressed most temperance piety to the great temperance advocate, Nancy Astor, the recipient of her opinions probably has to be taken into account here.) It is simple at one level, this desertion of an older politics: McMillan had a political theory and a practical plan for a socialist future: she wanted things to *happen*. After 1902, when legislation ensured that women were no longer able to take part in the local political system that supported the operation of the School Boards, she sought out the help of those with political influence (like Robert Morant at the Board of Education between 1905 and 1912) and those with money and power (like Nancy Astor in the 1920s). Forced to operate by persuading them, she too was persuaded.

But this simple explanation immediately provokes the difficult question: do sets of ideas, bodies of theory, chains of reasoning, political languages, carry with them *necessary* political understandings?[16] Was there something within the very intellectual construction of the socialism McMillan espoused between 1890 and 1910 that led her inevitably along the road to Liberal reformism and welfare philanthropism? This book will suggest that the *subjects* of a political theory have to be considered in answering this question: that the relationships in labour, and in affective life, between the theorist and campaigner and the social group for which she works are as important as the structure of the theory itself. In this case, the political subjects were *children*, and it is my general argument that this is the crucial factor in the telling of McMillan's political life story.

The children – McMillan's chosen sphere of political action – matter also for a more general history of the labour movement and the Labour Party in Britain, a history that stretches beyond the borders of this book. McMillan is *there*, implicated, in a history that shows the Labour Party moving from its position as representative of single constituencies of work to become the party that saw itself as the people's friend, and harbinger of the good life – for all, but particularly for the unskilled labouring poor. In fact, McMillan is more than just *there*: she is actually more important for an understanding of the Labour Party in the twentieth century than the more conventionally itemised 'labour people' – more important, in this way, than Ramsay MacDonald, Victor Grayson, Arthur Henderson . . .[17]

Between 1910 and 1930 the Labour Party shifted its focus of interest from the industrial conditions of the skilled and unionised working class to the conditions of working-class life in general. This working-class life was perceived, for the main part, by women. Its condition of existence was analysed, defined and documented in terms of health, infant mortality and welfare, maternity care and the lack of it, housing, the water supply, nutrition, education (particularly nursery schooling) . . . These issues were women's issues, and it was women who formulated them, spoke about them, wrote about them. It was women who performed the political task of using them to create an imaginative perception of the lives these conditions measured out, a sympathy for the people living under them, in the minds of skilled, respectable, traditional, card-carrying Labour Party members. It was women, using new political tactics like door-to-door canvassing, who took these issues back to the people who suffered the conditions they described, and turned wastelands of despair into Labour fortresses.

For the Labour women who were politically active in the 1920s and after McMillan's death, she had outlined an arena for the expression of an idealism – in the care, nurture, and education of young children.

8

But she did more: her work on the Bradford School Boards in the 1890s foreshadowed a much wider development in the 1920s: what McMillan did in that city, thousands of Labour women were to do in the decades after the First World War. In Bradford in the 1890s, McMillan defined a constituency in need of rescue; she promoted sympathy on its behalf; she campaigned personally (using much emotion, but even more hard-nosed 'scientific' evidence), and with an extraordinary political nous, for 'the slum child'. Her political progress in Bradford and (in a different key, but no less important) in Deptford described a politics coming into being, a politics whose legislative and structural flowering we may see in the establishment of the National Health Service in 1948. So by following McMillan's political trajectory we can move away from the administrative history that has attempted to describe the 'coming' of the welfare state and look rather in detail at one of the molecular changes of the periods 1893–1902 and 1910–20, which was eventually to bring a new politics into being in the years between the two world wars.

The political and emotional circumstances in which McMillan wrote the *Life of Rachel McMillan* in 1927 have been noted; but when that is done, it has to be said that it is remarkable how much faith the narrative keeps with the vision and convictions of the 1890s – when, for instance, looking out over the crowds of holidaying workers in Shipley Glen, McMillan (or Rachel: given the central device that organises the biography, she and her sister are interchangeable here)

> seemed to read the history of the working people of the North in this spectacle, to understand their struggles, their victories and defeats of a century, and to see clearly how we stood at a parting of the ways, growing slowly into a dim but new consciousness. [18]

However, the personal circumstances of the production of *Life of Rachel McMillan* do not entirely explain its particularities as a biographical/autobiographical text. There is also a historical and literary context to its writing that needs to be taken into account. Kathryn Dodd has drawn our attention to the large number of women's biographies and autobiographies published in the 1920s and 1930s. Dodd argues that as part of a general assessment of the First World War, and an attempt to find significance and meaning in the pre-war years, many women appropriated the masculine forms of biography and autobiography. We should also note Dodd's discussion of Ray Strachey's *The Cause*, which was published in 1928, a year after McMillan's *Life of Rachel McMillan*.

In *The Cause*, Dodd sees a narrative constructed within the framework of Baldwinite constitutionalism, with Strachey writing a history of British feminism and the suffrage movement that ignored militancy in a celebration of the achievements of exceptional middle-class women, who were understood to have both opened up the professions and to have succoured and uplifted the needy – notably working-class women and helpless children. It was indeed Baldwin's Conservative government that granted the universal franchise that gave all women the vote in 1928 – not in capitulation to feminist demands, but as a matter of constitutionalist inevitability. In this way, Dodd argues, *The Cause* can be interpreted as a kind of narrative analogy to this political understanding, where 'women's emancipation becomes . . . an index of progressive achievement, which both sexes can applaud.'[19]

So it is suggested that this classic text of feminist history is a 'celebration of the history and achievements of progressive liberalism', written as a kind of endorsement of Baldwinite constitutionalism; and something of this kind of rewriting is at work in Margaret McMillan's telling of her own life and political times in *Life of Rachel McMillan*, where the care and succour of little children, which had in fact at the time been carried out as a matter of political conviction and political policy, becomes the regenerative motor of the world and of the history McMillan recounts – a progressive cause that lay beyond 'politics'.

There were other autobiographical moments in McMillan's career as a writer, for as a leading member of the ILP she was frequently interviewed about her life, or asked to write a version of it. Through these journalistic accounts, which reached their apotheosis in the *Life*, we can see their author rewriting and reconstructing her own child-hood, and finding new places for it within her autobiography. One particular legacy of early-nineteenth-century Romanticism within Western societies has been the establishment of the idea of childhood as an arena of self-knowledge lying within each individual.[20] The specificity of McMillan's quest for her own lost childhood (a quest that has been seen as one of the organising principles of the life story as told in Europe since the late eighteenth century)[21] is that she reorganised and reasserted her own past not just in autobiographical accounts, but also within the life of others: poor children, working-class children, the 'children of the dark area'.[22] The body of theory that arose from McMillan's work with children was adopted as both ILP and Labour Party policy. Some of it also entered the statute books in the form of various enactments between 1906 and 1920 in the development of state policy on childhood, so delineating the meaning of children and of childhood within a particular cultural context has to be an important aspect of this book.

The modern study of biography as a literary and historical form has highlighted its tendency to elevate the life of an exceptional individual above the life of the unexceptional – that is, the way in which 'political movements, social and intellectual groupings, the aspirations of whole social classes, become the backcloth for the presentation of the principal actor'.[23] In the following pages I have taken a different approach, and allow McMillan's life story (only briefly presented) and her work to raise certain questions about the history of British social and political culture.[24] These questions involve the way in which working-class childhood was 'discovered' and used politically in this period; the role of women in local and national political life between 1890 and 1920; the development of social theory and social policy through the contrasting of country and city; the way in which the ILP – and, more broadly, the socialist movement of the 1890s and 1900s – drew on various bodies of thought that allowed them to make connections between material life and cultural life. I hope to show that McMillan's extraordinary output of journalism, and the romantic fiction that she published in the labour press throughout the 1890s, constitute a specifically *historical* evidence of this process – one, however, that demands of historians that they read texts as historical entities in their own right, rather than as the transparent illuminator of anterior historical reality.

This book was written out of a reflection on lacunae in present political times, where some forms of socialism no longer hold that our common and material life might be made better. It is about a climate of political thought in the past in which (in spite of all the paternalism and antagonisms of class relations involved) it was believed that the small people, living in little houses and going to bed at night, could have a better time of it; and that an improvement in the material conditions of life was the prerequisite for new ways of seeing and understanding. 'Our mental life is conditioned by the material; who can separate these?' wrote Margaret McMillan in 1897.[25] Once, too, a reasonable socialism had to have a theoretical place within it for the working class and (in some forms of socialism) for working-class experience. That not all working-class people were serious trade unionists prepared to spend time in study groups discussing the world's alteration, that many of them were unskilled, and un-unionised, and not serious about anything at all, caused leaders like Keir Hardie much anguish, for how could their 'horrible mode of life' (as one Bradford ILP-er called it) provide any kind of pattern for any kind of reasonable future? It is a claim of this book that McMillan attempted to deal with this dilemma, and provided a coherent and theoretical response to the problem for socialism that the unskilled working class represented.

A history of late-nineteenth-century British socialism is the framework for this biographical study, and the non-specialist reader may find it useful to bear in mind that the ILP was formed in 1893 out of a coalition of socialists and West Yorkshire trade unionists. It adopted a specifically socialist policy, with the common ownership of land and the collective ownership of the means of production and exchange as its aims. Yet it was always (and still is) contrasted in approach, appeal and theoretical underpinning with the harder, more secular, more scientific Social Democratic Federation (SDF), which was formed earlier, and occupied an avowedly Marxist political position. It is useful as well to remember that in 1900 the Labour Representation Committee came into being to act as a distinct Labour Group in Parliament consisting of trade unionists, ILP and SDF Members, with the brief of promoting legislation in the direct interests of labour. In the 1906 general election twenty-nine Labour MPs were returned, and the Labour Party formally constituted itself.

Two terms from the 1890s, 'ethical socialism' and 'the religion of socialism', are still used to describe the broad humanitarian appeal of the ILP, the process by which a sudden revelation of social evil and social injustice might convert the individual to the recognition that society was ordered unfairly, and to seeing 'the necessity for doing something amidst it all'.[26] One of the points of writing this current account of Margaret McMillan's political work is to subject to scrutiny these contemporary understandings and historical accounts of them.

The 'conversion' to socialism, made out of class guilt and the desire to improve the common lot of the common people, and the project of changing the social order according to socialist principle, can both be approached through the idea of 'culture', as it was used in political writing of the period. When men like Robert Blatchford, editor of the socialist weekly the *Clarion*, and Keir Hardie, as president of the ILP between 1900 and 1903, wrote of culture and the need of the working class for culture (as in one of the epigraphs to this book), they seemed to speak within the understanding established by Matthew Arnold, and to follow the whole project of intellectual, spiritual and aesthetic development outlined in the writing of John Ruskin. The project of awakening the working class to beauty, harmony and learning was a recognition of a profound spiritual need and, at the same time – especially in Keir Hardie's understanding – a possible means of bringing the dangerous and debilitated unskilled labouring poor into the fold of civilisation and class politics.[27]

Much of McMillan's work for and with poor children was to involve literally cleaning them up, and pouring clean air into the foul-smelling schoolrooms that entrapped them. Yet the visceral revulsion from the circumstances of working-class life shown by other members of the ILP was a rare eruption rather than a consistent theme of her writing – only twice, to my knowledge, discussed publicly.[28] Indeed, it seems that

McMillan made conscious efforts to confront her dislike of dirt and odour, and to deal with it by turning the dislike into a form of analysis. But to suggest this possible reaction on McMillan's part also raises other questions, which are forced again and again by the kind of work she undertook on behalf of the working class – particularly the point made by Raymond Williams, in discussing the Bloomsbury Group of the 1920s and 1930s and its relationship with working people. Here, it is argued, in these writers' depiction of working-class life, behind the impulse of social sympathy, lay all the old lines of social demarcation and class condescension. Did Margaret McMillan's work, and the writing in which she presented this life to a variety of audiences, operate in this way, as a similar

> formulation of a particular social position, in which a faction of an upper class, breaking from its dominant majority, relates to a lower class as a matter of conscience: not in solidarity, nor in affirmation but . . . against the cruelty and stupidity of the system and towards its otherwise helpless victims.[29]

The analogy cannot, of course, be made a perfect fit, for McMillan – as a woman with lower-middle-class origins – was not a member of 'a dominant majority'. However, the 'religion of socialism', its political vocabulary and the structures of sympathy and feeling that it permitted, could be said to have provided her (and other men and women too) with a project for a life, which was to abandon it for the sake of 'the people' and the uplifting of them. It is possible to argue as well (indeed, it is one of the arguments of this book) that through the figure of the utterly helpless – that is, the little child – McMillan was able to find herself as a more complete rescuer and saviour. But she saw that child (the figure of that child: in this book, children are both real children, living in time and space and material circumstances, and also figures, tropes, images, symbols) as a possible means of bringing the 'culture' that Blatchford and Hardie wrote about to the people, particularly to parents belonging to the unskilled labouring poor. Margaret McMillan's work and writing will allow us to examine this most complicated historical concept – the idea of a culture – in more detail: to discover, perhaps, in the close attention she paid to child development in her writing and her work, the alignment of a late-nineteenth-century understanding of culture with an older one: of the actual material improvement and cultivation of human beings, of bodies and minds in society.

PART TWO

Was it possible that the children of the working class, however fortunate, however plucky, could hold their own later with those who in the formative years drank deep and long of every fountain of life? No. It's impossible. Below every strike, concealed behind legislation of every order, there is this fact – the higher nutrition of the favoured few as compared with the balked childhood of the majority. Nothing evens up this gross injustice . . . But suppose that agencies were brought into existence that would not only lengthen the period of working-class children's education, but would enrich and refine the nervous system in the formative period – *what then*? Why then everything would be changed. The old hopeless, brutal, tragic and always *short* kind of industrial warfare would cease. Labour would have other advantages than mere mass or numbers. It would not stand cumbrous and helpless, like an antediluvian monster before an armed gymnast. Nothing stands against *real* culture, because real culture gives not only strength but the highest form of it. And this supreme gift is the condition, *not the reward* of victory. The people have to get it *before they win*, not afterwards. (Margaret McMillan, 'How I Became a Socialist', *Labour Leader*, 11 July 1912)

1

'Rachel'

THE McMillan sisters spent their early childhood in the USA, in Westchester County, New York, where their parents, natives of Inverness-shire, had emigrated in 1858. Before this, James McMillan had made several journeys across the Atlantic, his motive for leaving Scotland being presented by his second daughter in 1927 as a practical questioning of 'the rights of landlordism and the semi-feudal conditions of the Highlanders in his day'.[1] On his last trip home, in 1858, he met and married Jean Cameron, and returned with her to the States. There, in 1859, a first daughter, named Rachel, was born to them. A second, Margaret, followed in 1860; and a third child, Elizabeth, who was to die before her fourth birthday, was born in either 1862 or 1863.

Both McMillan's account of her father, and Mansbridge's later one, are unrevealing of James McMillan's social background, though his daughter placed him firmly in the tradition of Highland resistance to 'Englishness', and highlighted the warring elements of Celtic Catholicism and Presbyterianism in his background.[2] He seems to have belonged, like the young woman he married, to the Scottish lower middle class. In the USA after 1860, a proportion of his income came from shareholding in a fibre company, though it is unclear from where he got the money for investment.

The young family lived in some style, on the banks of the Hudson River. A woman in her late sixties recalled the impressions made on her five-year-old self by a style of architecture, a slave-owning culture, a climate of warmth and freedom:

In these early memories climate plays a great part and my clear memories begin with the hot time. The wooden house is a mere shelter in summer with long wide-open windows that are like doors opening in the stoep. It seems less a home than a kind of roofed series of gateways opening on the wide world. Darkies come and go through the farther gateway of windows. Their black heads look out from the upper storey and peep from behind the outhouses, where they disport themselves even at midday. They live all around us, as well as under the roof . . . It is a very happy life. Our parents are modern and American in their ideas of how we shall be brought up. They impose no heedless restrictions on us . . . It is managed somehow, that we little ones, Elizabeth and I, believe that the world is a splendid place. There is war of course. We know that. It only means that we sing 'Tramp! Tramp! Tramp! The Boys are marching' . . . and stamp with all our might . . .[3]

The re-creation of Westchester County as a garden paradise of childhood was an important feature of the homage to the American Nancy Astor that *Life of Rachel McMillan* represented. But at the same time, McMillan uses these opening chapters of the *Life* to prefigure many of her later political projects. They are in the form of the *Jugenderinnerungen* – the autobiography of childhood and adolescence – with its timeless present tense, its sudden surprise of detail coming into view out of the haze of memory, and its careful attention to the relative size of things:

> We were going, my father and mother (two shadowy figures) and my sister Rachel, who was older than I, but little like me, to see a new house, which was to be our new home. The wide road, the tall trees, through which a golden light filters, and the tall figures are also near, like pictures held in one's hand, but the tiny figure of my sister is very dim. I cannot see her at all, save as a little grey figure, moving near me, voiceless, and draped in shadows . . .[4]

In these memories, the Dutch settlers' house, built at the confluence of two rivers, represents and foreshadows the children's shelters in the open-air centre in Deptford, years later; America itself is a kindergarten, the future it holds in immanence signalled more precisely in the derelict hulk of the *Great Eastern*, which had been built at Deptford, lying abandoned on the shores of the Hudson, the little girls playing around it.[5]

In the summer of 1865, the remembered child was ejected from paradise. Three-year-old Elizabeth died, followed a few days later by the father of the family. Two months later, according to Margaret McMillan, her mother Jean took her remaining two little girls back home across the Atlantic, to her parents' home in Inverness.[6] It is possible to be much more precise about the class and cultural background of the McMillan sisters' maternal grandparents, and about the setting in which they grew to young womanhood. McMillan recorded that her grandfather, Robert Cameron, had been 'factor to a great landlord'; now, in retirement, he occupied a house in the Edinburgh Road, with members of the professional middle classes as neighbours.[7] The grandmother, Rachel Cameron, was described as a woman of formidable learning, able to read and write Gaelic, which was spoken in the household.[8] The grandparents worshipped in the

Free Church of Scotland, and the family history that Margaret McMillan outlined through her discussion of its religious affiliation suggests that the tradition of Scottish dissent, antagonism to the English ascendancy, and Robert Cameron's direct opposition to the Clearances, all shaped the family's sense of itself.[9]

This particular oppositional history, the tradition of radical religious dissent, was an important feature of the early ILP's creation of a public image with a radical inheritance.[10] Often, this particular 'Scottishness' fuelled a sentimental and marketable rhetoric, which McMillan was certainly to use, as we shall see, in her propaganda work for the Party and in her journalism.[11] Scotland, then, evoked a radical inheritance; but in the *Life* it was also the romantic place of true origin, depicted by McMillan before the American paradise in a lengthy passage about Glen Urquhart, her father's birthplace – a valley which, as she reported, she had visited only once in her lifetime:

> The country is of surpassing beauty. Glen Urquhart . . . is far up the loch. It has a mysterious, romantic loveliness, such as is not often seen or imagined outside the World of Dreams. The dark hills stand round in mystic silence, as if listening, and this peculiar listening silence is felt, too, in the valleys and along the banks of the dark clear loch. The castle looks over the waters, in which its roofless towers are clearly reflected. Little homesteads are tucked away, for the most part, in clefts of the hills, but nothing breaks the strange brooding stillness over the glen. Only on sabbath days a great many people start to life, as it seems, and walk along the quiet hill-paths and roads in sabbath clothes, holding Bibles and saluting one another, as they meet or pass, in quiet tones, as if they still felt and understood the hush of the hills and the water.[12]

The culture of decency and Presbyterian earnestness, here evoked in both historical and romantic terms, evidently presented the McMillan children with something of a shock. McMillan recalled how in Inverness, in 1865, 'a great stillness came into our lives. Hitherto we had been the objects of quiet but intense interest and solicitude. Now, we have no claims . . .'[13] The grown woman remembered how, in the house in Edinburgh Road, 'our mother . . . passed into shadow. It was as if she had done something wrong in becoming a widow . . . We were conscious that the old days of privileged love were over.'[14]

Jean Cameron's position as a young and dependent woman with two small children to bring up fuelled one family antagonism that lasted half a century. When Mansbridge quoted the passage above in his 1932 biography he received a letter from a Cameron relative, saying:

> I don't like page 6 of your Margaret McMillan book 'we have no claim' & that about my grandparents . . . I was left in the

same predicament with two little girls and a posthumous son but didn't burden my family. If lonely they feathered their nest all right . . . .[15]

The children were expensively educated, coached privately in the accomplishments of middle-class girlhood, as well as attending Inverness High School and Inverness Academy. McMillan was ambivalent about the myths of Scottish education that she used in describing the sisters' schooling.[16] The mixing of social classes in the schoolroom was applauded; so was a system of instruction in which the transmission of *knowledge* to the child was emphasised rather than the development of an individual, an education in which the teachers were 'university men'.[17] 'They may have talked – they often did talk – systematically, over our heads', wrote McMillan:

> But at that time and in that place children were expected to learn and listen to a great deal of talk that *was* over their heads. They learned things they did not understand as well as things they must grasp and know . . . The lessons were often given with enthusiasm, for the teacher loved the subject-matter even if . . . he cared little for the children . . . In those days there was little child study, but there was scholarship; and this was an advantage for the child in some ways. People did not study him, but he was allowed to study.[18]

She recalled the difficult reading matter of that Presbyterian childhood: an insistence on the irrelevance of a special literature for children was to remain a consistent feature of her educational advice to ILP and other socialist parents in later years.[19]

At the same time as it praised, *Life of Rachel McMillan* showed a revulsion against the physical setting to this austere education, a revulsion that was to surface again and again in the Bradford classrooms that she visited in the 1890s. McMillan recalled 'dirty walls, greasy slates, no hot water and no care of the physical body' in Inverness classrooms during the 1860s and 1870s. 'Reform. Reform. That's what Scotland needs', she wrote to an old school friend in 1930. 'What memories of suffering and cruelty I have of my native land.'[20]

The education of the two girls was almost certainly designed to fit them for the genteel labour market. In 1874 Rachel left Inverness for Coventry, to spend three years teaching at the Ladies' College there, which was run by two distant female relatives.[21] In the extended family, there was a recently established acceptance of women working. McMillan described one of the cousins who opened the Coventry school as a young woman 'rather modern in outlook. She revolted in her middle twenties against the idleness and restraints of her life.'[22]

Rachel McMillan returned home to Inverness in the summer of

1877. Robert Cameron had died in April and his daughter, Jean McMillan, in July. Rachel was to spend the next eleven years of her life nursing her grandmother, and her sister described how she attempted to professionalise the traditional role of the dutiful middle-class daughter by attending lectures on sick-nursing and reading widely on the subject.[23]

'Teaching', McMillan remarked of her sister's earlier move to the school in Coventry, was 'the only occupation in which gentlewomen with a knowledge of music and languages could engage.'[24] In 1878 Margaret McMillan herself was sent to Frankfurt-am-Main to study music – 'presumably', as Mansbridge remarked, 'to fit herself for a post as finishing governess, which in 1879 she actually became, in Edinburgh'.[25] Then, in 1881, she returned to Europe to work as a pupil-teacher in Geneva and Lausanne. This period of Margaret McMillan's life remains entirely hidden from view, though events in these schools were referred to in the autobiographical writing she produced before the *Life*, and some of the romantic fiction she published in the 1890s was set in continental finishing schools.

In 1883 she came home to a series of posts as a finishing governess in the English shires. These years are not discussed at all in *Life of Rachel McMillan*; in 1922 McMillan recalled that she 'could keep no situation and everyone thought I should be a failure'.[26] A situation with a rector's family in Ludlow, Shropshire, was the only one she ever specified, and that was held late in her governessing career, which lasted from 1883 to 1887.[27] Ludlow is notable as the setting for what McMillan came to call 'the moment', 'the real event', or 'the influence' – a spiritual occurrence that usually involved the absent Rachel. In the letter of 1922 quoted above, McMillan recalled Rachel – 'my angel' – sending Laurence Oliphant's books to her in Ludlow; and then, 'one night – well *it* came . . . the Invisible Powers'.[28] Five years later, writing the ostensible biography of her sister, the moment came to be described as belonging to Rachel, with McMillan reading about it in a garden at Les Grottes:

> I got a letter from Rachel which puzzled me. It described an experience of which I had no understanding and which I had no power to interpret. Something that had never happened to me – a sudden inrush of new consciousness. Later I learned that this thing had come to many, that it was no uncommon experience.[29]

In all the autobiographical accounts of the years represented here by the shifting 'moment' – the years 1877 to 1887 – Rachel appears much as she did in the opening passages of the *Life*: tiny and dim, someone whom Margaret cannot see 'save as a little grey figure . . . voiceless and draped in shadows . . .'[30] Rewritings of 'the moment' push Rachel further into the darkness;[31] but for McMillan herself they were part of the process of canonising her sister, and can be used as historical evidence of what actually happened in the 1870s and 1880s only with extreme caution.

The early episodes of McMillan's life (the account above takes us to 1887) are based almost entirely on her own published autobiographical writing, most of which was produced late in life, in order both to celebrate the departed Rachel and to fulfil the task of attributing the political work McMillan herself had done, and her achievements in child welfare, to her sister. In the story Margaret McMillan wanted to tell, Rachel was described as a significant narrative absence, an absence that served as a political and spiritual presence in her own life. We are caught here, then, between discussing Rachel as a literary figure, created out of McMillan's own project as a writer, and following the historical claim (which was also Margaret McMillan's own – the very point of the project that was *The Life of Rachel McMillan*) that Rachel was a formative influence on her, and played the larger role in the shaping of their political philosophy.

If *Life of Rachel McMillan* were to be examined solely as a literary text, then McMillan's use of the figure of her sister to tell her own story would have to be seen as a romantic search for the other self, with Rachel operating as a shade of this self, a shade to whom McMillan's own motive, intention and action were attributed. Following this line of thought, the reader would note as well a recurrent theme in McMillan's story, wherever and whenever it was told, by which political revelation and understanding were consistently attributed to other women: to an American girl in the school at Lausanne (who in other accounts is described as Russian), much later in life to Nancy Astor, and to many others. There was, for instance, a romantic story that was still circulating in Bradford in the 1950s, when an eighty-three-year-old former part-timer, Charlie Hunt, described how McMillan was the

> adopted daughter of [a] Lady Eveline and she sent her to berlin [sic] to learn music [where] a Russian Countess would be as a mother to her . . . This Russian countess was a Socialist . . . she began to talk about her work and Socialism to Miss Mcmillan [sic] and she converted Margaret to believe in Socialism . . . after her education she went back to Scotland . . . of course the Lady who had adopted her told her she would have to give up Socialism, and leave her, and cease to be her heires [sic].[32]

Having read these many fictions, the reader would then note McMillan's descriptive devices, that formulate Rachel as the Romantic girl-child of post-Wordsworthian sensibility.[33] From the moment of birth Rachel is portrayed as 'very frail'. McMillan reiterated this fragility, though (as in the following passage) she was quite aware that it was a matter of reconstruction rather than memory:

> Her little face was pale and overcast by suffering, for her first five years were marred by ill-health. Her fair hair fell in heavy curls on her forehead; her brow was nearly always shadowed by a frown, but a frown that suggested pain, not anger; and from under it, dark grey eyes looked forth with a kind of wistful and very puzzled expression, altogether overborne by a patience strange to see in one so young. I did not notice all this, of course; at that time I observed nothing, but I had a consciousness of Rachel as a being who was troubled . . .[34]

In the summer of 1865 a father and a sister die, but it is not those deaths that prompt Jean McMillan's recrossing of the Atlantic. Rather, in this narrative, it is Rachel's weakness and fragility that cause the journey to Inverness.

In the fictional and Romantic depiction of little-girlhood, the child has to die, weighed down by the preternatural sorrow she bears.[35] In fact, Rachel McMillan undertook an adolescence and young womanhood of arduous sick-room nursing, underwent (as we shall see) a rigorous training course in sanitary inspection whilst working full-time, and for some thirteen years, between 1896 and 1913, worked at an exhausting job that involved a good deal of travelling in rural Kent. Yet when she dies, in the pages of *Life of Rachel McMillan*, and within the confines of the character of child-heroine that has been created for her, it is the frail little girl who slips away into the dark.[36]

After 1874, when Rachel left Inverness for the school in Coventry, the sisters were evidently much apart.[37] They were to spend crucial periods together between 1874 and 1903, when they finally made a joint home; but for most of these thirty years McMillan lived at a great distance from her sister. In one of these periods apart, something happened to Rachel that has passed into the annals of late-nineteenth-century socialism in Britain, an event which, even if it did not occur, still exemplifies the moment of 'conversion' to socialism that was experienced by many in the 1880s and 1890s, and has been described in religious terms.[38]

Margaret McMillan described the way in which the intellectual climate of the Highland capital changed in the 1880s; she mentioned public speaking on the suffrage question as a typical 'echo of the great world' that reached Rachel as she went about her sick-room duties.[39] McMillan did not, however, discuss the revival of social thought and social consciousness in the Scottish churches that was certainly a new feature of cultural life in Inverness in the late 1870s and early 1880s.[40] Rather, she told of her sister's reaction to a piece of sensationalist journalism:

> Then something broke down Rachel's self-restraint. Stead's *The Maiden Tribute* fell into her hands. If a bomb had fallen on the house, it could not have caused a greater upheaval. She was fully awakened now to the existence of a dark world that ringed her sheltered life.[41]

This must have happened some time after July 1885, when W.T. Stead's series of articles on child prostitution in London, which ran in the *Pall Mall Gazette* for the whole month, was published in pamphlet form.[42]

In these articles – usually seen as a model for 'that personalised form of muck-raking that has become a permanent feature of modern journalism'[43] – Stead set out to reveal the extent of child sexual abuse and child prostitution in England. By purchasing a child from her mother and transporting her to France he tried to demonstrate the existence of a traffic in young English girls to continental brothels. The series included many graphic accounts of child rape, of little girls drugged, bound, and terrorised into sexual acts. *The Maiden Tribute* still operates as a moving and shocking piece of writing, one that produces strong reactions of horror and excitement in its readers.

In historical terms, we need to see Stead's crusade falling within a general theory of childhood in the mid-Victorian years, and as a component of a social purity movement, the stated intention of which was to change social attitudes about sex.[44] A very confused set of understandings of childhood operated within this movement for social purity. Female sexuality – including the sexuality of little girls – was viewed as both more meaningful and more dangerous than that of little boys. Confusion was extreme over the question of where working-class girls were to be placed on the dividing line between childhood and adulthood, for the work of such children was approved of as part of their class status, but at the same time their labour, and the movement in the public world that it necessitated, defined them as knowing and sexual in comparison with the purity of the little angel in the middle- or upper-class household.[45]

By emphasising Stead's *Maiden Tribute* as the formative text of her sister's socialism, Margaret McMillan exemplified the process that Stephen Yeo has described in 'The Religion of Socialism', whereby social pity across a great divide provided for sudden political allegiance – for a 'conversion' to socialism.[46] But mentioning this particular text also allowed McMillan to present the young Rachel as the ardent ideal-type of girl heroine. By association with the frail and terrified victims of Stead's account, Rachel's own innocence and frailty are reinforced. Indeed, the social mission of the young girl was to become a central theme of McMillan's later thought. It is to be found in the closing passages of *Life of Rachel McMillan* and in other writing from the 1920s, where the young girl's appointed social mission is defined as service to others:

> She is one with the armies Seen and Unseen, Known and Unknown, of the Saviours, the Deliverers. That is real life. Every girl wants it, and is looking for it, consciously or in the dark. My sister loved girls and understood them. She was herself, in youth, the ideal girl . . .[47]

A couple of years after this turbulent reading of *The Maiden Tribute*, at the age of twenty-eight, Rachel visited some cousins in Edinburgh and encountered there, in the capital, a wider range of ideas than had reached her in Inverness. The new socialist politics of the city emphasised the background from which Rachel had come, for the question of Highland land reform was the most important element in the emergence of socialist thought in Scotland in this period. It was a socialism structured by reaction to absentee landlordism (especially Highland clan chieftains absent from their lands), by a history of the Clearances, and more recently, in the mid 1880s, by a flowering of agrarian radicalism, with five crofters' candidates being returned to Parliament after the Third Reform Act of 1882.[48] All these factors were presented in *Life of Rachel McMillan* as a familiar family history, but were not detailed when McMillan described her sister's discovery of socialism in 1887. Neither did McMillan mention the formation of the Scottish Land Restoration League in 1884, nor the Scottish Land and Labour League, even though many of the people Rachel encountered in Edinburgh, those who influenced her, belonged to or moved through these organisations.

What McMillan did describe was the political and educational climate created in the capital by the local branch of the Socialist League, and the circle that gathered around John Glasse, rector of Greyfriar's Kirk and friend of William Morris, host to visiting socialist speakers, and tutor to the Socialist League study groups.[49] However, these absences in the political universe that McMillan depicted as a setting for her sister's socialist awakening may accurately reflect the political perspective of a sheltered young woman from a lower-middle-class Highland background.

It is possible that one of the cousins with whom Rachel stayed in Edinburgh was the McMillan who appears as a freelance socialist propagandist in the columns of the *Commonweal*, the newspaper of William Morris's Socialist League.[50] Certainly, she seems to have been provided with easy access to socialist circles in the city, which were fuelled that year by the miners' strike, local demonstrations of sympathy for them, and large public meetings against the Coercion Bill.[51] The Socialist League held study classes, and McMillan reported in 1927 that 'Rachel was a diligent attender at Socialist meetings', accompanied by the cousins' friend, John Gilray.[52] The reading group worked on *Das Kapital* in the early part of the year, using extracts translated from the German by John Glasse.[53]

Looking back on these fervent Edinburgh days of the late 1880s, John Gilray wrote of 'halls which often resounded to excited exposition of Socialist doctrine', and McMillan described Rachel: 'in dim halls, among keen-eyed, wild-haired, dusty comrades she sat, very still and attentive: her face alight with wonder' – though it really is not clear that McMillan was there to witness Rachel's progress towards socialist conviction. She writes Rachel's first meeting with John Gilray in dialogue, for instance, though on that occasion she certainly was not present.[54]

John Gilray, who was to become a close friend of both sisters in the 1890s, provided Rachel with copies of the *Commonweal*, with the SDF newspaper *Justice*, and with Peter Kropotkin's *Advice to the Young*. In a letter written in March 1887, Rachel described the effect they had on her:

> I am sending with this letter some of Mr Gilray's pamphlets etc. etc. on Socialism. I am very glad to have had them, and could never have collected them for myself or got anyone . . . to do so for me. I think that, very soon, when these teachings and ideas are better known, people generally will declare themselves Socialists. They are 'bound to do it', if they think at all. I instinctively felt they were good people, and now I believe they are the true disciples and followers of Christ . . . I further believe that most good men, who do good work, are, whether they know it or not, Socialists. It – Socialism – makes every noble expectation and hope realisable and opens up a sunlit track one can look joyfully along . . .[55]

In the 1927 account, McMillan was at pains to point out that the ideas Rachel encountered in Edinburgh in 1887 were 'not the source of her strength'. But however much the later telling demanded a denial of them, and however much the graphically described encounter between a sheltered young woman and socialism was dramatised and fictionalised in *Life of Rachel McMillan*, the description here provides confirmation of other accounts of conversion to socialism and remains an important delineation of McMillan's own socialist position, worked out a few years later, in London, in the early 1890s.

Rachel Cameron, the sisters' grandmother, died in July 1888. At the age of twenty-nine, Rachel McMillan set out on the path of paid employment for the first time in her life. It took her to London, though there is no record of how that move was decided on, nor how it was financed. 'She became', in her sister's words, '"helper" and junior superintendent in a working girls' home in Bloomsbury.'[56] The 1880s have been specified as a decade when careers opened up to middle- and lower-middle-class women for the first time, offering them a valid alternative to marriage. There was a large increase in the number of professional jobs available to them in the second half of the nineteenth century,[57] though we should probably not see Rachel McMillan's move to the Bloomsbury hostel as the undertaking of professional work in the modern sense. Like teaching or nursing, this form of labour involved a translation of a traditional female domestic responsibility to the public sphere, and in comparison with her sister, who had received a most extensive (and expensive) education as a finishing governess, Rachel was completely untrained. Margaret McMillan recalled that her sister was employed for £20 a year; she, on the other hand, almost certainly still working at the Rectory at Ludlow, would have commanded a salary of at least twice that amount.[58]

Four years later, after Margaret had joined Rachel in London, both sisters travelled to Bradford, both looking to the newly formed ILP and the socialist movement in general to provide them with a living. Margaret McMillan was initially employed to teach a course in adult education at the Labour Church in the city, and Rachel seems to have stayed with her until the end of 1893. In *Life of Rachel McMillan*, Rachel's decision to move back to London, to the Working Women's Hostel, and to take the Sanitary Institute's training in order to become a qualified inspector of nuisances, is presented as a matter of financial calculation, but also as curiously inconsequential:

'I heard Mr Ben Tillett at the Labour Church yesterday', she said. 'He thinks that the movement will have its first impulse here. He said he was glad we came here'. She went on to speak of our financial prospects. 'You won't earn anything. *I* must earn money.' We talked awhile, and then she said, 'I am going to train for a sanitary inspectorship'.[59]

The qualification as inspector of nuisances, which Rachel McMillan was to gain two years later, opened up a wide range of jobs to her in the fields of childcare and nursing. The training she received at the Sanitary Institute – in particular the theories of hygiene and mind–body relationship to which she was exposed – and the work she undertook between 1896 and 1913 as a teacher of hygiene, all influenced McMillan's evolution of a theory of childcare and child development.

The move was a rational one for a woman of Rachel's age (she was now thirty-five), for the field of women's work in the caring professions was expanding, and the hostel offered a place to live and study in central London. Both sisters were about to embark on careers that derived from a new professionalisation of childcare. Margaret McMillan's entry into this field was through municipal politics, for she was shortly to be elected to the Bradford School Board on the ILP ticket; but there are more similarities than differences between the two careers that converged in Deptford, in 1913, when Rachel gave up her job to work full-time at the Clinic and open-air school. Both had been made in 'the expanding field of childhood' which opened up 'significant opportunities for adults with literary and professional ambitions' from the 1870s onwards.[60]

Rachel McMillan went back to London to study for a 'Certificate of Competence in Sanitary Knowledge . . . to Discharge the Duties of an Inspector of Nuisances to a Local Authority'.[61] The duties of an inspector of nuisances, as defined by the Local Government Board, implied detailed knowledge of a wide range of Public Health Acts, model bylaws, and recent Sale of Food and Drugs legislation. Students working for the certificate dealt with food and water contamination and adulteration, and needed a grasp of principles of public health in the areas of drainage, disinfection and refuse disposal. What was taught was a body of knowledge that emphasised the community and interpersonal aspects of good health. Women who qualified in this way, as Rachel McMillan did in December 1895, were in great demand as health visitors (at least until 1908, when the Royal Sanitary Institute began to set exams in health visiting itself).[62] Health visiting had developed outside London from the 1860s onwards, and by the end of the century was in the process of transition from a privately funded and philanthropic service to a local authority provision. The title 'health visitor' was developed to describe women who visited mothers and newborn babies, though it covered a wide range of other practices. But whatever local arrangements might actually be, they involved instructing poor mothers in some kind of hygienic care of their children and household.[63] It would seem, then, that when Margaret McMillan recorded that on qualification Rachel took a post as 'a travelling teacher of hygiene under Kent County Council', it was her appointment as a health visitor she was describing.

Dates are a problem here, for McMillan says that her sister qualified early in 1895, whilst the records of the Sanitary Institute show that she did not gain her certificate until December of that year. McMillan also makes a brief reference to Rachel's going 'to Liverpool to organise work girls there', again (though the event is not dated) early in 1895. In fact, in late summer and autumn 1895 a Rachel McMillan is to be found as paid organising secretary to the Women's Industrial Council in Liverpool, undertaking most of her public speaking under the aegis of the local Fabian Society, usually on the topic of women's employment.[64] The detailed knowledge of health and factory legislation that this speaker displayed, her cognisance of the number and variety of women's trades and the environmental risks that their work involved (as well as the particular spelling of 'McMillan' – a point on which both sisters were most particular[65]) must suggest that like her sister, Rachel McMillan spent some time as a paid worker for the labour movement, in another northern city.

Her stay in Liverpool lasted from August to December, and she probably took up employment in Kent in the early part of 1896.[66] Kent did not at this time operate a health visiting scheme, and it seems most likely that someone described as a travelling teacher of hygiene between 1896 and 1913 would have been employed by the Kent Technical Education Committee, actually to teach classes in domestic hygiene in the rural areas. If this was Rachel McMillan's job, then it also involved the school-based instruction of girls in domestic science.[67]

In *Life of Rachel McMillan*, the 1890s are described as a time when Rachel's eyes were opened to 'the full tragedy of working-class life', a tragedy that was most clearly visible in the arrested development of working-class women: '"In many ways", said Rachel, "the cottage girls do not grow up. They remain always at the age of twelve or thirteen. The grown women do not merely write like children; in many ways they think like children."' Arrested development was a persistent theme of McMillan's own writing about working-class life. Here, in her description of Rachel's time in Kent, the perception is attributed to her sister 'that at every stage of childhood and youth, the tides must be taken that ensure later success'.[68]

Rachel lodged in Bromley, and it was here that Margaret McMillan joined her in 1902, after the end of her career in Bradford. From suburban Bromley, the capital seemed to have 'nothing to offer' in exchange for what had been forcibly given up. McMillan recalled a 'chill atmosphere', and a new loneliness, that she shared with her sister, a

> complete subsidal into a *new* isolation, more chill than that of the years before we joined the Independent Labour Party. The great revolt of the women, and the formation of the new Labour Party . . . all these movements swung past us like storms. We did not know how absolute our isolation was to be in the long years to come, but we knew almost from the first that we were alone. We went on alone.[69]

In writing her own story in *Life of Rachel McMillan*, McMillan described a complete isolation and darkness, so that she might present the emergence of the school Clinic, the camp school, and the whole enterprise in Deptford from 1910 onwards as a coming of the light. But in fact, *Life of Rachel McMillan* itself does not present this period as one of unrelieved gloom. The book recorded the conviviality of social life at Bromley; and Albert Mansbridge, in his 1932 biography, remembered meeting Prince Kropotkin, the Lansburys, Margaret Llewelyn Davies and the Countess of Warwick at tea parties in the McMillans' rooms at 51 Tweedy Road. 'In reality', he recalled, 'it was a salon.'[70]

It was here, in Bromley, that McMillan located the genesis of the health centre:

> One afternoon, on coming back from Deptford, Rachel sat with me in our room under the leads. We had resolved to take action, and as no party in London wanted us to stand for anything, this action would have to be entirely our own . . .
>
> 'Never mind,' said Rachel, sitting near the window . . . 'We intend to go forward.' A soft wind blew in, carrying with it a faint scent of flowers, and the peace of a cool autumn day brooded over everything. 'Let us draw up together the draft of a health centre,' she said, 'a place of healing in schools.'
>
> So we began to write, or rather to discuss, and we did not really agree. I wanted to make the whole scheme preventive: Bathrooms that should be classrooms; treatment for adenoids; new methods of speech-training and singing; training in the oral subjects to be given to all children . . . Rachel was not pleased with this scheme. She pointed out that most of the children we had seen were suffering from actual disease. 'Some can hardly breathe,' she said. 'Some are going blind. We have seen many septic mouths, I suppose, and crippled limbs. Your proposals won't deal with all that directly.'
>
> I was very vexed and she very troubled . . . We talked a long time . . . Suddenly . . . a wonderful smile broke over her face. 'Never mind,' she said, 'even if it isn't in the order of things as I see it, what does it matter? We shall leave it as you've written it.'
>
> I had written out what was in effect a scheme for a health centre, or school clinic . . .[71]

If the central device of the *Life* is the replacement of Margaret with Rachel, then this puzzling account was a means of both attributing the birth of the Deptford enterprise to Rachel (for this is what the story demands) whilst at the same time maintaining the historical truth, which was that it originated with McMillan herself. Indeed, her work as manager of Deptford schools took her into the area on a regular basis; her knowledge of continental systems of hygienic education informed her planning, and the development of the school clinic/open-air centre at Deptford was closely bound up with the campaign for medical inspection, which began to occupy McMillan from 1905 onwards.

The Deptford Clinic, and the school that developed out of it after 1910, brought Rachel from Bromley to Deptford in 1913, when she left her post in Kent to work full-time with her sister. She died in March 1917, much overworked by managing the Clinic and the camp schools, and nursing McMillan through a severe illness – all this through air-raids, the general dislocation of war and McMillan's frequent absences, as she toured the country in the campaign for nursery schools.[72] These years, between 1913 and 1917, are some of the most movingly described in *Life of Rachel McMillan*, elegiac in tone as they remember Rachel – 'my angel' – and the courage of the people of Deptford. The Clinic staff deserted, the people gossiped and maligned the Clinic; and

> in this deepening night of the soul, I saw Rachel. She was like a star looking from between dark clouds when all other lights have vanished. Again and again, the camps seemed doomed. Again and again she saved them. More than once I wondered what it was that she saw floating behind and between the wild streaming clouds and winds of that tormented time . . .[73]

It is hard not to read an extreme guilt in McMillan's reaction to her sister's death. The plain facts were that a woman in her fifties had been left to undertake the extremely arduous work of managing the school and the Clinic during a series of crises, with very little support from paid staff. McMillan's first publication after Rachel's death included a valedictory address to her sister that set the pattern for many future ones: 'So I go my darkened way alone. Dark it is, and empty the world, strangely dark . . . Oh my dearest! So I may meet you at the end of this dark road that I have to travel alone . . . so may I again hear your sweet voice breaking through the darkness.'[74] *The Camp School*, in which this passage appeared, is also notable for containing the first ascription to Rachel of the aphorism that McMillan made famous: '"educate every child as if he were your own"'.[75]

In the 1920s McMillan came to speak of the dead Rachel as a living presence, often in passages that are a wry mixture of mysticism and irony, as if she knew that evocation of a spiritual presence was the only form available for expressing great loss, loneliness and love.[76] However, her lyrical evocation of Rachel's presence moved quite away from irony when she wrote to Lady Astor – saying, for instance, in 1927:

. . . you see I *know* what it means – that hope is coming to the hopeless, the doomed children of the gutter and I know who is doing it all from unseen worlds. My radiant darling. She knows you well & loves you, under One who is not to be named lightly she lives and works . . . .'[77]

Her public pronouncements about her sister, particularly those she made to her students, also used the language of a lover in establishing Rachel as the girl-heroine of child-rescue:

> The base of my sister's character was neither morose nor tragic, but gay and ready for gladness – At the first easing of every strain she escaped into an almost child like [sic] and eager hope . . . Best of all it is to remember her in holiday times – in Kessara for example, walking knee deep in long grasses & bog myrtle on the steep slopes near Portree, laughing at me as I stood afraid to climb . . . Again I see her on board ship, in a storm off Lewis, the boat rocking up and down . . . every one [sic] else concerned or sick or angry because the Captain could not land us till morning, every one but Rachel, who loves adventure and does not know Fear – Rachel landing in the morning in a blast of sleet & rain, & turning a face all rosy in the wild gusts under her tam-o-shanter to the swuthering bare deer forest . . .[78]

A woman in her late sixties, surveying a long political life that she had enacted in a public space, appears to have used her dead sister to construct some kind of personal story for herself, a story in which there was motive and intention for what was done in the public world. This was achieved despite the paucity of information about Rachel's actual life, for it was neither Rachel's story nor Rachel's subjectivity that was figured in the pages of the book. Rather, it was Margaret's inside and outside that was written here; and the *point* of the life story that McMillan thus constructed was to explain a politics, to give it genesis, purpose, and meaning. The 'Rachel' of *Life of Rachel McMillan* was therefore a figure, a trope, whose function as a representation of privacy and subjectivity was to allow a story of political action and political achievement to be related.

2

Politics

IN McMillan's 1927 account her political path had its source in Scotland, in the loss of land and nationhood that a family history represented. In an autobiographical account written in 1912, she claimed that this loss was later confirmed and theorised:

> my awakening came I suppose, when I went to Switzerland to a school filled with girls from 17 to 22 years old. Some were Russians, and they were very astonishing. But the only girl of great ability I met was an American, who had lived mostly in Europe, and who gave me the most detailed account of the history of land-tenure in the Highlands, filling me with amazement by her knowledge of dates and places, though she has never been in Scotland at all. I came back much enlightened to my native land.[1]

She actually returned to England in 1883, not Scotland, and to the job of governess. The only record of the next five years is to be found in her character 'Mary Muse' and the relationship in fiction between a young, brilliant, misunderstood governess or companion and her obdurate, proud, ill-educated (and frequently High Church) employer.[2] What the real Margaret McMillan, as opposed to the fictional 'Mary Muse', produced towards the end of these lost years was the first in a series of six articles for the *Christian Socialist*, whose editor, W. H. Paul Campbell, provided the space for her first excursion into journalism. The publication of her first article brought her to London in 1889, to join Rachel.[3]

Paul Campbell edited the journal from 1887 to 1891, when it ceased publication, and his connections with the many socialist groupings of heterodox London mattered a good deal to McMillan's political education. The formation of the Christian Socialist Society in 1886 can be seen as a revival of the earlier mid-century movement, and its application of the principles of New Testament Christianity to social life,[4] but in fact this reawakening was a response to current events, using new political ideas and theories. Paul Campbell's own political position was worked out through a critique of current radical ideas, particularly the question of land reform raised by Henry George's *Progress and Poverty* (the same set of analyses that McMillan had encountered in the school in Lausanne), and through the political economy of Ruskin's later work.[5] In the four years of its existence his journal served as a clearing house for socialist ideas, and several of the people encountered by the McMillans in Edinburgh in 1887 wrote for it, including John Gilray and the young Yorkshire schoolteacher who was his fiancée, Barbara Fraser.

What prompted McMillan's first piece of published writing was the London dock strike of 1889, which lasted through the summer and early autumn. Her 'Sign of the Times' in October expressed a general middle-class reaction to the strike, a guilt provoked by revelation of the wretched lives led by the families of men subjected to casual employment. This was a sympathy across class divide that was reinforced, as some historians have noted, by relief at discovering that the barbarian hordes of dockers were, after all, respectable trade unionists.[6] McMillan commented on this impulse of sympathy, as well as taking part in it:

> Those who preached patience to the people as the sole remedy for the ills that oppress them must have felt considerable surprise recently, by the sudden manifestation of life in their own hearts, which was called forth by an act of spontaneous courage and decision on the part of the people. The English dock labourers struck, and the English public, in an uncontrollable impulse of sympathy, applauded.[7]

The dock strike was highly organised, and the socialist movement in London provided it with agitators, propagandists and educators. Paul Campbell's involvement in this world took the McMillan sisters down to the dock gates to sell literature – 'we addressed meetings even on the way home' – in what we must assume was the autumn and winter of 1889/90, in the aftermath of the strike and the triumph of New Unionism.[8]

Much of McMillan's later writing was to involve this kind of promotion and manipulation of social sympathy. In this first article, what was evident was her interest in the new relationship between the classes that socialism implied, and that the strike placed so dramatically on the political agenda. Compassion, felt across class barriers, outlined the inevitability of socialism, and the dawning of a new life through which she believed she saw a society actually living, in the winter of 1888/9. 'When the popular sympathy will have checked itself or have been checked,' she wrote,

> when the habit of cold calculation and criticism will have reasserted itself, when the nation, at the door of the sepulchre of the past, will again assume the wrappages of death for a little, we need not conclude that the sympathy given for a moment involuntarily

was but a caprice. Rather, it was evidence of a latent life . . .
growing daily stronger in the heart of the people . . .[9]

All six of McMillan's *Christian Socialist* articles were framed by a
critique of the established Church, and it is possible to read them
solely as an expression of her own recent experience in religious
households, and acquaintance with the social thought and attitudes of
the provincial squirearchy among whom she had worked. A few years
later she was to fictionalise the contempt for common life and the
emotional coldness in such households, in the romances she wrote for
the labour press. Now, the *Christian Socialist* pieces allowed her to
raise and explore questions that were to remain lifelong preoccupations: the material (particularly the bodily) life of working people;
and the ability of human beings to alter and change the conditions of
that material existence. The articles also show her encountering a
range of radical and socialist ideas, arguing along what we have come to
see as the familiar trajectories of Ruskin's aesthetic criticism employed
as social criticism, the debate over reform in relation to revolution, and
some ideas newly derived from Marxism about the value not only of
labour, but of working-class life itself. These were the sources for
McMillan's development of a socialist theory of material life.

When the *Christian Socialist* folded in 1891 and the Christian
Socialist Society itself disintegrated the year after, Campbell helped to
found the London Labour Church,[10] and it was under the Labour
Church banner, on the Dockers' Union platform, that Margaret
McMillan made her first appearance as socialist propagandist, on May
Day 1892.[11] In September of that year, Campbell also proposed her
membership of the Fabian Society, which, along with the Labour
Church, provided her with political platforms in the provinces.[12] By
early 1893 McMillan had gained a considerable reputation as a
propagandist and orator – and not just in London. The lecture circuit
and her journalism took her reputation to the North of England,
particularly to the Manchester area.[13] The move to Bradford in 1893
was not, then, that of a young, unknown woman. By the conventions of
her time she was in early middle age when she made it, and brought
with her a reputation for a charismatic and a highly effective platform
performance.

The ILP had been formed at a conference in Bradford in January
1893, out of a coalition between socialist and trade-union interests. The
Bradford trade-union movement had received widespread support
from various West Riding socialist groups during a prolonged strike at
the Manningham Mills, and the general election the previous year had
focused the attention of socialist activity in the North – in labour clubs,
Labour Churches, and the trade-union and labour press – on the

35

possibility of a national party of labour. McMillan's own account of the heterogeneous political and progressive forces that met in the Labour Institute in Peckover Street is often used as a classic description of the radical diversity that fed British socialism in these years. She remembered that 'the Social Democratic Federation were in force, and nearly all the members of the newly formed Independent Labour Party; Swedenborgians from Bingley and the valleys near, old Chartists, Secularists, and also inquirers and sympathisers . . .'.[14]

The considerable size and strength of the early ILP in Bradford was largely due to its trade-union base, for the Manningham Mill strikes of 1890–91 had won many unionists from Liberalism to the briefly lived Bradford Labour Union, which emerged in May 1891 to fight as an independent party for working-class representation in Parliament. By the end of 1892 the Labour Union had about 2,000 members, belonging to nineteen clubs scattered across the city. The political success of the Labour Union (it returned two representatives to the Town Council and one to the School Board during its brief existence) foreshadowed the early success of the ILP, though it was based largely on a membership that had been driven from the Liberal Party, rather than one that was attracted to socialism.[15] This conflict of trade-union interests and the social reform that was embodied in the ILP programme was to cause McMillan some political difficulty over the next few years.

The immediate goal of the new party that was formed in January 1893 was the election of independent labour representatives to Parliament. However, the policy adopted at the first conference included a programme of social reform, and a key feature of its approach was set out as the education of men and women into socialism, through the processes of propaganda.[16] McMillan moved, then, to a city that had given birth to a new national party and was one of its centres of influence, but was at the same time a local and regional centre, a political and geographical community that had provided for the growth of the new party out of regional circumstances.

The ILP was formed as a national party in January 1893 with a political programme directed along the parliamentary road, but it actually rose to political importance within specific localities and through municipal contests. Between 1893 and 1897 the national conferences of the Party ratified a programme based on socialist objectives: on the nationalisation of land, the collectivisation of the means of production and exchange, and the redistribution of income through taxation. Within this broad socialist framework specific struggles for reform were outlined, including a forty-eight hour week, the abolition of overtime, piecework and child labour, and social provision for the sick, the disabled, the old, and for widows and orphans.

Over the first five years of the new Party's existence, this basic programme was elaborated by a more detailed attention to education, to the whole question of child labour, and to the school-leaving age, which was the focus of the politics that emerged from the distinction between the schooled child and the working child. The way in which the working-class child was being changed from a component of the labour force into a subject of education was a historical development that exercised many more political constituencies than the ILP, and can be seen as one of the major political and social shifts of all Western societies in the late nineteenth century.[17] In the case of the ILP, the working out of a set of practical policies on the half-time system was the ground where two views of childhood were contested. The part-time labour of children, particularly in the textile trades of Lancashire and Yorkshire, brought the politics of rescue and child welfare into sharp conflict with trade-union principles and the pattern of working-class life, at both a national and a local level.[18]

Although a practical programme of reform was evolved, political power remained a distant prospect for the ILP, and it has been argued that the programme was never any more than an outline, a set of principles, with very little analytic effort being devoted to the question of how such reforms might be carried through.[19] Nevertheless, local politics did offer a space for the practical application of the programme, particularly where School Board and Board of Guardian elections were concerned, for here the franchise was broader than it was in parliamentary contests, with women ratepayers able both to vote and to stand for election.[20] The number of ILP representatives on local councils and boards rose steadily throughout the 1890s: by 1900 the Party had fifty-one members elected as Guardians and sixty-six representatives sitting on School Boards, the majority in the textile centres of Lancashire and Yorkshire. Bradford – 'Woolopolis' – was, as Keith Laybourn, the historian of the ILP in the city, has argued in his account of this period, one of the ILP's local success stories.[21]

Most histories of the local Party measure out the progress of municipal socialism in Bradford by discussing the conflict that existed between the 'coterie of trade unionists who led the ILP' and the socialists and radicals who joined and worked for the local Party.[22] Local businessmen, interested in the municipalisation of local services and social provision for the city's inhabitants, were prominent members of the Party and were often critical of the restricted horizons of trade-union socialism. Keith Laybourn finally attributes the failure of municipal socialism in the city to this conflict: to the way in which the local Party 'set its economic and social goals within a trade-union framework which was essentially democratic and evolutionary in approach'.[23]

The focus of this particular analysis, in which the local Party is seen to have failed in its objectives of building the socialist city, is on the election of ILP representatives to the Town Council. The majority of these ILP representatives between 1893 and 1902 were trade unionists, and municipal elections were consistently fought on trade-union issues. Particularly important here was the 'fair-contract' proposal, designed to bring about payment of trade-union rates to all contracted or sub-contracted workers employed by local administrative bodies.[24] The fair-contract question was involved in Guardian and School Board elections too, and McMillan dramatised and satirised the conflict between trade unionism and a broader municipal socialism in 1897, in describing her second School Board contest. In the Labour Club, where the ILP selection committee met, McMillan described how 'our chairman rose and cleared his throat':

> 'Comrades', said he, 'We are now on the eve of another School Board Election. Let us send two staunch men. You know what we want, and what we *will* have. We must pick men who know how to be *sound*. Men who know where the shoe pinches – men who are good trade unionists, and understand the ins and outs of contracts . . .' 'Dear comrades', said I, 'all this is excellent. It is *indeed*. But as it is a School Board election, perhaps a word or two on educational matters might not be altogether out of place'. I was in a cold sweat by this time, and our chairman knew it. He smiled indulgently at me, and looked as if he would make a joke presently . . . 'Is she all right on the Fair Contracts Question', cried the chairman . . .[25]

When the three Bradford School Boards to which McMillan was elected between 1894 and 1902 are examined, and the relationship of ILP educational policy to its political strategy in the city is taken into account, the analysis that McMillan offered in this wry dramatisation of 1897 is not really altered. The School Board was the least important of the local Party's political arenas, and the neglect of it by historians considering the development of a specifically Bradford socialism does in fact reflect its lack of structural importance in local politics. Nevertheless, its existence provided a space that allowed the development of ideas, theories and strategies that were of importance to the Party nationally, and in ideological terms. In order to make such a claim for the importance of the Bradford School Board we have to consider an older claim, of the 1890s and the 1900s, that ILP intervention in local politics made Bradford the most socially progressive city in Britain, and match this with the argument of modern historians, who measure Bradford's failures in municipal socialism. These modern arguments for Bradford's failures in municipal socialism generally ignore the School Board as a *political* arena, and so fail to recognise the evolution of a national ILP policy on child welfare, conceived in Bradford by a woman and a charismatic propagandist – factors that were crucial to the actual development of the policy itself.

Among the early women propagandists of the ILP, McMillan stands out – not simply for enduring as a political figure in a way that Katharine Conway (later Katharine Bruce Glasier), Caroline Martyn and Enid Stacey did not,[26] but for bringing the social problems of one city before a national ILP audience. It has been claimed that McMillan's activities were 'limited to Bradford municipal politics';[27] but this is true only if the immense output of her journalism and her public speaking on questions of childhood, community and class throughout the 1890s are quite rigorously ignored. A national ILP policy on child labour and child health was directed by the practical politics of one locality, so Bradford may have owed much of its – now claimed to be spurious – reputation as a progressive city to ideas that originated in the daily work of its local School Board, and the theorisation of that work by McMillan herself.

What is more, a consideration of the body of theory and political strategy that was worked out through interventions in the work of the Bradford School Board allows us to explore the difficult conflict between community and class that was a feature of ILP ideology. David Howell has pointed out that the Party's national political programme consistently presented *communities* of interest, sympathy and feeling as its frame of reference, rather than the unity of a class in the face of exploitation and oppression.[28] This was part of a self-consciously ethical appeal to a wide constituency, especially to the socially conscious middle class. At the same time, the Party saw the very poor as constituting a check on the development of a powerful party of labour, their material and moral degradation constituting a barrier to progress. In particular, Keir Hardie saw the uplifting of the unrespectable poor – the unskilled labouring class – as one of the first functions of the ILP, and his uneasiness in their political presence was shared by others among its leaders.[29]

For both the trade unionists and the middle-class socialists who belonged to the Bradford Party, the unskilled worker and his family were seen as incapable of providing a class-based politics, as a hindrance to every local effort. One of the local ILP leaders castigated the inhabitants of the poorest ward in the city as those 'unfortunate wretches', complaining that

the very people for whom we are working and toiling are our worst opponents – bitter and intolerant, unsympathetic and insolent, prone rather to live on charity than upon the rights of manhood and womanhood, and if ever such places are captured at all, they must be captured from outside, for not until the death rate, the insanitation and the horrible mode of life are changed shall we ever see the South Ward of Bradford taking an intelligent interest in the affairs concerning it.[30]

To assess McMillan's role in both national and local politics, we need to understand that her consistent efforts were on behalf of children belonging to the families of these 'intolerant, unsympathetic and insolent' citizens, people who stood outside the structures of community that the ILP sought to utilise – more specifically, were efforts on behalf of children whose parents were not voters for the new party and who had no ideological place within it, except as objects of pity.

It has been argued that 'the success or failure of the Bradford ILP's work is reflected in the changes it brought to working class life'.[31] In these terms it is found wanting, for it developed no coherent strategies for dealing with unemployment or poor housing in the years before the First World War. Yet under the heading of education (a category not usually considered to be part of a local political programme) the local ILP *did* pay material attention to working-class life, and the daily existence (or some hours of the daily existence) of some children in the city was made more comfortable and perhaps more pleasurable because of that attention (though most important changes in school life took place after McMillan had left the city in 1902).[32] The dirty and verminous children of South Ward and other very poor areas of the city did thus enter into ILP calculations, and a material attention to their needs was evolved as part of a political programme. To shift the criteria of success in this way does involve seeing children as members of a class, as McMillan certainly saw them and as her writing and oratory persuaded others to see them – that is, as the possible regenerators of a more general working-class life: of their families, of the unskilled labouring poor.

In this textile town, unemployment, which usually intensified in the winter months, was a constant feature of working-class life. It was exacerbated in all textile centres after 1890, when a series of trade tariffs was introduced, designed to restrict the import of cloth to the USA. McMillan arrived in Bradford in the middle of a severe depression, then, and unemployment was to remain particularly intense throughout her first months on the Board. Many of the children she encountered in schools, through her visiting work for the School Board sub-committees she sat on, had lived through several years of relentless family poverty. The failure of Bradford ILP and other local branches in Yorkshire to produce an effective strategy against unemployment has been outlined by Keith Laybourn.[33] The route away from coherent policy, and towards the romances of land nationalisation and resettlement on the land, was a common local response to a universal problem with which no local initiative could in any case hope to cope, and Bradford ILP took this path. But it was not the only one, and there are grounds for seeing efforts made to alleviate child poverty as part of the Bradford ILP's response to the crisis of unemployment.

In spite of commitments in adult education and her growing reputation as a Bradford-based propagandist for the ILP, McMillan's permanent residence in the city seems to have been uncertain until the summer of 1894, when she was selected as ILP School Board candidate, along with W.H. Drew and Leonard Robinson. Both these men were prominent Bradford trade unionists – Drew had been organiser during the Manningham Mills dispute – and both of them commanded a good deal of respect in the labour clubs and societies in which the election campaign was conducted. Yet McMillan was the ILP candidate who got in, 'by a very, very few votes and at the bottom of the poll . . . We were all very much depressed', she remembered in 1912, 'because as one comrade said, it was too bad to have only one out of three elected, and *her* only a woman.'[34] A local correspondent to the *Clarion* newspaper regretted the folly of running three candidates, when two would certainly both have been elected.[35]

The School Boards that were created under the 1870 Elementary Education Act were so constituted that they provided a political opening for minority parties like the ILP. Members were not required to have a property qualification (McMillan herself was not a ratepayer in Bradford, renting rooms in Hanover Square, off Manningham Lane). Voters had to be ratepayers, but they were not disqualified by sex. Each voter had as many votes as there were seats on the Board, and could use all his or her votes for one candidate. It seems likely, though we cannot tell, that much of McMillan's success at the polls was due not to the support of working-class voters but to the appeal of her ideas to certain sections of the socially responsible middle class and to the cumulative system of voting itself, which favoured minority candidates, allowing an impressed voter to cast all his or her votes for McMillan.

Until she was joined in 1897 by the Reverend Roberts, Congregationalist minister and secretary to the Bradford Ethical Society, McMillan was the only ILP member of the fifteen-strong Board. The trade-union/labour interest that was so strong a feature of the Bradford ILP in this period did not gain an actual voice at this level of local politics during the 1890s. As a setting to this political isolation there was a larger one: these mid-decade years have been called the 'triumph of Conservatism' in Bradford. At the 1894 municipal election all six ILP

41

candidates were defeated, and the Conservative Party actually had control of the School Board for the first time since 1871.[36]

But being the isolated representative of a political party (and being isolated, she claimed, on the Board itself – 'the other members ignore my existence for the most part', she said at the end of her first year[37]) did give McMillan certain advantages. She was able, for example, to develop her role as professional expert in matters of childcare, relatively untroubled by the educational perspectives of the local labour movement. In *Ladies Elect* Patricia Hollis has shown that women in English local government took upon themselves the care of children in this period, particularly where those children met the chilliness of the local state, in workhouses and board schools.[38] In Bradford, the School Board had long experience of the determined work of the Liberal member Edith Lupton, who had campaigned against the half-time system in the 1880s and tried to get corporal punishment banned from elementary schools.[39] If the other members of the Board ignored McMillan after 1894, it was not because they were unused to women members.

McMillan's own position as member of the intellectual middle class helped her to develop the persona of educational expert, for she did not have a job to go to, and the Board usually met during working hours. There were also considerable demands made on a member's time, apart from that used up by attendance at board and committee meetings, for during these years School Board members did many of the jobs that were later to devolve on paid officials, such as school and home visiting.[40]

McMillan's memories of this first School Board were dominated by the enmity of the Roman Catholic Church, embodied in Canon Simpson – 'at this time vice-chairman, and virtually the leader – or rather master – of the Board' – who had so profound an effect on her that thirty years later she made the Church's attitude towards the bodily welfare of its congregation the focus of her account of the eight years she spent as a School Board member. 'Here', she recalled in 1927, was a political opposition 'unexpected, undreamed of, but real enough . . . my opponent seemed to use new weapons that I did not know about – weapons forged in the underworld of life and consciousness.'[41] Though she claimed, in her 1927 account, that the local press ignored her during her first School Board, her arguments with Canon Simpson and the political style she developed in opposition to him were often reported verbatim.[42] These factors – the types of political opposition she encountered on the Board, and her isolation as an ILP member between 1894 and 1897 – meant that the local life of the ILP, particularly in its connection with the local trade-union movement, had neither to take cognisance of nor incorporate the body of theory that was being developed over educational questions.

As part of her administrative duties on the School Board from 1894 to 1897, McMillan sat on the School Attendance Sub-Committee (among others) – an appointment that was crucial in the development of her policy, for in this way she came into close contact with children working under the half-time system. Under existing labour and educational legislation, children were able to gain part-time exemption from schooling before the end of compulsory education if their parents were able to demonstrate a need for their wages. The half-time system, which was supported by a network of Acts of Parliament, endured until the end of the First World War, particularly in the northern textile centres. In Bradford, it was the School Attendance Sub-Committee that received applications for half-time exemption, and its interventions in this area were considerably increased in 1895 when it attempted to professionalise its work. The attention of the Board as a whole had been drawn to the physical condition of part-timers by its own medical officer, Dr James Kerr, and the Sub-Committee agreed to issue no certificates unless parents absolutely needed the money (a rule which involved much interviewing of parents) and to refuse application for exemptions by members of the Board itself, many of whom were local employers.[43]

This professionalisation of practice was done in the face of opposition from the one former child worker sitting on the Board, and the acknowledged interests of local working-class voters. McMillan had not only to oppose these local interests but also to face the real conflict of interests that emerged at ILP national conferences, where ILP trade unionists argued that the half-time system represented an economic reality of working-class life. In the national forum offered by the ILP Annual Conference, and as a journalist, McMillan attempted to deal with this conflict. In an article in the *Clarion* of May 1895 she dramatised it through a story concerning a half-timer, the child of a kindly, good-hearted but essentially obtuse trade unionist, 'Tom Bullitt', who is given to statements like '"I've a right to do as I've a mind with my own",' and '"I went to work when I was eight and I'm all the better for it".' Then Old Nature reads to the short-sighted father out of a history of the Factory Acts, and shows how it had once been considered shameful for working-class parents to send their children to the mill.[44]

Two *Clarion* articles on the same topic published later in the year show another of McMillan's journalistic tactics, and the way in which she was able to use its columns to place local issues on a national socialist agenda. Here, a detailed and statistically supported argument, which used recent research findings to show class differences in children's heights, outlined the psychological effects of work in childhood. The articles included a brief history of the way in which a modern conception of childhood had been created, citing Burns, Wordsworth, Eliot, and Walter Crane as literary and artistic sources for its development, and Herbert Spencer's psychology as a scientific one.[45] The *Clarion*, like other labour and socialist journals, was adapted for educational purposes by many audiences – the material adduced here would be used for lecturing and teaching – and McMillan had a clear sense of them, though some working-class readers may have found the heavy satire embodied in the figure of 'Tom Bullitt' a little hard to take.

The presence of women in the national organisation of the early ILP allowed a division of political labour, and the half-time system, child labour in general, and questions of family welfare were all judged to be women's work, in the sense that women wrote and spoke about these issues far more than men did.[46] Yet in the local context, in Bradford, the debate over the half-time system took these women's issues right to the heart of two political conflicts within the ILP: the relationship of a political programme to the realities of working-class life, and trade-union politics. Taking the body of McMillan's writing and journalism as a whole, over a forty-year period, what is remarkable about her presentation of working people's life is her lack of contempt for the exigencies that arose out of it, and the culture it produced. This lack of contempt becomes especially apparent if she is seen in comparison with other middle-class women involved in social rescue work, rather than as someone whose ideas were shaped by labour politics and socialist thought. The position she is then seen to express in her writing seems an attractive one. But it was partly achieved *faute de mieux*, by her single-minded concentration on children rather than on children in the context of working-class family life and working-class culture. The separation of children from their community and cultural context, and their isolation in a kind of literary pathos as figures completely deserving of sympathy and rescue, is apparent in this description of how she went about the business of the School Attendance Sub-Committee towards the end of 1897:

> The other day I stood before a number of children – all very poor, neglected, some living, or herding with a strange woman and strange bedfellows in one room, and sharing a tap with a dozen families and a basin with a dozen companions.
>
> 'Dears,' said I, 'you are *very* dirty. Would you like to go into a bath?'
>
> Great consternation on all hands. Some are silent and solemn as contemplating some awful To Come. Others shiver closer together.
>
> 'Well, would you like it?' said I. 'Tell me the truth.'

'No, I'd *noan* like it,' says the dirtiest girl. 'I'm *feared*, I am, of the water. It's cold.'

But the little girl at the end of the form is contemplative. She looks at me with her soft, dark eyes.

'Do you?' she ventured timidly. 'Does a person take all their clothes off?' said she.

'Have you *never* had a bath?' I ask.

'Yes, yes', says the little one, telling a familiar lie. 'I has a bath, I has, every week.'

'And don't you take your clothes off then?'

'Please, teacher, no,' says the child. 'Mother never makes us take off our clothes.'

'Is it your own mother you speak of?' I ask, looking at this poor, neglected little one.

'Please, teacher, no. My mother drowned herself in the dam. It's Ruth's mother as looks after me.'[47]

'Will you tell me', demanded McMillan of her ILP readership, 'how you are to teach this six-year-old child to be clean? I won't say patient, for the child is patient already . . . We ought to begin, you must admit, *at the beginning* . . .' – by which, of course, McMillan meant by washing her.

In November 1895 McMillan reported on her first few months on the School Board to the readers of the *Labour Prophet*, in a piece that demonstrated the awfulness of Canon Simpson to an audience wider than the readership of the *Bradford Observer*.[48] Much of the conflict with Simpson that was reported by the local press was over what McMillan believed was the Roman Catholic Church's attitude to the physical body – specifically, the dirty bodies of Bradford's outcast children. This McMillan could ascribe, in the heat of political debate, to the Church's desire to save souls at the expense of a comfortable and clean life here on earth.[49] In her *Labour Prophet* article of 1895 she wrote briefly about schools, and then noted: 'But there are no baths: and what is the use of doing anything with a child unless you have washed it?'[50]

Malcolm Hardman, in his description of the impact of Ruskin's social and aesthetic criticism on Bradford, has noted McMillan's many public statements on the question of washing children, and linked these with what he calls Ruskin's quaint belief that 'education "begins . . . in washing"' and has its final result in knowing '"what it is to see the sky"'.[51] 'Will you', urged McMillan of the readers of the *Bradford Labour Echo* in 1897, to whom she had just told the drowning story noted above,

just turn to the last page of the third book of your 'Past and Present' and read what Carlyle says there: – 'what is the first duty that I prescribe and offer towards? That the operative clean the skin of him . . .' Being washed 'thou hast an increase of tendency towards all good things whatsoever' . . .[52]

To the late-twentieth-century reader, so massively condescending (rather than quaint) do these injunctions to the working classes to wash themselves (or more particularly, in this case, to wash their children) seem that there is a real danger of ignoring the body of theory that lay behind the instruction, for whilst McMillan consistently appealed to the Romantic critique of industrialism that was embodied in a more general use of Ruskin and Carlyle by ILP propagandists, she was not here making a simple application of Ruskin's ideas to the Bradford situation. Rather, the rapid development of her theory of childcare and hygiene was a response to the situation she found herself in, working on the School Board after 1894.

The School Board had appointed James Kerr as Medical Superintendent of Schools in 1893, before McMillan had arrived in the town. His work in the inspection and categorisation of elementary-school children helped to evolve a highly medicalised view of working-class childhood, in which the contagious diseases spread in closely packed and poorly ventilated classrooms, and the dirty state of children's bodies, were established as the indices of deprivation and impoverishment.[53] Children in contact with each other, in the community of the classroom, were seen as a source of both danger and infection; but it was also this community that measured out the arena of possible amelioration. This perception of the body in community that Kerr's work gave to McMillan was to have an important effect on her development of an educational theory.

In the 1900s the focus of McMillan's political work was to be directed towards the national medical inspection of schoolchildren. Kerr was actually undertaking child-study in schools and making medical inspections of Bradford children from 1894 onwards, though in fact he had no legal authority to do so.[54] He rarely published his findings (except those concerning the physical condition of half-timers in 1895) but he built up a formidable body of evidence about child ill-health in the city. Kerr also embarked on a dramatic series of public examinations of schoolchildren, which intensified the growing professional understanding that it was dirt and disease rather than hunger which caused Bradford's 'defrauded childhood'.[55]

Within this professional perspective, McMillan educated the public – or at least, the attentive ILP readership of the *Bradford Labour Echo*, and the audience at the Labour Church – in theories of child development, physiology and hygiene.[56] This body of work – much of which started as lectures and ended up in the columns of the *Echo* and the national labour press – was a translation of the educational and physiological theories of Édouard Seguin and continental psychology for a lay audience.[57] The grounding of McMillan's ideas in these particular theories of mind–body relationship will be discussed later, but it should be noted now how very much she did expect her various audiences to take on board by way of theory – and how much they evidently did embrace, for her public lectures on education, on physiology and hygiene were always advertised as a particular treat by the local ILP press.

During the two School Boards of 1894–97 and 1897–1900 McMillan established herself as a local expert, and was interviewed and deferred to in matters of education.[58] Her aura of professionalism was intensified by the journalistic fiction that she produced for national newspapers like the *Clarion* and the *Labour Leader*, in which she used the moving and sentimental vignette of working-class child life in order to lay bare its psychology. Throughout this period she was also engaged in heavy programmes of adult education at the Labour Church (later the Labour Institute) and frequently away from Bradford, travelling as a lecturer for the ILP. In 1896, for example, she spent at least a weekend a month out of the city, speaking on labour and socialist platforms.

It is important, though, not to separate her roles as expert on childhood, adult educator, journalist and propagandist. In particular, much of the education she proffered to adults was concerned with questions of child development, and in her journalism she constantly sought new techniques for dramatising and fictionalising questions of physiology and psychology. The local Party certainly knew her value, and the reputation she had established as an orator: in 1896, after the local May Day celebrations, the *Labour Echo* reported on one of 'those vigorous and brilliant addresses which have made her famous'.[59] She was a socialist speaker with a fine sense of her heterogeneous audience, and the need to appeal to sections of it in different ways. In 1895, during the general election campaign in Bradford, she urged the 'struggle for a living wage – for life for all – and (till this is secured) for this only . . . the ILP lays aside other questions as minor. These can afford to wait . . .'.[60] Yet the Party line was consistently shaped by the educative principle, and here her mode of address moved between different political audiences: between the aspiring and self-educated lower middle class, schooled in Ruskinism and the Romantic critique of capitalism, and the working-class men who were being asked to cast their votes:

'Things', says John Ruskin, 'are not wholly alive or wholly dead. They are more or less alive . . .'. The calyx is a useful part of the

47

flower – very useful – but it does not have much at any time and it usually dies altogether when the flower is born. Well, the working people have been the calyx of the blossom of humanity, their life is subordinate. They never, or rarely, blossom. Yet that essential difference does not exist between them and their betters which exists between calyx and corolla . . . The labour candidate is come that you may have life more abundantly.'[61]

Margaret McMillan fought her second School Board election in autumn 1897, from the assured position of local expert on child welfare and education and with a national reputation as journalist and orator. She polled more at this election than she had in 1894 or was to do in 1900, and was joined on the Board by a second ILP representative, the Reverend Roberts.[62] The 'Progressive Eight' had been returned, the local Liberal Party agreeing to run only six candidates when the ILP ran two, in order not to split the progressive and left-wing vote.[63] McMillan was no longer working in an atmosphere of chilly Conservatism, though the Conservative Party was in the ascendancy on the Town Council.[64]

From McMillan's point of view, this second School Board was marked out by her efforts to have a system of mechanical ventilation and baths installed in elementary schools, though other members of the Board as a whole saw its increased concern with educational method, particularly in infants' schools, as the foremost feature of its work. In-service work for teachers in kindergarten methods was set up; visits to the Froebel Society in London and series of visiting lectures were organised.[65] All these initiatives were made by the Liberal representatives on the Board as much as by McMillan.

Accounts of McMillan as a reformer have tended to present her as a lone struggler, achieving great ends single-handed, and in this way the political context in which she had to work has been ignored.[66] Though she usually aligned herself with the Liberals over educational questions, they too formed an opposition – as did Conservative members, particularly over the question of expenditure.[67] The National Union of Teachers' (NUT) representative was both ally and enemy, particularly over corporal punishment, to which McMillan was vehemently opposed.[68] Never particularly enamoured of the teaching profession, she wrote in 1901 that teachers 'were made tradesmen by others and have made artisans of themselves . . . no NUT, however powerful it will become, will ever give elementary teachers that social status and social authority once possessed by every school master in Scotland'. To believe, and to point out in this public way, that there 'were evils inseparable from [an] education received in a hurry at a teachers' school instead of in leisure in a University', did not endear her to the teachers' representative on the Bradford School Board.[69]

In the 1900 election McMillan was able to present herself and the Reverend Roberts as both socialists and professionals in educational matters, claiming that as socialists they 'stood quite apart from all others, for they did not recognise any class distinction . . .'. At the same time, the voters were offered a detailed educational programme:

> . . . up to five years of age the infant ought to be at home . . . she did not believe there could be anything worse in the home than in a baby class in a poorly ventilated school. The children were so liable to contagion in the school that there should be the best ventilation and plenty of light and room. The children should be educated by playing and singing. They should break the discipline of ordinary regulations . . .[70]

She and Roberts also warned the electorate that Bradford's existing reputation as a progressive municipality should not lead them to think that everything in the city was 'along the lines of perfect education'.

The School Board elected in November 1900 was dissolved when the Conservative government's 1902 Education Bill became law. This piece of legislation abolished the School Boards and invested their authority, and the control and management of elementary schools, in urban district or county councils – to which women could not be elected.[71] When the ILP national conference debated the Bill in 1901, McMillan's work in Bradford was used as an example of what this limited enfranchisement of women – which had lasted for just thirty years – had achieved in local terms.[72]

Locally, and in the national labour press, McMillan protested against this legislation, particularly against the assault on the Higher Grade Schools that it involved. Technically and legally, School Boards had control only over elementary education, but since the 1870s the Board of Education had been giving grants not just for compulsory subjects but also for what were called 'specific subjects' – branches of mathematics and science, languages, commercial and domestic art – taught to children in the upper reaches of the elementary schools. This secondary education, the only kind available to working-class children, was also encouraged by grants from the Science and Arts Department for what were known as 'organised science classes'. These could be held in the evenings in school premises. In this way School Boards were, *de facto*, organising and controlling secondary education through what were called, in the North, the Higher Grade Schools.[73]

Bradford had established its first in 1895 when the School of Science opened, and there were three in the city by the time the Education Bill threatened their existence. McMillan particularly regretted the

49

demise of the evening classes in kindergarten principles and drawing for teachers, for in Bradford the Higher Grade Schools had formed part of an evolving system of in-service teacher education.[74] In this local and national struggle against their closure McMillan's professional concerns were put to work in a more general ILP argument, against the withdrawal of the only means of higher education available to working-class children: 'Let it be known throughout the land', declaimed the Reverend Roberts, 'that these schools of the people are to be destroyed in the interests of the classes.'[75]

In most labour and socialist struggle over the Education Bill, the board schools were defended as part of a system whereby working-class voters could control working-class education through their elected representatives; moreover, the threatened end of Higher Grade Schools implied a barrier to higher education for working-class children: the parliamentary debates preceding the Education Act and the administrative measures applied as a result of it showed secondary education to be a middle-class education in both conception and availability.[76] McMillan was aware of the class antagonism and conflict expressed in the lead-up to the 1902 Act. In 1900 she had visited the Education Minister, Sir John Gorst, with a Bradford School Board deputation, to apply for grant-earning status for the new commercial school in the city. 'They are not likely to forget that interview', she had written. 'This new development in education . . . was treated by the responsible Education Minister of the Crown with open hostility and scorn.' He had displayed, she said, 'the narrowest spirit of class feeling in education . . . Around all centres of Higher Education the Government will draw a cordon of gold . . . .'.[77]

In general, though, ILP support for the threatened School Board system was much less militant than that of the SDF and the Trades Union Congress (TUC), and some of the leadership supported the measures for rational administration that the Bill embodied. McMillan did not follow the Party line (or absence of line) here, and put forward pedagogical arguments for the continuance of working-class education in the Higher Grade Schools. In particular, she wrote to disabuse audiences of the belief that whatever was done in them could be done just as well in the upper reaches of the elementary school. In arguing for an education specific to age and stage of development, she was able to bring on the heavy ammunition of educational expertise – in this case, neurological work on brain growth – in order to demonstrate that the ages twelve to thirteen were the time of complex cerebral processing – 'the reaping time of the educator', who could do his or her work only in a Higher Grade School.[78]

But McMillan was ill. She resigned from the Board in November 1901 after two months' sick leave, and after returning briefly to her work she finally left Bradford in November 1902 and moved to London. The 1902 Education Act forced two other people to make the same journey from the city. Dr Kerr, unable to be Medical Superintendent to a Board that no longer existed, resigned to take up the post of Chief Medical Officer to the London School Board; and Robert Roberts, who had been secretary to the local branch of the Ethical Society as well as second ILP member on the Bradford School Board, took up a lectureship with the London Society, just as McMillan did when she moved south at the end of 1902.[79]

The London Ethical Society was part of the humanist and rationalist movement in Britain. As such it was also an educational movement, particularly preoccupied in this period with the promotion of moral and secular teaching in board schools. There was never a National Ethical Society with branches, but rather a series of metropolitan and provincial groupings, with the London movement concentrating at first around the South Place chapel where, between 1887 and 1892, Dr Stanton Coit was minister.[80] At this point, Coit had resigned to work with the West London Ethical Society and other local societies. In 1896 these joined together to form the Union of Ethical Societies.[81]

By 1898, then, Stanton Coit led an ethical society and an ethical union and was also editor of a newspaper, the *Ethical World*. This year also saw his marshalling together a missionary group, which he called the Society of Ethical Propagandists. Coit saw this organisation for propaganda as a possible career 'for young men, who for conscience sake, cannot take holy orders, but who still desire to become teachers of holy righteousness'.[82] These positions were salaried, but the propagandists were never paid enough to keep them from looking for a proper living. McMillan's move to Coit's organisation was part of a second wave of recruitment to the Society, when in about 1900 Coit started to use voluntary, part-time workers.[83] Even so, it does seem that McMillan was employed as a full-time paid worker, her reputation as an educationalist one of her main credentials.[84]

At this time, Coit was negotiating with Keir Hardie over the possible formation of a new newspaper that would merge his *Ethical World* with Hardie's *Labour Leader*, a combination that Coit suggested might lead to a new party, formed out of the ILP and the ethical movement, to be called the Democratic Party.[85] Ramsay MacDonald was one of Coit's early wave of paid propagandists, so in the late 1890s there was a good deal of contact and connection between the Society and the ILP hierarchy.[86] By recruiting McMillan Coit obtained a brilliant propagandist with an established reputation. Bruce Glasier, for one, thought that her style and general performance showed up the rhetorical poverty of the average London speaker,[87] and as in Bradford, the Society's publicity always offered McMillan's lectures as a particular delight. Her popular ten-lecture series of 1903 on 'Education Through the Imagination' formed the basis of her book of that title.[88]

McMillan's work for the London Ethical Society continued until the First World War, though it is unclear if she continued to be paid as a full-time worker. What the ten years of her involvement with the Society brought her was a series of audiences to whom she could express her view of childhood and education, which proclaimed a set of possibilities about the evolution of human society. In this way, her ethical propaganda was a continuation of the adult education she had undertaken in the Labour Institute in Bradford. When Albert Mansbridge recruited McMillan to his newly formed Workers' Educational Association (WEA) in 1903, he sought out a similar understanding of the potential of the educational process in a given society. In the case of the WEA (or at least, in Mansbridge's conception of its role) the idea was that by making available to a general public 'the discovery of the child', a broader understanding of human nature might be achieved.[89]

McMillan's administrative involvement in child education also increased in the years after 1902. She was elected a member of the executive of the Froebel Society in 1904, and to the Executive Committee of the WEA itself in 1909.[90] She became manager of a group of Deptford schools in 1903, an appointment that was to continue until the end of the First World War.[91] Her work in adult education, then, was informed by a continued contact with working-class children, brought together in the board school classrooms of poor London. Indeed, the WEA saw her 'years of active contact with the children of the people' as one of her chief qualifications for speaking on educational matters in general.[92] Most of her journalism in the first years of the new century concerned educational questions, and her books began to establish her dominant reputation as an educationalist rather than as a socialist and a propagandist.

Support from Joseph Fels, the American soap millionaire, philanthropist propagandist of the ideas of Henry George, enabled McMillan to open a small, experimental school clinic at Bow.[93] The Bow Clinic served the population of one school, operating out of the room belonging to the headmistress of the Devons Road School. The LCC rented this room to the Clinic, but had no further interest in its maintenance or progress. Actual authority for the Clinic rested in the hands of the Metropolitan District ILP Committee for the Physical Welfare of Children, though the Committee members had no right actually to enter the school. Fels financed other experimental London clinics like this one, but Devons Road School became the best known, probably because of the efforts of its two visiting doctors, Reginald

Tribe and David Eder, whose enthusiastic accounts of what was possible even under these restricted conditions brought it very wide publicity.[94]

What emerges from an account like this is the role that private charity played in the evolution of local authority and national provision of welfare services to children, and the way in which – as in the case of the ILP Committee for the Physical Welfare of Children – a local political grouping might become involved in the practical politics of child welfare. As the Bow Clinic served only one school it was not financially viable, and it was moved to Deptford to operate as the health centre for the group of schools where McMillan was manager. Framing these two local initiatives was the context of national legislation, for by 1910, when the new Deptford Clinic opened, it was legally possible for local education authorities to provide for the treatment of schoolchildren. The provision of treatment was the final result of the campaign for the medical inspection of schoolchildren, which had been the focus of McMillan's political work from 1905 onwards. This campaign, which later accounts have confined to the dusty history of educational provision, dramatised the conflict between the ideas of prevention and cure, a conflict which McMillan herself staged in her description of the genesis of the school clinic, under the eaves in the Bromley lodgings.[95] The obliqueness of her account suggests a real confusion between two principles, which may be used to illuminate the contradictions lying at the heart of the various theories of childhood expressed in the medical inspection campaign itself.

'We did not open a clinic at all', McMillan wrote, having described the Bromley conversation of 1903. 'We began to work for medical inspection.' The campaign for medical inspection of schoolchildren has the central place in the iconography of McMillan as a heroine of childhood. It marks the beginning of a period of her life in which she achieved fame outside socialist and radical circles, for she addressed a very wide range of audiences on the topic, and her output of journalism concerning it was immense.[96] Old friends (some of whom were to withdraw close comradeship over her single-minded pursuit of this goal), like Fred Jowett and Keir Hardie, were now Labour Members of Parliament, so the techniques of parliamentary lobbying, and a careful propagandist attention to the civil servants at the Board of Education, were available to McMillan.[97]

It was over this question, as well, that fissures between a Labour Party position and McMillan's vision of working-class education were quite dramatically revealed. In Bradford in the 1890s, work on behalf of the ILP had allowed McMillan to develop an expertise on questions of child welfare, so that by 1905 she was able to take part in the struggle between experts that shaped the school medical service, showing a grasp of medical principle and a detailed knowledge of continental systems that the parliamentary members of the Labour Party did not possess. The kind of technical argument that McMillan presented to her ILP colleagues led easily enough to charges of obsession, and in any case the question of medical inspection did not excite the socialist passions as the question of feeding children had – for instance, when the 1906 Education (Provision of Meals) Bill was debated nationally and in Parliament. What is more, it was difficult for ILP colleagues in Parliament to work out what McMillan was after as she lobbied them, especially as an embryonic medical service already existed. By the early 1900s some fifty education authorities had started the medical inspection of children under their care, and it was hard to mobilise enthusiasm for what looked like a developing system rather than a cause.

In trying to convey her views about the care and education of working-class children to the ILP over the question of medical inspection, McMillan also faced problems of status and position that had not existed in Bradford in the 1890s. First, she was a disenfranchised woman, as she had not been when she stood as a candidate in municipal politics. From 1906 she was a member of the National Administrative Council of the ILP but, at the same time, she stood outside the structure of political power in which the Party was now able to operate. Second, the political theory that lay behind her seeming obsession with medical inspection focused on childhood at precisely the moment when the working-class child, as an item of polity, was being taken over as a general political property, the time when 'in the first years of the twentieth century . . . the rather casual public interest in the health of schoolchildren suddenly became a widespread fear over the apparent deterioration of the British working class', a development that meant that 'a healthy working-class child was precious in a way he had not been before . . . '.[98] McMillan was able to tap into this alarm about the degeneration of an imperial race, and used the vocabulary of national efficiency in some of her propaganda.

McMillan had started lobbying for a Bill dealing with the medical inspection of schoolchildren in 1904, working particularly to convince a range of medical men of what she saw as the essential features of a possible system: published annual reports and supervision by a medical department at the Board of Education.[99] This last was an essential point for ensuring that child health and nurture would be established as part of an educational system rather than as an aspect of public health.

Administrative historians have described how the school medical service came into being secretly, as a corollary of medical inspection, with even the authorisation for inspection 'buried among more than a dozen other clauses dealing with uninteresting and involved house-keeping details of State school administration'.[100] In particular, the means by which the evolution 'from personal medical inspection to personal medical care was blurred and disguised' has been attributed to a 'political-administrative trick' performed by Sir Robert Morant with support by Margaret McMillan, as one of the 'most serious social reformers' of her day.[101]

McMillan had met Morant in Bradford when he had visited the city to investigate the embryonic system of school baths there.[102] In London she had sent him the scheme that she and Rachel had drawn up after the conversation beneath the eaves in Bromley. In shaping the legislation that finally authorised medical inspection, Morant relied much on McMillan's expertise and sought her advice on the structuring of the service – advice which he did not actually take, a point forgotten in the story told of the champion of childhood influencing the civil servant.[103] On the face of it, McMillan's relationship with Morant seems a clear example of the elision of ILP socialism with progressive Liberal reformism. His interest in preventive social medicine and his willingness to draw on the advice of experts in the field meshed with a keen family interest in the experiments in Bow and Deptford, and an attachment to the rescued children of outcast London felt also by his wife and daughter.[104] For both McMillan and Morant, it is argued, inspection promised to reveal such horrors of ill-health that treatment would be bound to follow.[105] In his drafting of legislation Morant relied on McMillan's experience, she giving him help that he was generous in acknowledging. 'This', he wrote to her in December 1909,

> is the *first* clean proof of the *first* Annual Report of the first *national* system of School Medical Inspection that this country has known: & I cannot resist giving myself the pleasure of sending it, in confidence, to yourself; for you are to me the person who has most signally & most effectively embodied, in a private individual, the best enthusiasm & most warming faith both in the possibilities of med. inspn & in the potentialities of a real honest preventative conscience in the State & in the People.[106]

But there were real differences between the two of them that were quite openly acknowledged. Morant wrote in 1907 that he had come to feel that

> for the good of the children & of the people, what subjects are taught, & how they are taught, *do not matter anything like so much* nowadays as (a) attention to the *physical* condition of the scholars & of the teachers, & (b) to the physiological aspect of

school. I think I lay more emphasis in my own mind on the *Preventative* side of this quasi-medical aspect of sociology than you do: & that you are thinking more predominantly of the Therapeutic Remedial side . . .[107]

That 'real honest preventative conscience in the State and the People' was exactly that for Morant: a change of heart and way of living that might be brought about by progressive legislation, but without public expenditure. Moreover, Morant saw questions of physical education as particularly appropriate for working-class children; the content of the curriculum and teaching method were in his view more properly aspects of secondary education.[108] Actually to mend the bodies of the victims of an industrial system cost a good deal of money, and though Morant achieved insertion of medical inspection clauses in the 1907 Education (Administrative Provisions) Act, and a permissive clause that allowed local authorities to provide treatment, he was very nervous about McMillan's lobbying for enforcement of the treatment clauses, telling her in April 1910 that 'were we to attempt such a Circular as you suggest, making Clinics practically compulsory in certain areas, we should be met at once with the reply that we have no powers whatever . . . to adopt any such attitude . . .'[109]

McMillan seems to have kept details of her co-operation with Morant from members of the parliamentary ILP, a wise reticence given his role in the drafting of the 1902 Education Act, the end of the School Boards and the demise of the Higher Grade Schools.[110] With her own political colleagues she was much clearer about the *political* project embodied in medical inspection. She hammered home the points about a medical department at the Board of Education and the publication of findings, in the *Clarion* and in letters to Keir Hardie throughout the early part of 1906, urging Hardie and other members of the parliamentary ILP to get an appropriate clause inserted in the Bill then before Parliament, in a form of words (McMillan offered them a clause to insert) that would inevitably lead from inspection to treatment.[111]

This Bill – a government Education Bill – folded at the end of 1906, and civil servants at the Board of Education and liberal leaders in the House of Commons made it quite clear in the process that they drew a distinct line between the inspection of children and their actual treatment.[112] She 'is very excited', reported John Bruce Glasier in the diary entry that records McMillan's first attendance at the NAC of the ILP. 'Full of complaints about MacDonald and Hardie over her Physical Inspection Clause . . . All very foolish on her part . . . speaks rudely to them both – she is fearfully hurt that they did not do as she wanted in the House . . .'.[113] In April 1907, at the ILP Annual Conference,

McMillan proposed that the Party support a new Private Member's Bill, and insert in it a clause to do with medical inspection.[114] This private Bill was withdrawn at the request of the government, and the Bill prepared by Morant became law in 1907. It embodied the medical inspection clause, and provided for the setting up of a medical department at the Board of Education.

McMillan had expected that compulsory medical inspection would bring about the school clinic she had been working for, but the failed experiment at Bow showed the constraints presented by local authority parsimony. Her campaign continued, and centred now on the question of financial responsibility. Under the new legislation the duty of medical inspection fell on the local authority, and responsibility for treatment upon parents. Much of McMillan's journalism over the next few years concerned the plight of working-class parents who, when their children were diagnosed in need of treatment, had to make arduous and expensive journeys with them across cities to hospitals, there to be condescended to by doctors who apparently believed that they were 'dealing with materials rather than a clientele'.[115] The local clinic, the type of organisation she had attempted at Bow and was to move to Deptford in 1910, was her proposed solution to these problems.

Historiographically, it is almost impossible to rescue McMillan's campaign – in ILP and Labour Party Conferences, in lobbying from the Froebel Society offices, in the national press, and through the WEA – from the dull reaches of administrative history. Certainly, the ILP – and in particular her old friends from the 1890s, Hardie and Bruce Glasier – never understood what was being asked of them in this particular campaign, nor the nature of the vision embodied in McMillan's imperfectly explained version of Clause 35b. They were able to remember the campaign of 1906–12 as an obsession, not as an essential feature of 'a system of hygienic education that will redeem the poor', nor as part and parcel of a planned process of change whereby dirty, diseased and malnourished children would be restored healthy, whole and beautiful to their parents, who would then be roused to a consciousness of their exploitation and deprivation; who would then rise up, and demand their rights as full citizens. When Rachel McMillan died in 1917, and a distraught Margaret went to stay with Lizzie Bruce Glasier, her brother John wrote: 'Poor lassie! As you say, she has been without spiritual sustenance for so long, and her very zeal for the medical treatment of children has obscured from her mind any clear vision of hope of a higher healing power . . .'.[116]

By the end of the First World War, McMillan was securely established as an expert on nursery education. She had published two books on the subject, and the focus of her public speaking had shifted in this direction. In 1923 she was elected president of the Nursery School Association, in which capacity she served until her resignation in 1929. This position confirmed her reputation as expert, though it failed to provide her with the kind of public platform she sought.[117]

Her relations with the NSA were continually acrimonious, in spite of Mansbridge's claim that they remained cordial until the end.[118] Some of the antagonisms were to do with the Association's failures over the question of democratic practice. 'I think the members of the NSA should take part more than they do', wrote McMillan in 1927:

Also that Vice-Presidents should be elected through the voting of the whole members, not by the will of the small group . . . the leaflet for the election should be passed by full Committee not written by a member and seen by one or two – I have worked mainly on Labour Party Committees, but even on elected Boards this is the *rule* . . .[119]

But there were much more fundamental divisions, with McMillan asking in 1929 if 'ours is the same movement'. The differences were to do with the social life that the nursery school intersected with: 'I am told you close at 3.30. That may be all right in some districts. But such a day would be worth little or nothing in any poor area! And I am working for the poorest children . . . .'.[120] 'I think', she wrote a few days later of these children, 'that the time of their deliverance has come. It will not come through the school that is advocated by the NSA.'[121]

The principles of a long day, in a large school – for the sake of economy – had been evolved out of McMillan's long experience in Deptford, particularly during the war years and the heightened emotion of the period following Rachel's death. Using private subscription, fees and grants received for the care of munitions workers' children, McMillan had opened new shelters to accommodate one hundred nursery-age children in 1917. Under the new Education Act of 1918 the London County Council built its own school for another hundred children on the same site, and this went into operation in 1921.[122]

Both schools operated under the same management committee, with McMillan a continual thorn in its side as she attempted to keep the costs of the Rachel McMillan Nursery School down, and to appeal to working-class parents. She told parents in 1921 that the charge was to be 1s. a day instead of the 3s.6d. fixed by the committee, and as a committee member reported, at the first rota of parents 'the atmosphere was decidedly tense . . . Miss McMillan is absolutely opposed to the 3/6 asked. Her attitude from the beginning has been that it is suicidal to ask this amount – to quote her own words – "Consternation is spreading among the people" . . .'[123] McMillan's presentation of the real needs of working people was a useful strategy in these negotiations, though committee members treated her representation with a measure of scepticism. One of them described another rota for means testing, reporting how McMillan and staff at the Nursery School had argued that

'we should never fill the school . . . parents hated committees and giving particulars of their income' . . . They had obviously been worked up by Miss McMillan and were almost in tears . . . everyone down there tries to make out that the psychology of the Deptford people is very peculiar![124]

It was through her work for the NSA, and the nursery school movement in general, that McMillan met Nancy Astor, though it was not until 1926 that the friendship (or at least the correspondence) between them became intimate. Astor represented a great many things for McMillan in the last eight years or so of her life – not just a family fortune that McMillan was able to draw on for the building of a training college to commemorate Rachel – including the political influence embodied in being one of the first women Members of Parliament. McMillan also maintained the friendship for the beauty and vivacity that Lady Astor epitomised. Astor, for her part, was convinced that 'the woman is a genius'[125] and did the most practical work for her in supporting the building of the Rachel McMillan Training College, including covering McMillan's debts at various points. The great apostasy of April 1929, when McMillan spoke on the Conservative platform in Astor's constituency, can be explained to some extent by following the trajectory of the nursery school movement through the 1920s, when it achieved in some quarters the status of a social mission that transcended party politics.[126]

In its publicity, the NSA itself suggested that local branches get platform speakers wherever they could across the political spectrum, and old ILP stalwarts like Katharine Bruce Glasier were roused by the vision of a new campaign. 'For years now', she wrote to the NSA in 1927,

I have belonged to your Association in spirit. I have helped to tell of Margaret McMillan's school at Deptford & all the movement stands for in literally hundreds of meetings . . . But I am beginning to feel that all my other hopes and works depend on your work – that even as a friend for Disarmament – total and complete – it is through the children & that perfect service that we can best find a way to open blind eyes before they lead us again into even more terrible trenches . . . nursery school bairns will not tolerate slums when they grow up! . . . the thought of Lancashire's need of nursery schools is beginning to crowd out all other thoughts in my old Socialist pacifist agitator's brain . . .[127]

It was not only Katharine Glasier who felt this way. One of McMillan's former employees, Mary Chignell, who had worked at the Deptford Centre between 1917 and 1920 and then took up a Bradford nursery school headship on McMillan's persuasion, was accused by the Education Committee in 1928 of using her school for the purposes of socialist propaganda. Her defence was a passionate assertion of the transcendental apoliticality of saving little children, her work the expression of 'a desire selfless and deathless – to see the consummation of the blessing which I most earnestly believe the Nursery School can bring to human life'.[128] For her, the nursery school offered a means of bringing about 'a social rebirth, a reinterpretation of life and society, of human tradition'.[129] When McMillan died in 1931, Katharine Glasier wrote to Nancy Astor:

I loved her so long (for 37 years) so cannot help wishing to bless you in the name of all who loved her & her perfect inspired work for the little ones of our slums . . . if only we could get an national agitation going! – clear of all party politics – just the *real* Christianity that loves his little ones & *saves* them as *He* bore us . . .[130]

The cause of childhood, conceived of as a social mission that transcended mere political divisions, could be viewed as the final resting place of a socialism that did not base itself in an economic understanding of a society's divisions, but saw rather the uplifting of broad masses of abandoned humanity as one of its central projects. In this way, we could see Katharine Bruce Glasier's assertion of a true Christianity through the saving of little children from the horrors of slumdom connecting directly with the sudden conviction of a young woman in Edinburgh, forty years before, that the socialists she had encountered there were 'the true disciples and followers of Christ'.[131] Is it possible to interpret the political journey that McMillan took in this way, to see it as a particular structure of ethical socialism, inevitably leading her beyond party, and class politics, to the garden of childhood and 'that perfect service' that work for them embodied? Certainly, other ILP socialists have been described as following this inevitable course (though not into the garden of childhood).[132]

However, McMillan's last campaign, and the religious fervour with which it was conducted, may show that it was not just the expression of a personal move from one politics to another, but rather a shared experience of the 1920s that cannot be attributed to the deficiencies of a particular form of social analysis. For we are left with McMillan's own political project, which was to establish childhood at the heart of a socialist theory, and her delineation of agency – the actual means by which great social change was to come about. If the rhetoric of the ILP is to be called maudlin and sentimental – and there is no denying that it was both – then that label ought not to mark the place where an excess is dismissed, and the historian moves on. Rather, a closer examination of the idea of childhood in the political context that has been sketched out should not only make the items of one woman's life story plainer but may indeed lead us to the place where sentimentality can be understood as both a political weapon and part of a political project – a topic of the next chapter, 'Childhood'.

McMillan died in a nursing home in Harrow in March 1931 and was buried by a Bishop, who read out a message of condolence from a Queen.[133] *The Times* obituary made something of her earlier politics, far more than did the Labour *Daily Herald*, which might have been expected to recount some of that other history in a week when the leadership of the ILP was being contested.[134] Both of them called her a great benefactress of childhood, seeing her passed beyond party to a communion of latter-day saints, who had striven for a new world through the reclamation of little children.

3

Childhood

> How cheery and high hearted he is, and yet at the same time
> one can see that hunger and the misery at home are bearing a
> little too hard on Fred. What do I propose? Reform the land
> laws? Bring in Socialism? Destroy Capitalism? Yes! But
> meanwhile? You see, Fred is 12. In four years from now it
> will be too late to help him. (Margaret McMillan, 'Camp
> Schools', 17 May 1912)

IN the late nineteenth century, and in the years up to the First
World War, childhood was reconceptualised in British society –
that is to say, children became the subjects of legislative attention
and formed the basis of various accounts of social development as they
had not done before. In a range of social and aesthetic criticism a
historical process was often described whereby attention had first of all
been directed at the children of the wealthier classes. Later in the
century, it was then argued, the children of the poor became the
beneficiaries of this increased understanding of the nature of
childhood.

Poor children were indeed investigated, written about, photo-
graphed and painted, surveyed and measured, in an unprecedented
way in the last decades of the nineteenth century, and it is tempting to
label this new awareness a kind of discovery of working-class childhood. But to do that would be to ignore the series of 'discoveries' that
were made at many different points and in different ways, throughout
the century. Indeed, it was with the legacy of these nineteenth-
century investigations of working-class childhood, which had assumed
different forms throughout the preceding century, that Margaret
McMillan herself worked, and out of which she wrote.

To suggest that McMillan *rewrote* working-class childhood between
1895 and 1920 is not to employ some metaphor, vaguely invoking
discourses of the social subject (in this case, that of 'the working-class
child'); it is rather to consider seriously the huge output of her writing,
the lectures she gave, and the books she published on this topic. The
figures of working-class childhood that McMillan presented to the
readership of the *Clarion* and the *Labour Leader*, and in the fiction
she produced for these and other journals in the 1890s, need an

analysis that can deal with the subjects of her writing as both invented and real – as literary figures, and as representatives of actual children living in particular social circumstances: in Bradford in the 1890s and in Deptford after 1910. It has already been suggested that the effect of McMillan's rewriting can be traced within British socialism, and that it was used to help form ILP and Labour Party policy on childhood. What helped shape this policy was not just sets of statistics concerning child ill-health and hunger, not just the sociological shape of deformed and defrauded childhood, but also, and at the same time, the moving, sentimentalised and 'sacralised' child-figures who dwelt in McMillan's prose and her platform oratory.

The term 'sacralisation' is used by Viviana Zelizer in *Pricing the Priceless Child*, in her discussion of the way in which 'a profound transformation in the economic and sentimental value of children' took place between 1870 and 1930. Through a consideration of child labour, public reactions to the death of children (particularly in street accidents), changing patterns of childcare, baby-farming, abandonment and adoption, and changing patterns in the practice of insuring children's life, Zelizer shows that in the United States in this period, economically useless children (useless because of their transformation from workers into scholars) became emotionally priceless – to their parents in particular, but also to wider communities than the family.[1] Living through these times, McMillan was both influenced by this shift in perspective and also played an important role in what may have been a specifically British transformation of the meaning of childhood: her work and writing, and their political use, allow an exploration of this general development in terms of class, and of the particular ambiguities that attached to the 'sacralisation of child life' when it was the children of the unskilled labouring poor who were under consideration. The difficulties involved in the reification of this particular category of children had much to do with their social class status. and the position of their parents within ILP thought.

Historiographical difficulties lie in the way of discussing the history of childhood, and as they are difficulties by which McMillan herself was actually constrained, it is worth outlining them at this juncture. To start with, it has often been noted that the history of childhood is intensely teleological, much of it presented to illustrate a progress made by a society towards an enlightened present. In this version of history, a horrific past – of child labour, or child exploitation, or child abuse – is overtly presented as a counterpoint to current circumstances. The history of childhood may have become more sophisticated since the mid 1970s, when deMause, in his much-satirised *History of Childhood*, told the history of the world in the change from the 'infanticide mode' of child-rearing to our present, but imperfectly established, 'helping mode.[2] But this teleology is in fact extremely difficult to abandon, for we live and write history (as Margaret McMillan did) by a central tenet of nineteenth-century reforming liberalism, which tells us that one measure of a society's civilisation and progress is to be found in its treatment of disadvantaged and dispossessed groups: women, slaves, children.

Children present a particular problem within the broad humanitarian struggle to make these groups part of the commonweal, for whilst not everyone has been a slave or a woman, all people have experienced childhood. Developments in scientific thought in the nineteenth century showed that childhood was a stage of growth and development common to all of us, abandoned and left behind, but at the same time a core of the individual's psychic life, always immanent, waiting there to be drawn on in various ways. A good deal of work still remains to be done on shifts within physiology – and later psychology – that established this particular perception, of human beings located within time by their own history of personal growth; but certainly, in the literary representation of children this implicit understanding of human subjectivity showed in the way the child-figure came to be used as an extension of the self, a resource for returning to one's own childhood, and as an image of one's extension in time.

Children had to be figured (turned into literary figures and represented) in the campaigns McMillan was involved in, and in the policy on childhood that she helped to evolve for the ILP and the Labour Party. This formulation of policy took place within a pre-existing history, in which intense concentration had been focused on working-class childhood at different points in the century before McMillan started to work and write in the area. One of the first points of attention was a series of debates, both literary and sociological, around radical reforming campaigns to regulate child labour, which took place at the end of the eighteenth century and the beginning of the nineteenth.[3] William Blake's poor chimney sweeper was the most enduring symbol of the social problem presented by the labouring child; and it is particularly important to note, for current purposes, that the little sweep represented the idea of the labouring child as danger and impurity, as well as innocence corrupted.[4]

This process of symbolising working-class children, and making them visible, is to be found at work in the great parliamentary inquiries into child labour of 1842, 1862 and 1867.[5] What is significant about the techniques of sociological investigation that these commissions employed is that they presented the transcribed words – the verbatim evidence – of poor and labouring children, and disseminated them to a wide audience. We could say, as well, that in the process of transcription these reports used the same new set of conventions for the depiction of working-class speech that novelists of the 1840s started to employ: the representation of dialect through a modified orthography embodied a way of both recording and actually *hearing* children's language.[6]

This making poor children visible through a presentation of their own words was also a feature of journalistic inquiry into working-class childhood in the mid nineteenth century. Henry Mayhew's depictions of young London street traders and other child workers are now the best-known examples of this kind of journalistic inquiry, but his work represents a lesser-known genre of the years 1860 to 1890, when labouring children were presented as figures of horror, pity and fascination – and frequently low comedy – in newspaper articles and short stories.[7]

This literal depiction of working-class childhood was connected to the emergence of photography as a means of representation. A large number of photographs, dating from the late 1860s onwards and produced by social welfare agencies, prison and workhouse authorities and by such forgotten photographers as John Thomson – one of a band of men who apparently roamed the alleys and byways, looking for young, appealing, and poor children to snap – measured out a continued 'discovery' of working-class childhood.[8]

Not only was childhood represented in these new ways from the 1860s onwards, but histories were written of it. McMillan herself wrote fragments of this kind of history, using the markers of literature and art to measure out a nineteenth-century invention of childhood.[9] John Ruskin's art history of working-class childhood was published in 1884, and it seems likely that McMillan's account was derived from his. In 'Fairyland', Ruskin noted the beauty with which children were depicted in the work of Rubens, Rembrandt and Vandyke, and then went on to describe how 'the merciless manufacturing fury, which today grinds children to dust between millstones and tears them to pieces on engine wheels', had compelled British painters to represent working children in 'wickedness and misery'. Using the same literary landmarks as McMillan was to employ, he suggested that 'in literature we may take the "Cottar's Saturday Night" and the "toddlin' wee things" as the real beginning of child benediction.'[10]

Some fifteen years before he wrote this piece, Ruskin had walked through St Giles on the way from his house to the British Museum, looked at the faces of the children playing in the streets, and considered 'the marvel [of] . . . how the race resists, at least in its childhood, influences of ill-regulated birth, poisoned food, poisoned air, and soul neglect'.[11] Other men had walked thus, some with cameras, others with notebooks, seeing as Ruskin did those faces, which 'through all their pale and corrupt misery' reminded him of 'the old "Non Angii" and recall it not by their beauty but by their sweetness of expression, even though signed already with trace and cloud of the coming life'.[12] McMillan's depiction of working-class childhood, the precise evocation of beauty in sordid surroundings, the *meaning* of the child thus depicted as an already thwarted possibility, lay within this tradition of literary, aesthetic and cultural criticism. In a striking – though probably not conscious – evocation of Ruskin's vision, Katharine Bruce Glasier recalled, after McMillan's death, an incident in 1896 when, after lecturing together in Oldham one October night, they watched 'the undersized workers pour out from a factory . . . and asked ourselves in bitterness of spirit: "How much would slaves of this kind have fetched in an old Athenian slave market?"'[13]

In 1884 Ruskin noted a number of artists who had 'protested, with consistent feeling, against the misery entailed on the poor children of our great cities – by painting the real inheritance of childhood in meadows and fresh air'.[14] McMillan's camp school in Deptford was an intensely practical manifestation of this Romantic critique of capitalism: children's adenoids were operated on, remedial gym straightened backs, and children put on weight rapidly. But *written* about, within this aesthetic and cultural tradition, the children who were healed and schooled there became figures that represented the multilayered meanings of 'natural' childhood. 'The love of spring may have been chilled for the moment by the cold wind of our industrial system', wrote McMillan in 1906, evoking the possibility of lowering national rates of infant mortality. 'But it is bound to revive. And it is love that will save the myriads who embark on the rough seas of life from going down so soon into the dark waters.'[15]   The child as potential rescuer or reclaimer of corrupt adulthood was a feature of the Romantic, post-Wordsworthian depiction of childhood, and as a literary territory this nineteenth-century understanding has been very well mapped out, particularly in the work of Peter Coveney.[16] It could be said that one of McMillan's literary achievements was the way she wedded this particular legacy of Romanticism within British culture to socialist thought in a new version of an established literary figure, 'the child', which operated as a kind of marriage between innocence and mortality.[17] This process is made clearer if we recognise that this child was always much more than a literary trope – was available as well as one of the means by which scientific and social thought mapped out the psychology of childhood and the stages of child language development throughout the century.[18]. 'The child' was also an idea that provided a context of understanding for the anthropological study of childhood, which in its turn established the norms of development with which we operate in modern society.[19] These developments in the study of childhood took middle- and upper-class children as subjects, and there are historical accounts of how Victorian society dealt with the divisions in social position and social function between different classes of children by sometimes denying that working-class children *were* children, in the post-Wordsworthian sense.[20]

Indeed, the observed *working-class* child represented corruption as well as innocence and the natural, in the tradition McMillan inherited and used. The idea of the working-class child (particularly the little girl) as a kind of danger and impurity was most overtly expressed in late-Victorian society in a publication that has already figured in McMillan's biography, in the furore surrounding the question of child prostitution and W.T. Stead's exposure of it in 1885 in his notorious *Maiden Tribute of Modern Babylon*, first published in the *Pall Mall Gazette* in July of that year.[21] The ambiguity – about sexuality, about childhood innocence – that the body of the little working-class girl represented in the scandal Stead revealed has been much analysed;[22] and there are grounds for seeing the potentially diseased state with which the young prostitute threatened the social body as only a heightened and baroque example of the threat posed by all working children, whose need to labour cut across newly established ideas about childhood as a state both innocent and separate from the adult world. Ten years or so after the 'Maiden Tribute' scandal, the more general exposure of working-class children's ill-health and disease, and the threat these presented to the body politic, fell within this understanding.

When McMillan started to publish her depictions of working-class childhood from the mid 1890s onwards, she did so for audiences that understood labouring children to constitute a form of social danger. This perception was sharpened by the revelation of ill-health among men offering themselves as recruits for the war in South Africa, in 1899.[23] The public debate that surrounded these revelations directed attention to deformed and diseased working-class children, and the way in which their ill-health threatened Britain's imperial prowess.[24]

This last argument is well known. The critique of the city, the implications of the discovery of the poor health and physical deterioration of the city's inhabitants that the debate worked with, and specifically the questioning of national efficiency occasioned by the Boer War, the publication of books like Arnold White's *Efficiency and Empire* and Seebohm Rowntree's *Poverty: A Study of Town Life*, the setting up of the Interdepartmental Committee on Physical Deterioration and the evidence it produced in 1904 – all focused new attention on the health of the city's children. Towards the end of the 1890s and beyond, this was the public context to McMillan's work with and writing about working-class children.

The other specific dimension to the discovery of working-class childhood in the period 1890–1920 was educational. Here, under a developing system of state education, the high social visibility of working-class children in the years after 1880 ought to be considered, with more of them consistently collected together in one place – the school – than society had witnessed before. In *Elementary Schooling and the Working Classes, 1860–1918,* John Hurt describes the conditions that were provided by the school system for the rapid spread of low-level contagious diseases in these years.[25] McMillan's political project on the Bradford School Board, for systems of mechanical ventilation in schools and the provision of washing facilities, were attempts to alleviate medical conditions that had been caused by the school itself.

McMillan's earliest journalistic fiction was concerned with what in the 1890s was called 'the woman question' – a debate about the role and function of women in existing societies, and in possible future ones. Within this framework, she had paid particular attention to the psychology of different types and classes of women, psychologies which she presented as evolved out of her fictional women's class and material circumstances. Many of these early pieces were autobiographical in origin: we have already noted the brilliant governess 'Mary Muse'; and in 'Zoë', published in 1895, 'Marjorie McGowan, the Scotch girl who had no home', encounters Zoë Coconcheff, the Russian revolutionary, among the parlour boarders of the French school in which she has found a job.[26] Up to 1895, then, McMillan's fiction dealt with the problems of young middle-class womanhood, cast loose upon the world and seeking a way of making a mark on it.

She seems to have turned her written attention to childhood for the first time in December 1895, when she published the story 'Gutterella' in the *Weekly Times and Echo.*[27] Here, the childhood of the working-class heroine and the child Gutterella's passionate love for her father are used only to prefigure her doom: Gutterella's inevitable course through the match factory, phossy jaw, casual sexual relationships, and death. For the next twenty years of fiction and non-fiction writing, McMillan was to use accounts of the corruption of childhood under industrial capitalism in this way, in order to make a more general point about working-class life – presented, as it was in 'Gutterella', as a 'solitary groping from cradle to grave'.[28]

At the beginning of 1897 McMillan published the two-part 'Lola'. Repeating the structure of 'Gutterella', 'Lola' is a moving account of a workhouse child's growth into womanhood, and ensuing deterioration unto death.[29] The figure of the workhouse child seems an odd device for McMillan to have chosen, for she was never involved in workhouse education, and although she showed a taste for exotic children (gypsy maids, Highland crofters' daughters and the like) Lola, in spite of her dark and brooding beauty, does not really fit into this category either. Rather, she is a workhouse child because then she can be utterly hopeless and abandoned, as is demanded in a certain type of romantic fiction of childhood. She is a girl, because within the literary culture attendant on this romance it is easier to look at girls and women, easier to probe their psychology, than it is to look at little boys. The fictional 'Lola', a girl and a workhouse child, allows McMillan to explore two central themes of the story: the influence of childhood experience on psychosexual development, and the notion of the unconscious mind. Unloved as a child, Lola cannot love in adulthood; is unable even to make friends with her fellow servants when she takes a job as a housemaid:

> The cook and the table maid . . . pitied Lola. They would have been kind to her, but she had such a strange way with her. She was not quarrelsome nor ill-tempered . . . But there was something about her that repelled. Her eyes never softened, her eyes never lightened even when she laughed, and she would have said good-bye forever in the same tone in which she said 'good-morning' . . . Something was wrong with her. She was like a plant without roots, that grows fast but falls at night. 'Unhappy the heart,' says a great poet, 'which has not loved in youth' . . .[30]

Lola marries, but leaves her husband within six months: she was, says McMillan, 'a wayfarer in life. Every house she alighted in . . . was an inn. And her husband was a chance traveller like the rest . . . it is certain that poor-law children, when they grow up, can be married like cuckoos . . .'. The only figure to promote love in Lola is a visiting educationalist, a woman who runs a model school in the country. Lola is haunted by the memory of her after their brief meeting, stands on street corners scanning the crowds and looking for her. Everyone else was 'part of the blank wall of the past, but she was like a dream-face, flitting forever between her and the cold stone'. Lola thinks of the child-rescuer on her deathbed.

In one extraordinary scene of Lola's young adolescence, she dreams (an event not usually allowed to fictional working-class children in this period), and through the dream McMillan allows her to express envy:

> Sometimes she dreamed that the big sea came and lifted her away. Far away she knew, there was life – stirring deep and glorious; new and strange things slumbered and played in it – things of which she had no hint, no clue. She dreamed not as happier maidens dream, but in a wilder element, with no point of return, no ark of peace, no glad sweet wakening – for she had no reminiscences, no

friendships, no regrets. The past was blank to Lola as a prison wall. She took the material for her dreams from the sights and sounds of yesterday. Always sights at which she gazed as an outsider. Always sounds whose inner meaning escaped her. One evening she had found herself in the grounds of a rich man. There was a great tent on the lawn, and within the tent a number of ladies and men were dining. Lanterns hung from the roof, and there were flowers and music. The ladies had jewels on their necks, and the crystal and silver on the table shone under a soft but brilliant light! Lola looked, and her brow darkened. Next day she heard the children in the Park prattling to their mothers and nurses, and the soft low tones with which the women answered them annoyed her. She went home quickly, carrying the loving words with her, like burrs on her dress.

By 1897, when this story was published in the *Clarion*, McMillan had already visited Charcot's clinic in Paris, and reported on it for *Clarion* readers.[31] At one level this piece is a useful reminder of the existence of the idea of the unconscious before Freud, its origins to be traced through the Romantic movement and in developments in neurological science in the second half of the nineteenth century.[32] But more particularly, the fictional Lola – her dreams, her repressed desire – allowed McMillan to explore the psychological effect of deprivation in childhood in fictional form. A month before producing 'Lola', she had told the ILP readership of the *Bradford Labour Echo*, in a passage quoted earlier, about the reluctance of a six-year-old girl she had encountered through school visiting to take a bath, and how the child had revealed – in a matter-of-fact way, scarcely remembering – that her mother had drowned herself in the local dam.[33] McMillan also frequently made the same point about the paucity of memory and its repression in poor children in her non-fiction writing. In 1902, in her ILP pamphlet *The Beginnings of Education*, she described another girl recounting her mother's death, in the same offhand way. 'Was the girl heartless?' she asked her readers.

> Not at all; the memory of that poor mother was already growing dim; but not because the child was unnatural. The very poor *cannot afford to remember*. Your fidelity, your tender thoughts of those who are no longer with you, cost something to the organism . . . Memory, more than any other faculty, is directly dependent on the blood supply, that is to say, on the food supply.[34]

McMillan's fiction was designed, as much as her other journalism, to express in a simple way some fairly complex ideas about physiology and psychology. At this level, then, we can see McMillan making the same points about her fictional children as she did on the political platform.

For instance, in her story 'Ann', published in the *Clarion* in 1898 and designed to show socialist children what it was like to be a child of the residuum, the eponymous heroine is turned out of the house by her family, makes her way to some woods, and there meets the water fairies, who make her notice her dirt for the first time. Here she also encounters Love, who teaches her how to dance. As a background to these events, Ann's first need had been taken care of, for the child ate a plate of sausages before the door of her home closed on her: food was the priority, necessary before children, rendered half-dead by the industrial system, could be awakened.[35]

'There is,' wrote McMillan in 1899, 'a strange lack of life and spontaneity' in such children. 'They are depressed, and their depression is obvious even in their noisiest moments. They do not complain. They never complain . . .'[36] Both the fictional 'Lola' and 'Ann', and the real Bradford children whom she described in her journalism, had been thwarted in development. More fortunate children, operating through play, gathered material 'for the higher mental life which is to follow, just as in the sub-conscious life of infancy, they once gathered materials for the conscious life of today'. The way in which she depicted working-class child life operated, then, as a warning to her readers: 'the mental life flows from the sympathetic and sub-conscious, and from these alone it is nourished. Woe then to those whose life-river is troubled near its source.'[37] So McMillan's fiction concerning children like these was a palatable way of both conveying information about them, and commanding sympathy on their behalf. 'It is that feeling for beauty, the potential beauty, of soul and spirit of all children, diseased and ragged though they be, that seems to me a unique note that Miss McMillan has sounded in literature', noted a *Christian Commonwealth* staff reporter who visited her in December 1911.[38]

A number of her stories were also written for the more-or-less privileged children of *Clarion* readers, and for those who attended Socialist Sunday Schools. These stories will be discussed in the chapter on 'Education', but it should be noted here how many of them, along with fictions like 'Ann', contained a reworking of McMillan's own childhood. To begin to trace this rewriting, we have to turn to her own autobiographical accounts of it – specifically an article written in 1912, and the major account (1927) that is to be found in the opening chapters of *Life of Rachel McMillan*. From the historical point of view, memories of childhood and their recording are particularly unreliable as evidence. In fact, McMillan dramatised the whole of her life in the 1927 account, presenting long incidents in dialogue that she could not possibly have recalled. This kind of fictionalising, done out of adult memory, is of a different order to the reconstructed childhood, where the writer has to rely on other people's accounts in order to tell the story of a childhood. Both these sources were used for 'the childhood' presented in *Life of Rachel McMillan*, and despite the difficulties they present there are ways of finding a historical reality within the unreliability: by paying careful attention to the *form* in which the childhood autobiography is presented.

'How I Became a Socialist', the precursor to the *Life*, published in 1912 in the *Labour Leader*, opens with a romantic reverie on childhood: 'the childhood of human beings is a strange period, mysterious as a northern twilight, dim and charged with great forebodings . . . [and] . . . adolescence, like childhood, is a time of dreams, of sleep walking.'[39] A recent analysis of the European *Jugenderinnerungen* – the autobiography of childhood and youth – has suggested that it is a form of literature that allows a writer to express an essential part of his or her own experience that cannot be accommodated within more traditional autobiographical writing.[40] The sense of self thus expressed, it is argued, usually presents itself poetically, if not in actual verse, and many of the early passages of *Life of Rachel McMillan* (like the extract from 1912, above) convey the oddness, disjunctures and dreamlike quality of remembered childhood experience, and do so in a highly wrought, poeticised style.

Particularly, McMillan presented her sense of oddness and dislocation in childhood by mentioning her deafness at this time. This deafness is abruptly introduced, attributed to scarlet fever, never discussed; its cure or remission is never pinpointed.[41] It is the silence of the childhood being described, the 'great stillness' that it embodied – especially the stillness of the house in Inverness – that allow McMillan to make a heightened visual presentation, and give what is seen – moving through the silence, suddenly coming into focus – a considerable degree of poignancy. McMillan returned again and again to the theme of deafness in her fiction of childhood, particularly that which she produced for a child audience. It provided the central device for her immensely long serial story 'Handel Stumm', which appeared in twenty-nine episodes in the *Labour Leader* between 1900 and 1901.[42] In 'Handel Stumm' a crofter's son, born in 1880, is marked out for great things in life by his deafness, and his triumph over it is directly due to a particular kind of physiological education.[43]

It is in his difference that Handel Stumm's greatness lies, and the twenty-nine episodes of the story can be seen as McMillan's most extensive working out of her own sense of difference and isolation, though this is at work in much of her fiction where isolated and sensorily deprived children are depicted. If we are to see in her writing (and in the political work that the writing elaborated) an insistent return to her feelings about her own childhood, then we need to note as well, along with some contemporary commentators, McMillan's self-presentation as a childlike woman. Julia Dawson, for instance, in her *Clarion* woman's column of 1904, described the middle-aged woman she had just interviewed as one 'who has never lost a year of youth and [who] is as much a child today as woman. She has all the brightness and originality of childhood . . . .'.[44]

Many of McMillan's fictions of child-rescue were embodied in an actual event of 1915, when two little boys were left in the Deptford Centre by their Lancashire miner father as he passed through London on his way to the front. The sisters took the children into their own house, and Peter and Totty made frequent appearances in McMillan's journalism from 1915 onwards:

> . . . one of our children is a collier's son from Lancashire. His father is at the front, and the child has never received any letters from his kindred. His physique is fragile; his age is seven. There is nothing to add to these few eloquent facts, except that his small face and head are beautiful, that his head is indeed very finely modelled and arrests attention . . .[45]

McMillan had always been susceptible to the sensuality of childhood, to the sudden startling beauty of a child's face blooming in the darkness of a Deptford street, and her affection for Peter and Totty was the apotheosis of this attachment. After Rachel's death McMillan travelled through occupied France and tried to arrange an official adoption with their father – a course of action, however, to which he did not agree.[46]

It was a theory of physiological education, especially that embodied in the work of Édouard Seguin (1812–80), that allowed McMillan to believe that working-class children could be rescued from deprived circumstances, made whole, well and strong, and educated to become agents of a new social future.[47] But Seguin's work apart, there was another set of ideas, popular in the 1890s, that allowed working-class children to be seen as possible agents of the new life. If the writing and propaganda work of Margaret McMillan and Katharine Bruce Glasier is considered, especially that of the 1890s, a certain notion occurs again and again: a telling phrase – 'little children have brought us all up from barbarism' – echoes.[48] It was only much later that Katharine Bruce Glasier revealed the source of this phrase – a now-forgotten but contemporaneously immensely influential book, Henry Drummond's publication of the *Lowell Lectures on the Ascent of Man*, in 1894. In *Socialism and the Home*, she wrote:

> Those who are familiar with the biographical writing of the brothers Reclus and Kropotkin, gathered into a wonderfully suggestive form by Drummond in his 'Ascent of Man', will

recognise the form of the argument that it has been the help-lessness of little children more than any other influence that has led us up as a human race to the possibilities of the Socialist state.[49]

Drummond's book was an exegesis on what the author called 'the evolution of love'. Darwinism, he argued, had been misunderstood, in that the struggle for existence had been confused with evolution itself. In fact, in Drummond's account two struggles are to be seen taking place in the history of the human race: the first for life, the second for the love of others: 'from selfdom to otherdom', said Drummond, 'is the supreme transition of history'. *The Ascent of Man* set out to reveal 'the stupendous superstructure of Altruism'. [50]

Drummond argued that in human history, it was 'in the care and nurture of the young, in the provision everywhere throughout nature for the seed and the egg, in the infinite self-sacrifices of Maternity' that altruism had found its main expression.[51] Within this account human children had a particular significance, because the human mother was able to recognise her children as *being like herself*, and thereby to move evolution on from a mere 'solicitude for the egg' to a full-blown maternity:

> . . . if a butterfly could live until its egg was hatched . . . it would see no butterfly come out of its egg, no airy likeness of itself, but an earthbound caterpillar. If it recognised the creature as its child, it could never play mother to it.[52]

With the creation of human children, 'Altruism found an area for its own expression as had never before existed in the world.'[53]

This structure of ideas informed a general understanding of McMil-lan's political work, and it is much more likely that it was derived from this source than from Herbert Spencer's observation on the question, which McMillan quoted as the epigraph to her book *Early Child-hood*.[54] Arthur Greenwood's memoir of McMillan, written in 1952, noted that she believed 'profoundly in little children as a precious chalice bearing within it the hopes of a finer life for all'. [55] Drummond's work, and her use of it – in all the Lolas, Gutterellas and deaf children she created – allowed McMillan to establish working-class childhood as both an arena for political action and a figurative device.

McMillan achieved her literary effect through a kind of rhetoric of sentimentality, and her childhood fiction still has the power to move the reader to tears. In 'Kindergarten', Franco Moretti tries to explain the means by which certain narratives make the reader cry.[56] He argues that moving moments in such stories are established when the point of view, or perception, of one of the characters coincides with the perception of the reader, who has just made his or her way through the narrative. Effects of pathos – being moved to tears – have also to do with the timing of this coincidence of points of view. The coincidence is particularly moving when, in Moretti's words, 'it comes too late' – the most obvious expression of this too-lateness, or tardiness, being the death of one of the characters. We cry then, because we understand that the course of events is irreversible; our tears are the expression of our powerlessness to alter it. As Moretti says, 'This is what makes one cry. Tears are always the product of powerlessness. They presuppose two mutually opposed facts: that it is clear how the present state of things should be changed – and that this change is impossible.'[57] McMillan's fictional depiction of working-class childhood, from the mid 1890s onwards moved between the idea of possibility – that things might be made better, that a regenerated child might regenerate a class, regenerate a nation – and her presentation of the process by which *this did not happen.* Her melodramatic child deaths, or the beautiful, ravaged dying of the child-woman 'Lola', stretched out on her workhouse bed, show what could have been, and what did not come to pass, both at the same time:

'Well, she's done with it,' said the doctor. 'Lola is dead! Do you remember her?' 'Me?' said the matron. 'There have been so many here, one can't remember them all. But I think we had once a girl with a strange name; it might be Lola.' 'It was Lola,' said the doctor. 'But this woman is too old to be Lola . . . Though to be sure,' she added, glancing at the white face on the pillow, 'she looks young enough now.' 'This is Lola,' said the doctor decidedly. 'She was a child of ten, twenty years ago, when she ran away from this very house. So she must be 30 years old now – that's clear enough. There are enough puzzles in the world,' said the doctor, irascibly, moving away from the bed. 'Don't *you* make more, if you please' . . .

They walked down between the rows of narrow beds, from which a score of cold, curious eyes looked forth on them. One old woman, sitting up, was moaning and weeping because 'they had given the box to Sarah Annie'. And a girl, dying of consumption, was moving her long, white fingers restlessly along the tucked-in sheet. They were all at home here. The younger patients had once been pupils at the school. Life for them had been merely a circuitous walk from the workhouse school to the workhouse infirmary.

The doctor looked at them, knitting his brows.

'Take for instance, this puzzle,' he cried, facing round suddenly on the matron, as they reached the door. 'You take them in, you wash them, you feed them, you clothe them, you teach them, you spend money on them, and they return here to die – at thirty. *There,*' said the doctor sternly, 'is a puzzle for you.'[58]

In this way did McMillan write about working-class childhood as part of working-class life, establishing its bleak trajectory as a figurative device; and so the notion of regenerated childhood as social salvation carried within it the sign that these things should *not* come to pass.

The fictional 'Lola', who died in the pages of the *Clarion* in 1896, was brought to life again in a series of pieces McMillan wrote for the *Highway*, the journal of the Workers' Educational Association, between 1911 and 1912. The series had the overall title 'In Our Garden', and the third and most reprinted piece was an account of the night when the first Deptford child slept out in the garden of the Deptford Clinic.[59] In describing the progress of Marigold's arrival, disrobing, washing, and settling down to sleep under the stars, McMillan made great literary claims for this Deptford seven-year-old, a costermonger's child, calling her, in her title to the piece, 'the English Mignon', and using as an epigraph the opening line from the infinitely sad song of yearning that Goethe's Mignon sings, later set to music by Schubert: 'Kenst du das Land . . .':

Know you the land where lemons are in flower,
Where the golden oranges glow in the dusky bower,
A gentle wind descends from the azure sky,
The myrtle is still and the laurel stretches high,
Is it known to you? . . . [60]

Wilhelm Meister, Goethe's great *Bildungsroman* of 1795–96, was much in the news in 1910–11, for an earlier version of the novel, entitled *Wilhelm Meister's Theatrical Mission*, written between 1777 and 1785, had just been discovered. A part-transcription of the manuscript reported in the British press highlighted the earlier version of Mignon's song.[61] In evoking Mignon, the strange, hermaphroditic, autistic girl-child of the two versions of *Wilhelm Meister*, McMillan attached a particular weight of meaning to her own Marigold. To the reader, the connections between the two child-figures are manifold. Goethe's Mignon is an abducted Italian child working as an acrobat with a troupe of travelling players when Wilhelm Meister first encounters her. She promotes in him 'intense pity' and an overwhelming sympathy and fascination.[62] The bodily postures of the child acrobats, of whom Mignon is only one, are seen as 'strange dislocations', and Mignon herself, though very beautiful, suggests a similar deformity, for 'her limbs promised stronger growth, or else announced a development that was retarded . . .'.[63] Meister buys the child from her exploitative employer, and she becomes his servant, though Mignon herself takes the young man as her father.

Mignon's silences and hysteria are part of what make her attractive to Meister, and what promote in him a great tenderness. Careless of her feelings, though, he does not see what Mignon herself cannot articulate, the young girl's developing sexual love for him. Mignon, who throughout the novel appears at the moments of Meister's romantic attention to other women, actually witnesses a sexual encounter between him and an actress in the bedroom where she has hidden herself to wait for him.[64] It is this scene that begins Mignon's descent into death: '. . . she suffered unbearable torment, all the vigorous emotions of passionate jealousy were combined with the unrecognised demands of an obscure desire'.[65] As child-figure and as a girl-child she has to die, and indeed does, welcoming the release from life, in front of Meister's very eyes: 'Look how your heart is beating' – 'Let it break . . . It's been beating too long anyway.'[66]

The import of Mignon for McMillan seems apparent enough, both in the child's strangeness and deformity and in her potential as reclaimer of sensibility in the adults around her. She is at once a representation of Meister's own inner conflict, his inability to grow and develop and of natural growth in general, inhibited by social forces.[67] The child Mignon is also preternaturally clean, and spends much time washing her clothes and herself.[68] Her music is the sum of her oddness and her beauty of soul; and McMillan described the 'English Mignon' singing her prayers to herself as she lay on her camp-bed in the Deptford garden:

> 'In houses,' whispers the little one, 'where it is dark and ugly, and people in the room, I will say them; but here I sing instead. Last night I sang all I know: "Jerusalem the golden", and "How bright these glorious spirits shine", and "There is a green hill far away". There isn't a *hill* here', said the child, 'but I like to sing that one the best . . . .'.[69]

Marigold's ardour and impulsiveness of affection and embrace echo that of Mignon: like Goethe's child, Marigold remains elusive, as when 'suddenly [she] flings her arms round her friend's neck, and, always holding aloof, looks at her with eyes full of love. She looks at Nurse, and keeps aloof even when holding her fast.'[70] What is more, the child-figure of the 1790s was the fruit of a double and shocking incestuous relationship, and it is possible that McMillan sought to indicate the horrors of her own child's home circumstances by evoking her.

It is probable that McMillan did intend the reader to make all these connections between Mignon and Marigold, and to bestow on the working-class seven-year-old of 1911 the same depth of interiority, dignity and meaning that Goethe gave to his child-figure. However, her only direct reference to *Wilhelm Meister* was when she presented the child's facial beauty. 'She wears,' wrote McMillan, the poor raiment of the slum child – a thin, soiled pinafore, long skirts and clumsy shoes; but on her head, over a triangle of short, thick golden hair, is a blue-knitted cap, which blot of vivid colour draws the eyes away from the poor raiment. Then one notes the beauty of the face, the broad, low brow, the exquisite lines of lip and chin, the nose, which like Goethe's Mignon is extremely lovely, and above all the ethereal blue eyes, set rather far apart under wide, dark eyebrows . . .

In *Wilhelm Meister*, Mignon marks the hero's particular failure of sensibility, and when she dies he understands, too late, the aetiology of that failure. Death elevates Mignon in social status too, but that elevation also comes behind its own time. Franco Moretti has called the death of Mignon the exemplar of Goethe's philistinism.[71] But the reader reserves outrage at Goethe's vulgarity for Mignon's funeral obsequies, where the embalmed child, endowed with the flush of life by the cosmetics that she had so painfully rubbed from her cheeks at the end of her career as an acrobat, lies in her open casket, whilst angelic crowds of little boys debate in chorus her various symbolic meanings:

> Boys: . . . she does not walk in the gardens any longer nor collect meadow flowers. Let us weep, we are leaving her here! Let us weep and remain with her!
>
> Choir: Children, turn back to life. May your tears be dried by the fresh air that plays around the winding stream . . .[72]

There has been some debate of late about whether what actually makes the reader cry is, as Moretti has claimed, that *it is too late*, or whether the convulsion of pity and tenderness is dependent not on the death, or annihilation of promise, but rather on the audience's sense that *if only* things had arranged themselves differently, opportunity for fulfilment would not have been lost.[73] *If only*, it is said, as a response made through the tears, confirms that there has been loss, or death, but also, at the same time, affirms that *it could have been*. So Steve Neale argues, in 'Melodrama and Tears', that at the moment of powerlessness to change things, which is what tears express, there is in operation a fantasy that things might be quite different. Another way of putting this might be to say that when tears come to the eyes, two levels of time are in operation – now, where things as they are say *it did not happen, it is too late*; and the conditional past, where *they might have been*.

This rewriting of Moretti's thesis has considerable purchase, except that Mignon's death says only: it is too late – and says precisely that *because* Moretti constructed the argument around different *child*-figures, not around adults, as in the revision of his argument. The horribly rouged dead-yet-living child lying in her open coffin may well suggest what could have been, for by her lying there her aristocratic heritage is revealed. But the embalmed child does not move us to tears, as does the living and dying Mignon. Indeed, as new and different meanings were accreted to the idea of childhood from the late eighteenth century onwards, we could say that children themselves became the central repository for the sense of loss and yearning that the words 'too late' embody.

This idea can be approached in a different though complementary way, by pointing to the massive development in understanding of human growth that the century we are discussing witnessed. The building up of scientific evidence about physical growth in childhood, the marking out of stages of development and the processes of language acquisition, all describe an actual progress in individual lives, which increased in symbolic importance during the nineteenth century, whereby what is traversed is, in the end, left behind and abandoned as the child grows up and goes away. In this way, childhood as it has been culturally described is always about what is temporary and imperma-nent, always marks out a loss in adult life, a state that is recognised too late.

What is more, the idea of things being *too late*, as exemplified in McMillan's rewriting of Mignon, expresses a conflict and ambiguity that must always attach to this kind of use of children in literary and symbolic terms. The manipulation of two levels of time (the here-and-now; the might-have-been) that the *if only* represents cannot really come into play with the child-figure, for children are quite precisely a physiological chronology, a history, as they make their way through the stages of growth. The solution of the writer trying to use the social fact of childhood in a symbolic way, and as representative of an adult state of mind, is usually to kill the child-figure. In *Wilhelm Meister*, Mignon dies at the realistic level because she has suffered too much, and because the narrative of her own life brings her to this point. At the symbolic level she expires because Meister has achieved adulthood, maturity and an inner integrity, and Mignon is no longer useful as representative of his former disharmony.[74]

We must suppose that by so deliberately operating this set of refer-ences, by making Marigold a version of Mignon, McMillan was both making a political statement – telling her readers, at a practical level, that help needed to be given to inner-city children at the optimum time for human development – and also, at the same time, manipulating much that was unspoken. Marigold is not doomed, as Mignon is, and she does not die; but whilst McMillan's child expresses hope, she also means: *it is too late*, a fact of which her author was quite aware. McMillan writes tenderly of her, asleep in the garden; then asks:

79

Will she go back to the dark ugly house? Yes. As the nights grow long and chill, she must go back. She will sleep again in a foetid room, and for this poor resting place the coster must pay such a heavy rent that there is little left over to spend on food and other things for Marigold.[75]

Marigold, it seems, could achieve the beautiful land of Mignon's song only for a very short time; she was a moment of hope, before she had to leave the garden. It is to gardens, real gardens and the gardens of the imagination, that we must now turn our attention. Particularly, we need to consider the garden in the Deptford slum, with its shelters thrown up for the healing of damaged children:

Know you the house, whose roof and pillars rose,
The hall is bright with light, the small room glows,
And marble figures hold me in their view:
Oh you poor child, what have they done to you?
Is it known to you?
                    Oh there, yes there,
Protector, goes the way that you and I should share . . .

4

Gardens

The ideal thing is that she should go into a garden, there to
find her own children, and people she knows looking after
them, and glad to see her and talk with her. (Margaret
McMillan, *Education Through the Imagination* [1923],
p.191)

IN the large-scale reclamation of working-class childhood and
working-class life that McMillan proposed, the idea of the garden
had a particular role. The physical embodiment of this idea, the
Deptford camp-school garden, was not only a place where children
were healed but was also the setting for McMillan's changing political
perspective, during and after the war years. We need, then, to deal
with real gardens – the flowers that were made to bloom in the urban
waste of Deptford – and with the gardens of McMillan's imagination.
These included, as has already been indicated, the lost paradise of an
American childhood and the loss of land that a particular Scottish
history delineated, and its attempted reparation through the movement for land restoration.

It is through Peter Coveney's pioneering work in *The Image of
Childhood* that we are familiar with the establishment of the Romantic,
post-Wordsworthian child in literature from the 1830s onwards.[1] His
argument is sometimes appropriated to a more general history of
childhood in which the late eighteenth and early nineteenth centuries
'discover' the child, with Wordsworth, and Rousseau before him,
being seen as key figures in the process. But in his *Child Figure in
English Literature*, Robert Pattison points to an essential difference
between the Rousseauesque presentation of childhood, as a stage on
the route to adulthood, and the Wordsworthian vision, in which
childhood is understood to be 'a condition which for the vast majority
of men is irretrievably lost as soon as completed'.[2] He asks us to see a
specifically *British* and post-Romantic understanding of childhood as 'a
lost realm, somewhere in the past of our lives, and the past of our
culture'.

In a more recent study of the 'golden age' of British fiction for
children, Humphrey Carpenter writes about a legacy of Wordsworthian understanding in which childhood is connected to the

Genesis story, and the idea that to children 'the earth appears as beautiful and numinous as it did to Adam and Eve'. In this way, then, 'Growing up becomes synonymous with the loss of Paradise'. Carpenter connects this understanding to Victorian and Edwardian children's writers' fondness for the symbol of a garden or Enchanted Place, 'in which all shall be well for evermore'.[3] Far less benignly, Pattison, on the other hand, argues that this post-Wordsworthian sensibility is linked to a much older Christian understanding: of childhood as sin and loss – emblem of the loss of grace and the expulsion from the Garden that is carried within and represented in each individual soul.[4] Pattison argues that the Rousseauesque vision of childhood had a limited impact on British social and educational thought, because of this conception of childhood as sin and loss.[5] Making the same general point, Coveney remarks on how little influence Rousseau and other continental theorists had on English educational practice, and comments that 'the first kindergarten was established in England only so late as 1851, the year before Froebel's own death'.[6]

It is indeed to Friedrich Froebel (1782–1852) that we might look for the translation of such ideas to a British audience – particularly after 1850, when the publicity machine of the Froebelian movement, the establishment of the Froebel Society in 1874, and extensive discussion of his educational theory in family magazines and childcare manuals all ensured his ideas a substantial middle-class audience. Private, charitable kindergartens, established in the poor districts of industrial cities in the 1860s and 1870s, did work that became official Board of Education policy from the 1890s onwards.[7]

The origin of these ideas lay in the late eighteenth century, when Froebel, working within a Romantic appropriation of Kantian philosophy, evolved an educational system for young children based on a notion of the human being as an organic unity, with the human mind as a spontaneously formative agency.[8] The 'child-garden' would allow the developing child to be active in a fitting way, and activity would permit the flowering of inborn capacities.[9] But although space, clean air, brightness and movement were specified as absolute needs of children, Froebel's 'garden' of children was not necessarily either a physical space or an actual garden. Rather, it was an organising metaphor for a particular kind of relationship between the child and the universe.

The use of the 'garden', then, was figurative, and it described a proper setting for child development. Much more clearly delineated within the theory was a kind of 'mother-made-conscious', for Froebel grounded his educational plans on what he perceived to be the social position of women in Germany in the early nineteenth century. Industrialisation had separated the roles of 'woman' and 'mother', and the training of women in his principles of child-rearing and early education, making many of them into professional mothers, was Froebel's self-proclaimed task.[10] One legacy of Froebelian thought, then, was a distinct 'educational mission' for women;[11] and this was to have some influence on McMillan, particularly in her argument for the training of young girls as nurturers of small children, and the education of mothers in the principles of mothering. This last was a particular development between 1910 and 1930, and will be discussed below.

The Froebel Society was founded in 1874; the Board of Education adopted 'kindergarten' as an activity for infant children in 1892; and the Society had started to offer a training leading to a certificate in kindergarten principles by 1884.[12] McMillan seems to have first encountered Froebelian ideas in Bradford, through her work on the School Board (though the *Labour Prophet*, for which she was writing before she left London, discussed the principles of Froebelian and kindergarten education).[13] In 1898 the School Management Sub-Committee of the Bradford School Board investigated kindergarten teaching in London board schools, and arranged for Bradford head-teachers to visit London. A School Board delegation visited the Froebel Institute itself.[14] These visits – and the gathering of information undertaken by McMillan and her School Board colleague, the liberal-progressive Mary Gregory – represent a direct call on McMillan's professional knowledge. The same kind of professionalisation of child welfare and infant education was at work when Florence Kirk, head of Bradford's Belle Vue Infants' School, took a course at the Froebel Institute in London, and then lectured local infant teachers in the methods she had learned, in early 1899. These teachers, in their turn, sat the examination of the Froebel Society.[15]

So in Bradford in the late 1890s Froebelian ideas provided a means by which female members of the School Board and women teachers could take on the structures of professionalism; but scope for the actual application of these principles was severely limited. The School Management Sub-Committee might recommend the removal of galleries from infants' schools, as it did in February 1899, but the provision of small chairs and tables to replace the ranks of desks and benches took three years to accomplish.[16] Free-arm drawing, sand-trays and spelling frames were introduced after 1898, but all these innovations (which McMillan was not alone in promoting) involved a reorganisation of the internal space of the school, rather than a move outside it. McMillan's work on the Council of the National Froebel Society, to which she was elected in 1904 after her move to London, shows her extending this aspect of her expertise, writing and talking on the potential of the *interior* space of the school.[17]

In McMillan's autobiographical account, the camp school – the school in the garden – arises unproblematically out of the first months of work when the experimental clinic at Bow moved to Deptford. Medical inspection of schoolchildren was compulsory by now, and treatment was possible, though no administrative structure existed for the financial support of such a venture. At this stage, then, the Deptford Clinic was funded by private charity and by fees paid by parents. Initially it operated as a treatment centre, opening after school hours, between five and eight o'clock. Its first reports, compiled by Doctors Eder and Tribe, were widely publicised and showed the sometimes astonishing results of very simple treatment.[18] A house in Evelyn Street, Deptford was loaned to McMillan and turned into a theatre for minor operations, and some time in 1911 a group of little girls recovering from treatment were put to sleep in its garden. 'Seventeen girls in all,' recalled McMillan,

> ranging in age from six to fourteen. They arrived all a-twitter late in the afternoon – arranged their night clothes and bed under the canvas, and played in the garden. Then washing in the boiler house . . . [they] came out all clean, with shining plaited hair, dressed in warm gowns, to take their place in the long row of beds in the open . . . The girls began to *dream* – to love to listen – to look *forward*. The night sky wakened them.[19]

McMillan saw this development as an essential part of the school clinic, arguing from 1912 onwards that the clinic was the nursery of the poor, that its nurse should be seen like 'a rich woman's nurse is – the nurse who tends the children in a Mayfair nursery' – but adapted to the exigencies of working-class life.[20]

Once McMillan's intention is understood, the idea of the camp school cannot be seen as an educational project in the modern sense, nor can it be completely subsumed under the heading of contemporary efforts in child-rescue and child welfare. Its most obvious difference from the open-air school movement of the time is the way in which it was designed to fit into the existing pattern of working-class life, not removing children from their homes and neighbourhood but providing an extension to them.[21]

As with most therapies of the period that involved healing in the open air, the use of the air itself was not questioned but treated rather as an obvious good.[22] In her journalism between 1910 and 1914 McMillan wrote of the unproblematic and unqualified good of children being in touch with nature, and it was this point that she emphasised to reporters and other visitors:

> Here the little girls gathered each evening, as the sweltering day turned to twilight; pale faces brightened at the sight of the sweet-williams and white fox-gloves which 'I can look at after I'm in bed'. Here, sleepy eyes looked from their pillows at points of

starry fire in the indigo blue depth; the night wind cooled their little heated bodies, and a primrose dawn called them awake. Will these children ever forget the healing joy of such nearness to the earth spirit as is possible even in Deptford?[23]

Later on, in *The Camp School*, in *The Nursery School*, and in the 1924 edition of *Education Through the Imagination*, we can see the theoretical apparatus being built around the camp school's existence, but none of McMillan's writing between 1910 and 1914 reveals one. Rather, it is McMillan's recent experience that gives clues to the prehistory of this 1910 development.

In 1903, at the garden party given by Bradford teachers to bid her official farewell, McMillan met Joseph Fels, the American philanthropist made wealthy by a lifetime spent in the manufacture of soap, already a devoted propagandist of the single-tax on land values as a solution to Britain's problem of poverty.[24] The land question and the reform of land ownership had done much to crystallise socialist ideas and we have seen McMillan's various encounters with these ideas, in her Scottish childhood and in her time in Germany and Switzerland as a young woman.[25] The 'Single-Tax' was the doctrine of Henry George, whose ideas, embodied in his most famous work, *Progress and Poverty*, had swept the British Isles from 1880 onwards.[26]

George's writing – and his strikingly publicised tours of Scotland and Ireland in the 1880s, when he visited scenes of agricultural distress in the middle of what was anyway an acute agricultural depression – helped to concentrate embryonic socialist thought on matters of political economy, and his work and writing thus helped to form a distinctly British socialism. George argued for a single-tax on the value of land as a cure for all economic ills. He argued that the value of land increased as the population increased, and that its value could not be attributed to either the efforts or the virtues of its owners, but rather to the human labour that had gone into creating it throughout recorded history. The solution to the vast discrepancies between wealth and poverty was a tax on land owners, according to the value of their land.[27]

Fels was interested not only in these Georgian economics but also in various educative reforms that promised the return of the people to the land, and what he had encountered by meeting McMillan in Bradford in 1903 was 'a personality with views and ideas of unlimited importance for the well-being of the future generation, very much in harmony with his own most intimate convictions, and worthy of every degree of support'.[28] McMillan had met someone with money, who was willing to spend it.

It seems from Fels's account that even as early as 1903 McMillan must have presented the idea of the health centre in educational terms, and broached the subject of open-air schooling, for the attraction of McMillan's proposal for him was twofold. Fels was concerned with an education that would promote a love of the land and the natural life in future adults. In terms of practical politics, he believed that a generation of children educated through such a health centre and in a camp school 'would have the land hunger, and also some knowledge of how to use land in town and country'.[29] McMillan's many references to the politics of land nationalisation in her propaganda for the Deptford Centre were partly an obeisance to Fels's role as a financial backer of the scheme. She was to encounter him many times after 1903, especially in connection with the Workers' Educational Association and its efforts to establish centres of rural education on the Danish model.[30]

What Fels offered on this occasion was £5,000 to help establish and equip a number of health centres for the treatment of schoolchildren in various districts of London. In November 1904 he and McMillan took the scheme before the Education Committee of the LCC, to be met with a good deal of political resistance and administrative parsimony.[31] After the failure of this meeting Fels withdrew his immediate and personal involvement, though not the financial support he had offered. A year later another scheme for health centres was forwarded to the Committee by the managers of the group of schools in Deptford with which McMillan was connected. This scheme foundered because the law as it stood prevented individual attention to the physical well-being of children.[32] However, legislation in 1908 allowed the Board of Education to give general powers to local authorities to provide for such treatment, and the first of McMillan's experimental clinics was opened at Bow in December of that year. Although Fels withdrew his first offer of £5,000, he made several smaller donations to the Deptford Clinic after 1910.[33]

In 1909, responding to a Fabian Society invitation to speak, Fels reported that he would be bringing McMillan along, and that she had been 'converted to the importance of the taxation of land values'.[34] Her 'conversion' may be seen as the price she had to pay for Fels's financial support, yet it is far more likely that it was the affective side of Fels's propaganda that appealed, and that she incorporated within her developing theorisation of the camp school at Deptford. In one of her first descriptions of the camp in the garden at Evelyn House – in *Highway*, September 1911 – she recalled Fels lecturing at Ruskin Hall in the previous week:

on 'Land', not on 'Nature Lessons' or 'Botany' or 'School Gardens', but on Mother Earth and the right of each to claim her . . . If only there were land for, say a thousand open-air bedrooms as humble as this one . . .[35]

In *Life of Rachel McMillan* and in *The Camp School*, McMillan dwelled on the events that followed the fiasco with the LCC and referred to the loss of the original offer of £5,000 many times, for it was a matter of deep regret to her. In these accounts, she presented Fels's obsession with Henry George and the single-tax as an idea that deflected him from the purpose she wanted him to fulfil, and in 1927 she made this ambivalent assessment of Georgism:

I have learned since that day that he was wrong, and yet right in great measure, for land tenure is below all social problems. The monopoly or abuse of it creates evils, veils them and protects the aggressor. Yet I am glad that we did not turn aside . . .[36]

Indeed, she attributed her own overt conversion to socialism, in the school in Switzerland in the 1880s, to encountering the ideas of Henry George; and the story of her own Scottish childhood, told in the opening chapters of *Life of Rachel McMillan* and rewritten in much of the romantic fiction that she set in the Highlands and Islands, had as a central theme the actual conditions of land tenure and land clearance that George had addressed during his Scottish campaigns in 1884 and 1885.[37] The Scottish Land Restoration League was formed in 1884 in the wake of George's visit, and it provided one element of the political culture that the McMillan sisters (or, more particularly, Rachel) encountered in Edinburgh in 1887.[38]

The Scottish childhood and adolescence that McMillan saw herself representing by 1927 (and perhaps by 1912) was a romance both of loss and of the possibility of restoration. She could not incorporate political economy within her theory of the restorative power of the earth, as her ambivalent assessment of George, quoted above, shows. But in the camp school she was able to restore working-class children to the earth as much as to the open air, and the earth that the children ran around on embodied a set of ideas that she had encountered in the political formations that developed around land restoration, after the 1880s.

In his book *The Political Anatomy of the Body*, David Armstrong has conceptualised large-scale shifts in understanding of disease in terms of what he calls 'social hygiene', a shift from a nineteenth-century understanding of its being located in 'the spaces between people', in 'the social body itself', to a new system in which people were understood to carry ill-health 'from the natural world into the social body'.[39] The Deptford camp school embodied no simple faith in nature, but rather in a specifically controlled and organised nature, which was the garden. The natural world was indeed understood to represent danger, in the terms Armstrong has described, and McMillan used Rachel's knowledge of social hygiene, culled from fifteen years' experience in rural Kent, to reveal the poverty of the natural.

Recalling her sister's work between 1896 and 1913, McMillan wrote at first a reverie of rural beauty: 'in May the whole countryside was a dream of beauty: wild flowers everywhere; hedgerows and lanes sweet with drifting scents; fields all abloom; gold and crimson and snow of heavy blossom on the trees . . .'. But then she warned that the dream 'did not blind [Rachel] to the tragedy of village life. In spite of the glory outside and the riot of flowers in the gardens, the children of the cottagers grew up like wild grasses on the shore. There was no nurture for them . . .'[40] It was indeed the theorisation of 'nurture' rather than a simple celebration of nature that supported the developing camp school, and McMillan recalled that in the 1890s, in the unhygienic hovels of the rural poor, 'Rachel began to dream of a new kind of garden . . . a garden of children. This is the true garden. All others come as the prophecy of the human garden of Paradise . . .'.[41] She indicated what nurture the organised child-garden might provide:

> In it should be the appliances for nurture and education. Out of the long sleep of prenatal life and the sleep of the first year, little children will waken in a place prepared for them. A glad inrush of sensation will come just at the moment of Life's first conscious waking – they will waken *well*. On this a system of education could be built at last![42]

This moment of dawning consciousness takes place in a garden, and is described in much detail in McMillan's various accounts of the Deptford camp school. The school (which always operated in conjunction with the Clinic, and will be referred to from now on as the Deptford Centre when it is not necessary to separate their functions) went through several manifestations, its first being the girls' camp, which operated from March 1911 until the outbreak of war. In the beginning, two tents were put up in the garden of Evelyn House. Gas piping and canvas formed beds, and a shower was rigged up by fixing a pipe and hose over the yard drain and surrounding it with a canvas sheet, weighed down at the bottom with stones.[43] After a few months the canvas collapsed, and a corrugated iron shed was put up between the fence and the house wall, with canvas shield forming the other two walls. Canvas provided the structure of outdoor wardrobes in the yard.[44]

The first lot of girls (about a dozen at any one time, the number sometimes rising to seventeen over the years), whose ages ranged from

six to fourteen, quite simply spent the night sleeping in the garden.
Marigold, the 'English Mignon', was among them.[45] They arrived from
home, according to the routine McMillan described, at about half-past
five, and had certain camp duties to perform but also time to play in
the garden. At half-past six, what McMillan called 'washing rites'
began, with the older girls looking after the younger ones. At seven the
beds were put out, and bedding was arranged – 'we dyed the girls'
blankets a beautiful blue – and the sheets and the pillows. The camp
looked very pretty.' The little ones were in bed by half-past seven,
with the older girls joining them, having showered later, at a quarter to
eight. 'At eight o'clock', wrote McMillan, 'all was quiet. The camp
slept, lighted only by a red lantern which burned dull and rosy near
the outhouse wall, and at the foot of the Guardian's bed . . . .'.[46]

The children had breakfast in the camp (on oatmeal, obtained from
Inverness: 'Once we got Lowland meal and once English meal, and on
both occasions the girls' weight went down at a run in a week!'), left for
board school at a quarter to nine, and ate the other two meals of the
day at home.[47] The simple principle behind all this was to get the
children out of crowded and badly ventilated bedrooms, and give them
a good night's sleep. Later, in 1914, when its educational aspects had
been much developed, McMillan called it 'an open-air residential
school, that does not separate the child from his home'.[48] Two years
before, in 1912, commenting on the Treasury grant-in-aid to local
authorities for the treatment of sick schoolchildren, she outlined what
the money might do if it were to be spent on centres like the Deptford
one:

> In the camp school, we could give them [the children] a first-rate
> education, also a splendid breakfast. Most of them can get some
> kind of dinner, if not at home, then at school. They could sleep in
> the open nine months in the year and in the camp building during
> the winter. This going home every day, taking a great deal that is
> precious *with* them, is part of the system. Parents would be in the
> camp every day and see what is going on. Close by is the Clinic
> with its staff; nurse and physical trainer, dentist and doctor . . .
> The camps would be under the supervision of the school clinic; or
> rather, they would be part of the school clinic.[49]

The camp school's second manifestation was in St Nicholas's church
yard, Deptford, where a Night and Day Camp for boys was constructed early in 1912.[50] It received a good deal of adverse publicity,
especially over the disturbance it constituted to the dust of Christopher Marlowe, who was buried there.[51] It was more beautiful, noted
McMillan, than any of the other camps, but 'it was no use falling in love
with all of this. Our hands were tied, our every movement watched,

our life a burden. Besides criticism, we had the wind and the rain and no cover.'[52] In April 1912 the McMillans rented a piece of waste ground near the Clinic, and on this site the permanent camp school was built. A sleeping pavilion was constructed, which also doubled as the schoolroom. A raised concrete floor was designed to allow free circulation of air, and the side-walls were sectioned, so that they could be removed. The front was permanently open, but with a storm screen that could be fastened down in bad weather.[53] The boys followed the same regime as the girls, though they took two meals a day in the camp. Teachers were engaged, working with all the children in the Boys' Camp, with the girls returning to the garden at Evelyn House to sleep. By the outbreak of war, the camp catered for seventeen girls and forty boys.[54]

For what seems to have been an experimental period in early 1914, six children under five years of age slept in the garden at Evelyn House, but a baby camp was not opened until April of that year: on what was known as the Stowage site, in Church Street, Deptford – a piece of land that had been originally purchased by the LCC for eventual erection of an elementary school. The Girls' Camp moved here, and the nucleus of the Open-Air Nursery School was formed in the Baby Camp, which was catering for twenty-nine children by the end of August 1914.[55]

At the end of this month, the clinic medical superintendent made his first report:

> . . . by the end of the summer, twenty-nine children were living and sleeping in the Camp. There was hardly any illness even during the hot months . . . There seems to have been marked mental improvement as well as physical . . . It has been generally recognised that the proper care of children under school age forms a serious gap in the measures that have been suggested to ensure a healthier and more vigorous people. This open-air camp for these babies is an endeavour to bridge the gap, and it is a method of treatment and child nurture that might well be encouraged and developed.[56]

The Stowage site was an acre in extent, and the garden developed slowly. At this stage, according to McMillan, it was the open *space* that mattered:

> Our rickety children, our cramped and . . . deformed children, get back to the earth with its magnetic currents, and the free blowing wind . . . To let them live at last and have the sight of people planting and digging, to let them run and work and experiment, sleep, have regular meals, the sights and souds of winter and spring, autumn and summer, birds, and the near

presence of mothers – to get these things we sacrificed everything else.[57]

'If the wind blows too hard,' she added, 'there is canvas to put up', insisting that 'of winter afternoons when it is soon dark, and of cold, and wet mornings, we must think *without fear*.'[58]

It was the nursery school that endured through the war years, and around which McMillan developed a detailed role for the garden in the nurture and education of children under five. The garden itself, she said, should be sheltered by trees – 'limes, mulberry trees and planes do very well in the most crowded district of south-east London' – and fruit trees and bushes should mark the southerly boundary. The ground itself should be terraced, to provide rock gardens and also to break the force of the winds. She specified a herb garden, for the purposes of sense training and the children's pleasure: 'the toddlers press [the] leaves with their tiny fingers and come into the shelter smelling their hands'.[59]

Ideally, the garden should provide vegetables for the camp kitchen, but the process of tending the vegetable plants was in itself beneficial to the children:

. . . nothing trains the mind and fills it with wholesome memories better than the carrying out of all this work in their sight, and with their help. They follow our gardener . . . down the paths and into the drills; and very early and without any formal teaching of any kind they learn to know the names of things.[60]

In the garden should be apparatus and low walls for the children to climb on, sand-pits, and a lawn – a place for them to run. But the garden should also contain its own wildernesses. One should be a rubbish heap – a 'rich place, a great rubbish heap, stones, flints, bits of can, and old iron and pots' – a place where 'there [are] no rules'; the other should be a flower garden, a large plot allowed to grow wild.[61]

All these arrangements constituted a specific place in which a child might *find herself*, in a condition often outlined by McMillan, which we may call *reverie*.[62] She described this state in Monica, who died after 'one conscious springtime':

She 'took in' the terrace wonderfully as the gate of a new world . . . one could see her, nearly every morning, in her clean pinafore, dreaming near the cabbage-bed, with one shoe left behind her on the path. No doubt Seguin would be glad to see her there. 'How few children,' he says, 'are allowed to remain dreaming, touching, and handling things on the knees of their mother . . .'[63]

In this particular account, the garden itself acts as a kind of mother. In McMillan's writing of the 1910s, the garden is able to do what working-class mothers are increasingly seen as unable to do: to promote speech in their children; to allow, as the vegetable beds did, the naming of things.

In the garden as a whole, two things might promote astonishment in the children, and thereby move them to speech. McMillan described three-year-old newcomers being shown round the garden by existing camp-school children; she remarked that 'they cannot speak at all, even at three years old. The herbs and simples which their remote ancestresses knew well appear to stir them. Their eyes are bright. Their mouths open.' Herbs, then, produced the initial shock of delight, and so did the roses. 'I am astonished to find,' McMillan recorded in 1917, 'that of all kinds, the low dwarf Hybrid Teas grow best of all in our Camp':

> they are so low growing, just tall enough for toddlers! When we got them to the rose beds, the open mouths found utterance. Their hands got eager. They stand in front of the rows of Hybrid Teas next, pointing tiny forefingers, but for the most part in silent wonder.[64]

What visitors remembered of the fully matured nursery-school garden of the 1920s was the sharp contrast it made with the squalid streets around it. From one of these streets a door led the visitor to a secret place, a 'new world', in the heart of a slum: 'the door leading in from Church Street opened into a garden full of autumn flowers. A bank of Michaelmas daisies with their mauve and purplish tints faced the main entrance, and climbing up some of the arches were "love in a mist", and late ramblers . . .'[65] The garden was not meant to be cut off from the houses surrounding it. In 1917, McMillan suggested that

> an ideal camp school must have a house or houses behind it . . . A fault of our present day schools is their awful isolation. This isolation is not natural, it is unnatural. Just as plant gardens were first made round homes, so *human* gardens should be started round human homes also.[66]

The Stowage site was overlooked by about thirty houses. It was meant to be observed, to provide a kind of show and object lesson for the local inhabitants. McMillan called the nursery school 'a theatre', a 'spectacle':

> All day there are groups near the entrance and eyes watching through the palings. They make me think always of the queues, waiting to go to the theatre. Here in London there might be a gay

drama played out under the eyes of admiring mothers in all quarters. 'It's *better* than a play,' said a poor woman, hiding a jug under her apron, 'better'n the pictures.'

'Come on,' cries a man at the corner, 'come and 'ave a look at the kids.'[67]

The spectacle was a lesson, particularly for the mothers who lived in the houses around. In her early accounts of the Deptford Centre, McMillan often described its benefits to the mothers of poor children, living just above the destitution line:

> All the 'red tape' loosens in their presence, and one realises that the soul of a people is something greater after all than the methods of an advanced section . . . The people want – not a great imposing place, miles away – but a familiar place, close by, where the best that is known about treatment and training can be under their eyes and at their service. They want a nurse who can be a neighbour, and a teacher who can explain why Joyce stoops . . . Everything that is imposing has to get off its pedestal if it is to be of any real use to the toiling, suffering masses in our great cities.[68]

The adult education available in the open and visible garden was delineated most clearly by Emma Stevinson, superintendent of the nursery school in the 1920s, in her book *The Open-Air Nursery School*.[69] But this theme also developed in McMillan's writing throughout the war years and in the early 1920s, though neither she nor the many journalists who made their way to Deptford mentioned this as a function of the Centre in its first few years of operation. Before the war, the target of the enterprise was always seen as the children, and a *Christian Commonwealth* writer came away in January 1914 convinced that camp schools might be made a 'great social weapon', and quoting McMillan on the possibility of their producing, in a couple of generations, men and women who would find it 'literally impossible to tolerate the economic servitude to which every new generation is now condemned'.[70] And it was the children, according to McMillan, writing in this early period of experimentation, who absorbed the short-term teaching as well. Some of them, she said, had already rebelled against their overcrowded homes, and put their beds up in their back yards.[71]

Nevertheless, in these early stages the education of parents was emphasised when the clinic itself was discussed. One of its potentials was seen to be the way in which it allowed them to make a cognitive leap, to realise that the disease and ill-health of their children was not just in the ordinary way of things, but produced rather out of material circumstances – particularly poor housing – that they themselves could change. Discussing the production of food in school gardens in 1909,

McMillan suggested that once the process was witnessed it would help working men to break the chains of dependence on their employers. She urged the Labour Party to make its appeal not to 'the human will, but to the intellect (however obscured) of the working classes'.[72] It was a development in understanding, in the making of connections – in cognition – that the whole scheme of the Centre might bring about.

In the period of experimentation, between 1910 and the outbreak of war, McMillan understood fathers to be parents as much as mothers. In one highly wrought – and very moving – piece written in 1910 she described a father in the dental clinic talking to the dentist, and being told what was wrong with his child, in an exchange in which – at least as reported – the dentist did not condescend. The father thirsted for knowledge, for a way of seeing how things worked, how they got to be the way they were; and a simple explanation of tooth decay started this cognitive process. 'It would seem', commented McMillan of this incident, 'that the very poor live in a kind of prison.'[73]

The emphasis on mothers (rather than parents) and on maternal care, seen most clearly in descriptions of the camp-school garden after the end of the First World War, can be attributed to two sources. First, the various experiments with the care and nurture of children over seven were largely abandoned during the war years (though one group of older children did remain to be educated by McMillan throughout the 1920s)[74] and the focus of attention turned to children under school age. The grant to institutions caring for the children of munitions workers during the war, and the Act of Parliament that allowed the LEA funding of nursery schools after 1918, formalised this shift down the age scale. These very young children, who were accompanied to school rather than making their own way there, brought mothers into the camp in a way that older children had not. Second – and as a background to this institutional change – was the development of the maternal and child welfare movement. The origins of this movement are to be found in the early years of the century, in the reaction to the physical deterioration that the Boer War had revealed. One of the strategies for amelioration that developed, among a wide range of welfare and philanthropic organisations, was the education of mothers, a form of intervention that increased from about 1910 onwards.[75]

McMillan did not particularly align herself with this movement, and the origin of her Deptford Centre in a theory of social and socialist reclamation can still be seen at work in her writing during the 1920s. Nevertheless, the staff she employed, the officials responsible for the schools (especially the one funded by the LCC) and the culture of medical sociology developing in these years, all turned her attention more and more towards the mothers of the children attending the

94

open-air nursery school. 'In the evening a crowd of mothers used to come', she recalled of 1914. 'They wandered about the garden. They gathered in the shelter. They looked at the bathing and dressing, feeding and play. Space at last. Fellowship at last, and under the open sky!'[76]

The garden, which might offer a temporary solution to the overcrowding and ill-health of working-class urban life, and at the same time, as part of a long-term strategy, might create the impulse for a more sweeping and revolutionary change in social circumstances, became part of a programme in mothercraft. Indeed, the garden itself played a diminishing role in McMillan's exegesis on the nursery school as the 1920s passed. The social and domestic circumstances that made getting Deptford children out of foetid and overcrowded bedrooms and putting them to sleep under the stars such an obvious solution to a pressing need had now started to ameliorate.

The garden, as both a paradise lost and the paradise regained through its re-creation on earth, is one of the most permanent paradigms of Western culture – a figure, an image, a way of seeing – which seems to persist through great tracts of historical time. We have been alerted to the seductions of this kind of immutability of terms by Raymond Williams, in his discussion of the long historical conflict played out as city has been contrasted to countryside in the literature of this culture over the last three hundred years.[77] Williams's warning should have some particular purchase here, as we consider the urban garden as a measure of the city-dweller's loss of countryside, and the child in the city demonstrating a yet more profound loss, and a more profound hope.

As we begin to measure out these ways in which children came to be available as metaphors of loss and hope, we should prosaically remind ourselves of two historical aspects to this development, both of which have begun to emerge with some clarity. The first is the figure of the child as a means available to social commentators for criticising the city, and holding up for examination its effects on the health and growth of its inhabitants, in the years 1870 to 1930. (This point will be explored in more detail in the next chapter.) The second aspect of this development that we need to bear in mind is the seeming transparency of the child-image. Robert Pattison remarks, in *The Child Figure in English Literature*, that when we encounter a child in a text, from no matter what distant past or unfamiliar culture, we divest that child of any symbolic meaning; see it smile, or cry, and believe that what we encounter there is a real child, always the same: a truth.[78] The historical importance of McMillan's writing is that she helped to create

95

this transhistorical figure, and at the same time located children in particular social and economic circumstances – explained them in those terms – as part of a political project.

What then was available to McMillan when, in the 1920s, she evoked the immutability of the child-image and spoke of children as 'the true garden . . .', with all other gardens only 'the prophecy of the human garden of paradise'?[79] The work of Froebel and the understanding transmitted by it would seem an obvious source, but Froebel himself was no advocate of a Rousseauesque open-air education, and sought rather to protect children from the dangers of nature. 'Kindergarten' was not originally a term that signified an actual garden, but rather an institution where children could spend time outside the family in the company of their peers in the presence of a trained adult; where 'the protective gardenlike atmosphere . . . would protect the child against the corrupting influence of society, and the dangers of nature'.[80]

Moving away from Froebel and looking at the actual planting of gardens for children, we could note that the early English pioneer of infant education, Samuel Wilderspin, advocated the planting of gardens around the slum infant schools of the 1820s, because he believed that trees and flowers were a provision for health, but also because the scented flowers would 'tend to counteract any disagreeable smell that may proceed from the children . . . '.[81] McMillan herself advocated sense training in the Deptford herb garden – not out of Froebelian conviction but out of a particular reading of Seguin, and the search for an environment that would produce the state of reverie.

Seguin himself had advocated garden schools 'in obedience to [the] axioms of Physiological Education' in order to make the 'schooling of the masses more active and practical'.[82] And whilst reminding ourselves in this way of the absences that underlie the connection between children and gardens at any particular point in the nineteenth century, we should note that in the early 1920s the layout of the camp-school garden itself partook of a particular theory of gardening and landscape, in which the principles of naturalness and wildness tamed warred with recently revived notions of order and design in garden landscaping. The mixed borders, the wild garden and the herb garden seem to represent several schools of thought in early-twentieth-century gardening, though we are not really to know if they represented McMillan's own knowledge or that of Mrs Hambledon, the Centre's gardener.[83] Certainly, the hybrid teas McMillan favoured were a very precise and *theoretically* determined choice of rose.[84]

We may note, as well, that McMillan constructed her garden in a slum at the same time as an intense debate about and planning of garden cities was taking place – indeed, she was involved in the planning of school accommodation in one of them, Welwyn Garden City. Endeavours at Welwyn and Letchworth (and there were many like them) attempted to improve the health of populations by placing gardens within conurbations, but in Ebenezer Howard's dream embodied at Letchworth, at least, little attention seems to have been paid to the actual form, function and planting of the *garden* in which people were to live. Rather, the garden operated as an organising idea for new relationships between populations, industry and culture.[85] However, it does seem that it was easier for planners to discuss the planting and arrangement of actual gardens when children were involved. The garden as a physical place – a place of actual healing and nurture – rather than as an organising metaphor, was realised in the care of children in these years, at least in the garden city movement; again, because of the immutability of the connection between children and gardens.[86]

All these metaphorical connections drew on specific sets of knowledge, and McMillan's own work in particular must focus attention on the immense amount of work done on child development in the late nineteenth century, the establishment of the psychological notion of stages of development, the detailed physiological accounts of physical growth that became available, and work on the process of language acquisition. All this scientific work established the general understanding of childhood growth as a natural unfolding of a preordained sequence. McMillan's popularisation of these ideas to a wide range of audiences, particularly through the pages of the *Clarion* and the *Labour Leader*, is the evidence underlying the argument of this book.

But other sets of knowledge were available to McMillan as she wrote and rewrote the child in the garden. In 1911, for example, she used a garden simile to express certain ideas about the unconscious mental life of the Scottish peasantry,[87] and it is likely that she was familiar with modern theories of the unconscious by this date, for her Clinic doctor, David Eder (who was to provide the first British translation of Freud's *On Dreams* in 1914), was busy promoting and publishing the new ideas in the journal *School Hygiene*, of which he was an editor and McMillan an honorary editor.[88] In Eder's work in this period, and in much of McMillan's writing, the garden at Deptford was viewed as a place where the hidden and unconscious life of childhood would be revealed. It remains to be seen how much darkness was understood to lie in the garden still, and in the working-class child caught there, in these new versions of lapsarian theology. A consideration of the city in which this garden was set – and the actual cities in which McMillan evolved her theory of childhood – may lead us to some conclusions on this question.

5

Cities

I N McMillan's political work and writing, the connection of childhood with a garden, both as an expression of the idea of human
growth and nurture and as an ideal setting, received a new shaping
and emphasis between 1895 and 1920. This reworking (which was not,
of course, McMillan's alone) had as its setting a more general social
circumstance and history whereby the city, in its relationship to
childhood, came to be radically condemned.

The following account is well known: the Boer War, and the
rejection of a large number of working-class recruits as physically unfit
to serve in it, plunged the nation into a debate over national efficiency.
After 1899 new attention began to be paid to the health of schoolchildren, and a whole new philanthropic and educational endeavour
attempted to reduce infant mortality and improve the health of young
children through the schooling of their mothers and the eradication of
maternal ignorance and incompetence.

Within this context – fears of national decline and the degeneration
of an imperial race – certain pieces of pioneering sociology had a
powerful impact. Seebohm Rowntree's *Poverty: A Study of Town Life*
(1901) reiterated the statistics of poor health among working-class
recruits to the army, but actually measured the health standards of
York's working-class community by the death rate among infants and
by the physical condition of two thousand children aged between three
and thirteen.[1] This sober attention paid to the condition of children,
and the book's carefully argued thesis – showing that a cycle of poverty
operated in working-class life, with most families experiencing its
worst effects while bringing up young children – directed quite specific
attention to childhood as a measure of a nation's health and physical
efficiency.[2]

Rowntree's book was one of many that drew attention to these
questions.[3] The majority of such publications discussed the question of
physical deterioration in the context of the city, and the debate was
popularised through conflicting interpretations of the statistics collected at recruiting stations round the country during the Boer War, with
deterioration being attributed to a degeneration of the race, or seen as
the inevitable result of living in an urban, industrialised environment.
Though the Interdepartmental Committee on Physical Deterioration,

98

which was set up as a response to these revelations, reported many witnesses who showed that health and sanitary conditions were no better for most working-class inhabitants of the countryside, the overwhelming evidence of the years between 1899 and 1904, when the Committee reported, seemed to condemn town life.[4]

This condemnation operated across the political spectrum. At the 1904 ILP Conference the free feeding of schoolchildren was argued for on the grounds that it would 'bring back the physique of the people to the standard it had obtained before the people were driven from the land into the towns'.[5] This early-twentieth-century censure of the urban environment fitted into an older and more extensive critique of the city, to be found in such publications as Cantlie's *Degeneration Among Londoners* (1885), Arnold White's *The Problems of a Great City* (1886), Fothergill's *The Town Dweller* (1889) and Williams-Freeman's *The Effect of Town Life* (1890).[6] What did shift, in this late-nineteenth-century assessment of the city as a place of darkness rather than of light, was the new attention focused on the children living within it.

McMillan moved through these arguments and through these alterations in sociological understanding of the city as a setting for childhood in terms of political rhetoric, using new ideas and new forms of language. For instance, after about 1904 her journalism employed the vocabulary of national deterioration, and she sometimes argued for reforms – such as free feeding of schoolchildren – on the grounds that they would produce a strong and healthy race.[7] One way of seeing the garden-in-the-slum that she created – and her active promotion of this version of open-air schooling after 1910 – is as the apotheosis of the critique of the city through the promotion of rurality, another version of which is to be found in the land nationalisation and movement for a return to the land espoused by the ILP.[8] But it is possible to make a more detailed assessment of McMillan's use of contemporary findings and theories about childhood and the urban environment, and her transformation of her sources. To do this, we need to look more closely at the cities in which she grew to political maturity and conceived a politics of working-class childhood.

In McMillan's writing, places of darkness and enlightenment were always urban. Edinburgh, for instance, was a place of political light and purpose; but in *Life of Rachel McMillan*, it was necessarily Rachel's city. This was not the case with McMillan's presentation of the London to which both sisters moved in the late 1880s. In the *Life*, the working girls' hostel where Rachel took a job, a tall, narrow house in Blooms-bury Square, is set 'in the midst of eager pulsing life beyond . . .

streets nearby crowded with artists, adventurers, Bohemians of many lands . . . people who lived an anxious, eager and perilous life'.[9] This is the bedsitter land that provides the setting to Isabella Ford's *On the Threshold* and other novels of the 1890s, novels that take as their theme tremulous girlhood or young-womanhood, on the verge of a social discovery that will lead to a new ordering of life.[10] The chapter 'London' in McMillan's book needs to be read as an example of this genre, especially for the way it evokes in dialogue the drama of genteel dread that the independent life forced on young women like Rachel: 'the note of anxiety prevailed. Anxiety that sometimes passed into a kind of terror and even into despair. Hundreds of girls were here who lived from hand to mouth, holding ill-paid jobs precariously, and in constant danger of losing them altogether.'[11]

McMillan used the hostel and its inhabitants as a metaphor for the emotional and political journey she had embarked upon, recalling in 1927:

> We lived the lives of adventurers. The one thing we had in common (Rachel and I belonged to them now) was that we must take our chance just as the press-gang victims took their chance yesterday . . . Outside, and close by, was the roaring, boundless human sea, strewn over with wrecks, some visible, but for the most part hidden and soon forgotten. It was a toss-up what became of any of us . . .[12]

In one of her fictional pieces written in 1894, McMillan's other self, the beautiful and passionate former governess 'Mary Muse', stays with her sister Primrose – 'a plump little figure in a shabby frock' – in the Home for Working Women; and there, having completed her great work, she dies:

> It was long past midnight when Mary laid down her pen. Her eyes rested upon the sheets [of paper] with a kind of estrangement. She knew that her work was done – that what had germinated in her had brought forth . . . She saw herself in factories striving to *know* the people, later, in the libraries, striving to interpret them. Now it was all over. She did not want to write any more.[13]

The hostel, one cell in the teeming tumultuous city, and the lives it contained and measured out, were a way of expressing her difference from Rachel in the 1890s; by the 1920s it had become a setting for their represented duality.[14]

McMillan's control of an environment she wrote about was often signalled by her use of comedy, and 'London' contains some of the funniest passages she ever wrote, in her description of the job she took

100

as companion and secretary to Lady Meux (of the brewing dynasty). The socialist secretary and outcast lady – '"You ought to know", she said slowly, "that I am a woman who is not received. Men come here, distinguished men, but not their women. I am outside"' – enact a comedy of contradiction and contrast – a comedy that makes a darker note sound constantly, for McMillan used 'Lady X' to contrast two Londons: east and west, dockland and Park Lane (and perhaps to prefigure the relationship with the other beautiful and titled woman to whom the book was dedicated; forty years later Nancy Astor also bought her clothes, and cast doubt on her politics, as did Lady Meux).[15] 'I began to appear at the docks and at the Democratic Club in expensive and beautiful clothes,' recalled McMillan, clothes

> that amazed and delighted the comrades (though one or two began to say I was a capitalist, or even a traitor). Rachel too was not a little vexed by this departure. She liked to see me in pretty clothes, but she wanted me to buy them myself . . . She went to see Lady X. Lady X. gave her a copy of Ruskin's *Seven Lamps*. 'You may read it my dear', she said. 'Certainly *I* won't. I have burnt Margaret's hat'. Rachel laughed and, for the present, Lady X. had her own way in everything.[16]

In the London circles in which McMillan moved between 1889 and 1893, the decision to devote a life to the socialist cause was frequently taken. For some, the existing settlement movement provided a pathway, as it did for P.H. Wicksteed, warden of the Mrs Humphrey Ward Settlement and friend and collaborator of Paul Campbell, who as editor of the *Christian Socialist* had given McMillan her first opportunity as a journalist.[17] In spring 1892 Campbell himself 'left his home in Streatham, and . . . pitched his tent in the wilderness of East London, with the definite purpose of adding another to the number of East End workers'.[18]

His move was part of the formation of the London Labour Church, which originated in Manchester under the leadership of John Trevor, a Unitarian who had formerly worked as an assistant to Wicksteed when he had been minister at the Unitarian Church in Little Scotland Street, London, in 1889.[19] Trevor believed that God was working through the new labour movement, and although a modern historian of British socialism sees the Labour Church as 'one of the most curious features of the spread of socialism in the North during the 1890s',[20] it quite straightforwardly provided a series of political platforms in Lancashire and Yorkshire for London socialist propagandists. McMillan's first provincial appearances were under its aegis, and it took her friends John Bruce Glasier and Katharine Conway to Bradford before she visited the city herself.[21]

Far from being an oddity to its adherents, the Labour Church was understood to have a clear role in the emerging labour movement. The secretary to the Bradford Labour Church wrote in 1893 about

the *absolute* necessity of its active existence, if the Labour Movement is to become a success . . . [and] the power it [the Labour Church] contains for lifting the question from the lower, sordid level which it now occupies, to a higher and nobler plain of thought, and generally imparting the solidity, that sense of brotherhood of humanity as a whole without which the movement must at no very distant date collapse like a bubble pricked with a pin.[22]

This strand of the movement, then, actively sought out refinement, and a woman with 'marvellous soul power'[23] had great appeal for its congregations. What is more, the northern Labour Churches operated as educational and social centres as much as places of worship, and one of McMillan's consistent appeals to her audiences was as an educationalist.[24]

Mansbridge suggests that McMillan first spoke in Bradford in June 1892 (though Bruce Glasier, who was in Bradford every weekend that summer, does not record the event).[25] But no matter when the first visit took place, the decision to settle in the city seems not to have been taken for another year. In June 1893 Katharine Conway told Bruce Glasier that McMillan was leaving London for Bradford at the end of the month, a decision they both saw as akin to theirs: to make a living from and dedicate a life to the newly formed Independent Labour Party. 'Two penniless propagandists!' wrote Glasier to Barbara Fraser. 'And Maggie McMillan too! Brave girl!'[26]

The moment of arrival in Bradford was portentous and symbolic: We arrived on a stormy night in November. Coming out from the entrance to the Midland Station, we saw, in the swither of rain, the shining statue of Oastler standing in the Market Square, with two black and bowed little mill-workers standing at his knee. Lord Shaftesbury had unveiled it in 1869 and it stood there, a tragic avowal of things that still went on in 1893.[27]

The symbolism of this moment has been made much of by commentators. By evoking the figure of the great nineteenth-century child-rescuer as she rendered her final account in 1927, McMillan placed the question of child welfare above that of political allegiance and ILP politics that had in fact (along with a job in view) brought about the move from London to Bradford.[28]

The place is dark, but it is lit nevertheless, by the machinery of commerce; and it is set in a countryside. In all her memories of it, it will be both contained by the hills that surround it, and cleansed by the winds blowing from them:

> Surging crowds filled the wide square and streets. To the right of the station a huge lighted car was taking the dangerous curve with a ringing of bells . . . The cobblestones rang under the heavy horse traffic. Through an opening, as we climbed the hill beyond the Station Hotel, the wind rushed out like a wolf, bringing with it a sense, in spite of darkness and traffic, of wide, wild spaces, very near.[29]

Here, now, in November 1893, Oastler and – perhaps more importantly – Lord Shaftesbury stand as McMillan intends them to, eloquently symbolising a history of child labour and exploitation. The work of a great philanthropist of the recent past indicates the social problem that Bradford's children still presented; and Shaftesbury's name indicates, too, that in 1927, if not before, McMillan wished it to be understood that the origins of her theory of childhood lay here, in that particular history and her encounter with it in this city.[30] The more recent history – which she did not mention in her 1927 account – was the intense local debate on the question of child labour that the city had recently experienced. Ben Tillet, ILP candidate in the 1892 general election, had made it a central theme of his long campaign in Bradford.[31]

What McMillan also remembered in 1927 about her arrival in this city was the warmth of a community united in common purpose, and the sense of having arrived at some kind of safe harbour:

> It seemed that we had been looking for them all the years – and here they were! This was home! They were as kindred, not friends only. (They always called me 'Our Margaret' . . .). They had been here all this time and we had not known it. Now one wakened as in one's own house on a sunny morning . . .[32]

The friendship and emotional security that Bradford provided are confirmed by John and Katharine Bruce Glasier's diaries for the early and mid 1890s. They visited the city frequently, and Barbara Fraser was close by, teaching at Luddenham. Bradford Exchange (the city stood at the confluence of railway lines) meant that people stayed overnight, as they toured the country on propaganda trips. 'We all went to dinner at Miss McMillan's', noted Glasier one Sunday in October 1896:

> Arrive at one o'clock to find Hardie, Mrs Pankhurst and Revd. Roberts. Hardie had to go off. A most lively afternoon. Miss M's droll descriptions of people most amusing. She hits off in a few

words and gestures the [undecipherable] of her fellow members of the School Board and gives us glimpses of aristocratic life. Her mimicing the 'Gay Gordon' & etc. Mrs Pankhurst as lively as a cricket and full of clever comment, criticism and scandal. I sit quite diverted. Miss M. also plays Mozart and Highland airs. Sings 'Lockabler [sic] no more'.[33]

Bradford, then, offered McMillan a place in an emotional world. It also offered her some kind of income, and work to do. The Labour Institute conceived of its work as educational, and its most successful lecture series were presented by McMillan.[34] Her name was on the list of travelling ILP propagandists who offered a lecture in exchange for a night's lodging, a train fare and a fee of 5s. She always maintained that no one 'should trust to getting a living in the movement . . . no one can earn a living by lecturing in the Labour Movement, or writing either. Most of the work is gratuitous, or paid nominally.'[35] Nevertheless, her increasing output of journalism was probably a major source of income in these years. In March 1894 she joined the staff of the *Clarion*, Robert Blatchford's socialist weekly founded in 1891.[36] He paid commercial rates and she was a regular contributor.

The first novel the Clarion Press published was Margaret McMillan's *Samson* (1895: her first novel, too – and her last). An attempt to transmute an observed working-class life into a criticism of an existing social system and, at the same time, to present it in its full reality, it suggests that she found some difficulty in her new encounters with working-class life. The social realism of the novel is attempted through dialect and the use of stock characters, like the Bradford mill girl with an eye lost in an accident with a flying shuttle (the local reviewer thought her 'a perfect treat'[37]). The character Samson, though, is pure argument: he is an SDF man with a narrow conception of the cause for which he is fighting, his restricted vision created out of the incessant toil of a working-class life.

Indeed, the attempt to render working-class life and the beliefs of 'the people' in *Samson* achieved a particular abstraction by McMillan's use of the Roman Catholic shrine at Holywell as a setting. Here the characters come, wrecks of an industrial system and quite divorced from their origins, to play out a drama in which their author can explore the hold of religion and superstition on the masses. She stands and observes her cast of working-class folk, first through the eyes of the upper-class dabbler in socialist theory who has brought Samson to the shrine, and sees that

the little crowd around the well was a very dingy one. It consisted almost entirely of people incapacitated for work . . . even here they looked ugly; and what is worse, dull. Combined with the harsh speech and sorry laughter, they irritated the beholder. They put him in a bad temper, they gave him tragedy without tragedy's grandeur, and mingled with his compassion and his sorrow, a kind of impatience . . .[38]

Through his experiences at the shrine, Samson himself is forced to look at the human beings who are the subjects of his socialist theory:

The water . . . seemed to be asking the question that Samson asked . . . – Was it possible that Humanity was so miserably weak and helpless? Had these people *no* power? Yet they stood at the springs of life . . . They were the parents of the future race . . . They would go home. And for what? Why, to swell the ranks of the sufferers of a later day . . .[39]

Reviewers saw in her shift between the perspective of the hapless suppliants at the well, and Samson's own vulnerable Marxism, an uncertainty of McMillan's own about the ideas and positions she explored in the novel.[40] She was never again to represent the sadness and waste of working-class life through either a politically conscious, or a male figure. 'Samson' was her first and last hero. After 1895 her use of the child-figure would allow her both a more complete identification with her literary creations and a way of removing herself from the awkward questions of human relationship raised by the shabby and broken people whom she represented in her first major piece of fiction, and with whom she had started to work in Bradford.

The vision that McMillan recalled in 1927 – the sudden perception, in 1893, of working-class life 'no longer a secret, or a thing remote or a creation of the imagination [but] . . . [a] close and thrilling reality'[41] – was certainly present in her journalism of the mid 1890s; but she recorded as well her physical reaction to that life, in a piece from 1894 called 'Drink in Labour Clubs', calling on the 'Good angel of Democracy . . . [to] send us – not a Socialist lecturer with Karl Marx at his finger tips – but a window breaker'.[42] A follow-up piece a week later included a simple lesson on the relationship between stale air and depression – although she did notice others things in the stuffy rooms in Peckover Street besides her own revulsion from smell and foul air:

The mugs are filled up again. A little while ago we talked coherently of the law of supply and demand . . . The pale fellow yonder kept a little knot of listeners around him. He talked – smile if you please – of something that throws a halo (to those who have sense) round the head of a struggling Oldham mill-hand. The spirit of tyranny peeped through the key-hole and trembled [though] . . . God knows, there is nothing to frighten him here . . . The pale young enthusiast will awake at midday in a paroxysm of despair, and will confuse carbon dioxide and original sin, heredity and tobacco smoke . . . The penitent . . . will throw up the study of social questions and find in the temperance cause a panacea for everything . . .[43]

These pieces and *Samson* were an attempt to reveal the 'life of the people' to interested and politically committed audiences, but this kind of revelation was not confined to fictional productions. McMillan brought some very grand friends to Hanover Square, including Margaret Verney and the Duchess of Sutherland, to see for themselves 'what the children and the schools and the life of a great manufacturing town were like'.[44]

In the first half of the nineteenth century, Bradford had been the fastest-growing town in the United Kingdom. Its development was based on a single industry, the manufacture of worsted (wool and cotton) textiles, with one of its specialities the production of children's dress material, another in mixed worsteds for women's clothing.[45] In mid century the three stages of the cloth production cycle (combing, spinning, and weaving) were largely mechanised, and the local industry entered an expansionary phase (assisted by the American Civil War and the consequent shortage of cotton goods) which lasted well into the 1870s, though the growth in population slowed down with improvements in productivity. After the 1870s the trade began to face competition from the more intensely mechanised worsted industries of the United States and Europe, and from the development of protectionist tariffs.[46] The adaptation of Bradford spinning machinery to produce the softly draping fabric that came into fashion after the demise of the crinoline – and which the French industry produced so much more easily – actually increased the workload for those involved in the trade in the city.[47]

In common with most textile centres, the Bradford industry had always employed a large number of women and children. As the depression in trade deepened in the late nineteenth century, their numbers actually increased as employers looked for ways of cutting production costs. Female weavers made up about half the total workforce in the 1850s but about two-thirds by the mid 1880s. In 1895 there were 23,000 women weavers and nearly 90,000 female spinners at work in the city.[48] Increased employment of women had created male unemployment, and it was insisted in trade-union circles in Bradford that women ought not to be employed. W. H. Drew, the local organiser of the Weavers' Union (and member of the School Board) told the Royal Commission on Labour in 1892 that 'the labour market is too crowded and [women's] exclusion would raise the wages of their male relatives'.[49] Both medical opinion and common sense in the textile centres held that the employment of mothers was responsible for high infant mortality rates, and this understanding was a Bradford commonplace too.[50] McMillan started her work with children in an environment where there was a strong culture of disapproval of married women's working, among both social welfare workers and organised labour.

Under piecemeal factory and labour legislation, dating from 1844 onwards, children under eleven could, in certain circumstances, receive exemption from full-time education in order to work part-time. At the beginning of the 1890s there were about 140,000 children working part-time in regulated trades in the UK, mainly in the textile industries. In 1894 just over 4,000 were working in this way in Bradford, the major employer of half-timers outside the Lancashire cotton trade. These children represented about 10 per cent of the elementary-school population.

Leaving aside for a moment the question of half-time labour (around which an industry of medical condemnation had built itself since the 1870s[51]), Bradford was an extraordinarily unhealthy place to be a child in throughout the whole of the nineteenth century. The overall death rate was just under 20 per cent between 1890 and 1895, a drop of only 6 per cent since the 1870s. In the 1870s, half the babies born in the city died before their first birthday; but the death rate for this group still stood at 32 per cent when McMillan arrived there in 1893.[52]

Respiratory disease was the largest killer of all age groups. Bradford was damp and low-lying, in a valley, and the smoke pall produced by factories burning several hundred tons of coal a day in mid century was notorious. Though it was somewhat cleaned up by the 1890s, Bradford was not literally a city of light – at least, not of daylight. As in all industrial towns, the difficulties facing anyone who wanted to deal domestically with the smoke and dirt were quite formidable The desperate shortage of household water experienced early in the century was improved by the 1850s, with water piped to about 70 per cent of the city's houses,[53] but a majority of Bradford's working population lived in tenements or shared divided dwellings without sanitary facilities to use the water provided. Only very slowly was a system of mains sewerage developed.[54]

Nevertheless, though Bradford still stood condemned in the 1890s by its high infant mortality rate, histories of public health in the city lead to the conclusion that life had improved for its labouring population in the second half of the century: the housing stock consisted of fewer back-to-backs; new working-class districts developed in the 1880s and 1890s, giving more households side sculleries; untainted food was easier to buy; and the majority of the population were, by the mid 1880s, Bradford-born and did not have to make the adjustments to a city environment that had faced earlier generations of immigrants.[55] A long history of migration to the city from a rural hinterland and from Ireland had helped to establish a lively political and religious culture, and McMillan's own account of the radical currents that merged in Bradford – 'Social Democratic Federationers . . . Swedenborgians . . . old Chartists, Secularists . . .' – has been taken as an exemplar of the varied strands of thought that fed into ethical socialism in the city.[56] It was this thriving and cohesive political culture and the support it offered her that McMillan was to remember with such affection, twenty years on. '"It's rougher and tougher than the South",' she has her landlady's daughters say to her that first Bradford Sunday morning in 1893. '"It's not like any other town".'

The work McMillan undertook in Bradford, particularly after her election to the School Board in November 1894, led her directly to the city of darkness, where the effects of poor housing, poor sanitation and poor food were measurable in its children. In particular, the children's bodies showed these effects. By concentrating on the bodies (and, to a much lesser extent, the minds) of elementary-school children, and the three themes of growth, food and dirt, McMillan began to evolve a theory of working-class childhood. By 1904 she labelled these three themes 'physical education', and suggested that all radical educationalists of the past had thought within these parameters: of 'washing and eating and opening windows . . . .'.[57]

Remembering the first shock of her visits to elementary schools, she wrote that conditions in the 1890s were 'worse than anything described or painted . . . the half-timers slept, exhausted at their desks, and still from streets and alleys, children attended school in every stage and state of physical misery.'[58] From the very first, then, McMillan's attention was drawn to two categories of Bradford children: half-timers, whom she said she could 'pick . . . out of a class as easily as I could pick red cherries from black ones',[59] and the children of abject poverty and dirt – those she was later to characterise as 'the children of the dark area'.[60]

Both the national and local ILP helped in the formulation of this distinction, for the question of half-time labour was a matter of trade-union politics that the new Party took very seriously indeed; and the ILP leadership saw the unskilled working class as a drag on the development of class politics and of socialism, with the uplifting of the denizens of darkness as one of its first political duties. In a local context, McMillan worked within a political culture that specifically condemned the parents of this last category of children, most of whom were understood to creep to school from the slums and alleys of South and North and West wards, spawn of its 'horrible mode of life'.[61] These wards of the city housed a large Irish population, and the representative of the Irish vote on the School Board, Canon Simpson, had a great effect on McMillan's theories of dirt and hygiene, as we shall see.

McMillan's first category of child, the exhausted half-timer, leads us directly to what has been described as a momentous shift in the nineteenth century: from a common assumption that children had a duty to contribute to the family economy, to the belief that labour in childhood was undesirable and that a society stood condemned by its existence.[62] The conflict between these two positions emerged at ILP national conferences: in 1895 and 1897, delegates from textile centres argued in support of the half-time system as an economic necessity for working-class families.[63]

McMillan's evolution of an argument against this position brought her into conflict with some working-class opinion – it was the attitude of a working-class father and trade unionist that she ridiculed in her piece 'The Trespassers' (1895).[64] When she formed part of a deputation to the Home Secretary on the half-time question in April 1895, she argued for abolition on the grounds that 'popular feeling on the subject in Bradford had changed, and the working people themselves were now becoming more and more conscious of the evils resulting from their children being employed under twelve years of age'.[65] But on home territory, at School Board meetings, she frequently dispensed with the opinion of parents, arguing in January 1895, that 'children working to support their parents was a spectacle that had never been seen in any but Christian countries. If parents were so blind as to be ready to mutilate the minds and bodies of their children, the Board ought to prevent it.'[66]

Very little of her writing on this topic placed the half-timer in the context of a family, or a family economy, and the same applied to her discussion of women's labour. She did use general arguments against married women's working in her pamphlet *Child Labour and the Half-Time System* – not in order to condemn women's absence from the home, nor to indicate their inability to care for their children, but rather because the intense physical labour of women workers in the worsted trade produced physical fatigue, which in pregnant and parturant mothers hindered the first stages of natural childhood growth.[67] In this way – in her attention to the individual bodies of labouring women and children – McMillan's argument diverged quite sharply from ILP thinking. Katharine Conway, for instance, in her ILP pamphlet *The Cry of the Children* (1894), insisted that the family was 'the acknowledged unit of the state', traced a history of urbanisation and industrialisation in which child labour indexed the deterioration of working-class life during the course of the nineteenth century, and proposed the family wage as a solution to the problem of the half-timer.[68]

The ILP in conference brought together conflicting and contradictory attitudes to the employment of children, but whichever set of assumptions is being considered, McMillan's concentration on children as physical individuals was decidedly unusual. Much of *Child Labour and the Half-Time System* was taken up with an analysis of statistics of physical growth in half-timers. McMillan sought to show thereby that in general 'youth is recuperative' – that factory children usually put on weight as soon as conditions improved for them, either in the factories or by their quitting such employment – but that on the other hand, the height of adults who had worked in childhood always lagged behind the height of those who had not.[69] The height of half-timers measured out an irretrievable loss of natural growth. What is more, she argued, growth in childhood was periodic, and the recumbent position favoured it: the half-timer, who had to get up at five and was kept awake in the afternoons by her teacher, was 'literally, not in a position to grow'.[70]

This physiological account of the deterioration of the child worker reflected a particular culture of medical knowledge, developed in Bradford during these years. It was much influenced by James Kerr, Medical Superintendent to the School Board from 1893 onwards, and by his colleagues at the Bradford Eye and Ear Hospital. Kerr's work in the decade following his appointment showed a consistent interest in the question of growth in children, and was one obvious source for McMillan's physiological analysis of the question of child labour.[71]

The physiology of growth, as delineated by Kerr and other medical writers, also underlay much of the attention McMillan paid to the feeding of children, particularly those of 'the dark area'. In fact, when she arrived in Bradford in 1893 the feeding of children was already being undertaken there, much of it originating in another meeting with a symbol of childhood degradation – a meeting remarkably like McMillan's own encounter with the statue of a bowed and blackened mill worker outside Bradford station. Robert Blatchford's falling in with a little street trader in Manchester, when he was working on the *Sunday Chronicle*, outside the Exchange public house, had led to his invention of 'Cinderella'. 'You know the facts', wrote Blatchford in 1930:

> How she asked me to buy her last box as she was going to a party at a Catholic Sunday School. How I noticed her and remembered that I had been keen on such parties as a poor child. How I [undecipherable] the idea of a club. How I gave it the perfect name, Cinderella.[72]

Blatchford's biographer said that the Cinderella Clubs, which were organised through the *Clarion* newspaper, were designed to 'give the slum children jolly good blow-outs' and that they 'blossomed into many wonderful things when Margaret McMillan touched Nunquam's crude conception with her genius'.[73] Several accounts of the history that led up to the 1906 Education (Provision of Meals) Act do in fact present McMillan as this kind of champion of child feeding. But her relationship to Cinderella was framed by her knowledge of nutrition in childhood – a knowledge that was bound to make the notion of a blow-out problematic – and McMillan made few political interventions on the question of feeding children, partly because it never became a major social issue in the city during the 1890s.

The Cinderella Club managed to feed destitute children during the months of winter depression and was never under real strain until the winter of 1903, when McMillan had left Bradford.[74] Her consistent public argument, right through the period 1893 to 1906, was that 'where the State compels a hungry child to learn, it is doing a thing, which is, on moral grounds, indefensible';[75] but during the Bradford years children's hunger was simply not visible in the way that their disease, dirtiness and physical deformity were visible. Moreover, McMillan's immediate reaction to the mass feeding of children after 1906 was frequently one of horror at the inadequate conditions and atmosphere of contempt for children in which it took place. In the 1890s she had seen children reduced to ravening for food at Cinderella blow-outs, the adults looking on, warmed by the thought of their own charity. 'A nice young secretary' of a Cinderella Club she had visited always said the same thing to her, she reported, when the food had been distributed: '"Doesn't it do your heart good to see them?" No it doesn't. I don't think it does any good. They look hungry and eat greedily . . .'.[76]

In the physiological systems of thought that she was using and transmitting in Bradford in the 1890s, food lay at the basis not only of physical life, but of mental effort as well. She described, for instance, Binet's work at the École d'Instructrice d'Épinal in Paris, to show that children's consumption of food increased with the scholastic effort demanded of them.[77] In a number of journalistic pieces, as well as in her book *Education Through the Imagination* – which she was working on as she left Bradford – she used these systems of thought to show that the faculty of memory was 'directly dependent on the blood supply, that is to say, on the food supply'.[78] The physiology that framed her thought in these years insisted on the body as an integrated system, and the feeding of children in conditions that called neither on their emotions nor on their desire for companionship could only be viewed as a palliative.[79] Indeed, as she remarked at the end of her first year on the School Board, 'what is the use of doing anything with a child until you have washed it?'[80] It is over the questions of dirt, cleanliness, hygiene and ventilation that a theory of development in working-class childhood can be seen emerging most clearly.

In the fiction she wrote to present working-class childhood to a general public, McMillan insisted on a sudden perception of a child's beauty, showing through the dirt. It might be the wrist – 'what a pretty thing a wrist is' – of a four-year-old in a baby class, as 'dirty and unconscious as possible', that showed what potential the bodies of children held; or the fictional 'Ann' of 1898 might show that a child like her might be awakened to life and a sense of her own beauty by the act of washing.[81] We have already seen how McMillan's argument found its place in a history of condemnation of the city and an industrial system, through a depiction of the appearance of its children.[82] To this critique McMillan could add the work of Édouard Seguin, to demonstrate that children like this could be physically reclaimed.

Seguin's system of physiological education, his own application of his work with retarded children to the education of normal children, and the understanding of a mind as shaped through sensory stimulation and muscle training will be discussed in greater detail later. His work on abnormal and normal education was available in the British Museum after 1894, and McMillan travelled to London to consult it.[83] She used it quite consistently after 1896, training the ILP readership of the *Bradford Labour Echo* in Seguin's psychology and physiology through a series of articles called 'School Board Notes'.[84] Translating Seguin's ideas about sensory stimulation, she was able to tell her readership that baths in school were not needed simply to clean the children up, but rather because the children of the poor had been rendered half-dead by the industrial system. Water would awaken the child's body, 'disease and death would fly from that meeting and recognition, and Pleasure (that great brain stimulus) would start new rhythms of life in the stagnant body'.[85] A month later, she wrote that it was possible

> in the most mechanical and deliberate way to set the feet of children on the upward path. Not by lectures and axioms, but by simple physical exercises . . . and by pure water. For our mental life is conditioned by our physical life. Who can separate these?[86]

Through this series of articles, it is possible to see McMillan attempting to develop a culture of physiological understanding in Bradford, and going to the polls, in the elections of 1897 and 1900, with a programme of education that expressed itself in physical terms. Indeed, it was over the question of hygiene in schools that she attained her widest reputation as a local politician: her frequent remarks about the willingness of the Roman Catholic Church to elevate the soul over

112

the body brought her into very loud conflict with Canon Simpson – 'she wished that clergymen were today like the Rabbis of old – sanitary teachers of their people' – and her remarks about the dirty state of many schoolchildren caused local furore from time to time.[87]

In Bradford, then, a particular and local critique of industrial capitalism was developed out of evidence that collected around the physical condition of schoolchildren. To add to McMillan's schemes for improving and healing children's bodies, we should consider as well the particular influence of Bradford on her ideas about clothing them, for if children were to be made beautiful by decent food and by washing, then their bodies should also be adorned in beauty.

Some of McMillan's most eloquent pieces of journalism described the shame and physical discomfort of children wrapped in other people's dirty cast-offs, and in 1912 she told her *Young Socialist* readers (or at least the girls), whom she was instructing in the making of simple 'art' dresses, that if nature hadn't intended working-class children to have pretty clothes, then they wouldn't see golden hair and blue eyes playing in the gutter.[88] The sensuality with which she presented children in her writing was extended to the argument for pretty clothing. She asked the same audience of young socialists if they knew 'how nice it is to be well-dressed – beautifully attired. I have known that a few times in my life, and it was a LOVELY, intimate, splendid feeling.'[89] Though much of her thinking about children's clothing was developed after she left Bradford, McMillan arranged for lectures in art, needlework and embroidery for pupil-teachers at the open and continuation classes in the city, and she knew of at least one connection between art, socialism and the betterment of everyday life in Bradford's recent history. In 1897 she wrote of William Morris's connections with Bradford, and remarked:

> . . . if you go into the Board-room and look at the patterns and stuffs which bear his name, you will feel a truly great man is not great in *one* thing, but in *all* things, and that all Art is great – even the art of needlework . . . The man who wrote the 'Earthly Paradise', and was one of the intellectual giants of this century, will show any factory girl in this city how she can choose colours and embroider a table cover . . .[90]

Did McMillan also know about John Ruskin's first Bradford lecture in 1859, and his injunctions to Bradford manufacturers to halt the production of cheap and nasty children's dress materials in favour of fabrics that were more substantial and appealing?[91] James Hanson, editor of the *Bradford Observer*, educational pioneer, and chairman of the School Board in 1894, disseminated this message over the years. McMillan spent nine years in a city that provided her with a context of thought for the beautification of working-class childhood, so that by 1912 she could suggest that eleven-year-old girls, working half-time, could sew themselves dresses in 'strong, plain colours', beautifully embroidered, out of fabric they themselves helped to weave.[92]

Long after 1903, when McMillan had left Bradford for good, Arthur Greenwood remembered her and Rachel paying him a visit in Huddersfield. 'On a cold winter morning I saw them off at the station on their way back to London', he wrote. 'On the platform, Margaret put her hands up on my shoulders, and said "Arthur, never come to London. It will break your heart".'[93] John Bruce Glasier gave an account of her extreme depression at moving to London: 'She is going to lecture for the Ethical Society', he noted:

> On Monday, she and I lunched at Dr Coit's and I saw her to the station on her way to her sister's at Bromley. She was very depressed at the thought of leaving her work in Bradford and beginning a new career in London.[94]

Echoing the account of an earlier move, from New England to Inverness, McMillan herself described coming to London as 'chill', and in 1927 drew attention to the end of a long period of Liberal rule on the London County Council and the beginning of Conservative sway.[95] The Conservative sway in which Bradford politics had been held since 1894 had not prevented her from doing most of her important School Board work within the context of Progressive Liberalism; but in London, to add to this alteration of circumstances, she found the social distance between herself and any centre of political authority, and the geographical distances involved in taking political action, extremely difficult to cope with. This point is made particularly clear in her negotiations with the LCC between 1904 and 1906, when she attempted to get a clinic opened with Joseph Fels's money.[96] What is more, the ILP in London could not provide her with the cohesive support that it had shown in Bradford. Her clinic at Bow, when it finally opened, was managed by the Children's Committee of the Metropolitan District Council of the ILP. McMillan did much of her publishing under its aegis, and in 1907 she chaired one of its committees to agitate for medical inspection. It provided her with contacts as well – sent Dr Eder to work at the Bow and Deptford clinics, for example – but the system of organisation and influence it embodied was necessarily attenuated and distanced, as it had not been in Bradford.[97]

Seven years elapsed between McMillan's return to London and her arrival in Deptford. In her own writing that arrival was much heralded, in descriptions of Rachel visiting the Observatory at Greenwich and

114

going down into the borough. Deptford itself is linked to suburban Bromley, where the sisters lodged, and to the larger city, of which it forms a dark quarter. It was, wrote McMillan in 1927, 'the place of the deep ford. Very deep and steep it is, the soft black yielding mass under the black waters of Poverty. At every step one goes down and down . . . '.[98]

'Why should I describe it any more?' demands McMillan wearily; but she does, in detail, specifically in terms of its history. She wrote of its former glory as a shipbuilding centre, its fine houses now broken up into tenements, inhabited by a broken and lost race of people: 'the streets here are eloquent. Their names arrest the historian . . . Like a fallen avalanche, the world of yesterday lies, buried but erupting often in unexpected ways under the squalor and misery of to-day.'[99] In spite of protests that this poorest area of south-east London had been delineated 'a thousand times and for at least forty years', she went on to show

> the stained and tumbling walls, the dark, noisy courts, the crowded rooms, the sodden alleys all hidden behind roaring streets. We know them now, from books as well as experience. Women who care no more. Girls whose youth is a kind of defiance. Children creeping on the filthy pavement, half-naked, unwashed and covered with sores . . . The place has had severe vicissitudes. The ugliest trade of all succeeded the fairest and finest. The cattle-market had followed the shipbuilding. This cattle market opened up other hideous trades. Girls flocked to the factories to cleanse entrails and do the foul work of the offal trade. This kind of work leaves its mark on a generation. It is not wiped out in days, or months, perhaps not in years.[100]

In all McMillan's writing about Deptford it is presented as a dirty and unclean place, in a way that Bradford never was; there, the wind blowing from the hills might always purify the dark streets.

McMillan first encountered Deptford schoolchildren in 1904, when she was appointed Manager of a group of schools: Alverton Street, Trundley's Road and Deptford Park.[101] Though all three were situated in East Ward, their children came from the wide variety of home circumstances that prevailed even in this most derelict part of the borough. In Deptford Park School in 1903 destitute children were being fed once a week by the District Committee, and at Trundley's Road the Managers drew attention to the migratory nature of the population; but at Alverton Street many of the children's parents were respectable artisans.[102] This last school, in particular, drew the Managers' attention to very young children, for whilst they praised the thoughtfulness of the headteacher, and his interest in the children's development, they were severely critical of the infants' room, noting in 1905 that 'as young children are passing through a stage of life when free movement is necessary for brain development, and when mental progress depends largely on the absence of arbitrary restriction, [they] . . . [regretted] to see the form of baby classrooms, and the whole aspect of the school as an environment for young children.'[103] They suggested that 'the school should be, as far as young children are concerned, a substitute for a good home.' This attention to very young children and their relationship to home life was to be a new and consistent development in McMillan's Deptford years.

In 1906, for the first time, McMillan directed her full attention to the question of infant mortality, using new comparative research on the birth weight of babies born to women working during pregnancy, and publicising new work on the value of breastfeeding.[104] As medical understanding of child development increased, and as McMillan used this range of work in her popular journalism, so she absorbed and transmitted the new, medicalised relationship between mother and child.[105] In Bradford, on the other hand, the working child had stood condemned in his or her independence and for the psychology to which wage-earning had given rise; for the way in which 'it dawns on him, on the day following his eleventh birthday, that he is in a new relationship to his parents – the relationship of a person who pays part of the rent . . .'.[106] There were no children like this in Deptford, no independent child-workers, who may have stood condemned but who had some effect on McMillan's early theorising about the possibility of childhood as social reclamation. The attention of the Deptford years, turned towards tiny children in relationship with their mother, forced a modification of this perception.

There is shock in McMillan's description of Deptford's children, and it is probable that she found their physical condition much more profoundly disturbing than anything she had encountered in Bradford. In Deptford, for the first time, she described a group of children who offered the gravest threat to all social institutions. 'The neglected children, who are in the minority, set the pace for all the work', she wrote in 1911:

> They dominate in subtle as in obvious ways the life and order and progress of all the others. It is they who determine that there shall be no fairy-tale books (for they would be rendered infectious in an hour), almost no toys . . . No one can guarantee the absence of every member of the nemesis class anywhere. They send one member of their order – and the night camp and playroom is infected. There is no part of the city or its institutions from which their influence can be . . . excluded . . . The collective power of

116

disease calls up other reinforcements, drains the sources of mental energy. The three-year-old victim of impetigo . . . makes a great social claim for himself . . . The nurse remains late, giving time, taking time, so as to make things easier for the baby from the bad street. He wins more than his share of sympathy, of tenderness, but he wins it at the expense of others.[107]

McMillan started to use a new language of condemnation during the Deptford years, partly as a result of sharper and more consistent observation of a much younger group of children than those she had encountered in Bradford. In 1913 she spoke to a reporter visiting the Deptford Centre about babies coming to the Clinic 'in a terrible condition, covered with festering sores, covered with horrid vermin; filthy'.[108] These changes in vocabulary and imagery are attributable to changed material circumstances, and to new forms of medical and paediatric knowledge that McMillan worked with. We should also note that her fictions of working-class life and working-class childhood take on a new set of values, as she increasingly presented working-class men, women and children as pathetic yet enduring, using the Edwardian 'slice-of-life' mode that consistently held the East End up as a symbol of wasteland and a threat, crouching on the other side of the river from the city of light and illumination.[109]

This symbolic wasteland of despair – the Metropolitan Borough of Deptford – had a population of 109,000 in 1911 and was one of the most built-up areas in south London, with a density of seventy-two people per acre. In the ward from which the children who attended the Deptford Centre came the density was 131; this ward also showed the borough's largest number of families living in one room. The infant mortality rate was high, above the national average, and again in East Ward it was higher still – 189 per thousand in 1910. The borough as a whole had fewer open spaces than most of its neighbours, though much actual wasteland was to be found there, for it had been criss-crossed by railway development, which left many patches of land, cut off from public use, unsuitable for housing, and serving as open-air rubbish tips. It was a borough lacking in middle-class settlement, and most men in East Ward were unskilled labourers, finding casual work in the brick, tin, sack and jam manufacturing trades. Other light industries scattered through the dark area were engineering and rag-sorting. Work for women was available in some clothing factories, and in the jam and sack trades.

In this situation of more extreme poverty and depression than McMillan had encountered in Bradford, very young children were highly visible, for Article 53 of the 1905 Education Code had directed the removal of children under five from the infants' departments of elementary schools. Across the country, there was a dramatic drop in the number of three-to-five-year-olds in school. In Deptford, after 1905, there literally *were* more toddlers playing in the gutters than there had been in Bradford in the 1890s, when the babies' rooms of infants' schools had contained many of them.

The people of Deptford were specified, too, as those of Bradford never were, in McMillan's writing from this period. Old women sunning themselves on doorsteps showed 'the power of many to keep what is good and fine in the old race . . . speak to them and you will see the gracious manners of long-dead mothers, grandmothers and great grandmothers . . .'.[110] As always, as in many other places, a bundle of rags stirs in her mother's arms, and a child-face gleams out like a star.[111] But here in Deptford, McMillan noticed the effect of poverty on working women in a way she had not before. In one of the most moving passages in *Life of Rachel McMillan*, she and Rachel pass down a Deptford street and are invited into one of the houses by a Mrs Tobias. It is another 'dark November evening', another 'rainy dusk', as it was when the statue of Oastler and the little mill workers, the shade of Lord Shaftesbury, welcomed them to Bradford. Here, it is a woman who shows most clearly the effect of grim poverty, hideous housing, the working-class life that is 'a solitary groping from cradle to grave'.[112] Mrs Tobias

> hated the ugly house. She hated the ugly clothes she wore. And she remembered, all her life, how her father had once taken her to a theatre. The light and the colour and the music made a stir in her dim mind now . . . The children were quarrelling over some stale buns, which their mother, in a burst of love and hope, had cooked yesterday in the oven. For she had sudden outbursts of gaiety, always succeeded by fits of blank ennui, or wild despair. In an artist it would have been temperament. In her it was temper – and spelt ruin.[113]

In a good deal of McMillan's writing about Deptford, both contemporaneous and reflective, mothers figure in a relationship to their children, as they had not in the Bradford years. The relationship now was not only one of nutrition, as her work on half-timers had helped her define, but psychological: mothers and children together taking on the structures of despair and loss that formerly only children had delineated. Her 'Slum Mother' (1908), for instance, shows McMillan working out, in vignette, the aetiology of the psychology represented by Mrs Tobias. Here, 'Mary-Ann' claims the insurance money on her dead child, and with husband safely put away for battering her, feeds the children and herself. She's wearing good borrowed clothes for the funeral, and soon 'the strangeness and awe of life [steals] in upon her', after all the years in which 'nothing had happened'. 'It is hope', suggested McMillan, 'that is breaking up the torpor of months.' But – the rent is in arrears, the landlord comes; she and the children go to the workhouse.[114] In a similar piece written in the same year, 'Clouds and Rain', another working-class wife, with two mentally retarded children and a brutal husband, is presented as having no future: 'yet, if nothing fair is to be her portion, she herself is beautiful . . .'.[115] This loss of hope and opportunity that such women increasingly represented for McMillan remained with her to the end of her days. She invited Nancy Astor to a mothers' tea party at the nursery school in 1926, saying 'that is fun, but a little sad too . . .'.[116]

This new attention paid to children in relationship to their mothers, and to working-class mothers themselves, was certainly influenced by the increasing politicisation of motherhood before and during the First World War. The garden-in-the-slum, and the moving picture of infant life that it presented to the mean streets around, was designed to forge a new relationship between the slum child and its mother – a relationship of knowledge, nurture and love.

In his discussion of late-Victorian and Edwardian 'slice-of-life' fiction, Raymond Williams considers the use of dialect by writers like Arthur Morrisson – particularly in Morrisson's fictions of urban life, *Child of the Jago* and *Tales of Mean Streets* – and the role this use played in the establishment of a form of realism, or naturalism: descriptive, representative and carefully observed.[117] He argues that though this form has been praised for its 'apparent exclusion of self-conscious authorial commentary', it actually marked a process whereby observation, or commentary, has been completely incorporated within narrative; has become 'a whole way of seeing, at a "sociological" distance'.[118] It is useful to consider the representations of working-class life that McMillan produced out of the Deptford years in this light, for her journalism increasingly adopted and manipulated dialectal representation. The shifts within this use are of importance, too; for when, for instance, the pathetic beauty or courage of childhood, or of working-class womanhood, needs to be presented, their speech is usually given in an almost conventional orthography.

These points will be returned to and considered in more detail; but the real conflict that lay in McMillan's use of this form of Edwardian naturalism must be mentioned at this juncture. She did not wish to exclude 'self-conscious authorial commentary', as Williams indicated her use might suggest. She was quite clear about the lessons she wished her stories to impart, and often wrote in her own voice to teach them. What underlies the shifting use of dialect in her writing from the

Deptford years was an understanding of childhood that was at war with itself: childhood as regeneration, with a clear role to play in the redemption of a class; and childhood as nemesis, as abandoned and potentially dangerous – as dangerous as the 'miles of awful slums, miles of awful homes, cramped, stifled, filthy hovels' around 'this little cleared out place'.[119]

These changes in form, and in the political understandings that such forms represent, must always take place in space and time; must be made out of all the books read, theories encountered and used: in specified and known cities. In McMillan's case, two cities, and the contrasts in working-class life they showed her, mark out a distinct shift in her political understanding in the decades before the First World War. 'London is brilliant', she wrote in 1912;

> London is the Brain of the World. But I love to think of Bradford. For there labour was shorn of all that is ugly and debasing. One saw it as in a morning light, half-freed and giving promise of what it will be one day, when divorced entirely from ignorance and failure.[120]

6

Women

Pah! Tess! I have been reading it again. I agree with the critic
who said 'there are too many cows in this book'. She with her
milk of human kindness – running *all* to milk. Men draw
splendid cows. I wish one of them could draw a woman.
(Margaret McMillan to Sally Blatchford, 2 February 1895)

ARGARET McMillan entered political life when 'the woman
question' was a matter of intense debate in radical and socialist
circles. Nor was the attempt to delineate woman's social and
familial role confined to discussion among advanced groups: from mid
century onwards evolutionary science had influenced sociological and
cultural analysis of woman's place, and had grounded this analysis
firmly in a culturally determined theory of sexual difference. Popular
biology and psychology suggested – as, for instance, did the widely
read works of Herbert Spencer – that differences between the sexes,
and a distinct role for women in the nurturing of the young, actually
increased the more highly developed a society became.[1]

Early feminism found its arguments and made its claims within this
context. In general, historians have delineated two feminist strategies
in the second half of the nineteenth century. Using the first, women
sought to enter the public realm on the same terms as men, and asked
for equal rights in property, in education, and over the question of the
franchise. The second major position within nineteenth-century feminism accepted – and, indeed, propagated – the idea of women as the
natural guardians of a society's moral order. What held these positions
together (the differences between them, it must be said, are more
apparent to the historian than they were to the women adhering to
them) were the implicit acceptance of a woman's role as wife and
mother, as part of the natural order of things, and the consequent
division of labour between the sexes attendant upon this role.[2]

Late-nineteenth- and early-twentieth-century feminism might advocate spinsterhood as the only means to a career, or to intellectual
fulfilment, but this argument was often grounded in an appeal on
behalf of the surplus woman, a plea which was able to evade the
question of the sexual division of labour. In fact, the question of a
surfeit of women, unable to find men to marry them, exercised a

121

considerable fascination in late-nineteenth-century society. The literature on questions of sexuality and feminism that enjoyed a particular
appeal in socialist circles might – like August Bebel's *Woman in the
Past, Present and Future* (1885) – set the argument in feminist terms,
raise the question of how the category of 'woman' had been fashioned
down the ages – but still draw the most striking attention to itself over
the question of the surplus woman.[3] Later, and into the new century, a
man like David Eder (McMillan's clinic doctor at Bow and Deptford)
might deal with these questions from a socialist and psychoanalytic
perspective; but even though his *Endowment of Motherhood* (1908)
attempted to break down the idea of a maternal instinct and to
eliminate class differences in the experience of being a mother (by
arguing for state support of pregnant and parturant women) the
question that framed its radical arguments was still about what a
society was going to do with its women.[4]

Within these broad social, cultural and biological understandings,
people attempted to understand themselves and the part they were to
play in the society they inhabited. As part of her own search McMillan
joined the Fabian Society in 1892, her membership proposed by the
editor of the *Christian Socialist*, Paul Campbell.[5] This was a move that
puzzled her friends; Barbara Fraser, the Yorkshire schoolteacher who
was to marry John Gilray, wrote: 'I can't calculate her mental orbit . . .
She has nothing of the typical Fabian about her.' But she noted as well
that 'everybody is becoming a Fabian or an Anarchist'[6] – and indeed,
the world of London radicalism that McMillan had entered allowed the
adoption of a variety of political positions, with ideas drawn from
religious and political sources that now seem inimical to each other.
Theosophy, for instance, occupied McMillan a good deal at this time,
as did the anarchism she had learned from Louise Michel while
working on two major articles about her for the *Labour Prophet*.[7]

It was not just the content of these ideas that mattered; it was,
rather, their very expression across divisions of class and gender that
excited and engaged. Young provincial members of the Fabian Society,
for example, circulated a notebook in which they recorded their
thoughts about free love, sexual emancipation and the possibility of
socialist revolution.[8] McMillan was not a member of this 'Fabian
Circle', but there was much of the same serious daring in a letter she
wrote to John Bruce Glasier in January 1893:

> Mr Gilray gave a lecture last night, and took occasion to rail at
> Theosophy. How he hates it – *you* and he. No doubt this is the
> result of long and profound study of its innermost occult essence.
> Was it not truth who was the sleeping maiden surrounded by
> Fire? You aggressive gentlemen may be people who have gone

through the fire. Meantime it attracts poor moth me! As for my wings I may singe them – and the Social Revolution be unhindered thereby . . . If this letter is not all it should be, just never mind. I am so glad you liked my article on Louise [Michel]. Yes Louise is the salt of the Earth – and there is a distinct plateau of Earth about her for all that. I didn't put it into the article of course . . .[9]

What is clear from other letters written to Bruce Glasier in these months is that theosophy gave McMillan a way of thinking about her own romantic and sexual feelings. As a philosophical system, with its dual appeal to ancient wisdom and a progressive programme for human perfectibility according to the feminine principle, it bestowed on women in general a moral superiority and a social mission.[10] Theosophical ideas allowed McMillan to present a position of her own in the face of other people's love stories. Writing of the proposed marriage of John Gilray and Barbara Fraser, she asserted that 'Marriage is bad and Free Love is worse'.[11] When John Bruce Glasier married Katharine Conway in June 1893 – in a pagan ceremony performed on Leith Sands, outside Edinburgh – he felt considerable trepidation at the thought of telling McMillan his news: 'What will she say? Oh I know! I have hardly courage to write to her!'[12] A few months before, she had told him that she held free love to be

> exactly like Holy Matrimonial Love. Same quality of thing; circumstances make it utterly abasing sometimes. But it is never anything but 'base', that is to say, *at the base of things*. To be there is good. To be higher is better. To fall is bad . . . While the male is encompassing the external possibility . . . the Woman is sitting as usual at the spring of life, form-giver, germ-nourisher, will-swayer and maker of Life . . .[13]

The religious and political influences that gave the socialists of the early 1890s a vocabulary – here taken from many heterodox sources, including theosophy, and other readings celebrating the transhistorical role of maternal love[14] – also provided women with an understanding of their special influence and potential role in a reformed society. As rhetoric, passages like this one of McMillan's have given the early ILP a very bad press in the histories of British socialism. But in this particular example of McMillan's high-flown usage, we need to note the irony of her approach, her manipulation of a complex set of ideas, and to recognise that Bruce Glasier was using religious and political ideas as much as she was to raise questions of how to make reasonable relationships across a divide of gender and social propriety.

It is hard to avoid reading a flirtatiousness in McMillan's correspondence with Bruce Glasier in the months before his marriage to

Katharine Conway – a flirtatiousness that was a product both of the ideas being employed and of McMillan's latent recognition of her sexual future as a 'brilliant', impoverished, independent woman tossed on the seas of heterodox London:

> If you . . . realised that every phase of life and development is a manifestation of One Inner Principle it would be a great deal easier to communicate with you. If you think it would be an advantage to know you, I could write to you ad infinitum – but entre nous, there are a million types of women none of whom you can truly know till you find out the relation between them all. I pray that [I as a type may soon be explained (deleted)] that you may learn something of the mystery of transition – the transition where all is accomplished and all is concealed, and which contemplating you lose the consciousness of relation and are compelled henceforth to throw names at people and exhort them to keep certain names (to wit Labour Church, Theosophite, The Federation etc etc etc).[15]

This swift and confident movement between different bodies of thought evidently had a powerful effect. After a Christmas visit to London in 1892, Barbara Fraser confessed:

> . . . she influences me a great deal. She did not exactly expound her doctrines . . . She is not quite a Theosophist, though she has some of their ideas . . . There is a good deal of 'soul-straining' involved in living up to her pitch, however.[16]

The feeling of a wide variety of audiences – that they had not quite grasped McMillan's meaning, that there was something she had failed to explain to them – was to be a consistent feature of reaction to her speaking and writing over the next forty years. Now, in Bohemian London in the early 1890s, McMillan felt the need to deny that she had attracted a cult following – 'Please don't talk about my "cult" – I have no cult any more than you or W. Morris. Don't call names!'[17]

Her effect was not solely on impressionable middle-class girls, searching for a new life through socialism. The factors that went to make up what was to become a legendary platform performance later in the 1890s were already discernible to labour audiences in her very early days as a propagandist. Joseph Edwards recorded in the *Labour Annual* for 1896 that on her first appearance as a public speaker on May Day 1892, 'she manifested in her address . . . such extraordinary powers as a thinker and speaker that there has been an increasing demand ever since for her services on labour platforms'.[18]

We have seen a group of young, provincial Fabians exchanging letters on the nature of sexual relations, the role of women, and the question of free love; and seen Margaret McMillan negotiate many of these ideas in her strange series of letters to John Bruce Glasier, in 1892–3. Another influential set of ideas, embodied in Edward Carpenter's *Love's Coming of Age* (1896), mobilised a wide range of responses in McMillan. She almost certainly used Carpenter's depiction of 'ladydom' for some of her 'Women of the Age of Gold' series, and quoted him a good deal when she was addressing the topic of change and growth in adulthood. But as for many other young socialist women, the question of 'free love' that Carpenter and other advanced thinkers raised occasioned some anxiety.[19] We have seen some of this anxiety in McMillan's letters to Bruce Glasier, and Enid Stacey, writing in the 'Fabian Circle' notebook, called the impulse towards free love 'a very strong force that is doing an incalculable amount of harm to our cause'. Her young male comrades, on the other hand, embraced the subject with much enthusiasm. 'I have said much of Carpenter', wrote one of them,

> but never came across his expression 'the impure hush of sex' which the Comrade quotes . . . assuredly our existing system of sex relations is altogether impure, immoral and unclean . . . in all its structure there is nothing so rotten as our 'sexual morality' . . . I consider it the imperative duty of all Socialists to deal with it as they deal with the other parts of the Social system . . .[20]

Isabella Ford's novel *On the Threshold* (1895) may perhaps offer a guide to the terms of the debate about women, sexuality and free love, as it was experienced in metropolitan London in the early 1890s. The novel concerns a group of young people living away from their families in Bloomsbury (where, in fact, Rachel and Margaret McMillan had been earning a precarious living a couple of years before, and where Rachel had just returned), all of them learning socialism, in one way or another:

> . . . we were all socialists more or less, and any disagreement among us concerned merely the particular manner in which we believed the ideal future would be realised. Kitty believed that the awakening of women was the key to the problem: Escourt believed that the future lay with the people . . .[21]

Isabella Ford devoted many pages to the advantages of women's presumed 'spirituality', its role in imagined futures, and to 'ladydom'. The deleterious effect of a separate-spheres ideology – stressed by Carpenter and by many other writers of the period and fictionalised by McMillan in her 'Women of the Age of Gold' series – is made the subject of continual debate throughout *On the Threshold*. '"I want you to tell me",' says one of its heroines to her aunt, 'why women's lives are like – like those' – I pointed vaguely out of the window towards the houses of her friends; – 'and tell me if there is not in your lowest, most secret soul, a longing, a great burning longing, for a real life, with real people in it; not second-hand kind of people with second-hand thoughts; but with real thoughts; and for real love which would care for all troubles . . . and which would help towards bringing light to all the dark places in the world . . .'[22]

Later, Kitty tells her friend: 'I do want happiness very much'; and this happiness involves *action:*

I want to do things, like going to Germany to study music, to study it really – women are such pottering creatures . . . I am not in love with anyone, and the idea of marriage does not attract or interest me very much, women's lives are so cut up when they marry . . .[23]

McMillan shared these yearnings (though of course she had been to Germany to study music, and by all accounts had studied it 'really') and shared, as well, the sexual and social uncertainty that accompanied what was her unusual – and vulnerable – position of independence in heterodox London. In 1895 Sally Blatchford, Robert Blatchford's wife, consulted McMillan over two hazards of marriage that she was encountering at that time, for she had recently lost a baby and was worried about her husband's fascination with 'the new woman', in whose company she felt vulnerable and ignored. McMillan wrote to her:

I can sympathise with you. I also have found myself in company with those who would not deign to speak to me. I used to feel it so much. I truly suffered. And for years I believed that they were very superior to me. But now I think that they were only very bad mannered people . . . I am not frightened of even *real* big people now. And I'm not frightened of what they think . . . I think a woman knows as much as men about big things, and simple women like me as much as others . . .[24]

Margaret McMillan's earliest work for the labour movement was directed at the question of what the movement offered women. She was speaking on 'Women's Place in the Labour Movement' at many venues in the North in 1892,[25] and over the next few years she suggested that the ILP might give all women the chance 'to be what you are, only more', by building a bridge across class divisions. In the sentimentalised anecdotage that was a feature of her journalism, she was to offer her readership the moving sight of a working-class

Bradford woman sitting in the Labour Club – still politically passive, but nevertheless *there*. 'You see,' she said, addressing working-class women directly,

> your more favoured sisters have tried to do it by philanthropy, by false culture, and they have failed. They are not interpreters; they make no hard ways or things plain. The cry of the people has reached their ears; they have prattled; they have not divined. After all, it was not theirs, it is yours O Daughters of the People. They say you are ignorant. Perhaps. It is a thrilling picture none the less, that of the joiner's wife in the Labour Club, with her knitting.[26]

Some of McMillan's very earliest journalism, produced before she left London, involved detailed descriptions of working women's conditions of employment, and like Rachel in Liverpool she called on the support of middle-class women for their labouring sisters.[27] She had also made clear economic and psychological connections between working-class and middle-class women in this early journalism, concluding one of her fictional pieces with the observation:

> In the Age of Gold, every man and woman is necessarily the victim of Gold. Those of us who belong to the working classes know very well where the shoe pinches. The horrible wrong that has been perpetrated on our sisters of the 'submerged tenth' is obvious enough. What we are apt to forget is – that we are *all* victims. We – not women of a particular class – but all women. The ladies who preach to us, the ladies who build homes and soup kitchens, the ladies who employ us, are suffering and stunted. They, no more than we, have attained their full moral and intellectual or even physical strength. For every woman wronged, all women do penance. It is a way that nature has.[28]

Part of the purpose of this chapter is to consider how McMillan negotiated these varying sets of ideas and how these theories of woman, and woman's place, affected her evolution of a political theory. In this development, the varying political cultures in which she found herself – like the radical and socialist metropolis of the early 1890s – were of clear importance. In her article 'Socialism and Scandal' Christine Collette has outlined the thinking on sexual morality and sexual relations of various late-nineteenth- and early-twentieth-century socialist groupings.[29] She has characterised the provincial ILP – with which McMillan was directly connected after 1893 – as a party that involved women at the local level and admitted them to the highest of its national councils, but which at the same time 'seems not to have inherited from the new life movement, the ideal that transformation should include experimentation with the ideology of gender'.[30]

The particular scandal that Collette discusses is the one involving the relationship between George Belt, full-time organiser of the Hull ILP, and upper-middle-class Dora Montefiore, member of the Social Democratic Federation (SDF).[31] Belt, former bricklayer's labourer and married man, was sacked from his post when details of the liaison emerged.[32] The scandal reached other provincial socialist circles, and national ones too, for Margaret MacDonald, member of the organising committee of the International Women's Congress – due to meet in London that year, and to hear Montefiore speak – was told about the scandal in Hull by her husband Ramsay MacDonald, who was himself on the National Administrative Council of the ILP. Margaret MacDonald told the story to other members of the committee, and was sued for libel by George Belt.[33]

One of Collette's points in outlining this story is to show that there was a real difference in approach to sexual morality between the ILP and the SDF. The latter, despite the misogyny of its leadership and its small number of women members, did nevertheless offer some space for the relationship between Belt and Montefiore, with Belfort Bax once arguing (over a different case) that 'It is . . . the best thing for members of the SDF to shut up their bedrooms when going out to meetings.'[34] This, Collette argues, was by way of distinct contrast with the ILP, where a much more bourgeois morality prevailed.

Margaret McMillan shrank from this scandal. In spite of the tenderness she often displayed towards her fictional fallen women,[35] she refused to have anything to do with the case. Dora Montefiore had often stayed with her in Bradford during the course of the liaison,[36] but it was the MacDonalds who asked for her support in the libel action. She wrote to Keir Hardie as president of the ILP in November 1899 begging him, as 'a personal favour',

> to get the case between MacDonald and Belt stopped. It will be disastrous to our movement. I have always kept my name clean, and I don't think I ought to be forced to give witness in a case that repels me. I shall certainly *not* do the MacDonalds any good if I appear as a witness . . . My friends are indignant that I should have anything to do with such a case . . . You too are in it. A Labour Leader. And a very bad position for you. No wonder we lose every election. None of us seem able to keep out of the Dirt – Faugh![37]

The question of reputation that had exercised Enid Stacey in 1892 still troubled McMillan in 1899, and this is one of the few indications she ever gave of the vulnerability she felt as a woman living and working alone.

After her series of six articles for the *Christian Socialist* between 1889 and 1891, McMillan's writing shows her as an investigative journalist, with a particular interest in the area of women's work.[38] The other major pieces during these years in London concerned Louise Michel, the exiled anarchist resident there.[39] McMillan's description of her acquaintance with Michel – "'la vierge rouge" of the Commune' – occupied much of the early part of *Life of Rachel McMillan*. Here she describes how she visited the International Anarchist School in Fitzroy Street, which Michel ran with André Coulon.[40] Of all the dramatised moments of the *Life*, the Louise Michel story is the most perfectly realised as comedy. It includes a hilarious scene in which McMillan takes Michel to call on Lady Meux in Park Lane, in the hope that Michel will be able to touch her for £10. The wild revolutionary talk of the heroine of the Commune sends the butler to lock up the silver and bring his deceased master's rifle to the head of the basement stairs.[41] Scripted as a kind of political farce in 1927, the account makes much of Michel's physiognomy, as an indication of her insanity. 'Her head', recalled McMillan, 'was alarmingly narrow at the top . . . it had no arch, but ended like the unfinished roof of a building.' The effect of these scenes set in Park Lane is created by the contrast between Louise, in her dirty coat and battered hat, and the Whistler portrait she encounters in Lady Meux, who is 'a dazzling vision' in pinks and greys.

But behind the comedy of disjuncture and contrast lies a more serious purpose which links with McMillan's appreciation of Michel, entirely serious in tone, written at the time of friendship between them, in 1892–3. In the Park Lane scenes of the *Life* the drama is enacted entirely between the women present, and McMillan draws the reader's attention towards the way in which the men in the room were excluded. Lady Meux happens to be carrying a bunch of red carnations when she appears in her dream of pink and grey. Michel is touched by her bearing of these symbols of anarchism. Lady Meux holds out the bouquet and Louise accepts it, 'with trembling lips. Perhaps she saw in Lady X. at this moment, a comrade . . . there were men in the room, but our consciousness of them was slight: she bestowed hardly a glance on them.' She speaks of World Revolution in the dining-room, and 'the men (particular friends, who formed a body guard to-night) laid down their knives and forks and looked steadily and for the first time at Louise, but even now she did not glance at them . . .'.

The drama takes place between the women and the point of recounting it is revealed in the events of the next few days, when McMillan returns to the mansion in her capacity as secretary and companion. Michel's ejection from Park Lane has in fact prefigured her own banishment, for a few days later Lady Meux says, '"You're going about with dreadful people. You speak in the Park . . .! To be in sympathy with *her* – well, that's the end" . . . '. 'Later', McMillan recalled, 'she became more tragic. "I'm not the stuff that traitors are made of!" And still later: "Decide or go."' And then McMillan tells how, as if following a stage direction, 'Lady Meux stood up, very beautiful. She was ready to die for Park Lane . . . "Go! You may blot me out of your memory", said Lady Meux.'[42]

This account, then, provides for a certain identification between Michel and McMillan, for she did indeed quit her employment and join the fight that Michel represented, 'for the debris of humanity'.[43] Her two articles on Michel, published in the *Labour Prophet* (in which McMillan noticed 'nothing remarkable in [Michel's] appearance – save perhaps her eyes') offered a serious biography, and an account of Michel's educational work, which McMillan set within a history of European anarchism. This account of anarchism placed great emphasis on the conflict between the base and the sublime, between the corrupt and the transformed in social life, which McMillan argued were also represented in the figure of the anarchist himself:

> . . . in many an Anarchist, the Base and the Sublime are inextricably mingled. He is himself representative of the degenerative instincts with which he is at war, and the living witness to the reality of those higher impulses which shall yet rule the life of an enlightened Humanity.[44]

The arguments constructed around the idea of baseness – particularly, as we have seen in the series of letters between McMillan and Bruce Glasier, the baseness of the sexual body – figured prominently in her thought during the early 1890s. Women were the particular subjects of this debate, and in social life the war between corruption and regeneration was lived and felt by women. In the dramatic scenes between Lady Meux and Louise Michel that have just been discussed, beauty and baseness, corruption and sublimity, mixed in the two protagonists.

'Lily Bell', the women's columnist of the *Labour Leader*, confessed herself (or himself: Keir Hardie writing in the guise of 'Lily') bowled over by McMillan's depiction of women in 1896 – a depiction made, in this particular case, on a labour platform in Glasgow the week before: 'charmed by the manner in which she lays before her audiences the result of her studies and research'.[45] McMillan had told the story of the raising of the statue in the temple of Minerva, so that by allegory she might show that 'women are the natural teachers of the race. The feminine is the intuitive faculty, the faculty of internal sight, that sees, and knows the truth'. Was there any need, 'Lily Bell' demanded, to point the moral of the tale McMillan had told?

> The temple of humanity wants to be crowned, and men have tried in vain to find their goddess in the woman of the past who has

been their own creation. Her attractions, and her feminine loveliness, which have appealed to their senses when in close proximity to her, have faded into nothingness when they have attempted to raise her to her rightful place. And the advent of her successor who comes in apparent roughness and unattractive form, is treated with scorn and derision.

It was no wonder, 'Lily Bell' reflected, that a society was still seeking after the truth, when the 'the truth seer, the woman, has been kept blindfolded in subjection for so long, and the male intellect alone glorified and deified'. S/he concluded that 'Labour is doing the greatest work in the evolution of women'.

This particular manifestation of separate-spheres ideology, ascribing to women a greater portion of morality and wisdom, appears with hindsight to have imposed severe constraints on those who lived within it. At the same time, however, it offered some women a space in which to be active and to exercise political influence – to 'do things', as in the fictional Kitty's cry for happiness in *On the Threshold*. What actual and practical field of action the labour movement and the ILP in particular offered to women remains to be discussed, but what is quite clear from the reaction to McMillan's Glasgow speech of 1896 is a more general support for women of refinement and education in the movement. On this occasion 'Lily Bell' wrote: ' . . . it says much of the ILP that it has been able to retain the sympathy and help of such a woman as Margaret McMillan'. S/he was not alone in this judgement. In the same year, McMillan's entry in the *Labour Annual* treated her as 'a woman of great and varied gifts, of the highest culture, with the inspiration of a prophetess . . . She is altogether one of the most striking personalities in the Labour Movement.'[46] The conjunction of various theories of women – particularly a belief in their superior moral capacity and spirituality – and a particular personal history allowed the emergence of McMillan as a female magus in the 1890s.

In 1895 the anonymous 'J.E.', musing in the *Liverpool Chronicle* about a recent visit by Caroline Martyn to the city, wondered 'when the story of Socialism in England comes to be written . . . what the historian will say about the little band of women who have done so much to infuse the movement with lofty moral principle'.[47] We now possess an answer to this question, which would appear to be 'not much'. We have seen, for instance, the most recent historian of the ILP describe how either death or marriage removed most of the early women propagandists from the scene, and assert that McMillan's own activities were largely limited to Bradford municipal politics.[48]

Despite this misreading of the evidence, historians of the ILP are in general agreement that as a party it offered, at both a local and a national level, a degree of participation to women that the blatantly misogynist SDF denied them. ILP branch membership was open to men and women on equal terms, and women were not relegated to separate support organisations.[49] Be that as it may, however, much remains to be discovered about the actual activities of women in local branches in the 1890s, and McMillan's own account of Bradford branch life in *Life of Rachel McMillan* disturbs the picture of parity a little. At her first lecture in the Labour Church, in November 1893, it was 'half a dozen women, hearty and hot', who had just converted the cellars of the old chapel into a tea room.[50] Miriam Senior, a pupil-teacher in Bradford at this time, recalled a quite clearly laid-out route for young women in the organisation, 'starting as was pretty usual . . . with the Social Committee which prepared the weekly teas . . . then taking charge of the Literature Stall'.[51] The Labour Church was not the ILP, of course, but much of the Party's activity was centred on the building in Peckover Street, and Miriam Senior also remembered a women's group of the ILP at Great Horton, 'with never ending work for the bazaars'.

Nevertheless, local branches did encourage women to take part in local politics; Emmeline Pankhurst's ILP career in Manchester demonstrates this as much as McMillan's in Bradford.[52] This local picture was not really reflected in organisation at the national level, and few women attended national conferences or took part in the formation of national party policy. Women were admitted to the highest reaches of the Party (Katharine Conway was a member of the first ILP executive) and there was a consistent female presence on the National Administrative Council from 1903 onwards. However, histories of the movement suggest that this minority of women had very little effect on policy.

This last conclusion is usually reached by considering the question of women's suffrage, and ILP attitudes towards it. The ILP did indeed seem the most sympathetic of all the socialist parties towards this question, and had retained a commitment to the extension of electoral rights to women and men from its very early days.[53] Lacking parliamentary representation and outside the realm of practical politics, all ILP policy remained an outline or a blueprint, a set of proposals rather than a practical programme of reform; yet this outline changed and altered with political circumstances. In 1904, for instance, growing suffrage agitation led to Conference accepting adult suffrage as the Party's objective, at the same time as advocating the extension of the franchise to women, on the same terms as men.[54] This tension in the ILP (and in the labour movement as a whole) was to do with claims for the emancipation of women on a limited franchise, in a situation where many men remained voteless because they lacked the necessary property qualification.[55]

At a national level and among the ILP executive, Keir Hardie was the only advocate of women's suffrage until Emmeline Pankhurst, Isabella Ford and McMillan were elected to the National Administrative Council.[56] To the others it does seem to have been a matter of complete indifference; for instance, John Bruce Glasier can be found arguing that voteless women could be adequately represented by the men in their family.[57] This hostility was reciprocated by women activists, both those who had served on the NAC and those who were prominent in local contexts. Emmeline Pankhurst, for example, drifted away from the party in the 1900s.[58]

It was quite clear to McMillan, remembering back over thirty years, that the question of the full emancipation of women was only ever implicit in the young ILP and that in the 1890s the Party had 'kept to its own real work': 'every question other than the social emancipation of the workers took second place'. She argued in *Life of Rachel McMillan* that 'the Independent Labour Party was not formed to champion women. It took that battle in its stride, and might drop it in its ardour. It was born to make war on capitalism and competition.'[59] Nevertheless, she had argued differently in 1895. In 'Women in Relation to the Labour Movement' she claimed:

> . . . the Reveille of the proletariat is the Reveille of women. Their emancipation must be simultaneous. Each in freeing themselves must free the other. At the bottom all their efforts have the same aim: self-realisation, a full and conscious life of social and personal activity.[60]

Because the cause of women's emancipation did eventually triumph – more or less – its history within the ILP and the labour movement in general can be easily appropriated to that eventual success and the obduracy of a Bruce Glasier, the indifference of a Snowden, the enthusiasm of a Hardie, can be seen as barriers and then stepping stones to an eventual triumph. It may well be, though, that by concentrating on women's suffrage and the ILP position on this question in the years before the First World War we ignore the actual and theoretical role that women, and the idea of women, played in the movement.

Even among prominent women in the ILP, who were most sympathetic towards the question of women's suffrage, a particular and specialised female political role was spelled out. Enid Stacey, whose careful piece on 'A Century of Women's Rights', published in 1897 in Edward Carpenter's *Forecasts of the Coming Century*, stands as a

comprehensive theoretical claim within the ILP for the full enfranchisement of women, understood certain social questions to be of
particular interest to them.[61] In 1895 she had suggested that the
half-time system, child labour in general, education, factory legislation
and the sweating system, old-age pensions and Poor Law reform were
the issues that should particularly engage the attention of ILP women.[62]
Whilst her theoretical piece two years later traced the history of the
women's movement, through the doctrines of liberalism and individual
rights, and whilst she asserted here that as the battle for narrow legal
rights was left behind, a broader range of women asserted a claim to
citizenship, her argument slipped from the question of rights to the
question of duties – especially 'the duties of a wife and mother', which
were to be extended and elaborated within society as a whole by fully
emancipated socialist women. In 1894 McMillan had urged women in
the ILP to become intellectual mothers as well as actual ones, and the
call to women's particular abilities, particularly the abilities acquired
through motherhood, was a consistent feature of her platform rhetoric.[63] She argued in 1913 that 'the vote is nothing if we are not to be
helped to discover entirely new fields of service, and to plant on these
a banner that has never yet waved over any field of social life'.[64]

Social maternalism, the means by which many middle-class women
in the nineteenth century could escape the confines of the domestic
sphere in order to practise charity in the public world and inscribe
good housekeeping on the working-class home, has received much
attention in recent years. Jane Lewis has argued that involvement in
local and municipal politics was in this way considered an extension of
women's traditional work.[65] Certainly, the freedom that McMillan was
given to manoeuvre in Bradford in the 1890s had something to do with
the way in which her work on the School Board was considered a
traditional kind of women's work. The movement for social hygiene,
with which she was intimately connected through Rachel's work, made
overt connections between women's abilities to tidy up a house and to
tidy up a society.[66] Indeed, it would seem, from their theoretical
writing and public statements, that prominent socialist women like
McMillan and Stacey derived much of their understanding of their own
work and the potential of other socialist women's work from these
structures of prescription and existing social activity.

But there were important differences between a political woman like
McMillan and the conventional picture of the nineteenth-century social
mother. McMillan was active on the Bradford School Board as a matter
of *work*; the professionalism that the Bradford situation allowed her to
develop made it quite impossible for her to be seen as a philanthropist.
It was because she wrote and lectured about questions of childcare and
education to a much wider audience than the Bradford one that she was

perceived as different from Mary Gregory, the other woman member of the School Board – Liberal, progressive: indeed, at one point running her own small day school in Bradford; but nevertheless understood to operate in a local and philanthropic context.[67] McMillan's work was not paid labour, but the journalism and public speaking that constituted a source of income in these years was clearly an elaboration – a theorisation and a propagation – of her School Board work. It was also political work that had constantly to be referred back to ILP policy, and which in her case became *part* of official ILP policy.

In fact, the ease with which it seems possible to appropriate new spheres of women's work to the idea of social motherhood is very probably deceptive. Middle-class women like Rachel McMillan, who took the message of domestic hygiene and infant care to the working-class home, were indeed following in the footsteps of many a previous 'lady visitor'; but at the same time, as paid employees, they carried with them a body of expertise. It was a medically validated theory of infant welfare and domestic hygiene that Rachel McMillan carried with her, to be sure, but this was not embodied in the doctors who had constructed it, but rather in the women who implemented it. Later, the McMillans did not see themselves imparting knowledge to the mothers of Deptford out of charity and philanthropy but out of a complicated, highly theorised and radical medical and physiological understanding of childcare and development, and (though this factor was on the decrease after about 1910) out of political conviction as well. It is so easy to elide McMillan's call to women to 'save the children' with vaguer notions about women's social mission that it becomes possible to ignore the way in which she elaborated her own politics around the idea of labour – both her own work as a middle-class woman and the labour of other women, especially those of the working class.

In the years before the First World War, McMillan moved in and out of the active campaign for the vote. She belonged to the moderate Women's Freedom League and the People's Suffrage Federation, but though her political alignment placed her in opposition to the militancy of the Women's Social and Political Union (WSPU), more than once it was militancy that galvanised her into action on the suffrage question. In 1906 Emmeline Pankhurst led a demonstration to the opening of Parliament, to protest at the omission of women's suffrage from the government's programme. Fights broke out, and ten women were arrested. McMillan wrote in support of the women in prison, taking particular issue with the conservative National Union of Women's Suffrage Society's condemnation of them:

I think we should rally to them.

I have never been a Suffragist – never thought the question out at all. But if the Suffrage Society of England apologise for these women *now*, what can we think of the wider and older movements?[68]

Jill Liddington has demonstrated convincingly how alienating working-class suffragists found the behaviour of the arrested ten women, eight of whom were from the well-connected and well-to-do middle class.[69] Particularly repellent to the radical working-class suffragists of Lancashire was the idea that they might 'be mixed up with and held accountable as a class for educated and upper-class women who kick, shriek, bite and spit', as the ten were alleged to have done in the House of Commons.

McMillan seems to have been quite unaware of such a reaction, or set of feelings. On this occasion, she was one of the many middle-class supporters of the Holloway Ten who were outraged at the idea of Richard Cobden's daughter languishing in prison. At the same time McMillan was able to translate the militant suffragettes into a persistent figure of her writing, the girl-heroine, who acted not for herself but in reclamation of her lost sisters. She argued: 'Not for herself did one of them put on the crown that does not pierce, but *burns*. It was done for the nameless mute woman who toils for a pittance and who buries one babe after another, glad that it is dead.'[70] The incident connected not only with a consistent theme of her writing, but also with her experience as a woman in the ILP. She recalled her own political career, and remarked:

> . . . men have been very kind to us in public life – very kind, very chivalrous, very reasonable . . . for sixty years or so ladies have behaved with graceful dignity and asked in dulcet tones for the vote. The men were charming to them, but they did not give them the vote. They gave them their approval and admiration instead.[71]

Seven years later, another petition to the House of Commons and another scene of violence against women – in this case against McMillan herself – galvanised her into action. As a member of the committee organised for the repeal of the Cat and Mouse Act (the piece of legislation that allowed the temporary release of hunger strikers from jail) she was thrown down the steps at Westminster, whilst – in the words of the young Rebecca West – 'the mob of policemen surged and stumbled over her'. That this elderly and revered woman, 'whose very appearance in the group should have been a protection to her, if her name and the work she has done . . . is remembered', was assaulted in this way provoked the same outcry as had the incident in 1906.[72]

The suffrage press might speak of McMillan's 'own special work' and the way in which it prevented her full participation in the women's movement, but what also kept her distant from it in these years between 1906 and 1912 was the question of women's politics within the ILP.[73] In 1906 the Cockermouth affair brought the differences between the ILP and the militant suffragettes into sharp focus. In August of that year the president of the Scottish Miners' Federation, Robert Smillie, stood as the Labour candidate at a by-election in Cockermouth, Cumberland. Several Manchester members of the WSPU and the ILP stayed in Cockermouth for the campaign, but against all expectation they refused to speak for Smillie, who was a supporter of adult rather than women's suffrage. The Conservative candidate won, and Smillie came a very poor third.[74] This incident was practically repeated at the Huddersfield by-election in November, with members of the WSPU arguing on both occasions, when they were questioned by their local ILP branches, that they were fighting for a true socialism.

The two women on the National Administrative Council of the ILP, Isabella Ford and Margaret McMillan, played the role of mediators between ILP and WSPU. As we have seen, McMillan had supported the ten militants arrested in October 1906, as had Ford. Before that, just after Smillie's defeat in August, she and Ford had written to the secretary of the ILP, Francis Johnson, suggesting that in future, 'to prevent further repetitions of the Cockermouth affair', the views of any ILP candidate on the question of adult and of women's suffrage be ascertained before adoption.[75] Ford and McMillan considered that 'anyone who hesitates on the question of Extension of Franchise, on the grounds of sex', was not a true socialist, asserted that 'the Cause of Women, of Labour and Socialism' were inseparable, and hinted that their own support might be lost at election time if the NAC did not make it clear that they had at least asked what a prospective ILP candidate's position on these questions was.

During the last months of 1906, then, McMillan hesitated between a suffragette and a suffragist position. The 1907 ILP National Conference found her firmly within the Party mainstream. At this conference a resolution was put forward demanding loyalty to the ILP as 'an essential condition of membership' and McMillan made the final gesture of mediation between the two positions, bringing 'a message of peace and good will' from women prominent in the fight for enfranchisement: '"we pledge ourselves never to go down to any constituency or take part in an election unless we go to help the Labour Party"'. She added, on behalf of Isabella Ford, Charlotte Despard, Ethel Snowden and Mrs Cobden Sanderson, that giving this undertaking 'meant a great deal to those for whom she spoke, for after all, women had some cause for making cleavage with the ILP. Women were still political outcasts and stood in an entirely different relation to the political issues of the day than men did.'[76] Keir Hardie's impassioned speech in favour of women's suffrage had already carried the majority at this conference (though not Emmeline Pankhurst, who resigned forthwith from the ILP, saying 'we are not . . . going to wait until the Labour Party can give us a vote'), and McMillan congratulated him on 'the masterly stroke' of getting women to join forces with the labour movement and yet remain true to his principles.

At this dividing point McMillan may have stood a political outcast, but she was an outcast with a clear political programme. The ILP offered her a much better platform for the propagation of medical inspection than did the militant women's movement. It was at this same 1907 National Conference that Ramsay MacDonald outlined the distinctive position of the ILP in comparison with continental socialist parties as its application of 'the general principles of Socialism . . . to the special political and social evolution of this country'.[77] McMillan's political choice in 1907 was a response to a party that saw socialism in this way, as 'a guiding idea for legislation, for administration, for all constructive work of a social character'. The party that could approve the vague measure that caused the Pankhursts to depart offered McMillan a quite precise support, approving the resolution that any future Education Bill should not only include medical inspection but should also make sure that inspection was supervised by a medical department at the Board of Education.[78] The ILP offered McMillan, as a woman with a political programme, space for political action.

After 1907, when dealing with questions of suffrage, McMillan paid a good deal of attention to working-class women and also to the more general category of working women, to which she saw herself belonging. In 1906 she had argued that out of the thirteen million women in England and Wales, four million 'earn our own living without any help from men'. She belonged, in the figures she quoted here in her *Clarion* piece, to that small 7–8 per cent who were employed 'in teaching or other professions', not to the vast armies of domestic servants and factory workers with whom she dealt in her propaganda and whose future enfranchisement McMillan saw not only as a reward for the contributions they made to the national economy, but so that they 'may be able to win something new and important for others'.[79] Disenfranchisement prevented working-class women from thinking in communal terms, but in the past things had been different:

. . . when man was a savage and a hunter, woman was by function a mother, and of necessity a worker. Working women were the first architects, the first agriculturalists, the first collectors of stores and tamers of animals, the first educationalists . . .

working women were the creators of civilisation and of the elements of that political life from which they are now excluded.[80]

It might be possible to argue that here McMillan sought to extend a vision of social motherhood to working-class women. Certainly, the enlargement of vision that the vote might bring with it was an essential, though unrealised, plank of the theory of adult education embodied in the Deptford Centre. Her position was an example of the repeated endeavour of this century: the attempt by women to change the terms of the political, to analyse 'that entirely different relationship to the political issues of the day' that she talked about at the 1907 ILP Conference. Hers was an assertion that 'the food supply, housing, industrial relations and conditions, the health and hygiene of the community, education and care of children, the Budget of the nation, and social relations with other people and countries' were part of 'the main body of politics'.[81]

In 1908 McMillan wrote of the ILP Conference in Huddersfield that though it was not 'a Woman's Congress . . . women were not forgotten; they never can any more be forgotten . . .'. She went on to show how women might 'stay asleep to social questions but they awake to trade unionism and social questions if they have anyone who depends on them'. As she frequently did, she personified a growing political awareness among working women in the figure of 'Ethel', responsible for an orphan family and determined that her little sister should not go into service:

> 'Why, Ethel?' Ethel's face reddens. She cannot tell me why Mary is not to serve in great houses, or small. Tens of thousands are quite as silent as she – and quite as resolute. When a multitude of people who are all in desperate straits make up their minds in this way, it is not they who are deciding something, but the Time-Spirit who is deciding it.[82]

The sentimentality remains enduringly irritating; but it is important to recognise that until the mud of the deep ford submerged McMillan's politics she possessed, within the terms available to her as a middle-class woman, an understanding of class division among women and a belief in the power of working women to bring about an alteration of their own circumstances.

In the accounts McMillan gave of her own political life, its central dramas were always attached to women. Indeed, this perception is the central device of *Life of Rachel McMillan*, where she tells her own life story in the guise of her sister's, attributing her first lessons in socialism to – variously – anonymous American girls with a knowledge of Henry George, fictional Russian countesses, real and imagined anarchists and nihilists.[83] In the drama of conflict between Louise Michel and Lady Meux McMillan finds her own path, to lead her from Park Lane to Bradford and the ILP. A fascination with upper-class women can certainly be discerned within this autobiography, and the ILP was to give more than one disapproving nod in objection to her enthralment to the duchesses – particularly the Duchess of Sutherland, to whom she attempted to teach socialism at the end of the 1890s, and to Nancy Astor, who occupied a similar (though much more elaborated) position in McMillan's imagination in the 1920s.

Her friendship with Millicent, Duchess of Sutherland, was watched with a fascinated trepidation by the labour world.[84] The 'democratic duchess', half-sister to another aristocratic devotee of socialism, Daisy Warwick, had first met McMillan in 1897, when she had been lecturing at the Labour Church in Leek, Staffordshire. According to one account the Duchess was 'hard by, at Trentham', where some of the Sutherland estates lay and where she was much occupied with the education of 'the people' and social conditions in the Potteries. The Duchess dropped in on the lecture and was riveted by the socialist speaker.[85] Stories of her subsequent 'conversion' to socialism abounded, and socialist opinion was divided over the friendship between the two women. Julia Dawson, women's columnist of the *Clarion*, thought that 'there is neither a lord nor lady in the land who would not be drawn towards any work after listening to an appeal on its behalf from Miss McMillan', and Katharine Bruce Glasier thought that she had 'real work to do among these duchesses'. Some, though, like Mrs Priestman, thought that all it showed was that 'our Margaret' was 'a mere snob'.[86]

It is a commonplace, in discussion of the history of women in the nineteenth and early twentieth centuries, to describe them occupying a position outside the political realm, separate from the body politic. However, McMillan's life, and her work within the ILP on 'the woman question', show her interacting with an organisation of ideas and policies around this question. The women she wrote about were thus representations of social entities, of ideas, of beliefs – and of a politics. Given the rhetorical organisation of her writing over forty years, they were bound, as well, to become representatives of McMillan herself. The figures 'Lady X' and working-class women like 'Mary Ann' and 'Ethel' allowed expression of McMillan's own difficult negotiation of class and gender.

7

Journalism

ISCUSSING work opportunities for middle-class women in 1894,
Amy Bulley and Margaret Whiteley observed that 'journalism
appears to be the fashionable literary pursuit for women'. There
was much demand, they suggested, for 'bright and readable, though
often flimsy, articles upon social subjects'.[1] 'New journalism', a
phenomenon born of typographical innovation, the growth of mass
marketing, and press campaigns on moral and political questions in
the 1880s,[2] had created a new field of employment for women writers,
and the authors of *Women's Work* were able to discuss potential
earnings with some authority. They reckoned that now, in the mid
1890s, the mainstream press would pay £10 a column for articles
by 'writers of repute', and told their readers that 'a lady novelist
and miscellaneous writer in London has been making £600–£700 a
year for some time.' An important feature of the 'new journalism'
from the viewpoint of the woman writer was the way in which
newspapers, by coming more and more to resemble magazines,
started to include serialised novels and short stories from the 1870s
onwards.

Bulley and Whiteley were no more complimentary about women's
fictional productions than they had been about their 'articles upon
social subjects', asserting that 'an immense amount of second-class
fiction is written by women, who seem to have a special gift for
producing tales that are readable and brightly written, without ever
rising above the level of mediocrity.'[3] However, the opportunities to
sell fiction were clearly there, and this context is of some importance in
considering McMillan's production for a range of labour and socialist
newspapers in the 1890s and 1900s. Finally, Bulley and Whiteley
advised all women writers, whether they had a reputation or not, that
they stood a better chance of making money if they were able to
combine documentary writing, or reporting, with imaginative story-
writing: 'a woman . . . who has a fair variety of subjects at command,
and can combine purely literary work with the day-to-day business of a
journalist, may make a very reasonable income from her profession –
say £400 a year.'[4]

What is interesting about this handbook of advice is its frank
discussion of remuneration, its plain assessment of writing as women's

work, and – even more interesting for current purposes – its unproblematic division of writing for the press into the two categories of non-fiction and fiction.[5] But the particular form that McMillan developed in the 1890s, particularly in her writing for the *Clarion* – a kind of argument by fictional allegory – cut across the divisions within which the *Clarion* (and other labour and socialist newspapers) worked. For instance, Robert Blatchford, editor of the *Clarion*, wrote romantic fiction and melodrama, and Keir Hardie, editing the weekly *Labour Leader* from 1892 onwards, wrote several 'slice-of-life' dramas of working-class life, low life and childhood himself.[6] But the movement between different voices and different genres that is a feature of McMillan's fictional allegories was not attempted by these two men. McMillan seems to have invented a form that is striking precisely because of the intense emotion invested in accounts that *at the same time* present themselves as factual, as matters of reportage. What is even more striking is the almost prosaic assumption on the part of the writer that intense feeling would be provoked in the reader, by comprehension of a kind of mutual grammar of sentimentality.

It has been suggested that the essential feature of the popular press, as it emerged in the late nineteenth century, was its conception of a grouping of people, an impersonal 'mass' to be appealed to as an audience. Earlier, it is argued, writers and journalists had proceeded by imagining a particular *type* of reader, belonging to the same class and background as themselves.[7] The popularity of a socialist paper like the *Clarion* must serve to qualify this argument, for the very structure of what was being sold or promoted in the socialist journal implied an equality between writer and audience.[8] A writer like McMillan complicated the picture still more, for she, like many of her readers, occupied a position outside the political structure (neither she nor they possessed a vote), and the subjects of her writing were women and the absolutely disenfranchised – children. What she did share with the other writers who contributed to the labour press, particularly that of the ILP, was what has been described as a 'personal journalism'. McMillan usually reported not on the activities of others, but on what she had been doing herself.[9] This was particularly the case in the series 'School Board Notes' that she contributed to the *Bradford Labour Echo*, and the many accounts that she gave of the Deptford Centre after 1910.

McMillan did not usually call herself a journalist (once, though, she gave that as her occupation when she stood for election to the Bradford School Board) and she actually spent more of her working life as an orator and lecturer than as a writer.[10] Indeed, she occupied the mainstream shared by other left journalists described by historians – in general they were men and women drawn from a wide variety of social backgrounds, with professional, salaried and business experience predominating (when considering women journalists of the ILP, we should add 'from the teaching professions' to the list), who offered a wide range of writing skills and also had an educational experience more extensive than that of their readers.[11]

McMillan's first excursion into a public and political world and national journalism had been through the written word, in the six articles she produced for the *Christian Socialist* between 1888 and 1892.[12] When the *Christian Socialist* folded, the *Labour Prophet* allowed her to interview Louise Michel and write two extended pieces about her which combined biography and exposition, outlining some aspects of anarchist thought in passages of poeticised prose. The anarchist, she wrote,

> is prompted to resist all pseudo-forces . . . and to proclaim for ever his utter *lack* of faith in all . . . rulers . . . who pretend to represent for him the embodiment of Forces, the first law of whose beneficent action is that he should be in immediate and unrestricted relation with them. Perhaps after all there is truth in this argument. The motive power and Design which have hitherto impelled Rulers . . . do not appear to be at one with that Power and Design that keeps the planets in their places and graduate [*sic*] the colours in a bird's breast . . .[13]

This rhetorical scheme, in which a conclusion is made by a radical and surprising departure from a train of argument – in this case, by the insertion of a striking and isolated visual image into a passage of abstract argument – was to become a stock in trade for McMillan. It depended for its effect on literally making the reader *see* something.

The same monthly journal of the Labour Church movement published McMillan's first and last pieces of investigative journalism. One of these – 'Silk Workers', which appeared in September 1893 – shows what was probably her first attempt to render attitude and state of mind through the representation of working-class speech. 'They weave beautiful fabrics', she wrote of the female labour force she was describing, but wear thin, ugly shawls and boots. ' "Well, it's hard, but they won't complain. There are many worse off than they" – a reflection that seems to have much comfort.'[14] Here, McMillan's relationship with the women she interviewed lay in her observation of them, rather than in her recording of what they said, so what is original about the conjunction she makes between beautiful cloth and ugly clothes lies in *her* eye, *her* apprehension, rather than in the women's assessment of their own situation – which is indeed presented as highly conventionalised and formulaic.

For the next twenty years, what McMillan was to *see* and understand of clothing (particularly the ugly garb of working-class children in a city that specialised in the production of good-quality children's dress material) was to allow her the most striking presentations of disjuncture between what was, and what might be. But the voice of the people she discussed was always to be absorbed in some way into her own, not necessarily by the crude device seen at work above (for McMillan's use of reported speech and her manipulation of the conventions of dialectal representation was to become flexible and subtle) but by the consistently presented difference between what she *saw*, and what she allowed her subjects to *say*.

'Lady Featherpoll – A Woman in Society', the first of her 'Women of the Age of Gold' series, also appeared in the *Labour Prophet* (the second, 'Mary Muse', was published eighteen months later, in the *Clarion*). After February 1894, the *Clarion* became McMillan's most consistent outlet. She produced eight pieces for it before the end of the year, and they serve to itemise the forms that she was already in the process of combining. There was the observation and reportage of 'Drink in Labour Clubs' in February 1894, and 'Music in Labour Clubs', a month later. 'The Women of the ILP' (March 1894) offered polemic and direct appeal on a political topic. 'A Halt on the Hill' (April 1894) and 'Two Friends' (November 1894) were both pieces of semi-fictional educative allegory in which ideas were presented through a dialogue enacted by two characters. These two last pieces had been preceded by 'A True Capitalist', published in the *Labour Prophet* a year before, where in dialogue between 'A Miner' and 'An Idler', the working-class voice shifts into McMillan's own, arguing that labour power is the true capital:

> MINER: Working men has been hurried into making bad bargains, driven by hunger and fear o't, from t'cradle t'grave, so as they don't know yet as they *are capitalists*, capitalists who advance everything and risk everything.[15]

In the two *Clarion* pieces written in 1894 the technique is more assured and the voice plainer, not because McMillan is particularly more accomplished at rendering dialect (though *Samson*, which she was probably working on in the second half of 1894, shows a formal understanding of the conventions involved in representing Yorkshire speech) but because the argument, rather than the voice, is more completely given to her invented characters. The 'Miner' of the *Labour Prophet* piece is now 'Dick', unlettered but intelligent, whose interlocutor and friend has been through higher education but has never had an original thought in his life. In April, 'Dick' speaks in dialect:

We've not lived human lives for generations and we're not adapted yet . . . there's a force in t'working people, a force bred o' suffering that has kept 'em human and out o' harmony with their environment and that force works underground now – works underneath the feet o' the clever people as is talking and writing about nothing at all . . .[16]

A few months later, and 'Dick' has lost the conventions of represented working-class speech and become the means by which McMillan can criticise a simple-minded adult education that teaches that all social evil is to be blamed on the environment, at the expense of analysing the psychic structures attendant on poverty and deprivation:

> DICK: . . . for centuries . . . the people have been rendered timid, docile, contented by the continual teaching of the duty of Resignation. They are now being assured that they are the creation of their own clothes and houses . . .[17]

By the standards of fictional realism 'Dick' is a clear failure, and he cannot be said to exist as a character. But then it is unlikely that McMillan intended him to. Her strategy here was quite different from that employed in 'Lady Featherpoll', where psychic structures, as products of class circumstance and class relationship, were explored *within* the narrative of a life story – albeit one that was only sketched out:

> . . . Justice is a virtue. She [Lady Featherpoll] cares little about it on its own merits. She buys off the rights of justice occasionally. That is why she will keep her maid up till three in the morning, and waken her out of her first sleep, at 4 a.m., to pick up her book, or give her a smelling bottle . . .[18]

'Dick', by way of contrast, was a technique of adult education: he served to highlight McMillan's relationship to sets of ideas, the people who were their subject, and their working through in a particular form.

McMillan's election to the Bradford School Board turned her attention to the children of the working class. Her journalistic role was now twofold: as an educator of an ILP membership through the pages of the *Bradford Labour Echo*, and as a writer who tried to convey imaginatively the experience of working-class childhood. She now sought out forms of writing that allowed her to instruct, and to convey technical – particularly medical and physiological – knowledge about childhood and child development. 'Lola', which appeared in the *Clarion* in two parts early in 1897, is very precisely a fictionalising of the essays on physiology and child development that appeared in the *Echo* from September 1897 onwards.[19] However, this form, which is

145

both a romantic fiction and a melodrama of working-class childhood, was not completely developed by McMillan until the 1900s. Particularly, after about 1910, the *Christian Commonwealth* and the *Woman Worker* published a good deal of it. It depended, as the much earlier 'Lola' had, on a presentation of working-class little-girlhood.

This body of allegorical fiction about working-class children was more perfectly sentimentalised and concomitantly more moving than her early pieces about working-class men, and it differs in important respects from her fiction of womanhood – the 'Women of the Age of Gold' series. 'Dick' and the 'Two Friends' had an objective existence within socialist theory, within the very set of arguments that she attempted to have them engage in. Their distance from McMillan, and her fictional distance from them, was immense, for neither out of her own experience (as in the case of the fictional women) nor out of her observation and work (as in the case of children) was she able to invent them for herself.

McMillan's journalism in the years before the First World War shows a refinement and elaboration of the techniques first used in the *Labour Prophet* and the *Clarion* between 1892 and 1895. Her output is difficult to categorise, partly because it was often dictated by immediate political need and partly because she moved between different forms in individual pieces. For instance, between 1889 and 1919 the majority of her writing could be counted as campaigning journalism: pieces written to draw attention to the half-time labour of children, the threat to the Higher Grade School, or – the topics on which during her career she filled the largest number of columns – the campaign for the medical inspection and then the treatment of children. Between 1905 and 1915 she wrote at least a hundred articles on this last topic, until the campaign for treatment merged with the campaign for nursery schools during the war years. These pieces often used the allegorical child-figure, produced as a final fictional conclusion to a factual piece, in order to make the argument plainer.[20] Indeed, this technique is to be found in much of her essay-writing and polemic, and in the descriptions of the work of the Deptford Centre after 1910. These pieces on the Centre itself were also part of a campaign, showing a variety of audiences what might be done about the health care and nurture of children.

McMillan wrote some forty or so pieces that, like 'Lola', could be described as the romantic fiction of working-class childhood. But again, later pieces like this were clearly part of a campaign to draw attention to the plight of deprived children. The large quantity of fiction specifically written for children (some ninety or so pieces in these years) can be attributed to McMillan's involvement in the *Young Socialist* magazine, but many of the stories published here were intended as allegories for adults as well as children.[21] Throughout the 1890s, journals like the *Christian Socialist* and *Ethics* called on her use of the essay. Argument on various topics, particularly educational topics, saw her use the educational allegory, though her use of it declined after she left Bradford.

The four hundred or so pieces of journalism ascribed to McMillan in the Bibliography to this book are certainly an underestimate of her output; in particular, the years after 1914 are under-represented. But even if it is reckoned that only about two-thirds of her journalism has been found, we should still see her producing about three or four articles a month, with the *Clarion* as her most consistent outlet before 1900, when she stopped being a regular contributor. The *Clarion* was indeed the newspaper in which her style and reputation were formed. Hardie's *Labour Leader* used her much more than it had done after 1900, but many of her *Leader* pieces were pre-publication seriali-sations of her books, like *Early Childhood* (1900), sections of which appeared in eight issues of the *Leader* between April and September 1899; and twenty-nine issues contained the interminable drama of Scottishness, deafness and physiology that was 'Handel Stumm' (1900–01).

The newspaper that shaped McMillan, the *Clarion*, was founded in 1891 by Robert Blatchford, when he and other journalists left the radical Manchester paper the *Sunday Chronicle* to found their own. The circulation of the new paper was soon to eclipse that of the popular *Workman's Times*, for which Blatchford had also been working, and within a few months the *Clarion* had become the best-selling socialist weekly of its day.[22]

The early circulation of the *Clarion* was about 30,000, and the runaway success of Blatchford's *Merrie England*, published in various editions between 1893 and 1894, added another 7,000 to this figure.[23] By the time its offices moved to London in 1895, then, the *Clarion* was, in national terms, a reasonably high-selling weekly (after the 1880s a provincial morning paper was reckoned to be viable on 20,000 sales, an evening daily on 40,000).[24]

From the 1850s onwards, when a cheap press became legally possible, weeklies were by far the most popular newspapers. Blatch-ford had worked for one in London, the sporting sheet *Bell's Life*.[25] All of them were radical, more or less sensationalist; all contained stories and illustrations, and their circulation was reckoned in the tens of thousands in the 1880s and 1890s.[26] Blatchford's particular achieve-ment was to wed this format to a socialist and labour perspective. His biographer called the *Clarion* 'a product of heredity and environment, by Artemis Ward out of Carlyle, bred partly in the Labour Church and partly in the Boar's Head, [that] could not have been like other papers if it had tried'.[27] It advertised itself as 'an illustrated weekly journal of Literature, Politics, Fiction, Philosophy, Theatricals, Pastimes, Criticism, and everything else'. In Blatchford's first lead article he placed it clearly within the context of the 'new journalism':

> . . . be it remembered that those who would teach must please, and that those who live to please must please to live. The essence of this new journalism – for it *is* a new journalism, and a journalism created by the men now risking this venture, is variety. We would therefore beg our serious friends that truth may lie under a smile as well as a frown.[28]

In histories of the press in Britain, the term 'new journalism' is notorious for its elusiveness and imprecision. It was used from the 1880s onwards to describe a wide range of developments that were once attributed by historians to the conjunction of paper becoming cheap, the repeal of various taxes on newsprint, and the demands of a public made newly literate by the Elementary Education Acts of the 1870s.[29] In recent accounts the term is taken to describe three developments of the 1880s onwards. First, there was the rapid development of advertising, directed towards a specified public and providing a major source of income for newspapers. Second, there were new sets of typographical conventions such as cross-heads and illustrations, and an overall break-up of the mass of print that had characterised an older newspaper format, making the new press much easier to read. Third, the subject matter of the new journalism was equally distinct, and along with these technical developments the 1880s witnessed the growth of issue-reporting and the build-up of campaigns around moral or political questions.[30]

This last development is usually instanced by W.T. Stead's 'Maiden Tribute of Modern Babylon' series in the *Pall Mall Gazette* during 1885, when – seeking to expose the alleged extent of child prostitution in London, and in order to hasten the passage of age-of-consent legislation then before Parliament – Stead purchased the child Eliza Armstrong from her mother, to show that it could indeed be done.[31] Throughout July a magnitude of metropolitan vice was revealed in his paper, under such cross-heads as 'The Forcing of Unwilling Maids' and 'I Order Five Virgins'.[32] Stead himself believed that the press ought to act as an extra-parliamentary pressure group, interpreting the will of the people to the government; though this, his own definition of the 'new journalism', was not what was generally understood by the term.[33]

In popular understanding, the 'new journalism' connoted the idea of entertainment, readability and scandal, which were long-standing features of the popular Sunday press of the mid-Victorian years – not a creation of the 1880s, but rather a commercially successful expansion of format directed towards a market that had existed before the Elementary Education Acts, and before the *Pall Mall Gazette's* runaway success of 1885. It was within these two trajectories – a Sunday press that had since mid century provided sensation, fiction and visual material, and specific developments in the 1880s and early 1890s – that Robert Blatchford talked about pleasure, variety and socialism in his first issue of the *Clarion*, in December 1891. The *Clarion* left out the scandal (or at least, it left out the sexual scandal) that was a feature of the popular Sunday Press, and omitted the racing tips, but Blatchford was quite clear that 'if we made the same mistake which other Labour papers have made, and devoted our columns entirely to labour questions, we should be ruined in three months'.[34] He wanted talent and good writing, and when he took McMillan on in 1894 he called her 'that clever woman', whom everyone knew could write.[35]

Robust in style, Blatchford's vision of socialism presented in the *Clarion* 'drew heavily on elements of the Romantic tradition and on popular working-class culture'.[36] 'News from the Front', an account of ILP and other socialist activity around the country, coexisted with cricket and football reporting, romantic fiction and a regular theatre column. It offered a complete contrast to a paper like the *Labour Leader*, where earnestness of content was matched by a dreary visual style. The sobriety of the *Labour Leader* allowed McMillan's serialisation of a book on child development, and four-part essays with titles like 'Four Ideals in Education: the Military, the Aesthetic, the Monastic, the Medical', but in the *Clarion* she could not proceed in so straightforwardly didactic a manner – had, rather, to seek new forms to embody the lessons she wanted to teach.

In his study of Blatchford's *Clarion*, Logie Barrow suggests that its readership was generally upper-working and lower-middle class, with many working-class readers gained through trade-union contacts.[37] There is a good deal of anecdotal evidence as to the light it brought to working-class homes, and McMillan herself, remembering its impact in Bradford, called it 'a new literature . . . suited to the needs and tastes of North Country people'.[38] It seems that the majority of its readership were employees, clerical workers and union activists, and it made a particularly conscious appeal to members of these purchasers' families. It ran fiction for children as well as for adults, and Julia Dawson's women's column was a feature it shared with other labour and socialist newspapers. In fact, the 1890s saw the emergence of women's columns in the popular press in general; we can interpret this now as part of a history of middle-class women as consumers, which saw family magazines turn into women's magazines – a history that sees all newspapers of all shades of political opinion start to heed the demands of their advertisers.[39] Barrow suggests that in fact the *Clarion* drew a larger female readership than did other labour and socialist papers, and cites female servants as a group frequently mentioned in its columns.[40]

It was a popular paper, understood to be so by its readers and those who wrote for it – jokey, bright and idiosyncratic. Yet at the same time it was a socialist paper, and its relationship with its readers was therefore different from that of the mainstream press, which increasingly, under commercial pressure, cut off communication with its readership and discouraged the kind of participation Blatchford invited.[41] The *Clarion* served as a listings sheet: secretaries of provincial Fabian Societies and ILP branches wrote their own accounts of local activities. For the historian, its events and announcements columns provide the best overall picture of labour and socialist activity across the country in the years before the First World War.

This obvious distinction between the *Clarion* and the popular capitalist press directs attention to the question of public opinion and audience in the 'new journalism'. The reconceptualisation of the reader in the nineteenth century – from the image of an informed individual, sharing the same political understanding and class background as the journalists writing for him, to an understanding of the reader as part of a mass, to be both swayed and *represented* – is typified in Stead's campaign of moral fervour in the *Pall Mall Gazette*, the insistence that its own stance was that of its readers – *was* literally 'public opinion'. But a paper like the *Clarion* did not have to manufacture an opinion in this way, for it could assume that its readers were at one with its project. Its project of 'making socialists' was, in fact, the education of the converted and an elaboration of their existing ideas and beliefs.[42]

There existed, then, a relationship of political interaction and political compliance between this newspaper and its readers: they could not be seen or written for as an anonymous 'public' that might be 'roused'. At the same time, the paper did construct a constituency that was different from itself and its readers, yet intimately bound up with the progress of the cause it fought for, and that was the 'masses' of the ILP imagination. Blatchford defined his function as a journalist in these terms: '. . . the masses are inarticulate . . . I am a writer and have the opportunity of doing the masses a good turn. I try to use that opportunity; and I think that I do a little good . . .'.[43]

These were the terms in which McMillan understood what she was doing when in 1908 she wrote to John Bruce Glasier (now editing the *Labour Leader*) offering him a piece of fiction in exchange for a free advertisement for her book *Labour and Childhood*. 'I thought', she said, 'of writing a short, realistic story founded on things I saw and heard on the Embankment. Not a love story, but designed to help the Unemployed Bill that will be going through the House.'[44] It can be argued that McMillan could never completely express in her writing the palpable sense of working-class life that burst upon her in Bradford in 1894, for what she directed towards working-class people, and how she represented them in her fiction and other journalism, was part of an educative programme designed to better their condition from outside. In this particular case, in 1908, the story she offered appeared in the *Labour Leader* four days later. The writer is accompanied to the Embankment by a fictional Norwegian who is able to show, by reference to social institutions in his own country, how things might be better ordered.[45]

In the 1890s the *Clarion* had allowed McMillan to deliver strictures and propose solutions with less solemnity and more wit. For instance, in 'The Two Conquerors' (1895), Hope, the young socialist, reads Darwin, and all is made plain to him: '"I see it", he cried; "It is life that struggles, life that conquers; it is life that transforms".' But his creator makes it plain that what he needs to learn is a more prosaic definition of life, particularly the life-giving properties of fresh air. So Hope meets Death, who often visits the Labour Club and who on this occasion has just been through the Labour Church, where He counted fifteen closed windows:

> Hope still sat silent. He was rather a short fellow – not particularly handsome . . . But he had steep brows and strange dark eyes. People with such eyes as these may do anything. You can't answer for them. They do not appear often in this world. They are a rare and priceless gift from the Invisible. They speak the word that has struggled for utterance in millions of hearts. They go down into the depths, and bring up the New Truth radiant and irresistible. And Hope was a Socialist and an ILP man.[46]

Hope dies, a victim of foul air: 'Next day a beautiful poem appeared in the Labour press. In another there was a paragraph written by a comrade showing that Hope was the victim of the "system". But Death knew better.'

Tendentious pieces like this, for all their light touch, reveal the instructive voice, and the plaint of the writer who is solidly and implacably *there*, moving Death and Hope around in order to make her point. In other pieces of a slightly later date, when the intention is to reveal the life of the masses and the psychology of people living in distress to a sympathetic but unknowing audience, McMillan would often retain a firm authorial voice throughout, directing her argument through a manipulation of her characters to which she constantly drew attention. It was a form of writing that took its readers into its confidence, told them what it was up to in direct address, but necessarily abstracted people into arguments, principles and embodiments of hope, despair and desperation.

Women journalists of the 1890s frequently complained about being restricted to feminine topics: to being asked to produce for the popular press the kind of comment on current events, fiction and children's stories that the authors of *Women's Work* were so disparaging about. The development of women's columns in the popular press during the 1890s was one that, as has been noted, the radical press shared, a product of the same commercial pressures that initiated them in the mass-circulation papers, but also as a result of pressure from women within the labour movement.[47] The women's columns in the *Clarion*, the *Labour Leader*, and (much later) *Justice* were generally seen to have the dual purpose of motivating women to an interest in socialist politics and enabling them to see domestic and family concerns from a socialist perspective. All their columnists operated, to a greater or lesser degree, within a framework that understood the division of labour, social and domestic, to be inviolable. This could mean that a women's column confined itself to recipes and dressmaking hints, or made detailed claims for the development of social motherhood within different political parties.[48] In either case, then, it is possible to see the women's column as a place in which the domestic could be asserted as the political.

But these columns were also arenas in which the claims of feminism and the claims of class politics were contested, and their most recent historian claims that in spite of their small success they represented the attempt of women who were keenly aware of issues of class and gender 'to carve out a space in which to focus on their [own] concerns in a world of male-dominated journalism and of "masculine socialism" '.[49] The argument continues by showing how the development of a separate women's press in the years before the First World War, and the broader platform it gave to contemporary feminism, provided for the decline of the women's column in the labour and socialist weeklies.

It would be a mistake, however, to see women's journalism for the socialist press as entirely restricted to these columns. Admittedly, its appearance outside the designated women's column was rare, but long before 1912–13, when Blatchford employed Rebecca West as a fully fledged *Clarion* writer, he had done the same for Margaret McMillan. Katharine Bruce Glasier, Enid Stacey, Caroline Martyn and Isabella Ford also wrote as individuals throughout the 1890s, Bruce Glasier being particularly noted for her fiction. But McMillan's position was unique among these women, both because she was a regular contributor to the paper and also because – far more important, this – her journalism was quite consistently about her *work*. From 1895 onwards, on the Bradford School Board and then out of her experiences in Bow and Deptford, she sought to show what she was doing in the area of childcare, and to explain the theoretical underpinnings of that work to her audience. This project divided her from the men of the ILP and the labour movement who also took to journalism in the same way. McMillan's fictional writing, for instance, shared some features with Keir Hardie's in its use of stock figures, the tropes of 'Scottishness' and the sentimentalised child-figure. But Hardie was not doing with those figures and devices what McMillan was attempting to do: dramatise a set of ideas, and describe a working life.

Indeed, the women's columnist of the *Clarion*, Julia Dawson, saw one of her own functions as the promotion and explication of Mc-Millan's ideas to a female audience; just as ten years later the newspaper of the Women's Labour League, the *Woman Worker*, was to take on board and promote her ideas about medical inspection and health centres.[50] In fact, to see the position of women in the labour and socialist movement at the turn of the century defined in terms of a simple opposition between class- and gender-based politics, with the separate sphere of the women's column as the clearest expression of this conflict is, in McMillan's case at least, severely constraining. Her journalism, the format she developed, and the attention paid to it as both theory and as a description of practical politics, shows the development of an authoritative voice, the voice of a leader as much as of a woman.

In its giving space to McMillan's development of a particular journalistic form, we should consider the arena offered by the *Clarion* for the construction of the sentimental child-figure. This was one of Blatchford's particular areas of interest, and his own home was one in which domestic child-study reached an apotheosis. He cited children as his own motivation to socialism, returning often to his meeting with the match girl in Manchester, writing that in 1894 he had felt like giving up political writing in favour of fiction, but:

> . . . then, I was in Manchester drinking in The Exchange, and there came a little match girl, and I looked at her and saw the pretty child face and sweet feminine soul of the baby already half deformed, and the flame of rage that such a sight always lights in me began to burn and I felt like a traitor who had gone over to the fleshpots and left the little ones to be trodden down and savaged by the Ghouls.[51]

'Lola' was quite precisely this little girl written down, with a history and a psychology; and only the *Clarion* could have given her existence. This fictional field of McMillan's that we can see emerging with

153

'Gutterella' and 'Lola' was an aspect of the 'invention' of working-class childhood – the way in which, across a number of disciplines and many forms of writing, from the scientific to the romantic, a new category of human subject was observed, defined and analysed in these years before the First World War. Of course, this development was not restricted to working-class children: child-study was widely and domestically practised, and resulted in a delighted apprehension and appreciation of children in many middle-class homes. Blatchford, like many other middle-class men, lived in such a domestic situation, and his vision of the little match girl was mapped on to the picture of little Winifred at home, as much as it was derived from a sense of this child as a potential social reclaimer.[52]

It is reasonable to claim, then, that McMillan *invented* her child characters, however much they were also the fruits of her observation of child life in the wastelands of Bradford and Deptford. Because she invented them in this way, and gave them speech, she presented no disjuncture between her own consciousness and the one she created. The place of disjuncture – one she certainly experienced, but expressed only obliquely in her writing – was where she attempted to convey this idea of childhood to the parents of the children she invented in her prose. In her early pieces in particular, the child-figure literally became an *argument* – with trade unionists and fathers who supported the half-time system; later with parents of the unskilled working class, who would not awaken to their children's beauty.

Newsprint is, as it was in the period under discussion here, the most widely consumed prose.[53] In this particular case it was prose distributed to a committed audience, all more or less understood to share a sense of social injustice and assumed by McMillan, the writer, to be in need of knowledge to mobilise that sense of injustice into political action. In this way, as a transaction between a writer and a number of readers, it was organised 'in certain changing social relations which [included] education, class habits, distribution and publishing costs'.[54] To this list of material relations which, Raymond Williams argues, dictate the relationship between writer and audience, writing for the socialist press also offered, quite overtly, a sharing of assumptions and of political experience. Did this shared agenda allow McMillan, in her particular journalistic project, to transcend received social relations? The writer in this case was a woman, who had to operate outside certain formal political structures – increasingly so after 1902. At the same time the writer was an authority on certain political questions, a theorist as much as she was a woman writing. Of course, she could no more transcend the social relations that existed between herself and the outcast of Bradford than could any other member of the local ILP, but by embodying ideas in figures representing this life, particularly in the figure of the child, she did manage to insert an *experience* (as much her experience of herself as that of the women and children of the unskilled working class) into socialist understanding in a way that would not have been possible had she written solely out of observation.

8

Socialism

MARGARET McMillan spent most of her working life involved in a political party that formally declared itself to be socialist and understood itself to be a vanguard party, working to bring about great social and political change. She was one of its elected representatives in the 1890s, a member of its Administrative Council from 1906 onwards. She spent a lifetime – or at least twenty-five years of that life – speaking for it and writing for it. In contemporary terms she was understood to be a worker for that party, one of the architects of its thought, and – however subject to *historical* qualification the ILP's brand of socialism may be – she was understood to be a socialist, at least until the First World War, in the same way as men like Hardie, and MacDonald and Glasier were understood, and understood themselves, to be socialists. And though the years after Rachel's death saw McMillan's virtual abandonment of the structures of political thought that the ILP had provided her with, her speech on a Conservative platform for Nancy Astor at the Plymouth by-election in 1929 was seen as a betrayal – if not by this time of socialism, then of the past, of something once believed. 'I was bound to tell you', wrote Ethel Snowden from 11 Downing Street, '[that though] it is not for me to reproach you . . . Labour people have been alienated by your action in supporting Lady Astor against a perfectly good Labour candidate. Especially when she had given you money . . . .'.[1]

If we set to one side the life-plan and its working out that McMillan presents us with in *Life of Rachel McMillan*, and if we restore to her the years between 1892 and 1912 – her immense output of journalism, her hundreds of appearances on labour platforms, her presence (however problematic) among the ILP leadership – that other biographical accounts have removed, then we can see her as a woman moving through circumstances, encountering ideas, living those ideas and also manipulating and altering them, particularly the structures and categories of late-nineteenth-century British socialism. An account of McMillan's interaction with this socialism can serve in two ways. It can show her as a typical figure, an exemplar of belief and background, so that her story and her politics may confirm major currents in ethical socialism, as already defined. At the same time McMillan's *use* of ethical socialism can serve to highlight aspects of ILP thought that have received little attention from historians. In particular, various conflicts within the Party over the question of education (particularly working-class education) are thrown into relief by a discussion of McMillan's political work.

The history of the ILP (and of the early Labour Party) often proceeds by image, by typicality – and by biography. For instance, David Howell, in *British Workers and the Independent Labour Party*, asks us to consider this picture:

> The socialist propagandist stands in the street of an industrial town in Scotland or the north of England in the mid-nineties. Typically he is in his late twenties or early thirties; his background seems to be that of self-educated artisan or clerk. His appearance tends towards bohemianism; he sports a red tie. Sometimes the propagandist is a woman of similar age, probably from a more established middle-class background. In either case, the oratory is emotional, sentimental and frequently effective. A crowd gathers. Some are merely curious, attracted to the rhetoric, as they would be to the hell-fire of the hot gospeller, or the blandishments of a patent medicine salesman. Others listening are more serious. They listen to the speaker and possibly are converted . . . the early propagandists of the ILP . . . carried on their missionary campaigns, braving apathy and hostility, buoyed up by optimism, concerned not with the minutiae of political dealings but the broad advocacy of ethical principles . . .[2]

Howell then asks us to look forward thirty years, to the tired faces of the nineties men who presided over the disintegration of the second Labour government, and then back again from this point, through their individual histories, histories which might capture some of the complexities of the ILP – at Philip Snowden, for example, autodidact and former pupil-teacher of the West Riding, famed for the 'come to Jesus' style of his oratory, whose wife Ethel wrote reproachfully to McMillan from No. 11 in 1929. Or we are asked to contemplate Keir Hardie, for whom Gladstonian Liberalism and trade-union radicalism provided the first perspective on his own illegitimacy and time spent as a miner, and who later employed his Scottishness and the image of a lost rurality in something of the way McMillan did. As the man who embodied the idea of the ILP throughout his career, he attached massive importance to the role of journalism in the 'making of socialists'.[3] 'One of the striking features of the labour movement as a cultural group', observes Kenneth Morgan in *Labour People*, 'is its evocation of former heroes, and the creation of an alternative history thereby. More than any other party it has praised famous men (and occasionally, famous women as well) and has perpetuated their imperishable memory.'[4] For men like Hardie, and for those who celebrated

157

their lives, autobiography and biography constituted an important assertion of an experience that might otherwise have been lost, a means of entry into a cultural formation.

How far was Margaret McMillan that typical figure on the street corner in the 1890s? She was a woman, and certainly from a more established class background than John Bruce Glasier or Keir Hardie. But hers were not the securely middle-class origins of Katharine Conway, Caroline Martyn, or Isabella Ford.[5] She had earned a living since the early 1880s, and her uncertainties and resentments about social place can be read in her writing during the 1890s and were still evident, even after her establishment as a female magus, to one reviewer of Mansbridge's biography of her, as late as 1932.[6] Karl Pierson has claimed that the most devoted apostles of ethical socialism 'were often men and women of the middle class who, for various reasons, had become estranged from their background',[7] and it is apposite to see McMillan dislocated from hers, by personal history as well as by geography. Men like Hardie and Glasier came from working-class backgrounds, but after the early 1890s lived the lives of metropolitan journalists. McMillan, by way of contrast, had an acquaintance with working-class life through her work that others among the ILP leadership did not possess. Certainly she did not live among the poor in Bradford, and the Deptford Centre was not a settlement; nevertheless, her work brought her into close contact with working people, particularly with the children of the unskilled labouring poor.

Of her reputation as an orator and a propagandist there can be no doubt. She was proffered, in listings, notices and advertisements, as a particular treat, and men and women came away from hearing her uplifted, to record their heart's soaring. Unfortunately, it is extremely difficult to work out what it was she actually *said*, on any one occasion, on street corners and platforms, for there are very few verbatim accounts of her speeches and talks. But, as Howell suggests, perhaps the words did not matter very much. One young man who listened to her in Nottingham Market Square in 1893 was to remember the sound of what she said, if not the content, all his life. Indeed, Percy Redfern seemed to think that the fact that she was not understood constituted part of the meaning and effect of her message. 'Margaret McMillan was the speaker', he recalled, reviewing Mansbridge's life of her:

What she said few could have understood. Her speeches were poetry. Her words were beautiful words about the loveliness of the world and the need for joy in the lives of the poor. The words floated out and away. The feeling of the presence of a fine spirit remained. The present writer was one of the crowd. He was young . . . But the impression made upon him was, in a poetic sense, definite. There did exist a splendour, a loveliness, which we could incorporate within our general social life . . .[8]

Robert Blatchford, who liked to call himself a Cavalier, a hedonist in love with life, often contrasted his own approach with the Puritanical earnestness of Keir Hardie.[9] He cultivated McMillan as a journalist precisely because for him, and for many more audiences of socialists, having a good cry was part of having a good time, and McMillan could always jerk a tear. Warm-heartedness and spontaneity were qualities that the ILP leadership cultivated, important aspects of the public image that was designed to contrast favourably with the narrow, Marxist economic determinism of the Social Democratic Federation.[10]

There was, as all recent histories of the Party and of ethical socialism in general show, a very large measure of truth in this image. Particularly, the ILP failed to take on board the central argument of Marxist economics, to question capitalism as a system – that is, to see capitalism not just as something that made for great injustice in the worker's life – poor wages, poor health, poor housing – but rather as a structure of economic organisation that systematically exploited workers at the point of production.[11] Neither, as Howell has pointed out, is there any evidence that ILP writers and propagandists understood that capitalism was liable to collapse, and they did not structure their vision of the future around this possibility.[12] In this way, it is argued, their rhetoric condemned an existing economic system, but never suggested that it might disappear or be overthrown. So, as a legacy of this imperfect economic understanding (and particularly important for considering McMillan's work and writing after 1906), it could be assumed that capitalism would evolve into a better form of existence, purged of its present inequities and harshness.[13]

This particular brand of economic understanding, forged in countless meeting halls and newspaper articles, resulted in two failures of perception on the part of the ILP in the 1900s. One was a failure to understand class relations in economic terms; they were seen rather as products of misunderstanding, individual and localised exploitations and unfairnesses, or of a failure to see the light of socialism. The second was a view of the relationship between the economic order and the state that allowed McMillan (and many others) to see the reform of existing institutions and general progressivism as a solution to the ills of a capitalist society.

Within such a culture of understanding we should perhaps expect to find McMillan praised, as Redfern praised her all those years later, for an absence of economic theory. She was certainly praised thus at the time by Katharine Bruce Glasier, reviewing her book *Early Childhood* in the official journal of the ILP in 1900: 'Miss M'Millan's Socialism has no need to declare itself in an economic formula or definitely attack our hideous class superstitions. The child's right to live, to be, or become its highest self is the "of course" that underlies every paragraph.'[14] Katharine Bruce Glasier was talking as much about herself as about McMillan here, for her own writing showed a consistent repudiation of economic theory as a means of social analysis, in favour of a social empathy.[15]

McMillan, by way of contrast, was careful in all her autobiographical writing to implicate *Das Kapital* in her early formation (along with Henry George).[16] Her six essays in the *Christian Socialist*, and some of her pieces in the *Clarion* during 1894–95, show a clear understanding of the labour theory of value, and the notion of labour as the worker's possession.[17] It could be argued that the analysis here was made in ethical terms, and that it was designed to promote sympathy for a series of victims of a system rather than to condemn the system itself. In April 1890, for instance, she wrote of the way in which the resource of working men and women was diminished by labour, and demanded to know, of women labouring in Midlands brick fields producing bricks to the value of one and fourpence a day, what might be considered 'a reasonable price for the woman? Observe,' she went on, 'she cannot continue long at this kind of work and rate of wages and remain a woman. The value of her work may be one shilling and fourpence a day, but the loss of it to her will be – her womanhood.'[18] Given the allegory by which McMillan chose to proceed in her popular journalism – her personification of evils, wants and desires, and her insistence on measuring the effects of capitalism in psychic as well as social and economic terms – it is difficult to see how else she could have made an analysis. There is an argument, then, for understanding descriptions like this as forms of rhetoric and persuasion, not just as soft and sentimental accounts of social evil wanting in proper socialist perspective.

A year later, in an article in the same journal, the *Christian Socialist*, she specifically rejected the socialism of appeal 'by the wretched condition of one class to the more disinterested members of another' in favour of proletarian self-help. McMillan asked: 'Why, since the truth was made manifest, do the workers still continue in bondage? There is but one answer. They have not yet recognised in themselves the wronged, and therefore the persons on whom the burden of Right is laid.'[19] She mentioned Bakhunin and his 'formula', and continued: 'Its scope is wide. It leaves no margin . . . to Chance or Charity. An unheeded and misrepresented formula in the days of Bakounine, it is fast becoming the watch-word of the labour world. "From each according to his ability, to each according to his need".'

McMillan was probably better read in Marxist economics and

socialist theory than other members of the ILP leadership. But to point this out is by the way when her political trajectory over the next twenty years is described, for on the face of it, the life she lived and the structure of ideas within which she worked dictated the evolution of her thought along progressive and reformist lines. She worked with and for a party where her central function was seen to be the making of socialists through a broad ethical appeal, and her involvement in municipal government and in legislative pressure groups directed her attention towards the idea of reform within an existing system. Most important of all, the social group with which she was most involved – children – had to be appealed *on behalf of*; could not, outside the realm of myth or fantasy, break the chains of their own bondage. Nevertheless – and in spite of all the ways in which it is possible to trace the absorption of socialist thought into welfare philanthropism – McMillan's work over the twenty years between 1895 and the First World War embodied an original set of ideas about socialist agency: not only concepts of *how* social change might come about, but arguments that sweeping change was both desirable and necessary. The restored working-class child – clean, healthy and beautiful – was meant to act as an agent of change, specifically by allowing his or her parents to recognise in themselves, in the words of the 1890 piece, 'the Wronged'.

The rhetoric that appealed to a sense of loveliness, the flow of beautiful words that left Percy Redfern with the sound rather than the sense in Nottingham Market Place in 1893, must frequently have masked McMillan's own difficulties in knowing what it was she meant. A shrewd reviewer of her novel *Samson* in the *Labour Leader* thought that its structure was probably dictated by 'a certain intellectual and moral indecision of her own'.[20] Years later, in 1911, another reviewer noted the same tendency in her writing. Discussing her *Child and the State* in the SDF *Justice*, the reviewer claimed to be in agreement with everything she said (she covered all the right topics); said that the book was 'very interesting and useful'; and then mused 'yet, somehow in our opinion, the book does not "get anywhere". One can tell the writer has fine ideals, but – is it the defect of her style? – they do not seem to break through so strongly or clearly as we should wish . . . .'.[21] Now, in the 1900s, McMillan's deviations from the diffuse definitions of socialism that the 1890s had given her were interpreted as a loss of faith. Writing to his sister in 1905 about McMillan's eulogising over the Duchess of Sutherland's work with crippled children, John Bruce Glasier (by this time editor of the *Labour Leader*) told her: 'she has an interesting article in the Leader this week. I took the liberty of interpolating a reference to Socialism at the end of it to prevent our pragmatic chaps suspecting that she was waning in the faith.'[22]

The 'faith' she had displayed in the 1890s had its own prehistory, which is both explicable in individual biographical terms and at the same time matches what we have learned from other sources of the intellectual basis of ILP thought. For instance, it is frequently noted of the ILP that many of its members were propelled into socialism by the writing of John Ruskin, and the way in which his work allowed aesthetic criticism to be used as social criticism.[23] But the precise content of this influence – what it was in Ruskin's thought that mattered at any one point in time – is not often discussed.[24] McMillan's intellectual formation can show a particular and political use of a set of Ruskinian ideas. During her time in Bradford, for example, she tried to persuade as many audiences as possible of the awakening properties of water, and this understanding of its therapeutic powers has been attributed to her reading of the physiologist Édouard Seguin.[25] But an equally likely source for her thinking was Ruskin's pronouncements of this question. His scattered writings on education had been collected together in 1894 by William Jolly, in *Ruskin on Education: Some Needed But Neglected Aspects*. There are many references to water, and Ruskin was unforgettably noted as pronouncing, in 'Fors Clavigera' that 'the speedy abolition of all abolishable filth is the first process of education'.[26]

Again, McMillan's early involvement with the journal *Christian Socialist* is a clear example of the path from Christianity to an ethical socialism that its adherents understood to be Christianity's true expression, allowing them to speak, in metaphysical terms, of ineffable powers. Nevertheless, there are items of McMillan's intellectual biography that serve to shift this conventional outline. For example, it is possible that she learned her notion of the unconscious from Belfort Bax's writing – in which, as Karl Pierson has put it, 'science did not exhaust the unknowable. There was within man's consciousness a "feeling" of "something beyond", an intuition of "being" as distinguished from the "phenomena" of "experience".'[27] But McMillan also knew the work of French neurologists in the 1890s, and after 1908 she had direct contact with the Freudian understanding of the unconscious through David Eder.[28] It was this understanding, rather than that of Bax, that she was able to use to outline the possibility of change in human *consciousness*. In the *Clarion*, in 1897, she used Edward Carpenter's *Love's Coming of Age* to explore the idea of growth and development in adulthood:

> . . . we weep and wonder even when our hair is grey. We trace a growth of a longer rhythm through the endless renaissances and decadences of the past . . . We . . . are compelled, in spite of all, to be young. We have to yield and fail continually, like crumbled

rock. On great occasions we are helpless. On great occasions too, we often rise superior to our former selves. We are like children, who distinguish new notes, new colours, bewildered, but taking possession. Through the windows of the last narrow house flits the glance of one friend, who grows old no more . . .[29]

This is seductive and moving prose; but it is certainly difficult to work out what she *means*. It is perhaps, at one level, the prose of psychological comfort, for it points to an apprehended purpose in life, to the 'periodicity in our lives – the rhythm in our blood . . . a tide in our affairs, though we cannot trace very accurately its well or lapse'.

But this piece on 'Growth' was also a clear exposition of recent research on class differences in physiological growth, in which McMillan cited the quite unmetaphysical neurologists and physiologists Crichton Brown and Donaldson.[30] Other trajectories should also be noted. McMillan's own presentation of anarchist thought some five years before had been absorbed to allow her to conclude 'Growth' with the assertion that 'no atom has been rendered void or old through the lapse of ages, being and breath are young. Life escapes in every paroxysm. Every despair is a new departure.'[31]

Part of McMillan's accepted role in the ILP was that of an intellectual, and she had received an education that gave her a wide acquaintance with continental thought.[32] She was certainly well read in a way that the male leadership of the Party was not. Nevertheless, any close study of the writing and platform rhetoric of the early ILP propagandists would probably show the same range of heterodox influences, their sources unacknowledged and perhaps unknown. For instance, McMillan's application of Seguin's physiological education, and her study of his arguments concerning the education of the poor, can be seen at work within a Saint-Simonian framework, in which the evident and first social strategy was to demonstrate clearly and practically that the life of the common people could be made better, and that change and improvement were possible.[33] But McMillan seems never to have mentioned Saint-Simonianism in her writing, nor to have been aware of the political legacy with which she was operating. However, it is important to consider the status of working-class life and working-class people within McMillan's political writing, for discussions of ethical socialism, especially the ILP brand of it, have dwelt much on the fierce criticism of and hostility towards working people shown by its adherents.[34] Often this has been attributed to a basic want of theory, the lack of 'a rigorous basis for investigating social relationships'. [35]

Deep structural divisions within the working class itself prevented the development of labour and working-class politics in this period.

Although the status of a labour aristocracy – skilled and unionised craftsmen – was being eroded between 1890 and the First World War, particularly through the growth of clerical work, it was from this élite section of organised labour that socialism, and the ILP in particular, drew its working-class support, rather than from the very large minority of working people who belonged to the army of unskilled, casual or seasonal workers. This minority, and the threat it posed to the skilled worker, set rigid boundaries to the development of a socialist politics based on the participation of the entire working class. McMillan herself entered the political world in an area of the country – West Yorkshire – where there was a particular concentration of poverty, in a town where the large-scale employment of women and children resulted in low wage rates and a low incidence of unionisation. Edward Hartley's often-quoted condemnation of the 'horrible mode of life' in South Ward, and the 'bitter, intolerant, unsympathetic and insolent' people living there who cost the ILP municipal defeat and did not know what was good for them, was echoed in many other places and by many members of the ILP.[36]

The poor – the unskilled working class – were therefore seen as a problem within ILP thought; seen to constitute a check on the efforts of the respectable, organised working class. The elimination of poverty became one of the ILP central aims, rather than the organisation of the unskilled, who remained obstinately uninterested in ILP blandishments. In this way, it has been argued, ILP socialism represented a movement on behalf of the poor, and was incapable of becoming a movement of the poor.[37] Yet it was towards this section of the working class, the 'unsympathetic and insolent' inhabitants of South Ward, and later the abandoned of Deptford, that McMillan turned her attention, and out of whose experiences she developed a theory of working-class childhood and its potential for reclaiming the poor and bringing them to socialism.

What exactly was McMillan's contact with the unskilled working class? Certainly it was greater and more extensive than that of other members of the ILP National Administrative Council (NAC), even though in Bradford she lived in the only ward in the city that could be called middle-class (Manningham) and did not settle in Deptford until 1914, commuting to it from suburban Bromley for five years. She did not share the life of the people who lived in these places; nevertheless, her work in both cities did bring her into regular contact with them; and especially in Bradford, she spent time in the homes of the very poor. She therefore had an experience of the way of life perceived as threatening that was unique among the ILP leadership. We have seen that her self-appointed strategy in the Bradford years was to present working-class life and its exigencies to an audience in order to gain the sympathies and understanding of that audience, and that only after arrival in Deptford did she adopt the rhetoric of horror and pity to describe the life she witnessed. But even in these later years, when work in the Deptford Centre led her to make distinctions between categories of working-class children, her representation of the life of the very poor remained broadly sympathetic, with an increasing emphasis on the psychology produced by despair and confinement, especially in the lives of working women.

It can be claimed, then, that McMillan did not share the hostility towards the unskilled that was common within British socialism, and that she made a place for them within a theory of social change. But can it be argued that she transcended or evaded the path that her party took, towards a rescue operation on behalf of a despised and un-organised working class? There are arguments which show that the work she was involved in – on behalf of children with no political claims, and using a body of ideas that were more and more connected with theories of maternalism – inevitably led her in this direction. This point could be connected to another, made by historians of the British labour movement who seek to show that the ILP was only ever a branch of reforming liberalism, not a socialist party in any true sense. Putting these two arguments together might therefore suggest that McMillan's stance towards the unskilled working class was much the same as any other member of her party, perhaps only a more sophisticated attempt to uplift a completely abandoned section of the body politic.

In *Labour and Socialism*, James Hinton has placed the ILP brand of ethical socialism firmly within the context of new liberalism and other progressive movements of the 1890s, the aim of which was to ameliorate the condition of the poor. He has argued that by the time the Labour Party was formally constituted in 1906, and ILP members sat in the House of Commons, their social policy towards the problem of poverty was an integral part of the Liberal revival, and their acceptance of the Liberal reform programme was virtually complete.[38] Indeed, McMillan's career after Bradford could be seen as a detailed footnote to this account, in which 'from the late 1890s ILP leaders were to be found working closely with New Liberal intellectuals to formulate an agreed programme of progressive reform'.[39] McMillan's collaboration with Robert Morant after 1906 is a well-known aspect of this story.

Yet there was a conflict – largely unacknowledged – within the ILP over many questions of progressive reform. If we consider, for instance, ILP policy on the family in the light of McMillan's interventions, its ideological content fractures and it becomes more difficult to subsume it under the heading of New Liberalism. Officially, in ILP policy, 'the home, with all that it implies in husband, wife, father, mother and children', was 'the acknowledged unit of the state'.[40] ILP support for the family wage was its clearest acknowledgement of the claims of the trade unionists who made up the majority of its working-class membership, but at the same time emotional and intellectual commitment to the family ran deeper than strategy, and the idea of state provision for working-class children conjured up the spectre of parental irresponsibility quite as sharply for many ILP-ers as it did for Liberals questioning the wisdom of providing school meals or giving short-sighted schoolchildren glasses. In 1909, in her pamphlet *Socialism and the Home*, Katharine Bruce Glasier trod carefully on this question: 'Wherever the home fails, then for the sake of the homes of the future the Socialists say that the state must step in as foster parent . . . [but] State maintenance of children as opposed to their home maintenance is alien to the whole history, hope and spirit of Socialism . . .'[41] This was the official line, but by adopting McMillan's view of medical inspection, and an understanding (an ostensible understanding) of the role that inspection was meant to play in bringing health centres like the one in Deptford into existence, the ILP did adopt and promote a view of childcare in which the child was situated not just in the family, but within a structure of care provided by the state.

Was it this structure of ideas that the ILP in conference embraced when it adopted McMillan's policy as its own in 1908, and that saw the passage of the Education (Administrative Provisions) Act in 1908 as its coming of age as a party?[42] Hardie's correspondence with McMillan during 1907 shows that he scarcely understood what he was being asked to do in the House in trying to get a particular version of Clause 35 written into the Bill concerning medical inspection then being considered.[43] Then again, at a Women's Labour League Conference in 1912, on the care of babies and young children, McMillan urged the necessity for the 'continuous supervision of the childhood of the nation by some one authority'. She hoped that when the next Education Bill was introduced, the Labour Party would 'ensure the care of babyhood, as well as of school children in all health Clinics or School Clinics'. Hardie's somewhat ungiving response to this proposal, in which he spoke at some length about not wanting substitutes for mothers, or forest playgrounds in school gymnasia, indicates that over Clause 35 he had not so much fought for something under another name five years before as helped to bring about an administrative structure the potential of which, as presented by McMillan, remained either a mystery or an impropriety to him.[44] Indeed, McMillan's position on the inspection and treatment of children was much closer to that of the SDF and the TUC than to mainstream ILP thought: the parliamentary ILP, particularly Hardie and MacDonald, was ambivalent about the full state maintenance of children; and educational questions, as presented to them by McMillan, fell within this broader category of state maintenance.[45]

Indeed, McMillan's understanding of the educative process often brought her into conflict with the radical inheritance of the ILP leadership. Lessons learned from a history of religious dissent, particularly in Scotland, led men like Ramsay MacDonald and Keir Hardie to fight educational battles over the question of secular education and freedom from priestly influence in schools.[46] This honoured and self-consciously used history of struggle against denominational teaching was interpreted by ILP members according to the individual and class histories that they themselves represented. By the turn of the century elementary schooling had become the most common and cohesive working-class experience, and the spread of socialist ideas in the 1880s and 1890s had allowed many men among the ILP leadership to construe their own childhood and educational experience within a framework of inequality. Brian Simon has pointed out that the autobiographies of men like Robert Smillie and Keir Hardie dwelt particularly on their childhood of labour and lost and thwarted educational opportunities.[47] The experience out of which they sought to rectify the educational system and to make it available to modern working-class children was vastly different from that of McMillan – and, more importantly for the argument here, from that of the very young children of a borough like Deptford, the children of the unskilled, unorganised, labouring poor.

Once, in 1899, McMillan took Robert Blatchford to task for refusing both actually to get involved in the dreary everyday business of managing board schools, and to send his own children to one. 'What is it you all say,' she demanded on the first point,

> that the work is badly done by a parcel of suburban tradesmen. Very good. Why don't you come and do it yourselves? Huxley went on the London School Board – and went off directly. Walter Crane has *resigned*. No one it appears has the civic spirit for this – but suburban tradesmen . . . Well, but suppose you wanted to do something other than throw words on the wind you would have to stop your investigating and writing, lend yourself to drudgery as the tradesman does – Ratepayers grudging expenses on one side, raw material on the other . . . the Will not to do one easy deed but a thousand dull and drudgery ones. No, can't do it. But then your brilliant advice and blame shouted from the shore is a thing to laugh at. You don't even see where we are! . . .[48]

Over the question of Blatchford keeping his children away from the common school, she was even fiercer and more sarcastic. She saw a connection between her own experience and the dirty children from whom Blatchford felt revulsion on his own children's behalf:

Yes – *of course* I should send my children to the Board School. I should want them to mix (as I mixed) with the poorest and dirtiest. I should give them two baths per day – but . . . *of course* my children should go to the Board School. They should not be bullied and beaten there, because I would not allow that, but they should see from Childhood how other children lived. Why don't we get things for our Board Children? Because you and the like of you won't send your children to our Schools . . . if you *did* send them you would all have insisted long ago that *the best* should be given . . . 'I like my children at home', you say . . . *You like!!!* In God's name what does it matter what you like? Are your children a kind of furniture then?

McMillan's admonition of Blatchford is important not only for her clear understanding of the political principle involved in the idea of the common school, but also for her recognition of the fear that lay behind his refusal to educate his own children there – as, indeed, a convulsive terror lay behind other labour leaders' apprehension of the wayward life of the very poor. McMillan made reference to class fear in this letter, telling Blatchford that if she had children and sent them to a board school she would confront the fear, 'should say "Yes. [to her hypothetical children] You see how horrible Dirt is. It makes one *sick*. Every one ought to be clean. But you mustn't run like a coward . . . but be brave and human *as a child*".'[49]

The educational policy of the British labour movement in general in this period has been attributed to an impulse to redistribute the goods of education, rather than a bid for its reconstruction by pedagogical method or curriculum content.[50] Was this the reason for McMillan's struggle with her own party leadership, to make men like Hardie and MacDonald understand that food, and good health, and filled teeth, and spectacles, were part of an educational programme? When McMillan's resolution for medical inspection of schoolchildren was heard with 'the deepest silence and respect' at the 1906 Conference (as she rehearsed yet again the statistics of ill-health and deformity in children) was it because she was already a *grande dame* of the movement, moving the delegates to pity for the rejected of society, pleading for those who could not help themselves?[51]

At moments like this we should certainly look to the humanitarian response to the children McMillan described, and to her own status within the ILP, as much as to an understanding or acceptance of her ideas. Nevertheless, it was out of this set of conflicts, antagonisms and misunderstandings – of education, of the educational process, of childhood – that McMillan carved a policy on childhood education for the ILP. After 1906 the effectiveness of this policy had much to do with the existence of the Labour Party and its annual conference, to which McMillan was one of the ILP delegates between 1908 and 1911. Here, her outline of physical education tallied with SDF policy on the state maintenance of childhood, and the other socialist party lent her more support – certainly more comprehension – than did the leadership of her own.[52] Indeed, McMillan's policy, and the way in which it seemed to provide an entry for a full system of state support of childhood, presented the ILP leadership with a problem, and if we look at the relationship of educational policies to the question of the reform and reclamation of the outcast nation, then children suddenly swing into sharp perspective, the troubled focus of class relations and class condescension.

The major break in McMillan's political career was made by educational legislation: the 1902 Education Act, which abolished the School Boards.[53] The ILP joined the vehement Liberal opposition to this measure, particularly because the Act gave funding for denominational education without any provision for its control and supervision.[54] This piece of legislation also directly threatened both the Party's ability to be involved in the public sphere, through election to the Boards, and its principle of community involvement. At the level of practical politics, the threat combined with an inheritance from its radical history, which held in deep suspicion all forms of priestly power, and over this question in particular the ILP drew closer to the Liberal opposition.[55]

The passion stirred by the education question in 1902 was probably the most important factor in the process that some historians have outlined: of the ILP becoming not a party of socialist opposition after 1906 (when the Liberals again came to power) but rather part of the support system for Liberal progressivism.[56] This question of education, highlighted by the 1902 Act, was therefore an important component of ILP ideology and also a means of self-identification and image-making in the 1900s. Through assertions of the right of children and teachers to take part in a system of secular education, and the right of the working class to post-elementary education, the Party saw its own history plain, and the place where it stood in the political arena. Within this understanding, childhood and education were not one and the same thing.

First of all, childhood was associated with the perception of *inequality*. 'We hold our theories of equality under the most glaring social and material inequality', claimed the ILP pamphlet *Commercialism and Child Labour*, 'and content ourselves with a mock philanthropy which preaches the cultivation of all the virtues, knowing full well that it is as easy for the rose to bloom in the sandy desert as for the life of good report to ripen in the "niggard earth" of existing social conditions.'[57] The most glaring feature of this inequality was visible in the way in which working-class children were not allowed to proceed up the educational ladder, to higher education. McMillan certainly dealt in terms of inequality when she discussed education, but her detailed and technical attention to the form and content of childhood learning places her outside the mainstream of ILP understanding.

At the 1906 ILP Conference McMillan spoke for her conception of childhood and education, and argued against the traditional ILP one. She told the assembled delegates that all their resolutions about secular and higher education

> betrayed a lack of proportion and want of knowledge of the real state of the children of the country. She was in favour of a university education for every working man's child, but let them begin in the right place. Every state aided school should have medical inspection, and the whole force of the Party should be concentrated on existing reforms in regard to elementary education.[58]

There was opposition here from some parliamentary members of the ILP – and it was to increase, for her words conjured up the waiting abyss of parental irresponsibility. Keir Hardie, in particular, worried about the moral effects of giving medical treatment free of charge to all children, just as some years before MacDonald had expressed concern about the feeding of all but the most necessitous. Brian Simon has noted that at the 1909 Labour Party Conference, when McMillan spoke for a very long portmanteau resolution that included the free medical treatment of children and the SDF resolution for the state maintenance of childhood, it was Hardie's intervention that turned the vote of the conference against her.[59]

McMillan's argument that the bottom rungs of the educational ladder were completely rotten had a particular personal resonance for a man like Will Thorne of the SDF, founder of the Gas Workers' Union, whose resolution demanding free meals, free medical inspection and advice, and a full system of physical education had been adopted by the TUC in 1905.[60] This resolution formed the basis of the TUC educational policy, which followed very closely the recommendations of the 1904 and 1905 Interdepartmental Committee on Physical Deterioration Reports by demanding that the Board of Education collect and publish statistics on the health of schoolchildren.[61] Will Thorne was instrumental in getting the eminent neurologist Sir Victor Horsley to support the policy of the TUC and to lend his support to the Parliamentary Labour Party on the medical inspection question.[62] Thorne saw child ill-health in school as a foundation of inequality, and lent

McMillan much more support than did the parliamentary members of the ILP.

As well as surfacing at the 1909 Labour Party Conference, differences over the Local Education Authorities (Medical Treatment) Bill emerged at the ILP Conference that same year. The measure was designed to allow local authorities to recover (or attempt to recover) from parents the cost of their children's medical treatment. McMillan objected to this proposal, believing that it would deter parents from seeking treatment – 'as for suing them for payment, one might as well sue the person lying unconscious'.[63] Ramsay MacDonald, on the other hand, objected to the Bill because it was non-deterrent: although parents were required to pay, they actually suffered no lack of rights if they were unable to. For him, the measure raised the spectre of socialism as a kind of state charity, with indigent and feckless parents supported out of the rates.[64] We are dealing, then, with sets of beliefs and understandings concerning childhood that cannot simply be subsumed under the heading 'education' or 'educational policy'. Particularly after about 1900, in ILP conference halls and in McMillan's campaigning journalism, we can see individual and collective histories of childhood and traditions of educational thought brought face to face with new bodies of thought concerning child development.

In *British Workers and the Independent Labour Party*, David Howell has emphasised ethical socialism's notion of society as an evolving organism, and its consequent eschewal of class struggle as a key determinant in bringing about either social change or the existence of a socialist society. In place of class, he argues, the idea of 'community' was asserted as the site of change – in all its ambiguity, he says, for at different times and in different structures of rhetoric, 'community' could mean a local community, or a national one, or a community of like-minded people.[65] McMillan presented children as a community of hope: 'the child' of her fiction and her ILP conference speeches was one of the theoretical underpinnings of ILP thought. A belief in the organic development of society was supported by the widespread use of an evolutionary theory in which children provided the key point of development. We have seen these ideas expressed particularly clearly through an appreciation of Henry Drummond's *Ascent of Man*.[66] An account of the social and affective function of childhood, like the one Drummond provided, allowed members of the ILP in conference, in the creation of Party policy, and on the propaganda platform to assert childhood as the focus of a cause that allowed the mere conflict of classes to be transcended. The relationship of the working-class child to the body politic, and to the socialist future, comprised a set of ideas that allowed a full expression of evolutionary socialism.

The child was figured across these forms of writing and political languages; but, shining and fair, she brought with her the dirty, adenoidal, corrupt shade of her former self, still infinitely connected to her outcast parents. What is more, children have to be acted on behalf of: children are true clients, those who cannot bring about change for themselves. They are also in a transitory state, for they grow up and become political subjects of a more permanent kind. Yet McMillan made great political use of them. Children allowed her to present the existence of the unskilled labouring poor not as some blind and motiveless horror, but as a thwarted potential. An apprehension of this life, through both the image and the sociological reality of childhood, enabled her, too, to measure the psychological and emotional costs of capitalism, and thus to approach the subjects of her writing and her theorising with a full human sympathy. It was inevitable, however, that an understanding of adults forged by analogy with childhood led finally to a more complete definition of working people as those who had to be acted *for*, uplifted and rescued.

So did McMillan reach the place that Hinton has described the rest of the ILP leadership reaching, the arena of welfare philanthropism and progressive liberalism, albeit by a more elaborate route? Once, long before, in 1894 when the *Clarion* and its readers had been debating questions of leadership, democracy and the relationship of leaders to people, McMillan had said that all leaders had to do in modern times was to ascertain the will of the people, and carry it out – adding that 'the fearsome task' in all this was actually anticipating *'the unfolding desire of a people just emerging into manhood'*.[67] McMillan took upon herself not only the anticipation of that desire, but its education. The route that the educative strategy led her along must make us see the erosion of a socialist perspective in actual events, actual relationships with different constituencies of adults and children – as the product of a particular history – rather than in the inherent failure of a body of ideas; so that we might say that it is the journey she made that remains important as much as its end-point, in a generalised movement to save the children.

A consideration of ILP socialism in relation to the idea of childhood offers one historical example of a society coming to terms theoretically, and in practical policy, with a large-scale reorganisation of the idea of human development and selfhood within a given society. It was one of McMillan's self-appointed tasks to educate her various audiences in the meaning and potential of childhood. In this way, she operated with educational forms and with methods of teaching – topics of the next chapter.

9

Education

WHEN McMillan is remembered today, it is in histories of education that the fullest accounts are to be found, accounts that ignore the socialist perspective within which she did much of the work they celebrate. She has been a particular casualty of the historiography that cuts educational questions off from the political and the social, so as well as restoring to its full contemporary meaning the idea of education with which she worked, it is also important to suggest what it was about the content of her thought, and means of trans-mitting it, that made it so very easy to appropriate it and her to the *vitae* of strugglers and saints of childhood restoration.[1]

A good deal of historical attention has been paid to one aspect of the educational process within the ILP: the coming to socialism through a convulsive recognition of social wrong. This moment of social learning has often been described as a matter of conversion, in the religious sense.[2] The individual, swayed by the moral force of the propagandist's argument, the shocking and sudden revelation of social inequalities, was desperately moved, and he or she turned to socialism, as formerly they might have turned to God: in the words attributed to Rachel McMillan, they were '"bound to do it", if they think at all'.[3] It is quite clear that McMillan's public speaking and her writing performed this function. She moved many to tears in her lifetime, and abundant evidence exists of her power to convert.

Yet a stereotyped picture of McMillan moving men and women to tears and socialism does not help much in explaining her writing or her political action in the period after she left Bradford. She joined liberal interest groups like the Froebel Society, and she wrote and worked for Albert Mansbridge's paternalistic Workers' Educational Association (WEA), not out of approval for the political vision they embodied, but because these organisations offered her the means to lobby and apply pressure – within her own party and the Labour Party, and in the wider society. The WEA in particular, which gave her a platform in its journal the *Highway*, allowed her to develop what she saw as the educative purpose of the Deptford Centre itself, which was to make parents and other adults aware of the regenerative potential of their own children and children in general. William Morris had argued that the function of socialism was to educate desire, to make working men and women want more and better: 'the leisure which Socialism above all things aims at obtaining for the worker is also the very thing that breeds desire – desire for beauty, for knowledge, for more abundant life, in short.'[4] A good deal of McMillan's purpose was to educate men and women, particularly those of the unskilled working class, in the potential of their thwarted desire for their own children.

The theory and practice of McMillan's pedagogy will be discussed in the next chapters, 'Bodies' and 'Minds'. Here, the purpose is to see McMillan in an educational relationship with adults and children of her own party (the children, in fact, being those who attended Socialist Sunday Schools), with working-class adults in Bradford and in London, and with the young women she trained as educators and nurturers of outcast childhood. In her different manifestations as educator and teacher she experienced qualitatively different kinds of human relationship, and these relationships had an effect on her political progress; particularly in the Bradford years.

The Socialist Sunday School (SSS) movement had as its aim the conversion of a significant proportion of British children to socialism, for the purpose of transforming society by political and industrial action. Fred Reid, the historian of the movement, defines the Sunday Schools as an example of a labour sect, drawing its membership almost exclusively from the working class, giving teachers and children opportunities to exercise responsibility and practise public speaking, in the tradition of nineteenth-century dissenting religious movements.[5]

The Socialist Sunday Schools originated in the West of Scotland in 1895, when Lizzie Glasier of the Glasgow Women's Labour Party started to canvass for the idea of 'Socialist classes being . . . formed in connection with every branch of the ILP, and all other socialist bodies in the country'. She argued that

hitherto, hardly any attempt has been made in Scotland in order to draw children into the Socialist ranks, yet it is obvious that if the world is to be led to the pure ideal of Socialism through an educational process of evolution, efforts ought to be made to get at the little ones when their minds and susceptibilities are plastic and impressionable.[6]

A branch was actually formed in Glasgow, early in 1896; but another root of the movement is also to be found in 1893 in Manchester, where many of Robert Blatchford's Cinderella Clubs had been taken over by the Labour Churches, and run as educational as well as philanthropic endeavours.[7] Reid distinguishes the Lancashire SSS from others around the country, because of their rationalist framework and their overt intention of providing a setting where 'children can be trained to think, and not merely to become Socialists or Labour Church members'. This rationalist principle, argues Reid, lost out to the ethical teaching of the rest of the movement, in which children were taught about the ethical basis of existing society rather than being provided with knowledge that would enable them to bring about a more just one.[8]

The idea of the movement was spread by Keir Hardie, writing his column for children as 'Crusader' in the *Labour Leader*. By 1901 the movement had its own journal in the *Young Socialist*, and McMillan was a consistent contributor to this monthly, writing some forty pieces for it between 1903 and 1912 and publishing here by far her largest corpus of fiction for children. Using Reid's distinction between the rational and the ethical in the turning of children to socialism, did McMillan's endeavours fall within the domain of ethical appeal? She wrote, she said, for 'dear Socialist children' who were for the main part 'neither rich nor poor', and she tried to awaken them to their responsibilities, particularly towards the children of the residuum.[9] Her fiction taught girls 'to despise mere wealth and position and pride and [to] reverence love and poverty and sacrifice'. In 'Schoolmates' (1903), for example, which taught this lesson, the fictional working-class Jessie refuses to become her school friend's paid companion and seeks out instead a life of service among the poor, teaching them 'to reverence what is truly great and to despise what is paltry and low'.[10] This, then, seems to be the training of working-class leaders of ethical socialism in the principles of a traditional self-sacrifice and piety: when McMillan contributed her piece to the 'Calendar of Socialist Saints', that ran from 1909 to 1911, she told her young readers that the meaning or 'the message' of Mazzini was his trust 'in the Young and above all in the Youth of the Working Class'.[11]

Back in 1895, before the ethics of mutual and social sympathy had come to dominate the sss movement, the intention had been to teach the children 'the rudiments of Socialism in a simple and attractive manner', and McMillan had undertaken the production of a 'Kindergarten Socialist Primer'; it was never completed, but a draft appeared in article form in the *Young Socialist*. 'Arithmetic' (1904) was an attempt to explain common ownership and the redistribution of wealth to children, and to introduce the rudiments of the labour theory of value. 'There are rules in arithmetic', she told the children; 'but is there any rule in the paying and the gaining, the selling and losing, the giving and taking, that make up human life?' Yes, she responded: 'there are fixed rules *everywhere*: the cheap dress isn't cheap because of the labour invested in it . . . .'.[12] In another story, 'The Swifts', Tom and Elsa (in a sibling relationship lifted directly from that of Tom and

Maggie in *The Mill on the Floss*) contemplate the behaviour of a group of birds, and McMillan uses their observations to outline the idea of social co-operation as opposed to economic conflict.[13]. In these stories the appeal to children's sympathy, and their instruction in ethics, was not divorced from a rational socialist education.

McMillan's support for the use of fairy-tales in childhood – against calls for their abolition by some sections of the movement who labelled them superstition – has to be seen as part of a more general educational debate taking place in the years before the First World War, for which the sss movement provided a forum, rather than as a purely sectional conflict between the ethical and the rational.[14] McMillan saw the Sunday Schools as a possible avant-garde in educational method. Reid has mentioned schoolteachers who, as converts to socialism, were drawn to the sss out of frustration with the restrictions imposed on them within the school system.[15] McMillan was particularly interested in this group, noting not just their experience and repertoires of teaching technique but the relationship that existed between them and the children they taught:

> . . . the dancing and the Tales, and the new intimacy between teacher and taught, that is all to the good surely. Just as the Sunday School was the forerunner of the day school, so perhaps – who knows – the Socialist Sunday School may usher in the new method . . . our children should draw freely . . . they should write more and talk more than is possible in the day school . . .[16]

If McMillan saw the Sunday Schools as an interesting arena for experimentation, she was equally treated as an expert within the movement, and teachers were urged to get hold of the books she recommended.[17] Her actual appearances at Sunday Schools were always recorded as an 'honour',[18] and other members of the ILP leadership also saw the Socialist Sunday School as a place where, under present restricting educational circumstances, her ideas might possibly come to fruition. Addressing the eighth-anniversary gathering of the Huddersfield Socialist Sunday School in 1904, Isabella Ford looked at the audience of parents and found her mind 'wandering . . . off to Miss McMillan's pamphlet on the "Beginnings of Education", where she speaks of the necessity of parents being interested in the right education of their children . . .'.[19] Indeed, the sss that Reid uses as an exemplar of the rationalist approach, the one based in Hyde in Lancashire, took as its two educational authorities McMillan and Herbart (1776–1841), the German philosopher whose psychology, along with the writings of Froebel, was used as a source for much educational innovation in nineteenth-century Britain.[20] Divided into six groups according to age, the four-to-six-year-olds attending the

Hyde School modelled with Plasticine, discussed large picture charts, played finger games and listened to stories.[21]

It seems that from its very inception the movement as a whole placed its pedagogy within this professional and progressive continuum. Indeed, the fact that McMillan was asked to write a *kindergarten* primer in 1905 shows that Lizzie Glasier and other members of the Glasgow Women's Labour Party were at least conversant with Froebelian education and with an age/stage delineation of child development. For progressive teaching material the Socialist Sunday Schools were in any case likely to use material put out by the Froebel Society, and by 1899 the Yorkshire and Scottish Socialist Sunday Schools, for example, were routinely basing their physical education at least on 'Froebel's Kindergarten Manuals', published by Sonnenschein.[22]

In the years between 1902 and 1910, when McMillan lacked an institutional base and direct contact with children, the sss movement and its journal provided her with a place to practise a pedagogy. Both the ethical and the rationalist schools of thought within the movement welcomed her as an expert on the question of education, and indeed, though McMillan's writing for the movement seems broadly ethical in appeal, it was the rationalist Sunday Schools of the Lancashire and Cheshire Union that paid the most serious attention to the theory of child development and learning that she propounded. It may be true that throughout this period the sss remained 'a communion of believers, a sect', as Fred Reid has argued. But it is also true that they provided one route for the transmission of ideas about education to an informed socialist public, and allowed McMillan to develop ideas about working-class education that were later to be put into practice in Deptford.

Margaret McMillan operated in an educative relationship to working-class adults long before she taught their children. By 1899 her reputation as a public speaker had been established through her adult education work. Her first lectures at the Labour Church in 1895 developed into a full series of 'Classes for Working Men' on the Greek myths.[23] These were given in ten parts, in May and June of that year, and formed the nucleus of Sunday lectures around the country during that summer. By August 1895 McMillan had prepared a series on the French Revolution, first given in Bradford and then forming an eight-part course at Leeds Labour Church in January and February 1896.[24] In March she started a new series on 'Art in the Middle Ages', 'bringing out as only she can', reported the *Bradford Labour Echo*, 'the beautiful spiritual meaning of these carvings in wood and stone'.[25] This series was received with positive rapture, the *Echo* calling them the 'most interesting and enlightening ever given in the Labour Church', and the Bradford correspondent of the *Labour Leader* reporting that 'in the words of one of her audience, it was the grandest sermon he had ever heard'.[26]

In 1897 she started a course on 'Modern Economists' at the Leeds Labour Church, delivering lectures on Adam Smith, Ricardo, Jevons, Mill, Marx and Ruskin throughout the month of March.[27] This was both the practice of conversion to socialism, and education in the principles of socialism, and it is important not to separate the many lectures she gave on child education off from this more conventional series. The same understanding that led her to convey theories of child development and the principles of physiological education to the Labour Church congregation of Bradford and the readership of the *Echo* lay at the basis of her support of the WEA, which at its inception was formed not just as an association for the education of adults but as a means of conveying information *about* education to the working class.

There can be little doubt about McMillan's commitment to this principle in the 1890s. The secretary of the Bradford Labour Church reported in the *Labour Prophet*, on the series 'Art in the Middle Ages', that 'she does not water down to meet the supposed low-level of a working-class audience. That were a profound mistake were it made and she knows her audience far too well to attempt it . . .'. In fact, she was recorded as saying to him that she found in her audience 'a quicker intelligence, a more virile and vital judgement in matters intellectual than is to be found in congregations where the cuff and collar . . . prevail'.[28]

McMillan's later plea for a national system of higher education, *The Child and the State* (1911), suggested that an educated working class would be intellectually more interesting than other sections of society, partly because being the largest social and economic grouping it was bound to include 'more various and numerous types', but also because working-class people 'are not limited by the fierce desire for gain and the impulse to sacrifice everything to this end'.[29] Even in the 1920s McMillan was to remember the excitement of encountering such audiences, of knowing herself to be in possession of skills that were needed and could be passed on – 'if one had lived abroad and knew French and German, she taught French and German in the cellar of the Labour Institute' – of horizons expanding, of a people waking from a long sleep.[30] Writing in 1909 of experiments in rural adult education in Denmark, she discussed the profound psychological change wrought in the peasantry by the experience of education, of 'faces . . . broken up – melted like sunned ice and showing the quick living water beneath'.[31]

It was in her discussion of education for adults that McMillan expressed most clearly her understanding of the psychological effects of poverty and deprivation. In *The Child and the State* she described a working-class woman who had attended a WEA class and who, speaking at a public meeting, had surprised her middle-class audience by breaking loose 'from her social idiom':

> the mill-worker copied no one. She spoke of what she had learned in the classes she had attended and of how it had lifted herself and her comrades into a new world . . . The work she had done in the classes had not helped her to earn a better wage as yet, but it had raised her up into a new life, and she was prepared to lay hold of this new life which seemed to her to be far beyond her. She became, in a word, her real self . . .[32]

By the time McMillan made these observations, the whole complexion of worker education in Britain was changing. During the 1890s the SDF approach to adult education – usually based on a study group with a leader, all working together on a text with a question in mind – could be contrasted with the ILP form, where the lecture, the speech and the sermon were more usual ways of approaching a question. In the 1900s socialist study groups started to proliferate around the country, many of them organised by the SDF and the breakaway Socialist Labour Party (SLP). In general these groups studied the texts of classic Marxist economics, although a whole range of textbooks became available at this time. Homegrown pamphlet literature like Blatchford's *Merrie England* was augmented by translations of Marx, Engels, Bebel and Plekhenov. The labour press expanded too, especially in the provinces.[33]

Marxist ideas, particularly Marxist economics, began to make a profound impact on the working-class movement, with serious textual study replacing to some extent the generalised emotional response to the platform exposition of ethical socialism. Not only was the ILP method of 'making socialists' challenged in this way, but the content of its teaching divided itself sharply from that of the SDF and the SLP. At this time as well, Ramsay MacDonald formalised the evolutionary and organic tendencies within ILP socialism in his *Socialism and Society* (1905), where Marxism was presented as outmoded, and the idea of society's evolution to a higher stage of development without revolutionary breaks was systematically argued through.[34] It was from this background of adult and political education, belonging to a party that eschewed Marxist analysis and economic understanding, that McMillan came to involvement with the Workers' Educational Association in 1903. Was this her natural home, as an ethical and evolutionary socialist?

The WEA was developed by Albert Mansbridge, a co-operator and Christian Socialist who had been involved in the university extension movement in the 1890s. The Association developed out of his work to extend the study of history and citizenship among working people; his appeal to the impartiality and apoliticality of Oxford and Cambridge teaching had great appeal for progressives of all political parties, and branches developed rapidly after 1904. Board of Education support was represented by the enthusiasm of Robert Morant, who suggested in 1907 that state support might be forthcoming for such an alliance between the universities and working-class organisations.[35]

The WEA, then, inherited the legacy of educational rescue work which had been manifest in the university extension movement, by which the educated and socially conscious middle classes attempted to bring about social harmony through the spread of knowledge. Mansbridge himself believed that there was no such thing as a 'working-class education. There is only human intelligence, advancing on darkness, creating order out of chaos, transforming not only the material world, but also the relationship of human beings . . . .'.[36] When the WEA produced a journal for the first time in 1908, it presented its role as supplying 'a platform, on which those engaged in manual labour may meet those engaged in the profession of teaching, to discuss the problems of education, and more particularly, the problems which concerned the workers'. Mansbridge castigated the labour movement for its silence on educational questions:

> Could the half-time system, could the employment of school children for long hours before and after school, could the pernicious system of large classes of sixty or seventy to one teacher, could the neglect of the Treasury to find money for medical inspection survive for a day, if the public of workers on educational matter were more vigilant and organised?[37]

Rhetorical structures apart, McMillan appears to have found herself at home in the WEA. She was elected to its Executive Committee in 1909, and though she was a poor attender at its meetings she did a more thorough job in reporting on the Danish system of rural education for adults, and in getting the Association to experiment along these lines.[38] The Danish system that she so frequently described was, on her own admission, highly paternalistic and conservative in intention, designed to weld national identity based on a theory of class harmony.[39]

In 1909 McMillan provided Mansbridge with public support over the Ruskin College crisis, when claims for a worker-directed education came into sharp conflict with the WEA brand of adult education.[40] Her support took the form of criticising the narrow economism of much worker education. Working people, she argued, were entitled to be introduced to the world of 'modern thought',

> and to live in it as a spacious home – not to be obliged as they are today to balance themselves on a broken fragment of knowledge tossed on a cold and troubled sea of ignorance to seize a broken wedge of political economy and career away on it like the poor homeless duck of Pierre Loti . . .[41]

Here, it is not clear if she is addressing the pleas of the Ruskin students, the TUC Trade Union Education programme that the WEA was to reject publicly in a few months' time, or the more general educational developments that have been noted in a variety of study groups around the country. It seems most likely, as she was writing in the *Highway*, that she was addressing WEA tutors and arguing that working people needed an understanding of social life derived from historical causality. They needed, she said, to understand a modern conception of the universe through a study of physics, astronomy and geology. Political and social economy should be placed within such a context of history and prehistory. Mansbridge alluded to this kind of general curriculum for adult education in his biography of McMillan, and remembered meeting Peter Kropotkin at the McMillans' in Bromley where, 'speaking with pride of our newly founded classes for working men and women', the Prince tore them 'to shreds. They should learn about the Universe and their place in it, he said'.[42] McMillan's rejection of economism may have been learned from a more radical source than Albert Mansbridge.

But to align McMillan completely with Mansbridge is to miss the point of what she was doing in these years, and her own theory of adult education. Above all, McMillan used the WEA to convey theories of childcare to a wide audience and to promote the idea of the school clinic. The *Highway*, in fact, provided the most consistent forum for discussion between 1908 and 1912, and the most extensive description of what was happening in Deptford.

McMillan saw the Deptford Centre – first the Clinic, and then the Clinic in conjunction with the camp school – as a system of education not just for the children involved but for their parents as well, and for the entire working-class community in which it was set. As we have seen, the Centre was designed to be *watched*, to be visible from the windows of the huddled houses surrounding it, and the people were meant to see *that it could be done*: that with very little money and minimal equipment, it was possible to take a dirty, malnourished, swollen-eyed child and make it healthy and beautiful. The people were thus to be awakened to a sense of how they had been robbed, promoted into political consciousness by their children. Her argument after 1908, in the pages of the *Highway* and elsewhere, was that the very poor were in desperate need of an understanding of *cause* in social life, of a way of seeing how things got to be the way they were. Within this perspective, working-class mothers, for instance, were presented not as degenerate, nor sunken in apathy, but imprisoned in a kind of loving ignorance. In 1910 McMillan watched the mother of a severely ill child and 'this great love burning close to this great tragedy', and concluded that the love was

> quite ineffectual, like a flame in a deep jar . . . this mother was blind. She was also very tolerant. She put up with the resentments of visitors who showed indignation and disgust of which she was a victim. What is passing in her mind as she goes her way, enduring always, hoping always, loving in the dark?[43]

The Clinic allowed for a cognitive leap – allowed men and women to see that their children's ill-health was not just in the way of things, but rather had *causes*: in dirt, poor housing; in the material conditions of life.

This understanding, this new cognition, was designed to have some impact on Deptford's unskilled working class. Remembering back in 1927 to the formation of the ILP, McMillan wrote that the intention of the new party had been to appeal to all:

> It reached forth not only to the skilled and semi-skilled, but to a new and vast army of sufferers who hung like a dead weight on the skirts of the working-class bodies, and who had wrecked their work in the past, the rear of the great organism called labour. It had been like the imprisoned tail of a creature whose lively head is free of the trap. In vain was the head advanced again and again with lively hope. It was doomed by its own members; and those defects would not end till the whole of the working classes and the classes below them could be freed together.[44]

In retrospect, then, McMillan placed all her educational work in the context of the New Trade Unionism, Blatchford's crusade for Cinderella, the fight for the bottom dog: a way of aligning the unskilled, politically unconscious working class with the élite of labour, to bring about social transformation. But as we have seen, ILP practice and ILP political theory had no actual place for the unskilled labouring poor. Neither, indeed, did the study groups of the trade-union movement, the SDF and the SLP, nor the Socialist Sunday Schools, which were all in the business of training working-class leaders. In the same way, the WEA appealed to the articulate, self-conscious and élite of the working class, possessing a consciousness of knowledge lacked, and of knowledge to be had.

Margaret and Rachel McMillan, *c.* 1871, Inverness

Margaret effects her own disappearance

Margaret and Rachel McMillan, *c.* 1874, Inverness

Margaret replaces herself with a banister

Margaret and Rachel McMillan
with Jean McMillan

Rachel McMillan, aged nineteen

Margaret McMillan, 1881/3?

Margaret McMillan,
Labour Prophet,
September 1893

Placings in socialism: at Hardie's head

Oastler uplifts the abandoned

Rescued children: Peter and
Alfred (Totty) Wood, *c.* 1916

The Girls' Camp at 353 Evelyn Street, 1911

The Boys' Camp at St Nicholas's Church Yard, 1911

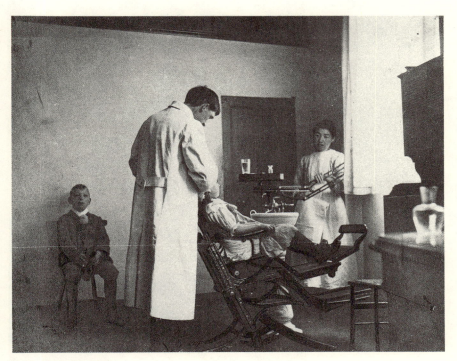

At work in the Clinic

The air-brushed image: Rachel McMillan, shortly before her death in 1917

Translation into Santa Barbara

There was no theory of political propaganda and working-class education that McMillan could have operated in, or used to develop her ideas. Indeed, the fact that the subjects of the educational process with which she experimented were children for the main part, and increasingly women, served to separate her ideas even further from the structures of influence and power that socialist and adult education shared with the liberal worker education provided by the WEA. In this way the practical experiment of Deptford, and the theory latent within it, could find theoretical expression only within liberal reformism and. welfare philanthropism. The circumstances of life in Deptford caught McMillan in the trap she was to describe so graphically in 1927, her particular entrapment being the daily round of trying to make things better for people sinking into the mud of the deep ford. She wrote to Robert Blatchford in 1929 from that depth, recalling:

> I tried to get things at Bradford – baths and open-air, and new singing and speech, but I had to come here and begin with the babies – I haven't any place among educationalists. That was all swamped long ago – it got lost in the seas of misery that rise round my head here, and will to the end. Never mind. The sea will be no more. 'There shall be no more sea.' . . .[45]

An educative process which had once been constructed in terms of agency became, in a description she wrote in 1912, 'a system of hygienic education that would redeem the poor'.[46]

In her early *Christian Socialist* articles, McMillan had argued that working people had to get knowledge for themselves; but there is little evidence that she ever took part in an actual system of education that allowed this. On the platform the rhetoric entranced, but the form of the lecture did not allow it to be analysed or questioned, and she usually taught sss children from a distance, through the medium of the didactic short story. She taught classes of adults in the Bradford Labour Institute, but these classes, apart from the language lessons, seem to have taken the form of the lecture or sermon. She taught few WEA classes, and in any case the form used was that of a tutorial group led by a teacher, who imparted knowledge after students had done their own individual reading in preparation. She does not seem to have experienced the group questioning of a text, with teacher and taught making their way through it. What she did experience served only to reinforce McMillan's image as giver of enlightenment and information, and there was, indeed, no place where her work and her analysis might seriously be questioned.

The fine and moving rhetoric of much of McMillan's journalism, which we have to assume was the written form of much of her oratory, is extremely difficult to follow because often she simply did not know what she meant, and she never experienced a form of interaction with working-class adults that challenged this form. The Deptford Centre, for all the opportunities it gave for parents to question what was being done for their children, was a show, a performance, in which the children were made actors and exemplars. This is not to say that the children blooming like the flowers of the field behind the fence of the Deptford garden were enacting some kind of falsehood; rather it is to suggest that what needed to be learned by their parents was staged, as McMillan staged her performance on the platform, in order to move her audience to a sense of the higher life.

A recent historical survey of European education for pre-school children notes how difficult it is to fit McMillan into the established history of early childhood education in Britain. In *Education Under Six*, Denison Deasey also notes that despite claims made for McMillan's influence on British education, official policy took only her emphasis on cleanliness and a physical education for working-class children from her writing on early education.[47] There seem to be few grounds for ascribing to McMillan the model on which, in the middle years of this century, nursery and other childhood education was constructed, as Elizabeth Bradburn has suggested. McMillan's insistence on a very long school day and on very large schools (for the sake of economy) always came up against the resistance of the teacher unions, and an official policy that accepted the Nursery School Association's recommendations concerning the homeliness in small nursery schools and units.[48]

McMillan wrote of her own experience of teaching in the Deptford Centre as quite limited, and interestingly mentioned a challenge to her approach made by the older boys – one of the few she can ever have experienced in her career as teacher and propagandist.[49] The type of relationship through teaching and the transmission of knowledge that McMillan did successfully establish at Deptford was with the young women she recruited for her training courses. Training at the Deptford Centre was offered as early as 1914, though it was not recognised by the Board of Education until 1919, when grants for a one-year residency in Deptford (on top of students' two-year training in other colleges) were made available.[50] By this time there were about thirty students working at Deptford – most of whom, in fact, received no grant, as they were taking McMillan's three-year course, for which no funding was available.

There were these two categories of student, and a further two: a group of young girls McMillan hoped to train as nursery assistants (non-professional workers of whom the NUT was extremely wary) and, in the war years and the early 1920s, a series of well-connected girl heroines and helpers, who were presented with the task of nurturing slum children as a social mission. Miles Franklin passed this way in 1916, between Chicago and Macedonia,[51] and Abigail Adams Eliot, who later ran the Ruggles Street Nursery School and Training Centre in Boston, was sent there in 1921 by the Boston Women's Education Association to study its methods in preparation for opening her own school.[52] McMillan increasingly saw the Deptford Centre as a place where the classes might meet her in harmony across a divide of young-ladydom – a divide that she herself, a quarter of a century before, had traversed in a much more subversive fashion.

McMillan saw the training she gave at Deptford as distinct in several ways from the usual teacher training. First, she was insistent that very young children needed trained teachers, and that 'the general view . . . that any kind of nice motherly girl would do for a nursery-teacher', and the idea that 'nurseries were . . . a dumping ground for the well-intentioned but dull women of today', were notions that a wide range of audiences needed disabusing of.[53] Second, she was quite clear that she was training young women to work in slum areas, with very poor children: she insisted that her students visit the children's homes and live in the streets around the Centre.[54] Third, she was clear that practice should precede academic work and the study of educational theory; that her students should work in every section of the nursery, washing, feeding, delousing and talking to children – 'not as mere labour, but as a preparation for mental work, and not as only ministering to bodies, but as a means of finding how the instrument of mind, the brain, develops and works'.[55] Only at the end of the first year did academic study begin, but even then the students undertook two or three hours of childcare a day. In the third year, practical work ceased altogether.

The students, many from sheltered backgrounds, were thus faced with an extreme poverty the like of which many had not known existed, and the extraordinarily hard work of caring for young children during a very long day. This form of training placed several of them in a situation of emotional shock and extreme tiredness, in which McMillan's message, her electrifying lectures, her expression of a wide culture brought to bear on the starved bodies of slum children, all had an impact that they possibly would not have had if theory had preceded practice. Most former students who were ever asked for their memories of this time were convinced both of the rightness of the sacrifice they had made, and of the genius of Margaret McMillan.[56]

At first McMillan had intended to keep the training centre small, and to operate by example to the other training colleges of Britain, in the same way as the clinic and the camp schools offered an example of what might be done. Fired by the growing nursery school movement, she seems to have conceived of a large training college from which she could staff the nursery schools of the land some time in 1926. In November of that year she wrote to Nancy Astor that she had been 'reading Lord Shaftesbury's life yesterday . . . I am urged by some influence to build a College, & I know it will go up presently'. She had been ill, and wrote again a few days later, saying 'for some reason I'm called back and quite well. I'm going to build a college – perhaps that's why I've come back.'[57]

Nancy Astor took this project as her own, and it was partly due to her considerable efforts that money was found for the building and that the Board of Education sanctioned the kind of training McMillan proposed. 'The more I see of this system,' Astor wrote to the president of Sears Roebuck, who had just made a hefty donation to the building fund, 'the more convinced I am that it is the only solution to the problem of the slum mind. It is no use giving healthy bodies to the slums if we cannot improve their minds.'[58] Later she said to him: 'Miss McMillan won't live forever, and she must train the women and give them her spirit.'[59] For both of them there was an urgency about the project, and what Astor did not reveal to McMillan was that some delays were caused by official reservations about the work in Deptford. One of Her Majesty's Inspectors who inspected the existing Centre in the 1920s told Astor:

> Miss McMillan is a genius, but an erratic one, and when I have persuaded an official to come to Deptford and have his heart melted by the work done there, Miss McMillan has not always made the situation an easy one: she is inclined to go off the practical side and become rather vague. Consequently they regard her as not very suitable for the carrying on of the serious business of a Training College. They do not doubt for a moment the goodness or wonder of the Nursery School but the Training College is a different matter.

She suggested that Emma Stevinson, the superintendent of the Nursery School, would be a more acceptable principal than McMillan, and added: 'I think it would be fatal if she knew I was writing all this to you. She is, as you know, very sensitive, and naturally feels she has done good work and can do more . . .'[60]

The Rachel McMillan Training College was finally opened in May 1930 (with Miss Stevinson as principal), and McMillan spoke of the project in terms that may well have caused alarm to the Board of Education officials attending the opening ceremony, saying that she

> . . . did not deny the importance of material forces, but the love with which the children in the open-air nursery school are surrounded is a diffused love, and that love is impressing itself upon the consciousness of a growing number of people today, and

186

is enabling them to provide that environment in which the child can live and grow. It is the work of our movement to restore them to nurture conditions . . .[61]

That nurture, as it was emphasised in McMillan's books, journalism and public speaking during the 1920s, was described in terms of an aphorism, attributed to Rachel, which provided the epigraph to both editions of her *Nursery School*: 'Educate every child as if he were your own'.

Some thirty years later, Anna Freud was to suggest to would-be teachers that it was psychologically dangerous for women to take on the structures of maternal thinking and attitude in their dealings with the young children they taught.[62] Surveying thirty years of prescription to teachers and practice in early childhood education, Freud suggested that the whole impulse towards child nurture and a new attitude towards children in school had occurred in Europe during the First World War, when 'teachers began to realise that the child's physical state had something to do with his learning capacity. Children were not getting sufficient food due to deprivations caused by the war, and . . . the first school meals were begun at this time.' She went on to suggest that first the child's need for sleep, and then for physical affection, was recognised. We can argue with the history that Anna Freud presented here, and show that this attention to the bodies of children in school had longer and more complex roots than those she described. And using that complex history – particularly its mani-festation in McMillan's development of a pedagogy, both for children and for those who were going to teach them – we can point out how very difficult it is, in a class society, for teachers actually to take on the structures of maternal love, 'treat every child as if he were your own', and make an identification with children who are so very unlike the teachers themselves.[63]

McMillan made strenuous efforts to make the children of Deptford like herself – to transform them, as she did Peter and Totty, by an education that included food, sleep and love. But the young girls who underwent her training did not always know these children as their own. Rather, they saw what McMillan did as a 'holy' mission, a bestowal on those children of what they lacked. They might exclaim in later life 'how wise she was . . . to train her staff to cleanse a child's head',[64] but it is difficult to perform that function and to think of the child as being oneself, one's own. What is more, the children *went back*, just as Marigold went back. In a passage strikingly reminiscent of the classic nineteenth-century form for looking into the homes of the poor that Alain Corbin has described, McMillan depicted 'Dennis', and his enduring contact with the dark place that spawned him:

Dennis lives in a . . . street [that] is a huddle of houses with dark, greasy lobbies and hideous black stairs leading down into cellars. It is so dark that when one goes down one sees nothing for a few moments. Then a broken wall, and a few sticks of furniture appear, and a dark young woman with glittering eyes looks down at us.

Dennis is a great pet in the Nursery. On his firm little feet he. runs all round the big shelter and garden . . . he breaks into a kind of singing on bright June mornings . . . his eyes alight with joy. In the evening his older sister comes, and carries him back to the cellar . . .[65]

In his biography, Albert Mansbridge attempted to explain why McMillan's educational writings had such a small circulation, and why there was 'little or no quotation from them in the educational literature of the time'. One reason he advanced was that she was thought of 'either as a pioneer or a prophet . . . but prophecy is hard to quote . . .', and indeed, the rhetorical organisation of her books, with their frequent pauses made to move readers to a sudden perception and sympathy – to move them to tears – did not make them obvious choices for student reading lists. Mansbridge's other speculation about the relative neglect of her writing was that its content was already known from more conventional sources, that 'her masters Rousseau, Pestalozzi [and] Froebel had provided the material for academic study'. [66] This in fact was not the case, for although McMillan was familiar with the work of these continental fathers of British progressive education, her theories were centrally derived from a quite different source, that of neurology and materialist physiology. Along with all the other factors that spelled neglect of her as an educational thinker, an unfamiliarity with the trajectory of this school of thought probably accounted for the major part of it. It is to this trajectory that we must now turn.

10

Bodies

I N 1900 McMillan finally published *Early Childhood*. During the
previous year Keir Hardie had given three columns a month to it in
the *Labour Leader*, where it appeared as a series on primary
education. Both the series and the book were addressed, as Hardie
observed, to the wife of Robert Blatchford's symbolic addressee, John
Smith of Oldham – to 'Mrs John Smith' – and was, Hardie thought,
'written more for the mother than the Dominie'.[1]

It is an important book in the McMillan corpus, for it drew together
and made explicit the theories of child development that she had been
working with throughout the Bradford years, and shows a continuing
use of the technique she had practised there, in the columns of the
Labour Echo, of simplifying and conveying an array of technical
information to a non-professional audience. Whether mothers of the
respectable working class read the book must remain a matter for
speculation, for all her books were orientated towards the professional
rather than the parent.

Eight years later, reviewing her three books on childhood in the
Highway – this one, *Education Through the Imagination* (1904), and
Labour and Childhood (1907) – J.W. Slaughter considered that
McMillan's achievement had been to make 'the discovery of the child'
accessible to a general public. This 'discovery', in Slaughter's estima-
tion, had profound implications for educational planning. 'It is only
within late years', he observed, that 'the necessity of a knowledge of
childhood as a condition antecedent to the arrangement of any
education programme' had become 'that prescribed by the child's own
nature and stages of development'.[2] *Labour and Childhood* described
this child as both a body and a mind; but the body came first, a
neurological and physiological entity that developed by its own
internal laws. McMillan showed that these laws could be thwarted, and
were thwarted in the case of the working-class child, who was cut off
from many of the conditions that provided for natural and normal
development.

In McMillan's description, the child's body was organised physiolo-
gically – that is, it comprised a collection of functions which interacted
with each other and were dependent on each other. Late-nineteenth-
century physiology has been described as a paradigmatic science,

189

marking a fundamental change in understanding of systems that spread to most other areas of biological thought.[3] In particular, the practice of physiology, which was highly and explicitly experimental, moved first from an assumption of idealism, in which matter was seen as secondary to its conceptualisation or abstract apprehension, to that of materialism, in which matter was understood to exist independently of any perception, account, or conceptualisation of it. Within this understanding, a system or an entity was studied through its parts, and the sum of those parts was taken to be a description of the whole. Later in the century, physiological accounts converged towards a more dialectical materialism in which the actual *interaction* between the different parts of a body, or other biological entity, were understood to constitute the description of the whole.[4]

The names of British and European physiologists – of the Berlin School; of Helmholtz, Brucke, Romanes, Cuvier, Carpenter, Virschow, Broca – are scattered throughout McMillan's writing.[5] She knew of the general trajectory of this work either from secondary sources, or from original reading. Some work, not translated into English, she probably read in the original German or French.[6] Certainly, the early-nineteenth-century developments in psychology and physiology that are represented by the work of Pinel, Esquirol and Itard were transmitted to her by Édouard Seguin's writing.[7] But Seguin died in 1880 and McMillan clearly had access to either first- or second-hand accounts of key developments in experimental psychology and physiology that took place in the 1880s and 1890s.

The body of a child as described by McMillan in 1900 was a physiological entity, in that the varying functions – movement, speech, thought – were presented as the sum of interactions within the body; however, it was the neurological system that mapped out this physiological organisation. McMillan told her readers that in babies the nervous system was undifferentiated, and that the child received early impressions through 'the sympathetic system, with its wide channels, its central ganglions'.[8] Not pausing to explain what a ganglion was (a nerve-nucleus in the central nervous system, from which nerve fibres radiate), she went on to describe how the arterial system that conveyed blood around the organism was large in proportion to the baby's body, and she located the place where mind developed within this system, describing how

> the living cells, whilst building up the pabulum or food-stuffs into their own substance, ever respond to the influences that play on them like breezes on a lake, but they respond in a peculiarly effective way during the earlier months . . . Occasionally we are reminded of the permanent character of these records by dim

recollection, and emotions awakened in us we know not how or why. The perfume of a flower, the tone of a voice, the sight of a face or of a scene which we cannot remember to have visited fills us with vague delight or tenderness. The origin of these mysterious emotions lies deep-rooted in the sub-conscious life – the life we lived when as feeble recipients we accepted the impressions which flowed in on us from every side and left their traces in us for ever.[9]

In the second half of the nineteenth century a theory of the unconscious mind developed out of British neurological science, and this development was understood and used by McMillan.[10] Discussion of it belongs to the next chapter; but it is important to note here how very firmly her audience was presented with a concept of mind that was rooted in the material – in the physical body. The baby was presented as

blind at first and deaf . . . he lies like a larva, choosing nothing, refusing nothing. He absorbs impressions even while he is asleep, for the nerve cells are never quite irresponsive, never rigid, save in death. And from this dim sea of subconscious life his feeble and wavering consciousness at last arises.[11]

McMillan described the baby and the small child gaining control of the finer muscles through movement, and then presented the order in which the limbs achieved this control. Each fine movement awakened intelligence – 'this is not wonderful', commented McMillan, 'in view of the fact that movements are registered in the brain, and involve the awakening of brain cells'.[12]

McMillan introduced the notion of a brain centre, and *Early Childhood* laid out clearly what she called the 'topography' of the brain:

. . . in a kind of arch many motor centres are ranged. And these are believed by many neurologists to be not merely centres of movements, but centres too, for the reception and record of innumerable sensations . . . the cerebrum is the organ of innumerable functions and activities . . . each part lives because it is stimulated through vibrations arising from without. It is the *nervous* current which is the mother of energy.[13]

This energy, then, in McMillan's account, was both cerebral and muscular: a tired child might receive a 'rain of stimulating vibrations' which, if they were dispatched to the brain, would generate energy – 'the muscles . . . now limp, regained their tenacity; nutrition became more active . . . '.[14]

In McMillan's account, the physiological basis of mind applied also to language. In *Early Childhood*, child language was described as a matter of production, as the actual result of a material formation – that is, 'the form of the mouth and the larynx'. Given this formation, any interference – from poor breathing, for example – would prevent the production of speech.[15] Thought itself was described as the ultimate operation of organs – particularly that of the 'Royal Organ', the heart – as muscle and blood moved within the system: 'the most casual thought, the vaguest emotion sends a red tide flowing to the brain . . .'. As specific intellectual endeavour took place – in studying, for example – 'the muscles are involved . . . the activity of the blood setting in a swift river towards the cerebral centres where the great movements are taking place to which we give the name of *thought* . . .'[16]

In recent years, detailed historical attention has been paid to the large-scale effects of the medicalisation of the human body in Western culture.[17] What can be pointed to here is the transmission of a system of understanding that was structured around the idea of growth and development, and allowed for comparisons between children. In McMillan's account, working-class children could be seen as thwarted in a natural and organic development. Indeed, her political point was to draw attention to the way in which a vast number of children were deprived of such a natural development. She turned to the child of her symbolic addressee, and said:

> Here is a boy called John Smith attending the elementary school. His age is eleven. He is short by two and a half inches of the normal stature of a boy of the upper-middle class. His chest is too narrow by six or seven inches. He breathes from the upper part of his chest. The nostrils are light, and the upper lip is probably stiff and motionless. Ask him to take a deep breath . . . [He] cannot . . . has not taken one for years.[18]

This account of John Smith Jnr represents a significant shift in perception of working-class children that can be located in McMillan's development as a writer and thinker, and speculated about in more general historical terms. In *The Political Anatomy of the Body*, David Armstrong reflects on large-scale shifts in understanding of the human subject, seen through the filter of medical knowledge.[19] He suggests that 'the gaze commenced with the child', by which he means that 'psychologists played an important part in the discovery of the normal child, in revealing the detailed stages of child development, in classifying behaviour problems and in developing techniques of educational surveillance and child-rearing . . . .'.[20] We can be more specific than this if we consider McMillan's conclusion to eight years of reading in medical and neurological literature, and acquaintance with children in Bradford's elementary schools. No longer in 1900 did she see the twisted bodies of child labourers caught in the stone of Oastler's statue. Certainly, the pale beauty of the faces Ruskin had shown her remained as a vision, but now, at the beginning of the new century, she looked inwards, saw little John Smith as a branching system of nerves, his brain centres imperfectly fed by his shallow breathing, his skin a barrier to sensation rather than its transmitter. It was this understanding of a child as a physiological interiority – a body containing depth and space within it – that she worked to convey in political terms, to the ILP and a wider audience. [21]

Early Childhood had, in fact, a clear political purpose, which was to show what a restorative educational programme might look like, and to demonstrate that 'all true education is, primarily, physiological. It is concerned not with books, but with nervous tissue.' [22] The kind of writing that it represents can be seen as the formal description of more overt political interventions made by McMillan – at the 1911 Labour Party Conference, for example, where she urged delegates to 'bend their energies to seeing that school clinics were planted in every city, so that the children of the poor would at last have the physical culture, the tender care, which would make it possible for them to become intellectual inheritors as well . . . '. [23]

Early Childhood was an argument for a perception of mind and intelligence developing out of the material body. The recommendations for training movement through play in this work of 1900, the specific direction of children to the making of large arm movements through free drawing, the muscular movements that would increase the power of the voice, the basal touch awakened through swimming – all these defined an early education that was to be 'concerned almost entirely with the development of the body'. Drawing, modelling, the activity of writing, and all kinds of manual training in school were important because they ensured a 'growth in motor control, a development of the basal sense of touch, a means of evolving in natural sequence and to full perfection the delicate network of fibres and cells which are the physical basis of mental and spiritual life'. [24] Later, the formal school curriculum could build on this foundation:

> The unconscious impressions of infancy should be succeeded in the school by others – more vivid, more connected – that is all. The best geography lessons, the best history lessons, are those which appeal most strongly to the senses, which stir the imagination, waken the sympathy, and exercise, not merely the cerebral, but the sympathetic system. [25]

When McMillan wrote in 1900 that 'all true education is primarily, physiological' she was making direct reference to the most consistent source for her work, the writing of the French physiologist and psychologist, Édouard Seguin (1812–80), whose work with abnormal children entered the mainstream of British educational thought after Maria Montessori publicised it, in the years after 1911.[26]

Seguin, who trained as a medical doctor, worked with Jean Itard and was involved in his experiments with the Wild Boy of Aveyron.[27] Seguin founded a school for mentally retarded children in Paris in 1837, and published observations on his method in *Traitement moral, hygiène, et éducation des idiots* in 1846. As well as dealing with mentally deficient children he worked with deaf-mutes, and in the teaching of the deaf placed himself within the educative tradition of Pereire and Rousseau.[28]

Until 1850, when he left France to settle permanently in the USA, he was a well-known and esteemed medical physiologist whose writing was educational in import. He was also a Saint-Simonian, who consistently understood his own endeavours in the light of Saint-Simon's *Nouveau Christianisme* (1824).[29] In 1866, remembering back to 1830–40, when Saint-Simonian ideas were being used in government circles in France, he spoke of that decade as a time when 'three schools were disputing the ruling of this century'. He defined these as 'the one called Divine Rights, because it attributed a divine origin to the oppression of the many by the few . . . the Eclectic school, whose highest aim was . . . perpetuation of classes . . . education to the presumed capable; in fact, a liberal school classifying from the embryo, unequalising from the foetus'. The third school of thought was what he called the 'Christian school . . . Saint-Simonianism . . . '.

The political context in which he thus placed his own work was a 'striving for a social application of the principles of the gospel; for the most rapid elevation of the lowest and poorest by all means and institutions; mainly by free education'.[30] It was for this reason that Seguin aligned himself with Itard and his work, even though Itard 'never so much as hinted at the possibility of systematising his views for the treatment of idiots at large, nor organising schools for the same purpose', because 'he was the first to educate an idiot with a philosophical object'.[31] This vision – of a form of physical and material education undertaken to show that the common lot of the common people could be dramatically improved – was the central political understanding of McMillan's life, and was almost certainly formulated around a reading of Seguin's work. Particularly, it helps in understanding the complex of ideas that she put into practice between 1909 and 1930, in Deptford.

Seguin's *Idiocy and Its Treatment by the Physiological Method* was written in English and available in Britain after 1866. This, and his *Report on Education* (1875), were probably the volumes that McMillan

194

travelled from Bradford to read in the British Museum.[32] Seguin's *Rapport et mémoire sur l'éducation des enfants normaux et anormaux* was also available in 1895. Never translated into English, it was certainly read by McMillan along with his other works. It contained Seguin's thoroughgoing speculation about the possibility of using his educational methods with ordinary children.[33]

It was, in fact, Maria Montessori who made the most famous experiments in this direction in her Roman slum nursery school, using Seguin's work as a guide – a history of the transmission of ideas that always annoyed McMillan. In 1923 she wrote that 'Seguin's work, carried on for many years after his death, was the text book and Bible which began to be taken as a guide in the 90s and which I strove to popularise at the time; but it was to receive a more dramatic recognition through the writings of Montessori in later years.'[34] Ten years earlier she had defensively told the readers of the *Highway* that 'the new education is not new . . . it was developed in Bradford fifteen years ago'. She described here the experiments at Belle Vue infants' school made by the Infants' Mistress Florence Kirk, and observed tartly: 'I do feel that charming as the little Romans may be, they are not more charming, trustful or artistic than the Bradford babies of Belle Vue.'[35] It remains a fact, however, that Seguin's theories entered British educational thinking via Montessori's work rather than McMillan's.

When Seguin called his method of teaching retarded children 'physiological', he meant that his understanding was based on a view of a structure of bodily organs inseparably connected with their function. To change, improve or modify a function, the appropriate organ – the wasted hand, the unseeing eye, the gaping mouth – had to be acted upon. The educator could do this, as the organs of sensation were external.[36] Seguin's method began with the training of the muscular system and the senses, through a variety of exercises and activities. Then he led children from the education of the senses to general notions, or understandings, and from general notions to abstract thought. Physiological education of the senses had to precede the development of mind.[37]

It was on this point that Seguin distinguished his approach from that of his teacher, Itard. Itard had repeated visual and auditory sensations endlessly with Victor, the Wild Boy, but had not led the child towards abstraction. It was at this point, too, that Seguin took issue with Friedrich Froebel, whose activities with children, he claimed, remained at the sensory level. Seguin was insistent that his methods led from what was imitative in the child to what was creative in human thought.[38] It was to this set of arguments that McMillan referred when in 1913, discussing 'Backward Children', she described a boy at the

195

camp school swinging from a tree, being told to get down, but an hour later being asked by the remedial gymnast to perform exactly the same set of movements. Nature, she argued, or 'the woods, do not offer the advantages of the higher order of school. The wild boy of Aveyron, educated in the woods alone, was an animal, not a human.'[39]

'Physiology,' then, described an interactive and interconnected system, contained within the body of a child, and a 'physiological education' was a means of acting upon that system. Physiology also described the child in a social setting. Seguin paid attention to the future work that children were likely to do, and tried to promote a respect for manual labour.[40] McMillan's emphasis on hands, the role of hands in labour and in the development of intelligence, and her interest in technical education has its origins here (though Peter Kropotkin's work on manual labour was also an important influence).[41] Other central features of her educational programme that can be directly traced back to Seguin were the importance of the physical setting of the school, detailed attention to the children's clothing and the food they ate, the role of water in the awakening of the senses, and the particular role of women as the natural caretakers of young children.[42] To say that she learned the educational vocabulary of love, nurture and physical activity from Seguin is another way of describing his influence, but it is also to point to him as a literary influence as well as a physiological and educational one. For instance, he highlighted the human hand in his account of normal and abnormal development in an exegesis of 1866 that still leaps from the page:

> If any part of us challenges definition, it is the hand, its excellencies being so many that a single definition cannot comprehend them all
> . . . When we say prehension, we mean the complex action of taking, keeping, losing hold; otherwise to seize, hold and to let go; these three terms are the beginning, the object and the end of the act of prehension. This act, so simple for us in its trilogy, is either impossible to, or incidentally performed [sic] by the idiot . . . [43]

This is a description of the human and social subject as much as it is a biological account. For McMillan, what was described were the little Bradford mill hands whose brain centres were atrophied through the simple repetition of monotonous movements. An industrial system stood condemned by what it had done to the hands of the people, where 'the whole burden of [the worker's] task falls on the forefinger and thumb of one hand'.[44] Indeed, it was the hand that her audience were asked to concentrate on in *Early Childhood*:

> Look at the hand of the defective child. The fingers are probably stunted and ill-formed – cold and blue – the nails broken, the

palm stiff. Indeed, the whole hand often hangs stiff and motion-less, moved like a dead thing from the wrist. Suppose a teacher wants to train his hand: how does she begin? By maxims? By lessons in reading and writing? No. By movement – by exercise.[45]

In the same way, McMillan's presentation of education waking a variety of learners from sleep can be traced to Seguin and his description of backward children waking from unconsciousness through physiological education.

However, McMillan did not take a system in its entirety from Seguin. She made, for example, considerable use of the work of the British neurologists, and her main description of the physiological entity called the child was made in neurological terms. Her presenta-tion of the mind of a child (which will be discussed in more detail in the next chapter) derived from pre- and post-Freudian psychology. Educa-tional thought – particularly that of the Froebelian school – and the questions of technical education raised by Peter Kropotkin were also clearly significant in the educational system she outlined. Neverthe-less, Seguin's work was the first source of both her understanding of a child's physical and mental organisation, and her placing of children in a political sphere.

More work needs to be done before it can be claimed that McMillan rather than Montessori took up Seguin's unfinished project first, and applied his work with abnormal children to the education of the normal – though this was certainly a claim that McMillan made for herself. What she did not question was the import of using work derived from the study of subnormal children in the planning of an educational pro-gramme for working-class children. It is important to do this now, and to ask: how far did this implicit connection pathologise working-class child-hood, and engender a perception of it as a type of abnormality?

Histories of mental testing locate the attempt to classify children according to innate abilities as a socially divisive practice originating in the late nineteenth and early twentieth centuries.[46] This aspect of educational history has been wedded to much larger-scale accounts of the medicalisation and psychologising of the human subject, with systems of knowledge and understanding seen to entrap a victim within a medical gaze that permitted no vision of amelioration or change.[47] Given this historiography, it must be pointed out that many saw the classification of children according to ability as a radical political measure at the time: McMillan herself went to the polls in Bradford in 1900 with the hopeful message that 'in the 30,000 to 40,000 children under the care of the School Board, there was every variety of aptitude and she did not yet despair of some classification according to these varying aptitudes'.[48]

Although McMillan wrote and worked in an era when segregation and control of defectives had replaced an earlier optimistic humanism of treatment and a belief in their educability (a humanism exemplified, in fact, by Édouard Seguin), she still drew that democratic impulse from this body of earlier work, and structured her own theory of childhood around the belief that the life of children condemned to physiological and neurological sleep by a social system could actually be enlarged. Seguin's work allowed her to perceive and understand two central points: first, that there was a developmental order and an optimum functioning of the human body; and second, that even for children deprived of this, amelioration was possible.[49] Her consistent assertion was that poor children were the same kind of children as more favoured ones, that their inabilities were not innate and fixed – even though 'some manage to believe still that the masses are born dull'.[50] The working-class girl, she said in 1909, 'is not a distinct species. It is not in her nature and its general law of development, that she differs from the so-called upper class girl, but only in her prospects and circumstances . . . '.[51] Although she was deprived of growth, of nutrition, of stimulation, these things could be put right – with political will, human effort, and a little money. It was this broad optimism that she took from Seguin's work, not a perception of working-class children as deficient or defective.

The system of education that McMillan described from about 1896 onwards, and put into effect a decade later in the Deptford Centre, was therefore focused on the improvement of children's bodies. When she asked, in 1895, what was 'the use of doing anything with a child until you have washed it',[52] she was not making a simple bid to clean up the child of the residuum, but rather expressing an understanding of neurological function whereby sensation was deadened by dirt. The children of the poor had been rendered half-dead by the industrial system. Water would, quite literally, awaken the child's body – 'disease and death would fly from that meeting and recognition, and Pleasure (that great brain stimulus) would start new rhythms of life in the stagnant body'.[53]

Later, when she had moved to London and was writing about the baths that Bradford had finally provided in its schools, she reflected sadly that they were being used to provide instruction. 'I wanted the babies to *play* in the bath – not to learn swimming . . . but only to get the pleasure and impressions that are the beginning of all capacity to learn.'[54] Even as 'a mere physical exercise' swimming positively improved the system that received these impressions: 'in swimming, the vital organs . . . come well into play, and the whole system is braced and strengthened'.[55] In particular, it broke up poor breathing habits.[56] In Deptford, in the camp school, there was no swimming bath available in a basement – which was McMillan's recommendation for elementary schools – but water remained central to the educational system practised, a 'method of general touch training'.[57]

The Deptford Centre demonstrated physiological education in operation, with its provision for sense training, the space given for large movements, and their refinement later by large arm drawing and modelling. It was an education framed by an understanding of the body's needs: its demand for food, for sleep, for movement and cleanliness. Yet the Deptford Centre was not a simple chronological realisation of theories of physiological education that McMillan had been able to put into practice only sporadically before 1909. An essential feature of the Deptford Centre was a relatively new attention paid to remedial work. The close and detailed contact with children that the London clinics at Bow and Deptford allowed, and the facts of child disease that medical inspection uncovered around the country as a whole, revealed deformities of which McMillan had not been aware when she outlined a system of education in the early 1900s. What evolved after 1910–11 was a system based on a perception of the majority of children as 'sickly and deformed'; physiological education was no longer a general system, applicable to the bodies and minds of all children, but a process of cure for a particular class of child.[58]

A deep ambiguity attached to McMillan's understanding of this development, though at some level she was quite aware that it had taken place. When, in 1927, she remembered her and Rachel's discussing the plan they were to present to Joseph Fels, she highlighted the sick and diseased bodies of London children, attributing the perception of them to Rachel.[59] 'We did not really agree', McMillan recalled.

I wanted to make the whole scheme preventative. Bathrooms that should be classrooms; treatment for adenoids; new methods of speech training and singing; training in the oral subjects to be given to all children . . . Rachel was not pleased with this scheme. She pointed out that most of the children we had seen were suffering from actual disease. 'Some can hardly breathe . . . Some are going blind. We have seen many septic mouths . . . and crippled limbs. Your proposals won't deal with all of that directly.'

She then went on to record Rachel's sudden, motiveless change of heart – her agreement to work for a health centre rather than a treatment centre. This strange account could be seen as McMillan's oblique recognition of what happened at Deptford. The garden-in-the-slum did have the form of a health centre, but the child playing there had, by the 1920s, to be seen as the fragmented creature that medical inspection and examination had made her. She was there to be cured, by the remedial system described in *The Camp School* (1917).

The next chapter considers the concept of mind that arose from McMillan's understanding of the body. The distinction is awkward in many ways, especially as what was being described was, for the most part, an integrated, holistic system. But if we are to understand McMillan as a political thinker who could seriously tell her many audiences, over many years, that mental life was conditioned by the material, then the aetiology of the material, the corporeality of her understanding, needs to be made plain – not least so that it can be seen how the theory ultimately failed her when translated into a political project. It may help as well, in biographical terms, to look at McMillan as a body in the world, working out a politics through the bodies of poor children. Albert Mansbridge paid serious attention to McMillan's neglect of her own body in the chapter of his biography called 'Margaret the Woman', giving his readers many anecdotes of tapes and hooks left undone, overnight visits made to strangers without any nightdress or change of clothes, fingers blue with cold as she wrote in a room 'without thinking that she could put a match to the fire'.[60] These are indeed the items that we might expect to find in such a *vita*, so that Mansbridge could present her among the company of saints, saying:

> . . . her body was but a means of expression. It had to do what it was told, and go where it was sent. Her real life was . . . otherwhere. She was not of this world, except in so far as her human body was concerned . . . There was a birth, food and sleep, and a death, that was all . . . She who cared not for her own body, sought to make straight, clean, and healthy the bodies of hindered children . . .[61]

The bodies of these children were diseased and often very dirty. She did confront her own feelings about dirt, but privately, only twice in thirty years in a public or political context (on occasions already noted).[62] She labelled her own disgust once in the 1890s, when she berated Robert Blatchford and told him that she would send her own children to the dirty schoolroom, saying to them: '"Yes. You see how horrible Dirt is. It makes one *sick*. Every one ought to be clean. But you mustn't run like a coward though you feel sick, but be brave and human *as a child*."'[63]

How are we to read the absence of reaction to stench and odour in McMillan's public writing? The question is a historically proper one, for we know from a wide variety of contemporary sources that the children she encountered in Bradford classrooms and in her south-east London clinics often smelled very bad indeed.[64] In his historical account of the perception of odours (which draws mainly on French sources), Alain Corbin describes the pre-Pasteurian period 1750 to 1880 as one in which the sense of smell gradually became more and more directed towards the poor in European society, towards the masses. During these years, the working classes came to be described in the same terms and with the same vocabulary as had the putrid dangers understood to lie in the natural world in an earlier era.[65] Fear and disdain for 'the people' were expressed in a vocabulary of rot, faecal swamp and engulfing filth; their existence seen to pose a threat to the ordered and increasingly deodorised bourgeois world. At the same time, as the nineteenth century passed, the stock of terms for the apprehension and description of smells actually contracted.[66]

Using the account in *The Foul and the Fragrant*, we can see how McMillan grew to maturity and adopted social theories and political constructs in a post-Pasteurian era in which sanitising enthusiasms were, in Corbin's words, 'launched . . . on the dirt of the wretched poor', at a time when various officials 'launched inspections of insalubrious dwellings, schools, barracks and bath-houses in sports clubs'. What is more, the last decades of the nineteenth century saw post-Lavoisian chemistry brought to a degree of refinement that allowed the most precise norms of ventilation for various types of building to be established.[67] We have seen McMillan using this meticulous environmental science – in particular, in her years on the Bradford School Board.

Corbin argues that 'it is from the sense of smell, rather than from the other senses, that we gain the fullest picture of the great dream of disinfection, and of the new intolerances . . .'[68] There could be no proper historical resistance to placing McMillan within this account and this setting – to acknowledging her involvement in the mythologies, prejudices and sciences of her age. But at the same time she was not (any more than any other historical actor) the passive transmitter of these ideas. Her case in particular shows a complicated and considered *use* of dominant mythologies and ideologies, for political purposes. There are indeed grounds for seeing the omission of smell from her political register of the body as a politeness – a reticence that refused to use the imagery that might label the children of the poor repugnant and bestial. Yet as the chapter 'Voices' will suggest, McMillan transferred her real and troubled repulsion from certain aspects of working-class life away from the olfactory to the aural: it was the voices of working-class children that she allowed herself to condemn – as ugly, deformed, grating.[69] We may see in this transmutation of the material – the dirt and smell of a crowded elementary-school classroom

– into the insubstantial – the play of ugly voices in the yard outside – something of what Mansbridge understood when he described the contempt in which she held her own body.

Mansbridge claimed that McMillan's own body 'was but a channel for flowing energy . . .';[70] but that etherealisation seriously missed the point of the materialist science from which she derived her educational and political theory. It also ignored the relationship she forged between her own bodily existence and that of the children she worked with. Photographs from the 1860s and 1870s contrast a short, dark and stout McMillan with the fair and slender Rachel, whose air-brushed image at the front of *Life of Rachel McMillan* shows not a woman of fifty, but an eternal and ethereal young girl. That this contrast mattered to McMillan can be read in her self-transmutation into the slender, elegant and brilliant 'Mary Muse' of her governess fiction.

In some way, however obliquely, she did recognise her bodily kinship with the children of the unskilled working class, and this recognition is detectable in all her movements of sensuality towards the children who were the subjects of her theories and her fiction. She recognised that her own sensuality, what she remembered of being clean and well dressed – that 'LOVELY, intimate, splendid feeling' – was what she wanted to promote in poor children.[71] She told readers of the *Clarion* that if they wanted to feed the poor, they 'must remember that they have five senses – also souls', and ought to condemn the ugly and hurried shovelling of food down the throats of abandoned children, asking 'Is it very beautiful?'; and replying:

> . . . you don't get beauty quite so cheaply – nor quite so easily. 'But this', cries someone 'is very sensuous'. Well, do you want [people] to get rid of their senses? And what would you be without them? And did Christianity come originally from the slums? No, but from an enchanted land . . .'.[72]

11

Minds

MARGARET McMillan's understanding of a child's mind was grounded in a topography of the body; mind was a creation of that body, and existed in an interactive system with it. This chapter will outline that conception of mind in greater detail, and will suggest what were the political implications for McMillan of the system of physiological, neurological and psychological ideas that she strove to popularise in the thirty years after 1895. It was in these related fields of knowledge that she sought to ground her political work, so we need to ask: what did neurology and physiology allow her to think and believe about working-class life and working-class childhood, and what did they permit her to describe? The sets of ideas within which she worked were subject to rapid shifts and developments in this period, and these also need to be indicated. These general changes in perception can be seen particularly in McMillan's understanding and use of the notion of the unconscious human mind (which she often called the 'sub-conscious').

It is generally accepted that by the 1880s 'the general conception of the unconscious mind was a European common-place';[1] McMillan worked within that conception and evidently expected her audience to be aware of it as well. In her account the unconscious was a product of sensation whereby impressions deposited minute traces in the child's mind, creating a sub-stratum, always there, immanent, its sources long forgotten.[2] (In McMillan's account the unconscious mind was not seen as the product of repression, as it was to become in Freudian understanding.) McMillan's general sources for this acknowledgement of unconscious processes were multifarious – all the philosophic and literary trajectories of thought available in the mid nineteenth century that Whyte has described in *The Unconscious Before Freud*.[3] What has also been described as taking place in this period is a 'British school of physicians . . . quietly developing a doctrine of unconscious mental activities as part of their professional task of trying to understand the patient as a mind–body unity'.[4]

It was to this field of knowledge, to neurology, and specifically to those researchers who described mind as a creation of neurological processes that McMillan turned for her description of the conscious and unconscious mind of a child.[5] It is not clear whether or not she read the work of Henry Head and Hughlings Jackson, whose names were and are most commonly associated with this development; but she was certainly familiar with their mapping out of mental processes in terms of the evolution of structure and function in the nervous system.[6]

If she did know this work at first hand, it is possible that she was introduced to it by James Kerr in Bradford in the 1890s, for it was this view of mental functioning that he consistently transmitted as a particularly appropriate one for teachers and other educators throughout his extremely long life. He told the Conference on School Hygiene in 1905 that 'the more the individual is studied, the more it is recognised that all qualities, the highest powers, the sublimer thoughts, have their existence merely as functions of nerves and muscles.'[7] By 1935 he was able to offer teachers a complete theory of the unconscious, based on the work of Jackson and Head.[8] He told teachers about Henry Head's discovery of a double set of nervous impressions, one instinctual – which Kerr called 'the life drive' – the other discriminating and intellectual. The first was useful for teaching, he argued, but could not be reached by direct instruction, only 'indirectly, by impression, emotion, suggestion . . . It is the subliminal self of earlier days, the subconscious . . . .'.[9]

It was not that Kerr did not know about the psychoanalytic understanding of the unconscious. He reported on the general use of Freudian theory in the USA to a British audience as early as 1915; and the journal *School Hygiene*, which he edited with David Eder, was a forum where neurological and psychoanalytic theories of the unconscious rubbed shoulders with each other.[10] Ultimately, though, for his purposes, the analytic theory of the unconscious was unsatisfactory because it did not allow mind to be seen in constant interaction with the material body.

Psychological theories allowed Kerr and Eder (in their very different ways) to express and elaborate political arguments, and it was for this reason that these theories were used, or ignored.[11] In recent accounts of the medicalising of human knowledge and of the human subject, ideas are often presented as both complete and compulsive in their organisation – bringing with them, as enclosed systems, *necessary* ways of seeing the world. However, if we consider the selections of knowledge made by someone like McMillan (and David Eder and James Kerr – though here it is possible only to suggest something of the choices these two doctors made), then knowledge is seen to be selected and employed for specific purposes.

McMillan's particular selection from the theories of the unconscious that were available to her were made for an exegesis on the possibility of a reformed working-class life. Such a vision of a future state was for her grounded irreducibly in the present possibilities of the human organism. Working-class children showed what had gone wrong with that organism as a functioning system, and what could be mended. The cause of dysfunction was social and so must the remedy be social. The psychoanalytic theories of the child mind that were available to her in the early twentieth century did not permit that kind of social vision, and she chose to use a different model of the conscious and unconscious mind – one that, it will be suggested, played a part in the disintegration of her socialist project.

At the Deptford Centre, the curriculum prescribed for the children suggested that education was primarily physical and remedial, based on the child's body – which, once made whole, would provide for the development of mind. But although the mind of a child, as described by McMillan between 1895 and 1930, resided within and was the creation of the body, the tenets of interactive physiology could not provide a complete description of it. Throughout the thirty years during which she mapped out the mind for various audiences, she can be seen drawing on various psychologies – and she said that her book *Education Through the Imagination* (1904) was 'a very tentative effort to apply some of the teachings of modern psychology to the curriculum of the elementary school as presently constituted'.[12] Finally, though, whatever heterodox set of psychologies she employed, she had to return the mind to the body because it was the body that suffered: it was dirty, crippled, sick and lousy, but it could be cured. Moreover, the version of sensationalist psychology to which she chose to adhere did not cut the children who suffered in this way off from a normal humanity. In an interactive social system, the children who were to be restored to a full humanity played a role in general social betterment, just as Seguin's idiots had done. At the beginning of the first edition of *Education Through the Imagination*, she remarked:

> . . . reference is often made in the course of the following pages to children of the poorer classes . . . Just as the defective and feeble-minded have furnished telling illustrations of the more obscure teachings of the neurologist, so the children of poverty illustrate through their misfortune and weakness the evil or good in various methods . . . [13]

All McMillan's description of children's minds was made within the context of a sensationalist psychology. The notion that the sensations were the basis of intellect owed much to various elaborations of Lockian psychology throughout Europe since the seventeenth century, and what neurology in its late-nineteenth-century manifestation allowed McMillan (and others) to do was to map that philosophic description on to a physical organism, and to locate it completely and absolutely within the body. This neurological understanding enabled McMillan to make a more complete description than the one she had learned from Seguin's physiology – one that remained resolutely material.

This was not the path taken by another disciple of Seguin and his physiological system, Maria Montessori, who believed that life itself was a form of energy, '"one of the energies of cosmic creation"', and that the process of growth was constructive of the human faculties, with each child's specific quantity of psychic energy directing it towards developmental goals.[14] McMillan's writing on the ideas of force and energy were indeed often obscure, and certainly in her later writing she did posit the existence of some force existing above and beyond the human.[15] Given this metaphysical and teleological tendency in her later writing, it is important to note that in her actual descriptions of child development the map of the child's being was described in physical terms strongly reminiscent of the neurological trajectories outlined by James Kerr. She told readers of *Education Through the Imagination* that there was

> good ground for believing that Imagination is of motor origin . . . its most elementary expression is the mere movement of organs and limbs . . . It is now believed by many thinkers that the whole question of mind development is concerned with the kind of movements natural to, or imposed upon children.[16]

Here she also outlined the way in which the conditions of working-class life and working-class childhood prevented the development of creativity. She prescribed free movement in the elementary school, arguing that

> spontaneous movements are not merely a form of exercise, they are a condition of rest. All formal work or specialised movement implies a certain degree of local rest. There is a storage of energy going on in quiescent parts of the body when energy is concentrated at a certain point – in special areas of the brain. But the effect of this storage is not declared until the tension is removed entirely, till the child is free. Only then are the currents of energy diffused. Only then can they course like loosened streams through the whole system . . . [17]

This extract is a good example of the way in which the imagery McMillan used to describe the formation of conscious and unconscious mind, drawn as it was from a Romantic lexicon, often disguised the materiality of her argument. What may lie behind the flowing streams here is a summary of Hughlings Jackson's work on the evolution and dissolution of the nervous system, a set of propositions that had received wide publicity in the medical and popular science press between 1888 and 1900.[18] Indeed, the large-scale neurological mapping of the unconscious mind was enjoying something of a revival in the early 1900s, when McMillan wrote *Imagination*, after a period of quiescence and narrowly empirical research.[19]

At the turn of the century, McMillan's presentation of the unconscious was of a dark and limitless sea – yet one that was formed from the shores of the material world. 'The child depends on his toys', she told readers of the *Leader* and *Early Childhood*:

> He depends on his environment. He depends on these because through them the sub-conscious life is nourished. And the important things for him are not the things which concern the conscious life, but the sub-conscious. The consciousness of any one person is small at any given moment. The word we speak, the word we have just heard is not us. It is a ripple on the top of us. Below is the self – the dark sea. The child is less conscious than we . . . many things escape his notice, but *he* does not escape them. Impressions flow in on him and form his sub-conscious. And from this sub-conscious life, he draws the materials of his thoughts . . .[20]

McMillan's popularisation of these ideas grounded the process in the physical, first of all by analogy:

> . . . just as the active nerve-cell is developed from the bed of nucleated and supporting substance called neuroglia, so all the higher faculties of the mature being are developed from the wealth of stimulating and sustaining impressions that aroused the infant soul to love and wonder . . .[21]

But the development of mind was not just analogous to the development of the nervous system; it was an actual physical process that centred on movement and the arrest of movement. The disorganised, large movements of the baby were interrupted or checked by an emotion, a surprise, that halted muscular activity. 'One day,' said McMillan, the baby

> is *interrupted*. He listens, he sees. This event, so dramatic and astounding to the mother, is a culmination. Below it and behind it, there are myriad nervous activities and movements which, multiplying and rolling on . . . like waves, have at last touched the high water mark where consciousness is tossed upward like spray. The unresting waves may now be charmed into stillness. The innumerable nervous activities disseminated throughout the

body . . . appear to receive a momentary check. Progress is manifested through an interruption . . . [22]

What McMillan needed to convey at this point was that 'in speaking of the character of actions of any being we are speaking of something which is the result of his organic life'.[23] It was this perception – of consciousness and unconsciousness, understanding and imagination and will – that she had tried to convey to the readers of Bradford's *Labour Echo* a few years before, when she had insisted that 'our mental life is conditioned by the physical. Who can separate these?'[24]

Early Childhood was ostensibly written for the hypothetical working-class mother, wife of 'John Smith', but *Education Through the Imagination*, written four years later, was for educators. Its aim, according to McMillan, was to ground 'the great fabric of pedagogical science' on 'the great facts' of physiological development – that is, to demonstrate that there was order in development, that the brain centres were augmented in a particular sequence, and that motor control was acquired subject to certain laws.[25] These 'great facts' were encoded in the presentation of the baby as 'a spinal creature' who moved through reflex action, serving at the same time an apprenticeship in language, through an appropriation of sounds in the environment. The spinal creature also investigated the environment actively and physically; thus was mind a product of sensation:

> mind images, or memories are the re-presentation in us all of absent things, or by-gone experiences – the echoes of sensations or colours, form, muscular impression . . . in the organism. Such as they are, they form the raw material . . . of all ideas and conceptions . . . [26]

This account written in 1904, designed to outline a possible pedagogy for the elementary school, was far less grounded in neurological description than was *Early Childhood*. It emphasised in particular the formation of 'memory'. In the system McMillan described, 'memory' was the result of impressions registered in living matter: 'the cells in continuous vibration catch the new messages and fix it [memory] in perpetual change and response'.[27] Memory was the conservation or storage of impressions; in this account its accretion depended on nutrition, and nutritive changes. Because some children were literally starved, the 'rapid registration and restoration [did] not take place'.[28] This absence of memory, of a storehouse of impressions, was the dominant feature of working-class psychology as described by McMillan in all her writing.[29] The point of an ameliorative educational system was to provide the body with food and the mind with impressions, so that a rich mental life could be created within the formerly stagnant body.

208

McMillan nevertheless presented the working-class child, starved of food and sensation, as being in possession of an unconscious life. It is important to note this, because one of the results of the appropriation of a popularised psychoanalysis to educational understanding over the last half-century has been to define poor children as being in possession of an inadequate mental life. McMillan was quite clear that she needed to tell her readers in 1904 that child development followed the same order and sequence in poor children as it did in more favoured ones.[30] The child in the Deptford slum was certainly cheated out of her rights as a human being, but was not perceived as *inadequate* for this reason.

David Eder, a practising psychoanalyst by 1912, used his afternoons at the Deptford Clinic not just to syringe ears, weigh babies and perform tonsillectomies, but also to make notes on 'the nervous traumas hidden in the starved little bodies of his child patients'.[31] He presented his findings to the North of England Education Conference in January 1914.[32] Whilst the audience listened with deep interest to the cases that 'illustrate[d] and confirm[ed] the "neurological" conclusions of Freud', and an account of sublimation exemplified by the Deptford Centre's children's 'healthy desire to be messy and dirty',[33] the Conference organisers had destroyed the transactions that included his paper.[34] For Eder there was no distinction between this work and the popularisation of a socialist agenda that he summarised for the *Christian Commonwealth* in 1910 as 'Provision of showers in all elementary schools. Warm and cold water and soap. Decent boots. Full insides and clean outsides.'[35] He believed that as all human society was 'moulded by desire', the 'Socialist position needs to be restated in biological terms, in terms of human rather than economic values'. For Eder psychoanalysis was a humane cause that might allow the construction of a reasonable social life.[36]

By 1923, when McMillan revised *Education Through the Imagination*, she was acquainted with psychoanalytic delineations of the unconscious mind, making specific reference to their deficiency in describing creativity in childhood and adulthood.[37] By 1923, as well, she understood the notion of compensation, and used it to describe Deptford children in this way:

> . . . all the thwarted instincts and impulses, the desires that are not realised, the hidden aspirations, envy, jealousy, ambition, love of power are lifted above the sub-conscious (whence they emerge in dreams) into a middle region of reverie. A child who is thwarted in her desire for power or appreciation or sympathy lives in an inner world, where all is arranged to meet her ambitions. Her heroes and heroines are greater than any of the people around her, and she is their child.[38]

McMillan was by no means as bold as Eder in seeking 'the sexual explanation of so many child neuroses', but in an oblique passage in *The Camp School* (1917), she attempted to describe the psychosexual formation of the first entrants to the girls' camp, in the summer of 1911. Bathing was on the curriculum as a 'method of general touch training', but to McMillan's surprise,

> . . . we found that in starting . . . we had to meet and deal with the very evil that was most difficult to reach, or even to write about, but which somehow sapped and lowered the *moral* [*sic*] of many children . . . Children who had slept with four others in the bed in their homes, clung in the daytime to their clothes . . . [39]

Was she here describing the false shame and prurience that her reading of Edward Carpenter, and Kerr's and Eder's exhortations in *School Hygiene*, had suggested might be banished by comfort, good food and ease of mind?[40] Or was she describing the perverted sexual formation of the slum, the same secrets of the shared bed hinted at in *The Child and the State* (1911), where she described the slum child's stock of 'hideous memories', remarking that 'only those who have overheard the invented tales of slum children realise how strong in them is the impulse towards gruesome and morbid imaginings'. Indeed, it was at this point that she recalled Louise Michel as the

> one woman who ever wrote the true history of a certain unhappy child . . . but no one would publish what she wrote. What is the most terrible result of overcrowding? . . . The physical nature develops in men and women with no corresponding mental advance. Not one woman, but many, now understand very well what lies behind the impregnable reserve of certain little ones . . . Who knows and will tell what is behind the evasive calm face of this pale child who breaks into a smile readily, a child whose real history would scorch the page on which it was written?[41]

Was it exposure to sexual scenes and incest that lay behind the trouble in the shower in Deptford, in 1911? In any case, a system of exercises, cold showers and massage worked wonders:

> The results were various as well as striking. As to the physical results, the doctor's report may be quoted . . . But I saw other results . . . the first was the obvious detachment of all children from everything but the upward struggle for fitness . . . it was impossible to doubt that a world of hidden distorted feeling, of half-strangled but swollen appetites had been smitten into something clean and fair. And this without any preaching or moralising.[42]

An earlier understanding of the notion of the unconscious mind had allowed her fictional 'Lola' to dream, and propelled the writing of working-class childhood in psychic as well as sentimental terms. It is possible that the Freudian conception of the unconscious, and the aetiology of sexual development which David Eder was able to describe out of his Deptford experience, allowed in part the tendency towards the pathologising of working-class childhood that can be seen developing in her work during and after the war years.

Within the topography of mind that McMillan possessed at the turn of the century, language was understood as a physiological function of the body. In *Early Childhood* speech was presented as 'first and foremost, a physical exercise', involving fine movements and the co-ordination of muscles and nerves: it had, McMillan explained, 'to do with the child's body . . . his lips and tongue, and lungs and larynx'.[43] Breath was the raw material of speech, large natural movements being the best way of getting air into the child's body. The content of speech, language itself, was understood to be acquired by imitation. Children 'learn by hearing other people speak and by imitating their sounds and movements . . . [the child] listens to the voices around him, and copies them faithfully.'[44] By the time *Education Through the Imagination* was published, McMillan had read widely enough in contemporary developmental linguistics to move away from this strictly imitative account of language acquisition to a presentation that recognised the child's own invention of grammatical forms.[45] Nevertheless, language as a means or expression of thought had little place in her description of a child's mind. The physiology and neurology in which her description was rooted could not help her here, for within the system described by Seguin, concept formation lay within the mind itself, not within language.[46]

That this understanding of language development and its relationship to the acquisition of literacy skills still pertained at the Deptford Centre in the 1920s is shown by the reading-teaching method used by McMillan and her staff. Children in the various camp schools were taught to read in exactly the manner prescribed by Seguin, with toddlers matching letter shapes to forms arranged in contrasting pairs, and learning letter names.[47] Other pedagogies and other accounts of the reading process were available at this time, but still in 1919 McMillan suggested that beginning in this way – by introducing children to the shape and form of the alphabet – was the best method, appealing as it did 'to three distinct senses, the muscular, the tactual and the visual . . . '. She explained that 'in teaching reading and writing, as in teaching everything else, we have two objects in view.

First, we are trying to enrich the sensorium and secondly we are trying to give new motor control.'[48]

The children built up one-syllable words with the wooden letters, taking the word to pieces again and again, then copying it on to the blackboards that encircled the room:

> . . . they also look at it, but this is not the 'look and say' method, for they look at it sometimes in pieces. And why should they not see it thus? Every great educator agrees that to break a thing up into its elements and then to make it a unity again is a splendid mind exercise.[49]

There were many theories of initial reading that McMillan could have drawn on that would have allowed her to see a child's spoken language as a basis for teaching an understanding of written language.[50] Indeed, Maria Montessori, using the same nineteenth-century sources as McMillan, had evolved a method of teaching literacy through the initial production of children's written texts.[51] But McMillan followed more strictly than Montessori the precept of physiological education (the one Seguin himself had learned from Itard's instruction of the Wild Boy of Aveyron) that the most helpful system was to break the written word into its smallest components.[52]

Once the children could read words spelt out with wooden letters, they moved to apparatus that consisted of words and sentences printed on cards. Having read a single word, the child ran to touch the 'table' or the 'flower', then followed silently the longer instructions given in sentences.[53] Writing was taught at the same time as reading, though the two were not connected in McMillan's description, as she saw written language as being 'Largely a question of muscular memory related to the recognition of form'.[54] The children were introduced to large-scale drawing of lines: first circles, then perpendiculars, then sloping strokes. Then they progressed to drawing letters that demanded the conjunction of lines, and soon after this they were introduced to drawing scrolls and other writing patterns. This state of motor control having been reached, the child was deemed to be ready to copy the words that she had been spelling out in wooden letters during reading practice.[55]

The teachings of neurology confirmed the correctness of the physiological approach, for as McMillan explained in 1919:

> Language and hand work are, in the beginning . . . very closely interrelated. The mere fact that the two brain centres that have to do the one with speech and the other with movements of the right hand, lie close to one another and are fed by the one artery, indicate how the hand, and especially the right hand, worked out the subject that is not called manual now, but is set apart from

manual subjects. Words, as well as tables, were made at first, largely by hands.[56]

For McMillan, then, language was a matter of physical organisation and of speech. Speech might be trained, ameliorated, and the language of the child made pleasing and beautiful (indeed, much effort in Deptford was devoted to the production of 'pleasant speech'); but it was not connected with thought, nor seen as part of a system of intelligence.[57] Indeed, when McMillan used the term 'language' she meant what developmentalists would now call 'speech'. Speech was for her the outward manifestation of mental processes, its closest analogy being the hand: 'Manual dexterity and language', she wrote in 1909, 'are the outposts of human mental life.'[58]

This system of understanding and description meant that declarations of language inability were easily made and it is significant that McMillan's only condemnation of working-class mothers before the 1920s seems to have been in the area of language. She wrote in 1905 of the slum child going to school, and of how, even at the age of five, he was 'in a strange condition aurally. His mother has not, apparently, spoken to him much; if she has, it has not occurred to him to listen to her.'[59] In 1907, trying to exonerate herself from reports that had her blaming teachers for the poor English of schoolchildren, she apologised:

> . . . many little children arrive in our schools today who are almost inarticulate. The mothers, overworked or absorbed by other matters, do not speak much to their little ones; so the latter arrive in school practically without any vocabulary and the teacher has to begin what should have been far advanced long before the age of attendance.[60]

Indeed, language can be seen as the hole in the system of thought by which McMillan chose to describe working-class life, and which pointed to its potential reclamation. It was this view of language that allowed her fictional characters a voice – many voices, in dialect form – but did not allow them to speak. In 1905 she had returned this problematic to Carlyle, describing him as the writer who

> gave us the most pathetic picture in literature of the dumb, toil-worn, toil-mutilated labourer – the great dumb giant who cannot speak. Every great master of literature has essayed to portray him; but of them all, Carlyle perhaps, gave us the finest picture of him, and Tourgenieff (in Moumon – the dumb giant labourer) the finest allegory . . . [61]

She went on here to describe the educational methods and a discipline that had, up to this point in time, kept 'the reserved little English rustic or timid denizen of the slum as quiet in class as a dumb creature, as sealed and locked in silence as the winter leaves . . .'. But no matter where the genesis of silence was located – in an inappropriate educational method or in the domestic muteness of the working-class mother – McMillan's system of physiological and neurological understanding, through which her political project was mediated, could only mend that deficit from outside, as it might supply food, a stimulating environment or a rain of impressions; it could not allow the articulated response of what was already known.

12

Voices

For a final treat I heard a few of the older children act a Shakespearian scene. This was a most wonderful experience. To listen to these little slum children expressing themselves in clear, good English . . . was proof positive of what Margaret McMillan can do. It was an earnest of what could be done everywhere if only these nursery schools were a regular feature of our educational system. (E.E. Hunter, 'Where the Slum Baby Thrives: Margaret McMillan's Great Work', *New Leader*, 21 October 1927)

WITHIN the the broad theory of body–mind relationship that Margaret McMillan appropriated and used, the senses were understood to be interchangeable – that is to say, in conditions of impairment, touch might be substituted for sight, sight for sound, and so on. Jean Itard's work, and Édouard Seguin's adaptation of it for work with deaf-mutes, belonged to a long tradition whereby touch and the vibration of the human voice had been used to instruct the deaf in speech.[1] Seguin's most important message in the propagation of his method with idiot children for use in normal schools was that 'their senses are trained, not only each one to be perfect in itself; but, as to a certain extent other organs may be made receivers of food in lieu of the stomach, and one emunctory take the place of the other, likewise the senses must be educated, so that if the use of any one be lost, another may perceive and feel for it.'[2]

McMillan's own childhood deafness, a disability only fleetingly and mysteriously alluded to, seems to have righted itself some time before her twelfth year.[3] But although it is mentioned only twice in her autobiographical writing, deafness as a theme was often returned to in her fiction. 'The Gifts That Cannot Be Stolen', first published in the spiritualist magazine *Two Worlds*, concerned 'Dumbo', a deaf-mute who learned to speak.[4] The twelve-part 'Fairy Tale by the Fairies' (1907–08) featured a Highland child called Mairi, made deaf by scarlet fever;[5] and of course, the twenty-nine-part 'Handel Stumm' had the eponymous hero congenitally deaf, taught to speak by Hirschler, an amateur of the physiological method, and his voice brought to full beauty by 'Luke Strong the illustrious voice producer', who used methods and produced results that echoed Seguin's account of the achievements of the illustrious Pereire.[6]

Margaret McMillan's own voice – her public voice – seems to have been heard first on May Day 1892. The impact of that appearance, and of subsequent ones, clearly depended on a great many factors besides the modulation of her tone and the dramatic meaning of a woman on a platform, in public performance – perhaps on an entire rhetoric and system of gesture and presence. She had been taught the rhetoric that was part of an actress's repertoire in the late 1880s, when Lady Meux had paid for her stage training.[7] She also took lessons from Emil Behnke, the author, with Lennox Browne of *Voice, Song and Speech, A Practical Guide for Singers and Speakers from the combined view of a vocal surgeon and voice trainer*, which had first been published in 1883.[8] Behnke described himself as a 'lecturer on vocal physiology, and teacher of voice production'.[9] His impact on McMillan was great, and was to have a lasting effect. In 1927 she remembered:

> This training was a new and amazing experience . . . For the first time it began to dawn on me that the original of all tools and weapons is in the human body . . . how Nature, when she made man, worked out the original of every kind of instrument . . . and means of music: and music can teach and pour through limbs as well as throat . . . It was wonderful. This was like light coming in at a new window . . . [10]

Part of Behnke's technique was to make the voice visible, demonstrating its physiological base to his students. One of them remembered how he had 'invented an arrangement of looking-glasses, by which the vocal cords could be seen. To watch them whilst sounds were being produced, was weirdly fascinating.'[11]

What McMillan learned in these years was to become part of her equipment as professional and expert during her time in Bradford and later. She acquired information that she continually sought to pass on to different audiences, readers of the *Clarion* and the *Labour Leader*. One of her first innovations in Bradford education was to arrange for Behnke's widow (who was to publish *The Speaking Voice: Its Development and Preservation* in 1897) to address the elementary-school teachers of the city, and for a teacher of voice production to remain resident there to give a series of lectures.[12] Behnke's daughter saw McMillan's role as a particularly pioneering one in this direction.[13] One of the reasons for this innovation was to do with the health of elementary-school teachers: in *Early Childhood* McMillan described 'Board School Laryngitis . . . the name given, not to one disease, but to a group of throat diseases peculiar to teachers', and she used the work of Greville McDonald to show that 'it is not to excessive use, but

216

unskilled use, of the voice that we owe the rapid spread of throat disease'.[14]

But far more important than the health of 'the woman who trains and teaches John Smith' was the effect of her voice on the developing child, for through the speaking voice 'the most important moral education of the race is given'. Years later, she was still looking forward to a time when the elementary-school teacher would have evolved to be worthy of the child's needs; when she might have stopped shouting, developed a charming personality, good health – and a beautiful voice. In 'Schools of Tomorrow' she imagined a time when teachers might have 'the charm of great actresses . . .', a future where 'they move with beautiful grace. Their voices are low, penetrating and musical and have a racial quality too, quite distinct from the voices of other lands. Their dress is simple and beautiful . . .'. [15] Given the organisation of the child – and because, as we have seen, 'the important things for him are not the things which concern the conscious life, but the sub-conscious' – the sensuous impression made by the teacher was far more important than the content of her teaching:

> . . . the *tone* of the teacher is more to him than her words. The colours of the pictures and walls affect him more than the subjects of the pictures: the unconscious looks, and movements, and manners . . . take hold of him through his plastic body, and form him . . . Far more important that the teacher should be gentle and cultured than that she should be able to teach him how to work sums.[16]

James Kerr, who learned much from McMillan on this point, was still telling teachers in 1935:

> . . . the brightness of the room, cleanliness of the floor, the teacher's voice, the way she does her hair, the buttons on her dress, the very motes in the sunbeam, through all of them, an unconscious and almost indelible education is going on . . . this absorption may be more important than what the teacher is consciously setting forth . . . [17]

Within the harmony of impressions feeding the unconscious mind, voice assumed the greatest importance because it touched more of the child's being and because 'it is the heart itself – the soul – that unveils and communicates itself in the tones of the voice'.[18] An imitative model of language acquisition reinforced this understanding. 'Go into the slums', claimed McMillan,

> and you will hear baby voices that are already harsh; in the classrooms of a well-organised kindergarten for upper-class chil-dren you may listen to the sweet tones of children who have had

good vocal examples to copy. Children reproduce the tones they hear; and as tone and inflection are the expression of feeling, they doubtless share in so doing the emotional life of the persons around them. So that voice production has . . . an enormous *moral* influence.[19]

McMillan remained convinced, throughout her career as an educator, that the human voice was the primary sense in social organisation, the one which both connected and divided people and classes more than any other. In a piece called 'Pleasant Speech' (1908), in reply to a reader who had raised questions about the social divisiveness of elocution lessons in elementary schools, she commented that 'not only the way of speaking but the voice itself and its inflections play a most extraordinary part in the matter of antipathy and sympathy' – and by this she meant, quite specifically, class antagonism and class harmony. She believed that 'everyone, even the most ignorant person, knows this, and is sensitive in vocal matters'.[20] We have already seen, in *The Child and the State*, her description of a working-class woman speaking in public and 'from sheer need of words' breaking 'loose from her social idiom'.[21] What is interesting in this account is the way in which McMillan described the audience as being uncertain at first about the woman's worth and culture, and then being convinced of it. She believed that class consciousness (in the social sense) was created in reaction to the human voice. In *Early Childhood* she asserted:

> . . . there is nothing a man or woman resents so much as that his social equals should speak more beautifully than himself. If one factory girl, for example, dresses more beautifully than another, her companions do not condemn her for this. She may even learn to draw, to embroider, to play the piano – she may marry above her, and no one will be jealous. But if her voice becomes musical, and she begins to speak beautifully – that is another matter. Her old friends are estranged. Even her mother is indignant – feels that her daughter has escaped her. And this feeling has very real justification. The changed voice *does* indicate changed . . . feel-ing . . . [22]

It is with the sound of working-class children's voices that McMillan's own feelings, her self-positioning in class relations, becomes most clear. In the 1923 edition of *Education Through the Imagination* she described the 'rough, strained, ugly voices of the school and the nursery', and how 'the noises of the playground tell us a great deal about the life, and work, and play, and *feeling* of the people of their day'; how those voices revealed the children's homes as places ruled by men and women who cannot express the gamut of happy emotion which might be and really *is* the birthright of human beings. All the music is quenched in them. It does not sing in their speech and quiver in their laughter. And so even the babies make a dreadful noise in play-time . . . [23]

As she observed in 1900, 'between classes, between strangers who wish to draw close to each other, the first spoken word betrays all that divides'.[24] What she called 'oral culture' in the schools would teach children the principles of breathing, of pronunciation and intonation, and 'its effects would be seen in a sudden increase of vigour, in new refinement, and growing sympathy'.[25]

An understanding of language centred on the voice, and on the movements of lips, tongue, larynx and lungs, was largely mechanistic. Within McMillan's schema, language was not understood as a means of cognition; therefore she did not use it to outline mental vacuity, lack of intelligence, or the whole complex of disabilities that pedagogies later in the century called language deprivation.[26] She came close to describing the mental life of the unskilled labouring poor as deprived and deficient in the second edition of *Education Through the Imagination*, but the sources of this description were an understanding of language inadequacy caused by physical deprivation, not a failure in cognitive functioning. Children breathed through their mouths because their nostrils were blocked by persistent infection. This habit reduced the amount of air taken in, which in turn prevented the absorption of nutrients from food. Catarrhal conditions of the ear were set up, and hearing was lost. And poor breathing prevented the blood supply from reaching the anterior lobes of the brain, which made the child look dull and vacuous.[27] In many working-class children, larynx and mouth were ill-formed, the throat sore and infected, the passage of air impeded. Working-class speech as a kind of deformity was most clearly expressed by McMillan in her proposals for teacher education in the projected Rachel McMillan Training College. Here she said firmly:

> The defective speech of the poorest class is not a mere peculiarity of class or humour of certain persons. The speech of the slums is not a dialect. It is the symptom of serious disorder, and it is to be treated as a kind of deformity, which indeed, from the standpoint of the organs involved, it is, just as the enlarged head or joints and twisted legs are the symptoms of rickets.[28]

Nevertheless, voice was a result (or a failure) of external factors, not the product of a pre-given or existing intelligence, and its faults were subject to amelioration and treatment. So although the voice, ugly, broken and made harsh by the deleterious conditions of an industrial system, was the site of class divide for McMillan, it was still subject to the interactive improvement that a physiological perception allowed was possible for the whole of a child's body. Having said that, it needs to be acknowledged that this understanding of voice, and its relationship (or non-relationship) to a theory of language, allowed a breach in both McMillan's educational and political systems, the place where its organisation around the notion of the donation of culture to a class becomes plainest.

McMillan elaborated her theory of the voice within the context of what she called (evoking Seguin's description of the immutability of the senses) the 'higher hungers' – for colour, and for sound. She described children possessing a love of noise for its own sake, and connected this to the human race's eternal desire for sound. Using the analytic devices of literary criticism, McMillan described music in terms of its metre (which conveyed no meaning but appealed to the child's instinct for movement, particularly movement to sound) and its rhythm, or the repetition of musical phrases (which conveyed 'a more or less perfect musical idea, just as a verse of poetry holds an idea'). Metrical accent was discussed in terms of its appeal to the instinct, and rhythmic as appealing to the intelligence.[29]

By 1923 McMillan was discussing music in the child's life both in terms of a hunger, a felt need on the child's part, and also in terms of an innate capacity. 'Has every normal person or child got a rhythmic intelligence to which one can appeal?' she asked. Her answer was still framed by the broad assumptions of nineteenth-century physiology: ' . . . nearly every child has such an intelligence and . . . it can be nourished and trained like most other gifts . . . at first through the muscles and senses.'[30] But there was more. Not only did the child have an inborn capacity to respond to sound and music; there was also something within that very organisation of sound that had a meaning apart from the child's appropriation of it. McMillan elaborated that meaning by discussing modern music, in which expectations of regular rhythm and harmony were disturbed. The features of the example she gave were '*freedom* and unexpectedness', where in spite of the listener's reluctance he or she 'is carried away on the new movement that breaks the old order, and is thus allowed to enjoy the new revelation'.[31]

The incorporeality of sound, its very immateriality, always permits a metaphysics. In the 1890s McMillan had written of an actress's voice allowing a child taken to the theatre to enter 'a new world – the world where spirits communicate through the power of sound'.[32] Inspiration, the poetic expression of political ideas, had always encouraged McMillan to use the metaphor of Voice – Voice as message, from the unconscious or from another world. None of that usage detracted from the broadly materialistic framework of her psychology and pedagogy, but the physiology on which they were based could not explain the generation of language, as opposed to the production of voice. It was in her discussion of sound and music in a pedagogical system (in the 1920s, under the impact of relatively new ideas about the classification of children according to innate capacities) that the absence of a theory of language became most strikingly obvious. On the one hand, it allowed McMillan to write about sound, voice and music in mystical terms:

> Just as the baby doubles his words, the Psalmist doubled his rhythms and phrases, and both obey the impulse and beat of the natural music that sings in the heart of Nature . . . a deep[er] thing woven into the secret places of the organic life and issuing thence in forms and powers that are not easily explained . . . [33]

On the other hand, it allowed her to believe that working-class children in elementary school had 'not much to express' and that 'they cannot, or anyhow do not, express this little'.[34]

Perhaps it was this absence of a theory of language which provided a place of entry in the system of thought she described for voices from outside, as much as the arcane imagery she used, that gave rise to the assumption that she was a spiritualist.[35] There is in fact no evidence that she took part in spiritualist belief or practice, and indeed she denied that she was a spiritualist on several occasions, before and after Rachel's death in 1917.[36] It is difficult, though, to know what to make of statements like one in 1923 when, discussing Rudolph Steiner, she wrote that 'the whole world is a whispering gallery to him and vibrations reach him from where we have no name'.[37] The ILP leadership in general dabbled in spiritualism. Keir Hardie enjoyed a good seance, and Katharine Conway took part in one at least, in 1893 when she visited McMillan in Bradford (though it is not clear if it was held at Hanover Square).[38] McMillan wrote to Nancy Astor in 1929:

> I don't go in for 'Spirit-raising'. No one has such a horror of it – 'Try them!' – No not me my dear apostle. I won't try 'em. I'll avoid 'em. Would run a hundred miles to get away from 'em all except the guardians that god sends. And I don't see *them*, or hear *them* alas. I've never been in a spiritualist church in England. So that's that.[39]

We can attribute some of the failure of McMillan's theory of physiological development, an environmentalism that was liberating and progressive, to the status of language within it. Yet it was with written language that she set about one of the major self-imposed tasks of her middle years, representation of working-class life for sympathetic yet uninformed audiences. The representation of her fictional characters' speech was fraught with difficulties, because of both the political positioning of her subjects and the view of language that created their words – for to a very great extent they were presented through their speech.

Raymond Williams has pointed to a long history of deliberately varied orthography in English literature, designed to show regional and national origin. In the late nineteenth century a 'systematic convention of class modes of speech' emerged, 'in a period of obviously increasing class consciousness which was expanding to just these parts of behaviour'.[40] In this historical and linguistic moment, Margaret McMillan set out to present her people of 'the dark area' to the readers of the *Clarion* and the *Labour Leader*. Versions of a 'rural dialect', a conflation of regions in a kind of Mummersetshire, had become common at least two centuries earlier, and the 1880s and 1890s saw the emergence of an urban dialect, non-specific to particular cities. McMillan's first attempts to render Yorkshire dialect show her with a very limited range of graphological technique, no more than dropped consonants and omitted aspirates. The 'Miner' and the 'Idler', the 'Two Friends' of 1893, could belong anywhere, to any conurbation.[41] McMillan worked hard at dialectal representation, though, and by the time *Samson* was published in 1895 she was praised by one reviewer for following so well the orthographic conventions that had probably been made common to both of them by the researches of the folklore societies in the West Riding.[42]

In her representation of the Yorkshire speech of 'An Old Chartist' in 1903, the dialect form is part of his dignity, an expression of his proper politics:

> He declared himself against Physical Force – he, the champion of the countryside, the unvanquished hero of a hundred fights! 'I'm noan saying it wouldn't be *pleasant* to hev stand up wi' them', he said more than half a century later. 'But would it ha' bin raicht?'[43]

He is given a political position here, and a dignity that partly derives from the evocation of the countryside; but McMillan is still *there*, present in intonation (expressed through underlining), in the syntactic structure, and in the rhetorical balancing of question and answer. It is indeed a commonplace observation that the writer must be present when she seeks to have men and women of another class express political convictions that are her own. It is an example of that incorporation of commentary that Williams has pointed to in the 'slice-of-life' novel of the late nineteenth century, in which the author can be seen to merge with the character in a voice purged of any confrontation with controversial ideas, particularly with the actual class relations that are subsumed in that 'real' citified voice.[44] That McMillan experienced these difficulties of representation – and did not entirely think she had resolved them – is obvious not only in her actual condemnation of working-class speech but also in her removal of dialect, of that which she considered ugly and debasing, from her female working-class characters. In general, it was men who were represented through dialect, characters with whom she did not have a great deal of intimacy.

McMillan's progress in the representation of working-class speech was influenced in another way: by the rapid advance of developmental linguistics between 1890 and 1920. The child-study movement proceeded in its investigations of development by refining a system of representing child language.[45] It shared a deviation from conventional orthography with an older fictional representation, but for quite different purposes. It is not clear what McMillan was reading on the subject of child language in the 1900s, but her writing during the 1920s shows that she had absorbed relatively new ideas about the phenomenon of babbling, and was less willing than she had been to present language as entirely imitative – more willing to recognise, to some extent, that it was generative.[46] A discipline that presented the individual dignity of the child subject, in the light of scientific and anthropological interest in its utterances, could have sat uneasily with McMillan's understanding of working-class child language as a matter of deformity. But in fact she had long practice in evading the difficulties with which poor children's speech presented her. For her, it *was* deformed speech, resulting from improper and inadequate nurture; she was prepared to write at length about how horrible it was, to assert that if 'you have always said " 'as" for "has", and have never troubled about the end of any word, the doors of literature do not open very easily'.[47] At the same time, however, these children who could move her by their beauty, their half-hidden sensuality, were the redeemers of mankind: 'the lost human life and language which the greatest preachers, artists and philanthropists had sought in vain to win back, is recalled by children'.[48]

The problem was resolved by rarely presenting their speech in class terms. 'Lola', one of McMillan's very first fictional reclaimers, does not speak as a child but, rather, makes very brief utterances as a young woman, speaking Standard English. 'Marigold', the heart-wrenching 'Mignon of the slums', is briefly placed by what is nowadays called a modified orthography, but speaks for the most part in tones of the utmost refinement.[49] Boys, like their fictional fathers of the 1890s, might be represented as speaking in a coarser way, as in 'Bob's Christmas Day' (1911). But Bob is a child under treatment for a scalp infection, ennobled by suffering and made thoughtful by the system of cure – a being more awakened than his father:

> 'Nice Christmas this here is', cried Bob's father bitterly. 'Where's them poor kids, yer sister and yer biby brother? In 'orspital. An' yer mother, where's she?' he added fiercely. 'Eh?'
>
> Bob looked eager like one glad to break the silence. He began to answer hurriedly . . . 'Mrs Rummell, in Colts Lane, said she saw her one day. She said as she stopped her an' arsked for the kids and me. "How's Bob?" she said, Mrs Rummells said. But I don't believe it's true, dad', said Bob . . .
>
> 'Garn!' said Bob's father roughly (he had had a little ale at dinner-time). 'Don't you carry on so. You and your Rummells'.

The children can form the material for side-play, the amusing and touching spectacle that promotes laughter and pity. 'Chris' and 'Emmie', two and three years old respectively, are home from the hospital (consistently spelled ' 'orspital' by McMillan) to spend Christmas day in their one-room dwelling. 'Emmie', particularly, is 'mysteriously refined . . . by much washing and tending', but can still promote the knowing and indulgent smile when they all sit down to tea with Norah, a neighbour's child:

> 'Bobby', said Em suddenly. 'Where's mummie? Ain't She coming back no more? . . .'
>
> 'Whist! You mustn't talk about her,' said Bob.
>
> 'Why?' said Emmie recklessly.
>
> 'You shut up!' said Bob, getting bewildered. ' 'Taint your business' . . .
>
> ' 'Tis our business,' said Em. 'Moren yours' . . .
>
> 'I heard people say your mother was a bad 'un,' said Norah, with the air of one who is making a real contribution to the general stock of information. 'She's gone off,' she added, 'with a lodger. She won't come back no more'.[50]

All the child characters hover between being the objects of amused condescension, and the author's pity. Earlier in her writing career, McMillan had evaded these difficulties by making her working-class children verbally refined. The two little Lancashire boys – real children this time – whom the McMillans took into their home and their heart in 1915 were actually refined in this way too. They had to learn 'what is practically a new language', but whenever they were given speech by McMillan, their tone matched their new breeding and culture. Totty was particularly symbolic of the child rescued. In all the pieces of journalism through which he flitted in 1915, one showed him to be particularly Édouard Seguin's own. 'Treasure is treasure even if it is left more or less neglected and covered with mire', wrote McMillan in 'At the Foot of the Rainbow': 'Nature . . . has been checked and interrupted all the time, as Seguin tried to show forty years ago. Indeed, that truly great man's life was spent trying to give Nature a new chance . . . in her spoiled human products.'[51]

McMillan rescued the spoiled human products she encountered, in fiction as much as in life, and in this way she was bound to give them a voice, bestow a language on them, rather than permit them to speak. But at the same time, and despite all her rejections of tawdry and conventional spiritualism, it has to be recognised that there existed in her a desire to transmute the material into the immaterial, to focus on the insubstantial voice rather than the body, as a way perhaps of evading the intractable political and emotional difficulties that those bodies – of real working-class people, living in the world – actually came to represent for her.

Albert Mansbridge made much of McMillan's voices. The 'Voices' were one of the ways in which he was able to appropriate her life to the *vita* of St Joan – ' "I always obey my voices because they come from God", so might she have spoken any day of her life' – a biographical elision discussed in the next chapter.

13

Legends

THE preceding pages have measured out a public and a political life. The records available, and the various biographical and autobiographical caesurae of McMillan's story – particularly the space created by Mansbridge's collection of material for the 1932 biography – prevent any drawing aside of an archival curtain to reveal the personal story and the real woman behind the public persona. It has been possible to use the immense output of McMillan's writing, particularly her fiction, to suggest possible motivation and development in her life – in her relationship with her sister, for instance, or in her negotiation, as a single woman of the Scottish lower middle classes, of the English class system during her governessing years. But doing this is a far cry from being able to present documented revelation of sets of relationships, or particular events. At the practical level, both the biographer and the reader have to accept that if there were secrets to be concealed, or true romances to tell (particularly in the case of Rachel, whose life remains suspiciously hidden for a professional woman of this period), then Mansbridge suppressed, or ignored, or was kept in ignorance of any such event or relationship. As his was the collecting, transcription and collating of evidence that provides the documentary core of what the historian has to deal with – in the shape of the McMillan Collection at Deptford – it is through this particular window on to McMillan's life that a biographer has to look.

But Albert Mansbridge's assertion that McMillan was essentially an unknowable and mysterious figure does not have to be taken as the final word on the subject, and in fact deserves to be explored as a problem of biographical interpretation. He described how 'at Bradford she was a mysterious figure, taken for what she said and did. Some of those who worked most closely with her knew nothing about her.'[1] He threw doubt on his own thoroughness in collecting information about her, saying: 'it is probable that during the course of her life she revealed most of her adventures and her thoughts – but never to one person', and explained the elusiveness of his characterisation of her by remarking that 'she was a different person to her different friends. This was not a pose. It was not insincerity. Her mood and quality responded to the mood and quality of others.'[2]

His solution to the fragmentary nature of the evidence he was given, and the absence of a consistent autobiographical account for a source, was to end *Margaret McMillan, Prophet and Pioneer* with a chapter entitled 'Margaret the Woman', in which he recorded the eulogies of his informants and collected together forty years of adulatory and stunned response to her presence.

Mansbridge can here be seen grappling with what Bernard Crick, in his introduction to George Orwell's life, has called the characteristic vice of the English biographical tradition: 'smoothing out or silently resolving contradictions in the evidence and bridging gaps by empathy and intuition'. Crick has suggested that all such 'fine writing, balanced appraisal and psychological insight' is the result of the biographer 'fooling himself by an affable pretence of being able to enter into another person's mind'. [3] In fact, Mansbridge made no such pretence. His final admission was of a fragmented subject, known to many, different to all, with no one possessing her story. Of course an obvious point here is that in the writing of a *vita*, the bad news has to be omitted. The resentful cousin who supplied Mansbridge with information about the little family from New England feathering their nest in Inverness in the 1860s and 1870s also remembered 'a visit of Margaret McMillan when an old factotum called her Maggie. Her reply was I'm Miss McMillan to you'. She had other stories, she wrote, that would show Mansbridge his heroine's feet of clay. [4]

McMillan's jealousy of her own position as educational innovator surfaced publicly in her pronouncements against Maria Montessori, [5] but those who worked with her suffered it too. Mary Chignell, former special school head who worked at the Deptford Centre between 1917 and 1920, claimed later that she created both the theory and the practice of the Nursery School, particularly in 'the fulfilment of another ideal – to which I brought more experience than Miss McMillan – the establishment of the Nursery School as a culture centre for the parents and the people of the neighbourhood where it is placed'. [6] Working in Bradford in the 1920s, in a nursery school headship that McMillan had urged her to undertake, she was accused by the Education Committee of using her school for the purposes of socialist propaganda. In a letter seeking the support of the Nursery School Association, she suggested that the Director of Education had 'got hold of Miss McMillan and roused the devil of jealousy in her – never long dormant – by saying that I have claimed something in the making of the Nursery School which belongs to her'. [7] McMillan did seek to control and own the ideas she evolved, and lost friends this way. John Bruce Glasier called her attack on the Labour MPs who had failed to do what she wanted in the Commons over the medical inspection question 'sheer jealousy and spite. She is shocked to think that anything can be done in spite of her . . . I have ceased to respect her.' [8]

Mansbridge outlined McMillan's affective life in terms of her legendary presence and reputation, and perhaps here suggested that he recognised, albeit in an oblique way, that it showed an important conjunction of public demand for the figure of seer and prophetess, and McMillan's willingness to adopt that role, as a solution to the problems presented by her family and personal history. In 1922, for instance, McMillan provided an old Bradford friend with an autobiographical outline, so that Margaret Sutcliffe might write a play about her. The programme notes that accompany *The Legend of Margaret McMillan* explain that 'legends tell lies in order to give the public a truthful impression'.[9] In the same way, Mansbridge's collecting together the items of this legend a decade later were an attempt to delineate its *meaning*, for different audiences.

The audiences for the public making of McMillan's life story were in fact many and various. We have seen her move before the ILP gathered in conference halls, transfix gatherings in Labour Churches and labour halls; seen crowds held under the flickering gas lamps, a young man entranced in Nottingham Market Place, the huge May Day crowds in Shipley Glen, for weeks promised the treat of Tom Mann, Keir Hardie, Isabella Ford and Margaret McMillan, seeing them now, applauding rapturously. G.A.N. Lowndes assembled a series of testimonies to her platform presence in his book *Margaret McMillan: The Children's Champion* (1960). 'People walked five or seven miles into Bradford to hear the speakers', recalled one of his correspondents.

> Long before the scheduled time, the hall was packed with some 4000 or more people when Margaret McMillan was due to appear . . . After fifty years I still have a vivid memory of her standing, tall, erect, very calm, like a prophetess of old, dressed in black. Beginning very quietly, her lovely voice would gather in force and power as she warmed to her theme . . . Gradually she spoke 'with hands, arms, and her whole body' . . . One evening . . . an extraordinary event took place. She carried her hearers on wings into high places. They soared, as it were, amongst the stars, breathed the breath of the infinite . . . Her inspiration was so great that, instead of applause, that vast audience, deeply moved, rose in silence as she left the platform . . .[10]

These were the audiences that formed McMillan. Later, we have seen her move men of government, Cabinet ministers receiving deputations. Mansbridge will make the analogy plain, but even without him we know that we have witnessed these scenes before, as the young, ardent, asexual Joan of Arc makes her plea before other sober men, for another great cause. We forget, as we watch the re-enactment, that

McMillan was thirty-five when she moved the President of the Board of Education on behalf of Bradford's half-timers in 1895, approaching forty when she rose 'with indignation writ large on every feature' and challenged Canon Simpson for keeping dirty the bodies of the poor, nearing fifty when Robert Morant listened gravely to her arguments about medical inspection, and was convinced by them. The saint of childhood is herself eternally young, and just as McMillan had air-brushed the portrait of Rachel that forms the frontispiece to *Life of Rachel McMillan*, in order to make the fifty-year-old look like a young girl, so Mansbridge's son painted a posthumous portrait of Margaret McMillan that canonises her as a youthful guardian of childhood.[11] In his biography Mansbridge tells us how she reminded many men of Joan of Arc, and ends the chapter 'Margaret the Woman', and his book, with a quotation from Shaw's *St Joan*.

But if not St Joan, then Lord Shaftesbury will stand in for McMillan, or Florence Nightingale, or Santa Barbara. Throughout his last chapter, Mansbridge consistently performs a sleight of pen whereby descriptions of sages and heroines of the past are substituted for descriptions of McMillan, as in this example:

In his description of Florence Nightingale, Lytton Strachey speaks of her work as he might of Margaret McMillan. 'Her soul, pent up all day in the restraint and reserve of a great responsibility, now at last poured itself out . . . with all its natural vehemence . . .'.[12]

Her life is offered by Mansbridge to all women, as an example:

So, in reality, Margaret the conqueror is an inspiration to all women, hindered in their normal expression, to conquer by love and by loving serve, though the day be dark and night looms ahead; to love as much as possible, before the chance goes. In the strength of her inspiration, life will radiate love, fulfilling itself and moving perfectly in the rhythm of the glorious purposes of God. Yes, I am alone on earth, I have always been alone.[13]

And who is it who speaks at the end, Margaret or St Joan?

It is, in fact, a particularly late-nineteenth-century Joan of Arc who speaks, for as Marina Warner has shown in her study of the saint and her *vitae*, each legend is transmuted by the needs and desires of its particular historical audience. The early nineteenth century in Britain saw the development of a secularised Joan of Arc: the saint was presented as a force of nature, 'alert and obedient to the inner promptings of the innocent human heart'. Accompanying this development was a deep interest in Joan's childhood, and in the childlike qualities she later displayed.[14] An emphasis on her upbringing and education was what the mid nineteenth century inherited, and John Ruskin, for example, used Thomas de Quincey's account of Joan's open-air education in the forest at Domrémy to make the claim for a pedagogy located in the natural world, in 'the pleasant places which God made at once for the schoolroom and the playground of our children'.[15] By the end of the century Joan was fully established as a child of nature.[16]

What McMillan herself could demonstrate – actually *show* – of regenerated child life attained immense capacity to *move*, to change serious men's minds. In the early 1920s the School Medical Officer for New Zealand, Lieutenant-Colonel R.B. Phillips, went down into Deptford, with not a little reluctance. He had tried to read *The Camp School*, he explained to Albert Mansbridge, 'and failed. The book was altogether too feminine and sentimental.' But a day with its author and the children touched him in quite a new way. 'I took farewell [of her] at the gate of the school', he recalled:

> A small person of three or four years was holding onto [*sic*] her skirt. (When a statue is made to Miss McMillan one or more children holding on to her skirt and looking up to her face should be included . . .) . . . Much to my embarrassment, the little girl held up her face for me to kiss. She evidently quite expected me to do so . . . I think this illustrates very well the happiness and confidence of the children in the school . . . Without such a thing having been even remotely alluded to in the course of our conversations together, the piety of Miss McMillan was so much part of her being that one could not fail to observe it. Undoubtedly herein lies the mainspring of her life's work – 'Inasmuch as ye have done it unto one of these little ones . . .'[17]

Obituaries in 1931, and Mansbridge's account, called her pioneer, saint, children's champion.[18] Administrative history in particular presented her as a great reformer. In his history of the maternity and child welfare movement in Britain (1935), G.F. McCleary called her 'the one most remarkable woman of her time';[19] and we have seen how a classic account of the development of the welfare state in Britain makes her role as social reformer pivotal in the creation of the school medical service.[20] But this isolation of McMillan as a remarkable and charismatic figure began long before her death, in the early 1890s. Her 1892 May Day address in Hyde Park was frequently noted at the time, and often remembered. In the first *Labour Annual*, Joseph Edwards recalled that 'she manifested . . . on that occasion, such extraordinary powers as a thinker and a speaker that there has been an increasing demand for her services on labour platforms.'[21]

The young socialist schoolteacher Barbara Fraser recommended her to John Bruce Glasier in 1892, saying how 'Maggie McMillan . . . quite fascinated me. Really, there is no other word to describe the effect she had on me . . .'.[22] By October she was telling him: 'I can't calculate her mental orbit . . .', and after a Christmas spent with the McMillans at Tadema Road: 'her will power is so strong and she is so magnetic that she almost persuades me at times, of the necessity for getting above one's natural wishes and affections . . .', but once she had got back home she added: 'there is a good deal of "soul-straining" involved in living up to her pitch . . .'.[23] The drama of her self-presentation in personal relationships was no less effective than it was on the platform. Barbara Fraser remembered 'Maggie . . . telling me the other day – in quite a Sibylline manner – how we would conduct ourselves if it *should* come to the barricades. I am glad to say that she gave you an honoured place in the foreground of the hottest battle alongside Rachel . . .'.[24] This ability to hold the smallest and most private of audiences is manifest in Bruce Glasier's account of the wit and accuracy of the mimicry McMillan was able to perform for the entertainment of her guests in Bradford in 1896.[25] At this time, in fact, he considered McMillan 'a woman of marvellous soul power', and in recommending her to his fiancée Katharine Conway, he added: 'I went through the Royal Academy with her – she and you are the only women I have met who understand art.'[26]

By the time McMillan went to Bradford, then, in November 1893, she had a public and a private reputation as an exceptional and fascinating woman. A small group of socialists, all of them about the same age, recommended her to each other, and part of their desire to know her better was a desire to discover what she really thought. That her thought, the theories she expounded, achieved the status of a system (Barbara Fraser called them 'her doctrines'[27]) for this group of friends had much to do with her status as a possessor of knowledge. She was indeed highly educated and very well read, and what lay at the basis of her public and educational success in Bradford Labour Church was the sense she managed to convey of *transmitting* knowledge, of passing it on.

It was her knowledge that entranced 'Lily Bell' in the *Labour Leader*, and her ability to systematise and synthesise different fields of knowledge. Reporting on her public appearance in Glasgow in late 1896, 'Lily Bell' told his/her readers that McMillan had 'studied the deeper things of life with so clear an insight, and so wide a capacity of understanding their relation to each other . . .'.[28] Her particular appeal emanated from the way in which she laid 'before her audiences the result of her studies and research', and the disciplines that 'Lily Bell' said she integrated were evolutionary biology, education, chemistry, anatomy and physiology. This present account of McMillan's life has itself been constructed around her role as populariser of scientific ideas, and her transmission of them to a wide variety of audiences for political purposes. In her fictional writing of the early and mid 1890s McMillan cultivated such an image, and a reputation for knowledge and learning. In a 'Women of the Age of Gold' piece written for the *Labour Prophet* in 1894, 'Mary', the ex-governess living with her sister in the Home for Working Women, completes a great theoretical work, and then, laying down her pen, sees herself 'in factories, striving to *know* the people, later, in the libraries, striving to interpret them'.[29]

We should see, then, a continuum between her reputation as private individual, the impact she had on friends and acquaintances, and her public persona. But if by 1896 a series of 'vigorous and brilliant addresses . . . [had] made her famous', we must look further than the ILP platform and public meeting to find the sources of her performance. As we have seen, some time between 1889 and 1892 McMillan had trained for the stage. She took lessons in voice production from Emil Behnke, but also studied under Henry Neville. In 1878 Neville had opened an acting studio in Oxford Street, which was still operating in the early 1890s. It was here, we may assume, that McMillan took lessons from him. In 1895 Neville co-authored, with Hugh Campbell and Robert Brewer, *Voice, Speech and Gesture*, the fruits of his years as a teacher of drama.[30]

Neville's section of this textbook dealt with the classification and notation of gesture and the range of rhetorical styles suitable for the pulpit, the law court, the stage and the political platform. 'In order to gain a just idea of suitable action and expression', he told his students, 'it is necessary to remember that every passion, emotion and sentiment has a particular attitude of the body, and physiognomical expression, which should be carefully studied and practised with force and frequency.'[31] For McMillan, such an understanding of the relationship of body to mind was fundamental. We should see such lessons (if indeed they were what she experienced) as giving her both a means of personal expression and a component of the integrative physiological system of education that she evolved. Neville made the argument at another level too, saying: 'Our first object must be the cultivation of the soul, which should be rendered sensitive to the various emotions, the pure, true, magnetic instincts that govern us not only as children, but as grown up people . . . .'.[32]

Did McMillan learn techniques that allowed her to present herself as both ageless and any-age? The childlike qualities that witnesses noticed were constantly mentioned in the adulatory attention she received in the labour press. Julia Dawson, for instance, wrote of her in the *Clarion* women's column in 1904 as someone who 'is as much a child today as a woman. She has all the brightness and originality of childhood, combined with the wisdom and experience of womanhood. *This* is the secret of her greatness.'[33] Robert Blatchford's daughter Winifred remembered being taken once in the 1890s to visit 'a place called Miss McMillan's, at Bradford'. There the child found 'a pretty cosy room where a wonderful lady lived . . . a tall, gallant woman with kind clever eyes that have a delicious trick of screwing up at the corners . . .'.[34] Her father – who, as we shall see, put some serious thought into analysing the components of McMillan's appeal – offered a particular insight into the immutability of her physical presence when he recalled for Albert Mansbridge an incident of 1895:

> Miss McMillan loved my wife. My wife was a woman's woman and that is the very best kind of woman. She came to see us in Streatham in 1895. We three sat up talking. When we began to talk Miss McMillan looked a tired sad woman of middle age . . . As she talked she grew younger and better looking and still younger and still more handsome, and before we parted for the night she was a very beautiful young girl. Imagination? No. I said to my wife, 'Did you notice anything strange about Miss McMillan?' and my wife said: 'I should think I did. She frightened me . . . She kept getting younger and prettier. She turned into a beautiful girl.'[35]

Blatchford recounted a similar incident that took place a few years later in Bradford, and concluded: 'Well. She was a Highlander and a spirit . . .'. That McMillan was aware of this ability is possibly to be read in her attribution of it to Rachel, for Blatchford also told Mansbridge that 'she said to me one day: "My Sister Rachel can be as young as she likes, as lovely as she likes, *when* she likes".'

The force and power of McMillan's platform performance can be traced through the labour press of the 1890s, and beyond. How different was it, in presence and reception, from that of the other female orators of the ILP? In the absence of detailed research on the development of women public speakers in the nineteenth century, we can only draw some comparisons between McMillan and Conway, Stacey, Martyn and Ford, and speculate about public understanding of the female presence on the platform. The women members of the ILP were all advertised with enthusiasm and reported with rapture, and at the level of performance they were often more of a success than their male comrades. We should not underrate the novelty and power of witnessing the female figure on the platform, especially the power of a woman addressing questions of how to live sexually as well as socially. The intense questioning of the young men, clerics and artisans, in the typical ILP audience was partly answered by the woman, who in her youthfulness, social status, and femininity embodied the yearning in her audience for something finer. Katharine Conway's beauty was often remarked on, and it was clearly a factor in her appeal. But McMillan was not conventionally pretty: if she is the Scottish 'Marjorie McGowan' of her 1895 story 'Zoë', then she knew herself to have 'plain, honest features'.[36]

She evidently cut an imposing figure, and other ILP orators paid tribute to her powers, but it is difficult from press reports to find out exactly what she said on any one occasion. Reporters usually summarised her speech, and made much of their own reaction to it. 'The beauty of her similes' might be mentioned, or her 'intense, even fiery conviction of the truth', but these are comments about performance, not content.[37] She evidently thought about performance until the end of her days, one of her training college students recalling how in 1930 she constructed a lecture by following 'the classic principles of oratory, dividing the speech into its six distinct parts, saying "That will do for the exordium, now for the peroration".[38] This particular student was to give the lecture on McMillan's behalf, for she was now severely ill. She told her 'and remember, never begin a speech too loudly. You get people's attention better by talking quietly to begin with.' Not only quietly, but disarmingly too. One of the few transcripts of her public voice is to be found in a report of the 1899 ILP Conference, where McMillan stood up and said: 'I am going to speak to you for five minutes, and I do not know in the least what I am going to say. I have been thinking of infant schools, and what I should say at the Conference next Saturday . . .'[39]

This ability to be both a figure isolated on a platform and a woman sharing herself and her thoughts may well have been a feature of all female oratory in this period. Even so, a rhetoric of gesture and movement (the decoding of which may have been a matter of conventional reading to her audiences) was particularly important to the socialist agitators of the 1890s, who often spoke to large crowds, so that what was said could not always be heard. Many socialist meetings were small and intimate, but in large gatherings a rhetoric of gesture and the rhetoric of a feminine presence may have spoken louder than words.[40] When an educated woman, seen to be sharing her knowledge and her self with an audience, spoke about a history of women, or a particular role for women in social evolution, then we have 'Lily Bell's' testimony, at least, to the electrifying nature of the whole performance.

Though we do not have a detailed or accurate transcription of McMillan's public utterances, we can safely assume the core of their content. Much of her published writing grew out of her public speaking. We cannot know the extent of her revisions, but we can see what in general she spoke about. David Howell, in *British Workers and the Independent Labour Party*, discusses the limited usefulness of ILP platform rhetoric, describing how

> the tedious journeys from town to town . . . the intoxication of an enthusiastic meeting could . . . inhibit the germination of new ideas. Indeed, repetition was almost inherent in several propagandists' perceptions of the socialist creed – simple, emotional, without the need for complex theoretical elaborations . . .[41]

Possibly, this picture needs modifying in two ways. First, we should look at the exchange between audience and performer, the complex meaning of a public presence, and the decoding of gesture, movement and dress that marked out the popular form of the public lecture, sermon or speech. Until detailed research is done, we can only say that within this complex of understanding the female presence had a particular *meaning* which cannot simply be explained by invoking simplicity, emotiveness and repetition. In McMillan's case we can record that she had been tutored in a technique of emotional expressiveness and that her balancing of remoteness and intimacy was *noted*, at least by those who reported on her performances. What is more, we should observe that for all the sentimentality of her utterances, and her certain repetition of them, the public platform actually witnessed her development of a coherent and elaborated – and theoretically complex – idea of childhood and its regenerative power for socialism between 1895 and 1910.

'Lily Bell'/Keir Hardie was transfixed by her Glasgow performance in 1896; but often McMillan was thought to have a special appeal for women, as both actor and sage. An important component of this appeal was the way in which it cut across classes and made all women aware of their female mission. *M.A.P.*, the journal of social gossip, became interested in McMillan after the Duchess of Sutherland's spectacular 'conversion' to socialism after hearing McMillan speak at the Labour Church in Leek, in 1897. 'What is Margaret MacMillan [*sic*] like?' asked *M.A.P.*.

> That is a difficult question to answer – so difficult that probably no two of her many friends would answer it alike. First and foremost she is a Celt, pure Celt; but she is a Celt enriched and broadened by varied experience in America, in Europe, and in every class of society. Swift of insight, unusually bare of prejudice, imaginative as a poet, she arrives at a conclusion long before laggard minds are within a thousand miles of it. Miss MacMillan [*sic*] lives a simple, not to say austere life with her books and her idealism as chief companions, in the cosy nest she has made for herself. Years ago, she decided to set aside all luxury and to devote herself to the Labour movement . . . In fireside talk she is perfectly delightful;

full of quaint, subtle and elusive humour, and quick to make thumbnail sketches of friends and acquaintances.[42]

There are all the elements of the exemplary life in this description – the isolation, the devotion to a great cause, the flashes of humour to show the 'real' woman. By working within this tradition of spiritual biography, many commentators were actually trying to assess and come to terms with her singleness, her childlike qualities, and her apparent lack of a sexual life. It was this absence that Mansbridge obliquely referred to when he wrote of women like her 'hindered in their normal expression'.[43]

There was an elaborate theoretical approach to the problem that McMillan thus represented. Its conservative expression can be found in the work of a writer like Herbert Spencer;[44] but we should note that left-wing observers of McMillan's presence and performance were more likely to be approaching the enigma along the lines Edward Carpenter had drawn. In *Love's Coming of Age* Carpenter had discussed 'the women of the new movement', suggesting that they were

> naturally drawn from those in whom the maternal instinct is not especially strong; also from those in whom the sexual instinct is not preponderant. Such women do not altogether represent their sex; some are rather mannish in temperament; some are . . . inclined to attachments to their own rather than to the opposite sex; some are ultra-rationalizing and brain-cultured; to many, children are more or less a bore . . .[45]

Carpenter's outline could only have made McMillan more of a puzzle than Spencer's delineation of the social mother, not least because she so clearly used 'brain-culture' as the foundation for great attachment to children, and seems not to have had any sexual relationships at all with either men or women.

Robert Blatchford, reflecting on forty years of friendship with her in 1931, was honest about his reaction to what he called McMillan's ' "virginal strange air" '. 'A strange, beautiful, gifted woman,' he mused; 'great; but odd.' He recalled how in the 1890s they 'were afraid of each other':

> If I had to speak in public . . . and saw her amongst the audience, I felt tempted to run away. Once, at Stoke, I was to take the chair and she was to speak. We were at tea before the meeting with a score of friends, when she said suddenly: 'I wish you were not to be at my meeting: you make me nervous . . . there is no reason why I should be nervous. There is no reason why I should care a damn but I *do*' . . . Now what were we afraid of? She only saw the

Galahad part of me. She did not know the careless 'you be damned' Army Sergeant. I think she made of me a blend of a hero and a child . . . I stood in awe of that strange woman . . .[46]

She paraded her oddness, her sense of difference from other women, before John Bruce Glasier, watching herself ironically do this the while. She did the same to Blatchford. He recalled how he once called on her in Bradford, and she kept him waiting. 'Then she floated into the room, all smiles and – what do you think she said to her editor and hero? She said "So you have come, you funny little thing" . . . .'.

A few days after he sent off these reminiscences to Mansbridge, Blatchford wrote again. He wanted McMillan's biographer to understand the relationship he had had with her. He had decided to call it love, but a love that could be described only by referring Mansbridge to 'a wonderful book' by 'Stacpoole, called "The Beach of Dreams" ' Blatchford outlined the plot:

A young rich French lady and a rough big English sailor are cast away on the wild desolate island of Kergulen. They have many adventures and at last escape and get a ship to Marseilles. I want to quote one short passage. The society lady is explaining the relations between her and the sailor. She is explaining to an old sea captain.
'A little roughness what is that to freedom and the life I have learned to love and the man I love. For I love Raft, Captain Boutempts, just as I know he loves me. Oh, do not mistake me, it is not the sort of thing they call love here among the houses and streets; it is not a woman that is speaking to you, but a human being.'
And the old sea captain understood. But Stacpoole says, acutely: 'No Paris poet could have understood her. The old fisher captain did.'
I think the wonderful Margaret loved me like that and I loved her as one of Jean d'Arc's rough soldiers may have loved the shining maid. 'Something all too wise and good for human nature's daily food.'
Well, I think now you have seen all my cards.[47]

It is quite clear that McMillan understood the effect her performances had on others. Sometimes she was at pains to refute the charge of 'seriousness': 'Isn't it strange that I make other people feel so serious. Dear me. I find the world very amusing . . . I like the world very much indeed. It isn't a desert drear at all.'[48]

Up to the very early years of this century, accounts of McMillan's public performance or of her personality were often adulatory, but they represented at the same time a series of serious attempts by commentators to assess the formation and impact of a charismatic personality. In this way, a striking personality, an awesome intelligence, and an oddity were recorded. But after her attention was turned more completely towards children, and her reputation as a writer and a politician became more completely bound up with questions of child welfare, it is possible to see the construction of a legendary figure, a saint of childhood, taking place. In these accounts of the 1900s – as in this one from Mallon's 'Portrait Gallery' (1908) – the misunderstood or ignored message is frequently mentioned. At the same time, earlier saints and prophetesses are introduced, by way of deification. 'To dreamers of a new world', wrote Mallon,

> McMillan pointed out that in continuous accession of children, a new world is always being born, and, that through our mistreatment of them, always being lost; to babblers of revolution she retorts that revolution will come when we decide to feed the revolutionaries . . . she says that the way to Utopia is a white road that even an education minister might see . . . This, for nearly a generation, has been her consistent message. We rejoiced in her complete knowledge . . . We said that she had a shining bold look, like Santa Barbara . . . in a great fresco. We loved to think of her as protectress of the children. But we called her 'crank', and said she had one idea . . . In the Middle Ages they did these things better than we. Had Miss McMillan lived 500 years ago, she had lived as the Saint of Poor Children forever.[49]

At this stage in the development of 'the legend of Margaret McMillan', her *knowledge* was still deemed to be a component of her sainthood. Much later, after her death, when the legend was not only transcribed but actually used within educational writing, anti-intellectualism became an important dimension of her reputation. In Miriam Lord's account (1947) she is presented as having 'no scientific training, no academic pedagogy, no knowledge of education . . . yet [she] reached the sure truth hidden from experts'.[50] This repudiation of her considerable intellectual abilities did not take place in her lifetime – or at least not before the 1920s, when her writing and her expertise were credited with their full political and propagandist worth.

At the 1914 North of England Education Conference, held in Bradford (the same one at which David Eder delivered his shocking paper on the conflicts of the unconscious in his little Deptford patients) William Leech asserted that 'the greatest living educationalist is Miss Margaret McMillan. Every single advance made in the last fifteen or twenty years is directly traceable to her genius. This wonderful seer and prophetess has disturbed and harassed and trained the public conscience . . . one woman has set going a whole revolution.'[51] At the same time, though, as the prophetess in the wilderness was described, commentators also began to relate her achievements in terms of the distance they measured from the great ideal, to tell the story in terms of the great 'if only': 'For six weary years', said Winifred Blatchford in 1913, 'she has been knocking, and has gained – what? Just a grant for a clinic in Deptford . . .'.[52]

We need to return to the 'if only', to a structure of understanding that has been discussed earlier in these pages. In a revision of Franco Moretti's argument about sentimentality and tears in 'Kindergarten', it has been suggested that the point of convulsive recognition, the moment when the tears fall, is to do with a set of feelings, a response, that could be labelled 'if only' rather than with the sense of things being 'too late', as Moretti originally claimed.[53] Earlier in this book it was argued that as Moretti's thesis was constructed around the representation of *childhood* in various texts of the late nineteenth and early twentieth centuries, and not around the adult perspectives discussed in the revisionary 'Melodrama and Tears', the original argument holds, for childhood is always, when represented, a lost realm: it is always represented 'too late'.[54]

When this melancholy and mordant understanding is applied to grown men and women, a very peculiar evasion and repression take place, closely akin to what Marina Warner describes in the transmutations of St Joan into the flower of childhood in this period:

> When virtue is pictured as innocence and innocence equated with childlikeness, the implication is obviously that knowledge and experience are no longer media of goodness, but have become in themselves contaminating. This is a very despairing outlook, in its way as black as Augustine's original sin, for it supposes that original goodness will in all likelihood be defiled . . . It surrenders the attempt to represent virtue in a mature phase . . .[55]

To describe the legend of Margaret McMillan is to point to her as a victim of this understanding. It is also to point to an individual and political conflict with a sentimentality, a set of symbols, and a social system that, no matter what political efforts McMillan made to improve the material conditions of working-class children, actually returned those children to the idea of loss and hopelessness.

PART THREE

Biographical Questions, Fictions of the Self

T HE shade of an autobiography – a story of the self presented as a biography of another – has moved through the preceding pages; and that shade has been a major source for the writing of this book. In her *Life of Rachel McMillan* (1927) McMillan purported to write the biography of her sister, and in fact wrote her own. This elision of forms, of biography and autobiography, is a further item in what has been argued to be McMillan's particular importance: her manipulation and use of genres (particularly in her fiction writing) and rhetorical forms (in her political journalism and platform speeches). What is more, an argument of this book has been that literary usage constitutes a specifically historical form of evidence, of the ways in which ideas get used, manipulated and transmuted in historical contexts, so to discuss literary form and literary usage – the form and use of biography and autobiography – by way of closure is not just to provide this book with an index to its own deconstruction. Rather, it is to come to some conclusions about the historical developments and changes that McMillan was agent of and actor within.

Modern literary studies separate autobiography from biography very clearly, with autobiography having the more detailed and sophisticated attention paid to it. Whilst biography is generally understood to be both popular and theoretically unexciting (a point that will shortly be returned to) autobiography is usually analysed nowadays as a complex and problematic form.[1] This is largely because of a modern intellectual interest in the fragmented human subject, an interest which forces a series of compelling questions about the act of splitting oneself off from oneself in order to write a life story. Yet there are historical cases like that of Margaret McMillan, who blurred the distinction between the two and who must make us reconsider the source of the division between the two forms as it has been established in the literary theory of the last century and a half. Indeed, there may be a longer and more general history that suggests a certain indivisibility of the forms, for both writers and readers.

Literary forms are both permissive and preventive. On the last score, they prevent writers and readers from doing things – from thinking in particular ways, making particular causal links, performing particular acts of interpretation. This final chapter opens with a discussion of such constraints and permissions: those that the bio-graphical form has presented to the writer of this book, discussing a historical figure, a woman, now, in the 1980s; and the constraints that the form of autobiography offered to McMillan, writing her own – very odd – life story in 1927. The current constraints, the restrictions that the form enforces as far as this book is concerned, are to do with the current state of feminist biography (and the history of biographical form that it carries around its neck), with the legacy of a certain kind of women's history; and finally – and as it was in the beginning – with the subject herself, and the ease with which various retellings of her story have been given hagiographical shape.

Raymond Williams has argued that in spite of its seeming simplicity, biography, along with memoir and history, is a difficult and perplexing form, partly because in so rigorously asserting its generic factuality, as opposed to the fictionality of myth, or epic, or drama, the writer can disguise his or her use of epic or drama in the narrative.[2] Yet the way seems quite open for the biographer to use this insight in the writing of a new life story. For instance, it would have been possible, in describing McMillan's apostasy in 1929, when the veteran socialist spoke on a Conservative platform in support of Nancy Astor's nursery school campaign, to have written in the tragic mode, and at the same time to make the reader aware that this was being done. With an actual self-consciousness about literary form and rhetorical organisation, it could be argued that this current biographical study has carried with it its own engine of internal deconstruction and foregrounded its major source, which is McMillan's own *Life of Rachel McMillan*, showing how the living Margaret canonised the dead Rachel, so that this *Doppelgänger* bore the whole narrative of McMillan's life. The biography McMillan wrote (and this one, which has just been read) could serve as an exploration of the romantic variant of the form, in which the biographer seeks a shade of herself in the subject she delineates, in the pages of her book.

There is no harm in watching the determined accretion of stories around other stories, autobiographies around other tellings of a life (and no harm, either, in finding much pleasure in the watching). But the historian has to deal with all these recastings of form, all these retellings, as matters of historical evidence; and on the face of it, it does seem that the historical narrative, *whatever form it takes*, is in some kind of conflict with the written life story, in both its biographical and autobiographical modes. This conflict can be seen most clearly if we consider history, biography and autobiography as forms of narrative, and history as a narrative form that has its own – highly convincing – rhetoric of persuasion.

The persuasion might be outlined like this: this book was conceived of as a historical project – that is, the life story here presented is understood to illuminate ideas, ideologies, class and gender relations, and the social practices of a particular period of British history. At the same time, a particular life is seen as being shaped by those ideas, relations and practices – a shaping that the biographical subject is cognisant of at some points in her life, quite unaware of at others. The account has been presented as a form of history, and that presentation must be viewed as its own rhetorical device, allowing the writer to present a plot that seemingly *had* to be shaped in a particular way, according to what the documents used for its composition authorised, or what they forbade. The writer of any kind of historical narrative can always present herself as the invisible servant of archive material, as merely uncovering what already lies there, waiting to be told.[3] It is as well that the reader of this current study is alerted to the fact that the historian is able in this way to appropriate to him- or herself the most massive authority as a story-teller.

And even if the historian does not do this, even if she tells the story in a more speculative way, allowing that things might have happened in a different manner, or that there are different interpretations available, then still the huge weight of notes at the end of the volume of history (which are indeed necessary, and constitute one of the decencies of the craft) appear to say: here, look: you may write down the accession number, take the train to the distant city, call for the papers, undo the bundle; and see then that it is the truth that is being told here; or at least, see that the interpretation made of what lies in those papers is both possible and reasonable. Again, the authority of the historian as narrator is confirmed.

It is important to raise these questions about the fictionality of the historical enterprise, not because there is a great deal of mileage in the notion that none of it happened, or in the idea that the story could be told in any old way (that this version is just one among many equally valid possibilities); but rather, in order to make it plain that in terms of writing (of the kind of literary activity that history writing is), by structure, plot, characterisation and narrative organisation, history is a fiction.[4] When narratologists and philosophers argue that there can only ever be a history of the potentialities of the present, they are suggesting that writing about the past must always be done out of a set of current preoccupations, and that the literary enterprise of history-writing tells a story about the present, using items from the past. The truth, or the objectivity, that historians claim lies in the particular structure and narrative organisation of these items, around themes that in this particular case have already been delineated – around, for instance, the idea of late-nineteenth-century socialism, or the development of work for middle-class women in the 1890s, or the professionalisation of childcare in the pre-First World War years, or whatever – where the arguments of other historians are heeded, and current interpretations of these developments are confirmed or adjusted or denied. Within this understanding of truth, or objectivity, the current study would lay claim to it too, especially on the topics just outlined.

Stories, says Louis O. Mink, truly become narrative only when they take on the same meaning for the listener as for the teller; and they come to an end when there is no more to be said, when both teller and audience understand that the point that has been reached, this end-place, this conclusion, was implicit in the beginning: was there all along.[5] In spoken and written autobiography, a simple variant of this narrative rule is in operation. The man or woman, leaning against the public bar or writing a book, is the embodiment of something completed. That end, the finished place, is the human being, a body in time and space, telling a story, a story that brings the listener or the reader to the here and now, or to this rounded and finished character in the pages of the book. Written autobiography ends in the figure of the writer, and the narrative closure of biography is the figure that has been created through these pages.

In narrative terms like this, these forms of writing – biography and autobiography – must always remain in conflict with the writing of history, which does indeed come to conclusions and reach ends, but actually moves forward through the implicit understanding that *things are not over*, that the story isn't finished, can't ever be completed, for some new item of information may alter the account as it has been given. At the centre of the written history lies this recognition of temporariness and impermanence. The writers and readers of historical biography need to recognise this narrative conflict at its heart: the pull between the impermanence of writing history, and the closure and completeness of plot and character that are wanted from biography.

English biography as a literary form is usually said to have emerged in the seventeenth century as part of a larger body of writings that dealt with spiritual journeys undertaken in individual lives. The Puritan autobiography is the best-known – and most investigated – component of this genre, and a brief discussion of it as a literary form and as a way of understanding and interpreting life stories – as a form of cognition – is a useful way of approaching the problems involved in writing and reading modern biographical accounts of individual lives.[6] These questions are elaborated by the particularity of telling and interpreting *women's* lives.

This early autobiographical writing was designed to situate a life within the context of God's purpose, and at the same time to give an account of its *meaning*, through that very placement within the time and space of a particular spirituality. For the development of the

246

secular form, the important point is that time and space were specified in some detail: religious and social milieux were often itemised, and it is this detailing of the material world that was important for the development of the autobiography. The standard histories of autobiography that we possess describe a development, over the last four hundred years, of a specifically historical consciousness – that is, an understanding of the self as formed by a historicised world, by an environment or setting that exists and changes independently of the human actors who find themselves within it.[7]

In many literary and critical accounts of autobiography it is Goethe in particular, in *Dictung und Wahreit*, who is presented as first formalising the notion of self-formation as an interplay between the self and the world around the self.[8] In this way autobiography is distinguished from such forms as memoir and reminiscence by the status and function of *experience* within it. In the memoir, for instance, a series of events, or other factors, is viewed as dictating the narrative course. The writer may translate these into inner experience, but that inner experience – lived and felt experience – is not its focus, as it is in autobiography. The biographer – the external recorder of another person's life – can often be seen steering a course between these two principles of causation, the internal and the external, that were developed within the forms of memoir and autobiography.

When seventeenth-century spiritual autobiographies and later developments in the form are labelled 'interpretative', it means that for their authors and their community of readers, the purpose of the life story lay not so much in its narration, but rather in the interpretations that could be made of it.[9] In the same way the spiritual biography, a parallel development, was exemplary in form, its purpose being not just to give an account of a life but also to make a demonstration of the possible purposes, meanings and uses that might be made of that life story by others.

This is the point at which to raise the question of popularity and desire, for readers evidently want something from the form – and get it, if best-seller lists, in which a biography or two usually figures, may be allowed to delineate the approval of readers. The biography of women, produced out of publishers' women's studies lists over the last ten years, has shared a more general success and owes much to what makes the form generally popular: the confirmation it offers that life stories *can* be told, that the inchoate experience of living and feeling can be marshalled into a chronology, that central and unified subjects reach the conclusion of a life, and come into possession of their own story.[10]

Biography also partakes of a kind of historical romance, or romance of history. The historical romance can be defined as a *hope* that readers hold (their particular expectation of any particular text being a reflection of a much wider one) that that which is gone, that which is irretrievably lost, which is past time, can be brought back and conjured before the eyes 'as it really was'; and that it might be possessed. Biography takes us much closer to its subject matter than does other historical writing, and within the romance of getting closer, women must and do figure with greater depth and delight than men, for as all schoolchildren know, when they are set to copy figures from the history books the queen is a more interesting figure to trace around than the king, possessing a plethora of lace collars, and farthingales and ropes of hair.[11] It is by the satisfactory *detail* they offer – which can be sartorial, emotional, domestic – that women are the visible heroines of the historical romance, and the biography usually offers a very clear telling of it.

It may be satisfying, but it is also dull, for there is a less sexy and more practical point to make here about the popularity of biography as a form – that its seeming innocence also outlines its *boringness*. Biography does not have the theoretical glamour of the problematised popular forms, such as detective fiction or the gothic. It can present itself as respectable and worthy, particularly when it operates under the banner of history; but it is not the intellectual firecracker that autobiography has become; there is 'something inescapably second-rate that seems to cling to biography and its practitioners . . .'.[12] It may be hailed, as Robert M. Young has recently hailed it, as the 'basic discipline for human science', but this is to claim no more than that all of us find abstract ideas or the theoretical structure of unfamiliar disciplines easier to understand and appropriate if they are presented in their evolution through the life story of philosophers, scientists and other theoreticians.[13]

Speculation about the popularity of biography as a form can be weighted with an observation about the work that has been done in the field of women's history over the last fifteen years. One legacy is an altered sense of the historical meaning and importance of female *insignificance*. The absence of women from conventional historical accounts, discussion of this absence (and of the real archival difficulties that lie in the way of presenting their lives in a historical context) are at the same time a massive assertion of the littleness of what lies hidden.[14] A sense of that which is lost, never to be recovered completely, is one of the most powerful organising devices of modern women's history. The sadness of its effect is also to be found in much working-class history – where, indeed, a greater number of lives lie lost. But a comparison between the two forms – people's history and women's history – demonstrates that in the latter case, loss and absence remain loss and absence, while in the writing of working-class history they do not. Its organising principles – the annals of labour, class struggle, the battles (particularly the 'good fights' of trade-union history) that can be seen to foreshadow a greater and final revolutionary struggle – all these allow the lack of detail about working lives a greater *prefigurative* force than women's history can allow the women whose absence it notes from the written and recorded past. Oppression and repression have a *meaning* within the narrative structure of people's history and labour history, but not in women's history.

We could say, then, that women's absence from conventional historical accounts is 'meaningless', in this particular way. At the same time, it is important to distinguish 'meaninglessness' from the literary delineation of 'uneventfulness', which has been a structuring idea within the biography of women for longer than the last fifteen years. Lives of heroines have been written as the eruption from uneventfulness into public life, and that early life has been presented through a domestic detail that asserts how little really happened in it. The nineteenth-century heroine of modern biography remains perforce an exceptional and unusual figure, whose life story explains only itself. This is partly to do with the absence of analyses of women's structural relationship to the societies in which they become actors, but the exceptional female figure is also partly produced out of the biographer's use of a personal, or individual, frame of time. Early uneventfulness, in which nothing much happens to the heroine, is thought to produce and structure what happens later, within a public arena. In this way the public life is presented as a reverse image of the old, private and uneventful life, rather than as a product of the interaction between subject and the political and social circumstances she finds herself in. So, as in the tradition of exemplary religious biography from an earlier period, spirituality (that which is created in adversity, in isolation, in a life where 'nothing happened') is understood to shape and form later conduct.

A theoretical and historical understanding of the insignificance of women's lives in the past does indeed place the biographer of a woman who lived a public life in a political space in some conceptual and organisational difficulty. The problem was this: in the political culture where Margaret McMillan operated, women were not an absence by simple virtue of their disenfranchisement, nor by the social and legal barriers to their action; rather, their absence and obscurity were organised by a wide variety of political thought, and by various theories of femininity. These actually allowed women to operate politically across a wide arena, and it has been one of the purposes of this book to outline the historical setting that provided that sphere of action.

A further difficulty was presented by the way in which old assumptions about an individuality formed in struggle and isolation are sometimes reinforced by a modern psychology of women in which particular domestic struggles are universalised and calls are made for the structure of biography to follow a delineated female life cycle.[15] A struggle with a father is then seen to mirror and foreshadow a social struggle, against the assumptions of a patriarchal society. Women's dependency and failure to break from it is understood as a transhistorical factor and allows a life story to be constructed in terms of relationships with others and the vicissitudes of those relationships. That a particular pleasure lies in such personal accounts, and that readers search after such personal and domestic detail in male biography, and wish that there were more of it, should not blind us to the fact that a biographer has made a choice of narrative construction, and decided to elevate the affective and the personal above political and social context.

Margaret McMillan left no collection of papers, no journal with which to peel away the layers of public form, in order to reveal the true woman. There could be no attempt to unveil her for the delectation of an audience, for there are no secrets to tell about her. Within the form, such secrets are usually sexual, and McMillan appears never to have had a sexual relationship with any one. In the preceding pages her relationship to children, to her own childhood and that of the working-class children whose cause she espoused – and in particular, her passionate and sensual depictions of various children, both real and fictional – may seem to function as that kind of central 'secret', the relationship that explains the trajectory of a life. But in fact, what was important about McMillan was precisely that these were not solely individual and personal relationships; rather, her public and political significance lies in the fact that she gave expression to a large-scale cultural shift in understanding of the self, which was to do with ideas and theories of development and growth in the human subject, and a new relationship to them. 'The child' (that is, real children, and child-figures) embodied this understanding, and it was conceptualised across a wide variety of public forms at the turn of the century. As a politician, a socialist and a journalist, McMillan's own reconceptualisation had particular and far-reaching historical *effects*, but it was not hers alone.

She seemed, then, to be a woman who demanded a public life; in some way she prevented the delineation of an inside that is 'personal' and 'real', and lies beneath the public persona – and appeared to ask for a biographical telling that took as its central device the arresting rhetorical moment of the woman on the public platform, or even more appropriately – and we have a witness to this – the woman in the public square, in the Market Place, Nottingham, during the miners' strike of 1893, and Percy Redfern the draper's assistant leaving his counter and going outside to be uplifted by her words, 'touched by something vaguely, unattainably fine . . . '.[16]

It was Mikhail Bakhtin who, in discussing Greek rhetorical autobiography and biography, showed us the public square, the place and form of the ancient state, and the civic funeral orations and memorial speeches delivered there, in which spoken and valedictory biographies 'there was not, nor could there be, anything intimate or private, secret or personal . . . [where] the individual is open on all sides, he is all surface . . . '.[17] To have actually found Margaret McMillan in a public square is a moment to gladden the heart of the historian. But though that moment may be used to draw the reader's attention to the dead weight of interiority that hangs about the neck of women and their depiction, it is not of course possible to dissolve the boundary between inside and outside. However, the moment can be used as a trope that might alert the reader to the *historical* argument that lies at the centre of this book: that what might be seen as McMillan's 'insideness', her meaning, which was her remaking and reassertion of childhood, actually spells out the public space of cultural change. What is more, McMillan's writing and her own, odd evasion of autobiography might lead us to the speculation that in the act of figuring oneself the self is not split and fragmented but most powerfully integrated, so that in this particular case the woman might stand there and speak, in a public place.

The speaker, though, is bound to tell stories about herself. McMillan told many, particularly writing and rewriting the narratives of childhood that had their origins in her own. To consider a life story in fictional terms is not to suggest that its subject told lies about herself, or practised more genteel or general concealments. It is rather to propose that as well as all the other things that they do with a life, people live through – and make public presentations of themselves by using – a society's fictional forms. What is available to people depends on their history and their education as well as on their class circumstances, and the forms of popular romance, of myth, or dramatic performance are only the most obvious choices.[18] In the current case, it has been useful to speculate about the stage training McMillan received, and the refinement and manipulation of the popular form of the public lecture that it probably provided her with.[19] Less speculatively than this, we have seen her use the melodramatic form of popular newspaper fiction, adapting it to her purposes of presenting a theory of working-class childhood. Throughout this account as well, her references to contemporary European realistic fiction have also been noted from time to time, and McMillan's use of a sub-genre, the Edwardian 'slice of life' and its comedy of class relations and class misapprehension.

Returning to speculation, we could suggest that such performance, in person and in writing, allowed her to negotiate the difficulties of being a single woman, from an uncertain class background and a difficult childhood; suggest that it allowed her a way of circumnavigating the awkwardness she felt about herself. This awkwardness was apparent in the series of letters she wrote to Bruce Glasier in the early 1890s, and in what Robert Blatchford remembered of their relationship in those years. The feeling of being out of place in the world was inscribed in the childhood she wrote in *Life of Rachel McMillan*, and was remembered for Nancy Astor in 1930. 'Once', recalled McMillan, 'when I was 8 I was asked to my first party. I was so glad that I got ill – & couldn't go.'[20] Mansbridge remembered her in the 1920s, 'sitting aloof and alone, regarding the passing guests at a garden party or reception. She would sit there brooding . . .'.[21] It is not necessary to pathologise her to recognise that the condescension she described the fictional Mrs Heavytop meting out to her governess was very probably what she experienced herself: 'I also have found myself continually in company with those who would not deign to speak to me', she wrote to Sally Blatchford in 1895. 'I used to feel it so much. I truly suffered.'[22]

To have found herself and a mission in life through work with children was not an unusual solution to the problem of a woman's life in this period. What has been presented as particular and interesting about McMillan's writing of childhood, and the connection of her own selfhood with working-class childhood, is that it formed part of a *socialist* vision. The political particularity is useful: having begun to outline the ideological framework to McMillan's claims for children, we may be in a better position to uncover and specify other theories of childhood, in this and other historical periods.

Her theoretical understanding of childhood was as a phenomenon that could act as a form of agency, a means of bringing about great social change; and it told her that her own life was to be lived through and for others. At first, it was various audiences – others – who labelled her a female magus, the possessor of great wisdom and almost mystic powers and knowledge. But after Rachel's death it is possible to see her own mythic appropriation and use of her childhood, an appropriation effected by eliding her own story with that of Rachel, and telling it in the guise of her sister's.

In *The Life of Rachel McMillan*, we need to note the absence of information about McMillan's past until the telling of Rachel's story in 1927; the childhood of silence that is only briefly attributed to a clinical deafness; the beached hulk on the shores of the Hudson, prefiguring Deptford; the wanderings, real and spiritual, through Europe and the English shires; the many initiations that McMillan described – the bombshell of *The Maiden Tribute* in Inverness in 1885; Hyde Park Corner, May Day, 1892; the changeling story, a version of which the old half-timer Charlie Hunt remembered for Miriam Lord as late as 1952, when he wrote about McMillan's supposed adoption by a Lady Eveline and her abandonment of great wealth for the cause of the people.[23] There were also many mystical moments of seeing, some of which have been noted in the preceding pages. The constant movement between herself and the dead Rachel in the *Life*, the handing over of herself and her past to the image of Rachel – whom she did indeed, as Mansbridge observed, make 'an object of worship' – meant that in making her sister a saint, she made herself one too.[24] This transition – what might be called a fiction of self-effacement – is particularly to be seen in McMillan's description of moments of revelation, or inspiration. She mentioned these for the first time in 1913, when she was asked to describe 'The Faith I Live By'. She wrote about 'that verge of life where youth vanishes' and where

> it – the Influence – became an Intelligence. It spoke with a 'voice almost audible to human ears, but with a touch entirely sensed by natural physical organs (the touch sense is old), and then I was driven into the Labour movement and followed the indication of every event or happening with utter obedience, regretting not to have followed it . . . .[25]

Ten years later, the 'moment' had been moved from a broad materialist framework and labelled mysticism. In the 1923 edition of *Education Through the Imagination*, using Bucke's *Cosmic Consciousness*, she described how, in the lives of famous people, 'at a given moment', when they had come to maturity but were still young (she specified an age range of twenty-nine to forty) an incident would occur 'in the nature of a new initiation'.[26] In the letter to Margaret Sutcliffe (1922) in which she provided biographical material for *The Legend of Margaret McMillan*, she specified the 'real event', saying that it took place 'in Ludlow, in a rector's family'. 'When *it* came . . . the Invisible Powers . . . I gave up my post and went to work in the East End . . .'.[27] By 1927 this moment had been transferred to Rachel. McMillan recalled her time in Switzerland, and how she had been sitting 'in a garden at Les Grottes, Geneva' one September evening when she received a letter from Rachel that puzzled her:

> something had happened to Rachel, something that had never happened to me – a sudden inrush of new consciousness . . . a swift realisation where she had thought there was vacancy. Watchful love, strange intelligence, a throbbing companionship near, invisible . . . Joy, great joy . . .[28]

To note that 'the moment' was shifted from the living Margaret to the dead Rachel is not to suggest that something like this never happened to Rachel, nor that McMillan herself never experienced something similar. It is rather to claim that McMillan's telling of her own story in the guise of Rachel's was no mere reaction to Rachel's death, but the culmination of the fictional enterprise of McMillan's own life. Mansbridge saw something of what happened to McMillan in the worship of Rachel and the telling of Rachel's story: 'she endowed her with all the exellences [sic] she could conceive, and in so endowing her, gained power to express them . . .'.[29] All the Lolas and Gutterellas and Mary-Anns and Bobs had permitted her to rewrite herself, express her own sense of loss, of hope deferred. The child – the idea of that child – who could be rescued, but was not rescued, led her to the place where she lost herself in Rachel.

Her last fiction, then – the fiction of 1927 – was the culmination of many writings, the final working out of an agenda that can be seen drawn up in her two 'Mary Muse' pieces of the mid 1890s. In any case McMillan signals these short stories as self-revelatory in a way that others are not, by the eponymous and anagrammatic name of her heroine – and surely by the fact that McMillan *cares* so much, cares that the sister-figure Primrose in the story is faded, and small, and dumpy, and nervous, whilst Mary Muse is tall, and slender, and beautiful: possesses all the graces that she paid homage to in Rachel when she removed her own form from photographs, replacing Margaret with a bannister, or a studio backdrop.[30]

The first 'Mary Muse' story opens in Clearance territory – that is, in a real and historically created place where a tenant farmer uncle makes ready to pay his rent to the landlord, some time in the 1860s, the reader guesses; and also in the terrain of myth, the lost place of the Highland radical romance. As the uncle and aunt talk, and make plain the themes of expropriation, absenteeism and class conflict, the two orphaned nieces sit on the back doorstep, dress their dolls and discuss their future:

'What will you do when you are big?' said Mary at last.
    Primrose removed a pin from her mouth and answered promptly:
    'I will live in a fine house, and have little children – a great many of them – *real* ones – to take care of . . . Then you will bring *your* children Mary, to see mine, and I will say "How do you do Mrs Halleybulley?" and then you will say, "Oh, my dear Mrs Mulligans, my Adelaide has such a cough". You will have one little girl called Adelaide, won't you?'
    'No', said Mary.

'It's one of our finest names, you know', said Primrose, timidly.

'I won't have an Adelaide – I won't have any children,' said Mary. 'I want other work when I am big.'

Primrose opened her eyes wide. 'What will you do?' she asked in amazement . . .[31]

It is love and motherhood that McMillan has Mary Muse either pass through, or conquer, in pursuit of her mission. In the Heavytop Rectory, where she is governess, the nephew of the house loves her, but Mary burns his portrait – the reference to 'raking the cinders together over the face of the heir of the Heavytops'.[32] When Mary finally completes her great work, living now in the Home for Working Women in London, and sits up all night in her cubicle correcting her proofs, she thinks that 'not in vain had she purified and concentrated within herself all the forces of motherhood!'

At the end of this *Clarion* piece, written in September 1894, Mary dies, as we have seen. But she returns again (or her story is returned to) eighteen months later, in 'Mary's Lover'. Mary has been speaking at socialist gatherings, and a working-class woman in one of her audiences has sent her son to fetch Mary to meet her. The Warden of the Home is alarmed at his appearance, and Primrose – 'a snub-nosed young girl who sat there sewing' – makes a brief appearance to urge that Mary be allowed to go – ' "she always does the right thing" '. Part of the story's purpose is to show men of limited vision, like the young temperance orator walking her to his mother, that women had a place on the public platform, in public life, and in the realm of important ideas. But much more than that, it sought to make some common ground between the old working-class woman, 'the whole story of strenuous toil, of dumb effort, written on every line of the aged face', and the beautiful young agitator and writer, to add depth to the son's observation that ' "there ain't no accounting for wimmin folk, young *or* old" '. It is the old woman's motherhood that Mary praises, and that praise brings tears to everybody's eyes. As the young man walks Mary home, he

> continued to expound to Mary his opinions as to the place, function, limitations and deserts of women. The stream of words flowed like the streams of people, and to Mary nothing in it was distinguishable; it was swallowed up by other words, unspoken yet clear enough, that seemed to ring like the clear presence of the aged woman in the clean kitchen where the pewter dishes shone . . . words broken by the sighs for the powers that had waned over washing tubs, and the faculties that had shrivelled in an atmosphere of petty cares; words mingled with Desire that had outlived failure, withstood age, and rose conscious and clear when desire ought to be failing.[33]

When the angry warden questions Mary about her late homecoming –
' "You, a well brought-up girl!" ' – Mary defends herself in what seems
to be support for the immutability of women's work for social good, in
this exchange fraught with misunderstanding:

'It takes a long time to learn to do anything well', said Mary.
  'I am brought up, it is true. And so is he. And you are brought
up Matrona. We are all brought up – wonderfully!'
  'My dear, do you mean to say *my* training was not excellent?'
said Matrona, getting indignant. 'My father was a god-fearing
man, and my mother never left her home, except to go to church
or market. She wouldn't have spent an hour in reading or
recreation of any kind. She was a model woman. But you have
such strange notions. You think you can teach us old people
something, I daresay – we who were capable women before you
were born. It takes a long time to gather wisdom – a very long
time indeed, my dear child.'
  'I know. It takes *ages* to *get bright pewter*,' said Mary . . .

Margaret McMillan did indeed evade the common lot of woman-
kind, of seeing her faculties shrivel in an atmosphere of petty cares.
She chose the public path that she let lie before 'Mary Muse' in the
scrubbed working-class kitchen, and long before that, on the back
doorstep of the Scottish farmhouse. Did she thus achieve the fulfilment of desire that she attributed in its thwarted state to her fictional
subjects of the 1890s, particularly to her several 'Women of the Age
of Gold'? The answer to this question has to be approached through a
consideration of the subjects upon which and with whom she performed her life's work – not women, not working-class women, but
children. We still await the common history of a cultural shift that
might help us towards a complete answer. In general, though, it can
be said that during the nineteenth century the state of childhood
came to be understood as an extension of the self: an extension in
time, into the future, and an extension of depth and space, of
individual interiority – a way of describing the place lying deep
within the individual soul: always a lost place, but at the same time
always there.
  We, as late-twentieth-century inheritors of this Romantic and
post-Romantic configuration, are probably most familiar with a psychoanalytic description of the depth and interiority mapped out in
childhood, and carried unconsciously through life. We have seen
McMillan use and work with some of these ideas; but at the same time
– her biography makes this clear – the means of symbolising the self
through the image of childhood was available from many other sources
at the end of the last century. McMillan's work and writing reveal such

heterogeneous sources, for example, as the mainstream of nineteenth-century realist fiction, and neurological science.

We have seen, too, the particularly interesting uses McMillan made of a wide variety of literary reconstructions of childhood, in particular her effacement of herself in the chapters of *Life of Rachel McMillan* that contain Rachel's *Jugenderinnerungen*. We have gained some insight into the way in which the literary and cultural construct of 'childhood', in which children appear as serious representatives of the human condition, is one that is bound to be in conflict with itself, for it has to operate by denying in some way that childhood is merely a stage in human development, and that children grow up and go away. (Another way for the contradiction to express itself is in some kind of denial that children are different from adults, and the bestowal on them of an adult understanding and an adult sexuality. That version of the contradiction was violently exposed in the 'Maiden Tribute' scandal of the mid 1880s, particularly in the sexualised status it gave to lower-class little girls.)

If we return to Goethe's *Wilhelm Meister* – and to Goethe's Mignon, with whom this particular argument began – we begin to see that in that novel, and in structural and symbolic terms, Mignon provides the hero with a means of contemplating his own thwarted development and immaturity. Goethe *had* to kill the child because she was both symbol *and* reality, had to destroy her out of a recognition that a real and living Mignon, operating on a novel that worked by the conventions of realism, could not be the representative of Meister's psychic wholeness. Mignon's death may be a vulgarity, but it is also a recognition of this point.[34] Working in the social world rather than the space of the novel, McMillan did not face herself with such sharp and difficult choices; indeed, she may come to be recognised as one who, whilst attempting self-effacement in the image of childhood, also paid serious attention to its temporariness as a social state, and in a quite material way worked to allow children to grow – tall, healthy, beautiful – and of course to grow up, and go away.

I first encountered McMillan's writing when I was teaching young children in the late 1970s, in a reading that has to have taken place, but which I cannot actually remember, however hard I try. I always worked in very poor schools (that is, schools in poor areas) where the children were much preoccupied with the exigencies of the adult life around them. Reading McMillan gave shape to what seemed to me the obvious way of proceeding: I wanted to give the children a meal and put them to bed for a few hours before doing anything else. Often, I wished there were a bath in the school.

I was teaching in the heyday of deprivationalist thinking, of the construction of various theories of language acquisition and language impairment that all reached, it seemed to me, a very old conclusion by a new and tawdry route: that in some way the children of the unskilled working class were stupid, and probably ineducable.[35] This was a belief held with a good deal of social pity and social kindness by some left-wing teachers as well as many conservative ones. I gritted my teeth a lot, and thought that they were not only wrong but politically incorrect into the bargain; so to read McMillan's accounts of the calm assumption that *of course* it all belonged to those children – the ability to read, to be intelligent, to have a good time, to read books, possess high culture as well as low – was a great comfort.

I started to work on McMillan believing that I would find out more about the way in which intelligence, cognition and language had been added to the checklist of class divisions and class condescension over the last century. McMillan's story turned out not to tell me a great deal about this development, and of course along the way I discovered that she too had used a theory of language deprivation, though in the 1910s and 1920s it did not carry the weight of condemnation that it was later to have; for McMillan it was a means of description rather than an explanatory device. The world changed as well, in the decade I spent working on McMillan. Whilst it seemed then that the idea of linguistic and cultural deprivation was the greatest and most restrictive burden placed on Class IV and V children in school, we have now returned to a starker agenda, for some time in the last ten years, when no one was noticing, a hard-won consensus in the establishment of which McMillan had played an important role – that as a society we fed our children, and ensured them the baseline of good health that allowed them to benefit from schooling – just quietly disappeared.[36]

I watched McMillan's disappearance into the children she encountered, her self-effacement in the 'continued accession of children' – what her old friends thought of as her 'obsession' – and saw how the idea of social motherhood had come to rest in both the training of teachers in mid-twentieth-century Britain, and – more interestingly and importantly – the daily experience of self-effacement in the job of work that teaching is.[37] I think I came to understand, through a growing acquaintance with McMillan's writing and thought, that when we weep for children it is for ourselves that we weep; in the attempt to rescue them, we search for our own lost self. I recognise now, I think, how very little distinction we make (are able to make) between real children and our fantasy children; that as we talk to, watch, teach and write about children, we want something from them, desire them: want the thing we can't have, which is the past: our own lost childhood.

Now, with an account of McMillan's life and work completed, a question is made clear that was not clear before. What are the social implications of the kind of symbolising of childhood that McMillan tried to put on a political agenda? What is the import of our various theories of childhood, implicitly or overtly held? There is much work to be done here, though we do have sketch-maps stored towards an answer, mainly drawn up by the literary theorists whose work has been used in the preceding pages. It seems to me that this is how we must start, in literary and representational terms – by recognising that children are the first metaphor for all people, whether they have children or not, whether they are literate and in the business of constructing literary metaphors or not: a mapping of analogy and meaning for the self, always in shape and form *like us*, the visual connection plain to see.

As children are produced materially out of women's bodies, and as in all known societies women, whether actual mothers or not, have played the greater role in their care, we should expect variation in the uses of childhood made by men and women; but not that much variation, as it is in the power of children to represent the loss of the self and the extension of the self into the future that the theoretical purchase lies. McMillan knew this usage when she sought to make the metaphorical *meaning* of children available to their parents, especially to men and women of the unskilled labouring poor, whom she saw as starved of this inheritance as well as all the others. Their children were not only to be the means to culture; they *were* the culture that they had 'to get . . . now . . . before they win'. 'The lost human life and language which the greatest preachers, artists and philanthropists had sought in vain to win back, is recalled by children', said McMillan, and describing the Bradford schoolchildren taking their drawings home to their parents, she commented:

> If the voice of their own children – and the art of their own children, true, not imposed from without, but expressing feelings that have already been lived through – if this be ineffectual, then all the popular concerts, free art galleries and philanthropic entertainers can never hope to succeed.[38]

Ten years later she possessed a vocabulary for the condemnation of working-class parents, but still made the same political point, arguing that

> the sorry lack of ambition on the part of the masses lies at the root of all failure. They will not believe in themselves or their children, but only in their rulers. And as 'ruling' is a trade and a very well paid one, the masses are the best disciplined and least enlightened people in the world.[39]

She turns, she looks; a child stares gravely back: it is the world's salvation, herself, who stands there.

Notes

The place of publication is London, unless otherwise specified. The abbreviation PP stands for the Parliamentary Paper Series.

PART ONE

Introduction

1 For an account of the teleological approach of most history of childhood, see Hugh Cunningham, 'Slaves or Savages? Some Attitudes to Labouring Children, 1750–1870', unpublished paper, 1987. The kind of history of childhood that is analysed here may be found in Lloyd deMause, *The History of Childhood*, Souvenir Press, New York, 1976; or more recently in Thomas E. Jordan, *Victorian Childhood, Themes and Variations*, State University of New York Press, Albany, 1987.

2 See below, pp.233–5. For an introduction to the idea of the rhetoric of the visual in nineteenth-century political oratory, see Paul A. Pickering, 'Class Without Words: Symbolic Communication in the Chartist Movement', *Past and Present*, 112 (August 1986), pp.144–62.

3 Albert Mansbridge, *Margaret McMillan, Prophet and Pioneer: Her Life and Work*, Dent, 1932.

4 D'Arcy Cresswell, *Margaret McMillan, A Memoir*, Hutchinson, 1948. George Lowndes, *Margaret McMillan, The Children's Champion*, Museum Press, 1960.

5 Elizabeth Bradburn, *Margaret McMillan: Framework and Expansion of Nursery Education*, Denholm Press, Redhill, 1976.

6 Margaret McMillan, *The Life of Rachel McMillan*, Dent, 1927.

7 The 'childhood' – the *Jugenderinnerungen* – is distinguished from the *Bildungsroman* by Richard N. Coe, in *When the Grass Was Taller, Autobiography and the Experience of Childhood*, Yale University Press, New Haven, 1984, pp.1–40. For a recent account of the *Bildungsroman*, see Franco Moretti, *The Way of the World: The Bildungsroman in European Culture*, Verso, 1987. See below, pp.72–80.

8 See, for example, its use by Stephen Yeo in 'A New Life: The Religion of Socialism in Britain, 1883–1896', *History Workshop Journal*, 4 (Autumn 1977), pp.5–56.

9 See, for example, Basil Bernstein, *Class, Codes and Control, Volume 3: Towards a Theory of Educational Transmissions*, Routledge & Kegan Paul, 1977, p.132; and Jane Lewis, *Women in England, 1870–1950*, Wheatsheaf, Brighton, pp.36, 43.

10 See the Bibliography for a complete list of archive sources. The McMillan Collection at the Rachel McMillan College Library, Deptford, has been moved to Manor House Library, Lewisham since the research for this book was completed.

11 British Museum, Additional Manuscripts, Mansbridge Collection, C (i), Albert Mansbridge to Mrs Stanton Coit, 5 June 1931, and Albert Mansbridge to David Eder, 5 June 1931. Both letters indicate omissions and suppressions in the biography Mansbridge produced.

12 For a brief introductory account of the nursery school movement, see Nanette Whitbread, *The Evolution of the Nursery-Infant School: A History of Infant and Nursery Education in Britain, 1800–1970*, Routledge & Kegan Paul, 1972, pp.53–80. See also Grace Owen (ed.), *Nursery School Education*, Methuen, 1920, and P. Cusden, *The English Nursery School*, Kegan Paul, 1938.

13 See below, pp.139–40.

14 Reading University Library, Astor Papers, MS 1416/1/4/68, Margaret McMillan to Nancy Astor, 2 April 1927, and MS 1416/1/179, Margaret McMillan to Nancy Astor, 11 August 1927. MS 1416/1/1/74, Margaret McMillan to Nancy Astor, 23 February 1928: 'O my dear! How dreadful to worship Party – It's like worshipping Punch and Judy.'

15 Margaret McMillan, 'Drink in Labour Clubs', *Clarion*, 24 February 1894.

16 On this point, see Gareth Stedman Jones, 'Rethinking Chartism', in *Languages of Class, Studies in English Working Class History, 1832–1982*, Cambridge University Press, Cambridge, 1983, pp.90–178.

17 Kenneth O. Morgan: *Labour People, Leaders and Lieutenants: Hardie to Kinnock*, Oxford University Press, 1987.

18 McMillan, *Life*, p.80.

19 Kathryn Dodd, 'Historians, the Evidence of Texts, and Ray Strachey's *The Cause*', unpublished paper, 1986. Ray Strachey, *The Cause* (1928), Virago, 1988.

20 For introductory discussions of post-Wordsworthian constructions of childhood, see Peter Coveney, *The Image of Childhood, The Individual and Society: A Study of the Theme in English Literature* (first published as *Poor Monkey*, Rockliff, 1957), Penguin, 1967, pp.68–90; Carolyn Steedman, *The Tidy House*, Virago, 1982, pp.61–94. See also Ann Thwaite, *Waiting for the Party, The Life of Frances Hodgson Burnett*, Secker & Warburg, 1974, for a brief but suggestive account of childhood as a new interiority in the period under discussion.

21 See Coe, pp.41–75, on this point.

22 McMillan first used this phrase in 'Save the Children, A Plea for the Social Treatment of Disease', *Labour Leader*, 17 November 1911.

23 Dodd, p.13.

24 For biographical accounts of McMillan's life, see Notes 4 and 5. See also the new account in Elizabeth Bradburn, *Margaret McMillan, Portrait of a Pioneer*, Routledge, 1989. This has not been consulted for the present study.

25 Margaret McMillan, 'School Board Notes', *Bradford Labour Echo*, 22 October 1897.

26 Yeo, p.49, quoting William Morris, from G.D.H. Cole, *William Morris: Selected Writing*, Nonesuch, 1948, p.671.

27 For the cultural project of British socialism and the Ruskinian tradition, see Stanley Pierson, *Marxism and the Origin of British Socialism*, Cornell

University Press, 1973, pp.22–38. See Fred Reid, *Keir Hardie, The Making of a Socialist*, Croom Helm, 1978, pp.151–3 for the definition of culture as social rescue work. See Raymond Williams, *Culture and Society* (1958), Hogarth Press, 1987, pp.71–195 for the conceptualisation of culture inherited by men and women like Hardie and McMillan.

28 See below, pp.105–6, 116–17, 168.

29 Raymond Williams, *Problems in Materialism and Culture*, Verso, 1980, pp.155–6.

PART TWO

1 'Rachel'

1 Margaret McMillan, *Life of Rachel McMillan*, Dent, 1927, p.3. (Hereafter McMillan, *Life*.)

2 McMillan, *Life*, p.3. Albert Mansbridge, *Margaret McMillan, Prophet and Pioneer: Her Life and Work*, Dent, 1932, chapter 1.

3 ibid., pp. 8, 10.

4 ibid., p.6. For the *Jugenderinnerungen*, see Richard N. Coe, *When the Grass Was Taller: Autobiography and the Experience of Childhood*, Yale University Press, New Haven, 1984.

5 McMillan, *Life*, p.8.

6 ibid., p.12.

7 ibid., p.15. *The Inverness Directory*, 1893, shows that Hawthorne Cottage was surrounded by the houses of dentists, drapers and solicitors.

8 McMillan, *Life*, pp.15–16.

9 ibid., pp.14–15.

10 David Howell, *British Workers and the Independent Labour Party, 1886–1906*, Manchester University Press, Manchester, 1983, pp.133–4.

11 Much of McMillan's romantic fiction was set in the Highlands and Islands. See, for example, the twenty-nine-part 'Handel Stumm', which appeared in the *Labour Leader* between September 1900 and March 1901. Other stories with a Scottish setting included Margaret McMillan, 'A School in the Western Isles', *Ethics*, 5 September 1903; 'Sorcha's Dream', *Weekly Times and Echo*, 5 March 1905; 'Ishbel's Return', *Weekly Times and Echo*, 23 September 1906; 'The Robber: A Tale of the Hebrides', *Weekly Times and Echo*, 16 September 1906; 'The Alien', *Weekly Times and Echo*, 26 May 1907. Her Scottishness was sold as part of her platform appeal. See, for example, Bradford *Labour Echo*, 21 January 1899, and an account of her address to the Caledonian Christian Club in London, in the *Inverness Chronicle*, 27 February 1905.

12 McMillan, *Life*, pp.2–3.

13 ibid., p.15.

14 ibid., p.16.

15 British Museum Additional Manuscripts, Mansbridge Collection, C (i), I. (Cameron) Jeaffreson to Albert Mansbridge, n.d.

16 For an account of the mythologies involved in Scottish education and its history, see Robert Anderson, 'In Search of the "Lad of Parts": The Mythical History of Scottish Education', *History Workshop Journal*, 19

(Spring 1985), pp.82–104.

17 In 1927 McMillan was making a comparison between the Scottish educational system of the mid nineteenth century, when schoolmasters were university graduates, and the English system of the 1920s, when elementary-school teachers were trained at teachers' colleges.

18 McMillan, *Life*, p.19.

19 See, for example, her advice in Julia Dawson, 'Our Woman's Letter', *Clarion*, 26 February 1904, and the chapter 'Literature and Children' in Margaret McMillan, *Early Childhood*, Swan Sonnenschein, 1900, pp.98–112.

20 Rachel McMillan College Library, McMillan Collection, A/86, Margaret McMillan to the Revd John McKenzie, n.d.; noted by Mansbridge, pp.9–10, as being dated 7 July 1930.

21 For the Ladies' College, see annotated material in Rachel McMillan College Library, McMillan Collection, A/9.

22 McMillan, *Life*, pp.21–2.

23 ibid., p.24. See Ann Summers, *Angels and Citizens*, Routledge 1988, pp.1–28, for a general introduction to the professionalisation of nursing in the mid nineteenth century.

24 McMillan, *Life*, p.21.

25 I have not been able to trace McMillan's employer, whom Mansbridge named as a Mrs Drummond of Craiglockhart, in either census material or local directories.

26 Bradford Record Office, Miriam Lord Collection, 22D/77/3/5. Copy of letter from Margaret McMillan to Margaret Sutcliffe, 12 December 1922.

27 By a process of elimination it is safe to assume that McMillan was employed by Edward ffarington Clayton, Rector of Ludlow. His was the only rectory within a radius of ten miles that had little girls and young women living in it in the late 1880s. For ffarington Clayton, see *Ludlow Advertiser*, 30 November 1907; *The Times*, 25 November 1907. This very grand family (the Reverend Clayton had married one of the Windsor Clives, of the family of the Earls of Plymouth) was probably McMillan's source for her satires of gentry and country house life.

28 McMillan, 'How I Became a Socialist', *Labour Leader*, 11 July 1912. See also below, pp.253–4. For Laurence Oliphant, see Anne Taylor, *Laurence Oliphant, 1829–1888*, Oxford University Press, 1982, pp.219–20, and her account of his *Sympneumata, or, Evolutionary Forms Now Active in Men*, Blackwood, Edinburgh, 1885, which in obscure language sought to define a power called Sympneumata: 'This was the faculty of superhuman vision, hearing, strength, and resistance to disease and death . . . it was the duty of those beings possessed of Sympneumata to impart it to their fellows . . . Thus, slowly, would the regeneration of the race occur, and men and women be restored to their happy condition of before the Fall. Prior to that event, male and female had been joined in one being and sexual love was pure . . .'. Given the context in which McMillan was remembering this event of the 1880s, and the privileged place that Oliphant gave to women in the struggle for purity, it is most likely that this odd book was the one Rachel sent to her.

29 McMillan, *Life*, p.25.
30 ibid., p.6.
31 Arguments for McMillan's own adherence to spiritualism have been developed out of these descriptions; but we should probably look to the platform appeal of 'Scottishness' in this period, audience expectation of Scottish mysticism and Highland 'feyness', and its shaping of some early ILP rhetoric. But on Keir Hardie's spiritualism, see Kenneth O. Morgan, 'Writing Political Biography', in Eric Homberger and John Charmley, *The Troubled Face of Biography*, Macmillan, 1988, pp.33–48. On the ILP fondness for a good séance, see Janet Oppenheim, *The Other World: Spiritualism and Psychical Research in England, 1850–1914*, Cambridge University Press, Cambridge, 1985, pp.88–9. See below, pp.220–21, for a further discussion of these questions.
32 The American girl of 'How I Became a Socialist' becomes 'Zoë' the nihilist, in the *Clarion* story of that title, 9 March 1895. Bradford Record Office, Miriam Lord Collection, 22D/7/9/15. Testimony of Charlie Hunt, 1955.
33 For some discussion of the literary transmutations of this figure, see Robert Pattison, *The Child Figure in English Literature*, University of Georgia Press, Athens, 1978, pp.1–65.
34 McMillan, *Life*, p.6.
35 See Peter Coveney, *The Image of Childhood, The Individual and Society: A Study of the Theme in English Literature* (originally published as *Poor Monkey*, Rockliff, 1958), Penguin, 1967, pp.11–161.
36 McMillan *Life*, pp.184–7.
37 Arthur Greenwood, *'All Children Are Mine': The Inaugural Margaret McMillan Lecture*, University of London Press for the Margaret McMillan Fellowship, 1952, p.6.
38 Stephen Yeo, 'A New Life: The Religion of Socialism in Britain, 1883–1896', *History Workshop Journal*, 4 (Autumn 1977), pp.5–56.
39 McMillan, *Life*, pp.26–7.
40 Donald C. Smith, 'The Failure and Recovery of Social Criticism in the Scottish Church, 1830–1850', Ph.D thesis, Edinburgh, 1963, pp.383–97.
41 McMillan, *Life*, p.27.
42 For an account of 'The Maiden Tribute' campaign, see R.L. Schults, *Crusader in Babylon: W.T. Stead and the Pall Mall Gazette*, University of Nebraska Press, Lincoln, 1972, pp.128–92; and *Pall Mall Gazette*, 6,7,8,10 July 1885. The series was published in a pamphlet in the following week: Schults, pp.153–4. See *The Maiden Tribute of Modern Babylon. The Report of the "Pall Mall Gazette's" Secret Commission*, 1885.
43 Deborah Gorham, 'The "Maiden Tribute of Modern Babylon" Re-examined: Child Prostitution and the Idea of Childhood in Late Victorian England', *Victorian Studies*, 21:3 (Spring 1978), pp.353–79.
44 Sheila Jeffreys, *The Spinster and her Enemies: Feminism and Sexuality, 1880–1930*, Pandora, 1985.
45 Gorham, 'The "Maiden Tribute of Modern Babylon" Re-examined', *passim*.
46 Yeo, p.11.
47 McMillan, *Life*, pp.200–01.
48 Howell, p.133.

49 For John Glasse (1848–1918), see Smith, pp.360–70; C. Desmond Greaves, *The Life and Times of James Connolly*, Lawrence & Wishart, 1961, pp.30–31, 40–45. See also John Glasse, *The Relation of the Church to Socialism*, Edinburgh Branch of the ILP, Edinburgh, 1900; *Modern Christian Socialism*, Co-operative Wholesale Society, Manchester, 1897. The Edinburgh branch of the Socialist League had a clear sense of its own innovative history. It had been formed in 1884, and under its auspices William Morris had lectured. John Gilray, who wrote an account of these early days, called this event 'the first indoor meeting of a public character for the preaching of modern socialism ever held in Edinburgh'. The Society changed its name, and many of its members became involved in the Scottish Land and Labour League; but all these groups contributed to the atmosphere of intense public debate over socialism and social issues that Rachel encountered on her visit. Writing his column on 'Socialism in Scotland' for the *Commonweal* of February 1887, A.K. Donald noted that 'In Edinburgh, which is the most bourgeois town perhaps in Britain, we are able to get the halls filled Sunday after Sunday by the very best class of workman. You have simply to look at the faces of the audience and it becomes apparent that these men are not to be trifled with. They mean business and now that they are convinced of the necessity of appropriating their exploiters, no power on earth will turn them from their purpose . . . .'.

50 Though he does not appear to have lectured in the Meadows until autumn 1887, and according to McMillan, Rachel visited Edinburgh much earlier in the year. *Commonweal*, 2 October 1887.

51 One of a series of laws proposed and passed in the 1880s, which were designed to defuse Irish agrarian unrest by giving the Irish administration special powers, including the suspension of habeas corpus.

52 McMillan, *Life*, pp.27–8.

53 *Commonweal*, 25 June 1887. Bernard Campbell Ransom, 'James Connolly and the Scottish Left, 1890–1916', Ph.D, Edinburgh, 1975, pp.8–9. Greaves, op.cit., pp.30–31.

54 Gilray, pp.8–9. McMillan, *Life*, p.29.

55 McMillan, *Life*, p.30.

56 ibid., p.33.

57 Though as Martha Vicinus and others have pointed out, as late as 1901 only 45.5 per cent of spinsters were occupied in some form of employment. Martha Vicinus, *Independent Women: Work and Community for Single Women, 1850–1920*, Virago, 1985, p.27.

58 McMillan, *Life*, p.33. See M. Jeanne Peterson, 'The Victorian Governess: Status Incongruence in Family and Society', *Victorian Studies*, 14:1 (1970), pp.7–26, for some discussion of governesses' salaries.

59 McMillan, *Life*, p.79.

60 B.J. Bledstein, *The Culture of Professionalism*, Norton, New York, 1976, pp.68–9, 118.

61 Sanitary Institute, *Examinations in Sanitary Science for Local Surveyors and Inspectors of Nuisances*, Sanitary Institute, 1892.

62 'List of Associates of the Sanitary Institute', *Journal of the Sanitary*

Institute, 16 (1895–6), p.522. For the development of health visiting, see Jane Robinson, *An Evaluation of Health Visiting*, Council for the Education and Training of Health Visitors, 1982, pp.4–22; Robert N.J. Dingwall, 'Collectivism, Regionalism and Feminism: Health Visiting and British Social Policy, 1850–1975', *Journal of Social Policy*, 6:3 (July 1977), pp.291–315; W.M. Frazer, *A History of English Public Health, 1834–1939*, Ballière, Tindall & Cox, 1950.

63 G.F. McCleary, *The Maternity and Child Welfare Movement*, P.S. King, 1935.

64 McMillan, *Life*, pp.91, 81. *Liverpool Labour Chronicle*, 1 August, 2 September, 2 December 1895.

65 London School of Economics, Records of the British Association for Early Childhood Education, Nursery School Association Papers, Box 18, Margaret McMillan to Miss Sanger, n.d.: 'If you reprint my pamphlet would you mind seeing that they spell my name as I spell it, and always in the same way. One of the idiosyncrasies of the N.S.A. was that they never *could* spell my name or my sister's . . .'.

66 *Liverpool Labour Chronicle*, 2 December 1895. A report of the Women's Industrial Council meeting, to consider 'the appointment of a paid Organising Secretary in place of Miss Rachel McMillan'.

67 Kent County Council, Technical Education Committee Minute Books, 1891–1903, CC/MC12/1/1–7. E. Melling, *A History of Kent County Council*, Kent County Council, Maidstone, 1975, pp.12–15. George M. Arnold, *Some Account of the Work of Education Under the Kent Technical Education Committee*, Maidstone, 1903. I am very grateful to Sue Garland, Assistant Archivist, Kent Archives Office, Maidstone, for helping me on this point.

68 McMillan, *Life*, pp.93–4.

69 ibid., pp.98–9.

70 Mansbridge, p.54.

71 McMillan, *Life*, pp.108–9.

72 In the 1920s, McMillan conceived her plan of a training college in memory of her sister. That was the last stage of her Deptford project. See below, pp.184–7.

73 McMillan, *Life*, p.154.

74 Margaret McMillan, *The Camp School*, Allen & Unwin, 1917, pp.174–5. (Second ellipsis by McMillan.)

75 ibid., p.178.

76 British Museum, Additional Manuscripts, Mansbridge Collection, B2 (iii), Margaret McMillan to Albert Mansbridge, 20 July 1927: 'Yes. I've got a pension. Rachel would have been glad. I feel she *is* glad . . .'.

77 Reading University Library, Astor Papers, MS1416/1/4/68, Margaret McMillan to Nancy Astor, 2 April 1927.

78 Rachel McMillan Collection Library, McMillan Collection, A2/7, 'In Holiday Hours'. I assume that these are notes for a lecture.

2 *Politics*

1 Margaret McMillan, 'How I Became a Socialist', *Labour Leader*, 11 July 1912. This Highland history is implicit in an earlier possible meeting of

McMillan with John Stuart Blackie, which Mansbridge described. In his biography of McMillan he quotes from a letter (which is not preserved in the Mansbridge Collection) from McMillan's Edinburgh employer, Mrs Drummond, who recalled in 1931 that 'John Stuart Blackie was a frequent visitor. He became attached to her. They had many long talks together' (*Margaret McMillan, Prophet and Pioneer: Her Life and Work*, Dent, 1932, p.12). Blackie was also working on 'The Philosophy of Education' in *Essays on Social Subjects* (David Douglas, Edinburgh, 1890) in these years. John Stuart Blackie, Professor Emeritus of Greek at Edinburgh University, had by 1879 become Chief of the Gaelic Society, and was working on his *Gaelic Societies, Highland Depopulation and Land Law Reform*. The questions raised by Blackie in the years before the formation of the Scottish Land Restoration League and the Scottish Land and Labour League may well have offered McMillan a political perspective on the family history learned in Inverness. John Stuart Blackie, *Gaelic Societies, Highland Depopulation and Land Law Reform*, David Douglas, Edinburgh, 1880.

2 See below, pp.254–6.
3 McMillan's six articles for the *Christian Socialist* were 'A Sign of the Times', October 1899; 'The Church and Socialism', December 1889; 'Liberty', April 1890; 'Labour, the Mother of Capital', June 1890; 'Evolution and Revolution', August 1890; and 'Help', April 1891.
4 G.C. Binyon, *The Christian Socialist Movement in England*, SPCK, 1931.
5 W.H. Paul Campbell, *The Robbery of the Poor*, Modern Press, 1884.
6 James Hinton, *Labour and Socialism: A History of the British Labour Movement, 1867–1974*, Wheatsheaf, Brighton, 1983, pp.46–8. W.H. Paul Campbell, 'Notes on the Great Strike', *Christian Socialist*, September 1889.
7 McMillan, 'Sign of the Times' (1899).
8 McMillan, *Life*, p.38. British Museum Add Ms. 46289, f.24, W.H. Paul Campbell to John Burns, 10 September 1889.
9 McMillan, 'Sign of the Times' (1899).
10 With P.H. Wicksteed and J. Bruce Wallace. See Peter d'A. Jones, *The Christian Socialist Revival, 1877–1914*, Princeton University Press, Princeton, 1968, p.313. For the Labour Church, see Stanley Pierson, *Marxism and the Origins of British Socialism*, Cornell University Press, Ithaca, 1973, and 'John Trevor and the Labour Church Movement in England, 1891–1900', *Church History*, 29:4 (December 1960), pp.463–78. See also John Trevor, *My Quest for God*, Labour Prophet Office, 1897; Stephen and Yeo, 'A New Life: The Religion of Socialism in Britain, 1883–1896, *History Workshop Journal*, 4 (Autumn 1977), pp.38–9.
11 *Labour Prophet*, June 1892. Joseph Edwards (ed.), *Labour Annual*, Labour Press, Manchester, 1895, pp.212–13.
12 Nuffield College Library, Fabian Society Papers, C4, Minute Book, entry dated 12 September 1892.
13 She spoke in Manchester and Salford in June 1892: *Labour Prophet*, June 1892; in Ordsall in May and October 1893: *Clarion*, 28 May, 7 October 1893.

14 McMillan, *Life*, p.75.
15 Keith Laybourn, '"The Defence of the Bottom Dog": The Independent Labour Party in Local Politics', in D.G. Wright and J.A. Jowett, *Victorian Bradford, Essays in Honour of Jack Reynolds*, City of Bradford Metropolitan Council, Bradford, 1981, pp.223–44. Keith Laybourn and Jack Reynolds, *Liberalism and the Rise of Labour, 1890–1918*, Croom Helm, 1984, pp.1–94.
16 See David Howell, *British Workers and the Independent Labour Party, 1886–1906*, Manchester University Press, Manchester, 1983, pp.293–300; Hinton, p.58. See also E.P. Thompson, 'Homage to Tom Maguire', in Asa Briggs and John Saville (eds), *Essays in Labour History*, Macmillan, 1977, pp.276–316.
17 See below, pp.62–8. This shift has been generally neglected by historians, but Eric Hobsbawm reflects on it in *The Age of Empire, 1895–1914*, Weidenfeld & Nicolson, 1987, pp.149–50.
18 Howell, pp.343–85.
19 ibid., p.345.
20 John Hurt, *Elementary Schooling and the Working Classes, 1860–1918*, Routledge & Kegan Paul, 1979, p.75.
21 Laybourn (1981), p.224.
22 ibid., p.234.
23 ibid., p.241.
24 ibid., p.233.
25 Margaret McMillan, 'Levana', *Clarion*, 14 August, 1897.
26 For some account of the women propagandists of the ILP, see Yeo, 'A New Life'.
27 Howell, p.165.
28 ibid., p.358.
29 Fred Reid, *Keir Hardie: The Making of a Socialist*, Croom Helm, 1978, pp.182–3.
30 *Labour Echo*, 30 November 1895. Quoted by Reynolds and Laybourn, p.319.
31 Laybourn (1981), p.240.
32 J.H. Palin, *Bradford and Its Children: How They Are Fed*, ILP, n.d. Keith Laybourn, 'The Issue of School Feeding in Bradford, 1904–1907', *Journal of Educational Administration and History*, 14:2 (July 1982), pp. 30–39.
33 Laybourn (1981), pp.229–33.
34 *Labour Leader*, 28 April 1894. *Clarion*, 9 May 1894. McMillan, 'How I Became a Socialist' (1912).
35 *Clarion*, 1 December 1894.
36 W.D. Ross, 'Bradford Politics, 1880–1906', Ph.D, Bradford University, 1977, pp.208–54.
37 Margaret McMillan, 'My Experiences on the School Board', *Labour Prophet*, November 1895.
38 Patricia Hollis, *Ladies Elect: Women in English Local Government*, Clarendon Press, Oxford, pp.132–92, *passim*.
39 ibid., pp.179–83.
40 Hurt, p.96.

41 McMillan, *Life*, pp.86–7.
42 Evidently to much local delight and amusement. *Labour Echo*, 4 September 1897: 'the last meeting of the Bradford School Board was a remarkably quiet one. The Very Reverend Canon Simpson was absent and Margaret McMillan had doffed her war paint.'
43 *Bradford Observer*, 24 January 1895, Report of the Bradford School Board Meeting of 23 January 1895. Bradford Record Office, Bradford School Board Records, School Attendance Sub-Committee Minute Book, 52D75/7, Meeting of 17 December 1895. School Attendance Sub-Committee Minute Book, 52D75/7/4, Meeting of 23 March 1896.
44 Report of the Fifth Annual Conference of the Independent Labour Party, 1897, p.22. Margaret McMillan, 'One of the Trespassers', *Clarion*, 11 May 1895.
45 Margaret McMillan, 'The Half-Time System', *Clarion*, 12 September, 19 September 1896.
46 Enid Stacey, 'Women's Work and the ILP', in Edwards, pp.116–18. Katharine St John Conway, *The Cry of the Children*, Labour Press, Manchester, 1894.
47 Margaret McMillan, 'School Board Notes', *Bradford Labour Echo*, 18 September 1897.
48 *Bradford Observer*, 24 January 1895.
49 Later, in much of her popular journalism, she was to evolve an argument in which Christianity's rejection of the physical body and material life was seen to lie in the way of social reform. Margaret McMillan, 'A Forecast of Civilisation', *Ethical World*, 21 October, 28 October 1899.
50 McMillan, 'My Experiences' (1895).
51 Malcolm Hardman, *Ruskin and Bradford: An Experiment in Victorian Cultural History*, Manchester University Press, Manchester, 1986, p.309.
52 Margaret McMillan, 'School Board Notes', *Bradford Labour Echo*, 18 September 1897. Thomas Carlyle, *Past and Present* (1843), Chapman & Hall, 1893, p.201. See below, pp.111–12, 198–9.
53 For James Kerr, see below, pp.110, 204. For his appointment and a general account of his work, see *Education in Bradford Since 1870*, Bradford Corporation, Bradford, 1970.
54 His inspections reached a wide audience. See 'Notes from the Front', *Clarion*, 6 April 1895.
55 *Bradford Labour Echo*, 1 May 1897. *Bradford Observer*, 22 July 1897.
56 Margaret McMillan, 'The Ventilation of Schools', *Labour Echo*, 15 May 1897. 'School Board Notes', *Labour Echo*, 18 September, 25 September, 22 October 1897. 'Physical Training', *Labour Echo*, 12 November 1898. 'Rest', *Labour Echo*, 21 January 1898. 'Baths', *Labour Echo*, 13 May 1899.
57 For Édouard Seguin, see below, pp.194–8. McMillan made specific reference to Seguin's work in 'School Board Notes', *Labour Echo*, 19 November 1898, though his theories of mind–body relationship are at work in all her *Echo* pieces.
58 '"Good morning. Sorry to find you indisposed", and taking a chair I endeavoured to return the cheery smile of the first educationalist in Bradford.' 'Miss McMillan Interviewed', *Bradford Labour Echo*, 23 May

1896. 'Tomorrow . . . Margaret McMillan will speak in the afternoon on "Children and Exercise" and in the evening on "Children and Rest". Miss McMillan, as our columns can testify, is an expert on such subjects, and those who fail to give themselves the pleasure of listening to her will miss a treat.' *Bradford Labour Echo*, 21 January 1899.

59 *Labour Echo*, 9 May 1896.

60 Margaret McMillan, 'To the Electors: ILP Special No. 1', *Labour Echo*, 9 July 1895.

61 Margaret McMillan, 'To the Electors', *Labour Echo*, 11 July 1895.

62 *Bradford Observer*, 19, 23, 25, 29 November 1897.

63 Ross, pp. 268–9.

64 ibid., pp. 255–94.

65 Bradford Record Office, Bradford School Board Records, School Board Minute Book, 52D75/I/10, Meeting of 24 March 1897, reported in the *Bradford Observer*, 26 March 1897. Special Meeting of 28 May 1897, reported in the *Bradford Observer*, 29 May 1897. School Management Sub-Committee Minute Book, 25D75/II/8/8, Meetings of 24 May, 25 June, 6 December 1898. Meeting of 10 January, 21 February, 24 April 1899. *Tenth Triennial Report of the Proceedings of the School Board for the Three Years Ended November 30, 1900*, School Board Office, Bradford, pp. 117, 118, 135, 148–50, pp. 154–5. *Labour Leader*, 15 April 1899.

66 Howell, op. cit., p. 347.

67 Ross, pp. 220–53.

68 Bradford Record Office, School Board Records, School Board Minute Books, 52D75/I/10. Meeting of 28 September 1898, in which McMillan quarrelled with John Cryer of the NUT. Reported in the *Bradford Observer*, 29 September 1898.

69 Margaret McMillan, 'Schools and School Boards', *Cooperative News*, 20 December 1900.

70 *Bradford Observer*, 13 November 1900.

71 Brian Simon, *Education and the Labour Movement, 1870–1920*, Lawrence & Wishart, 1965, pp. 208–46. Margaret McMillan, 'The Higher Grade Schools', *Clarion*, 17 August 1901.

72 ILP, *Report of the Tenth Annual Conference of the ILP*, 1902, pp. 24–5.

73 Simon, pp. 176–9.

74 Bradford Record Office, Bradford School Board Records, Education Committee Minute Book, 52D75/I/11, Meeting of the Board in Committee, 7 June 1899. 52D75/II/3, Meetings of 13 July, 18 July 1900. *Tenth Triennial Report of the Proceedings of the School Board for Bradford During the Three Years Ended November 30, 1900*, pp. 118, 133–4.

75 R. Roberts, 'The People's Schools', *Labour Leader*, 1 January 1901. See also R. Roberts, 'Board Schools and Ethical Education', *Ethical World*, 25 August 1900.

76 Simon, pp. 194–5, 197–9, 232–3. Margaret McMillan, 'Schools and School Boards', *Clarion*, 20 July 1901.

77 Margaret McMillan, 'The Government and the People's Schools', *Ethical World*, 29 September 1900.

78 ibid.

79 Bradford Record Office, School Board Records, *Eleventh Triennial Report of the Proceedings of the School Board for Bradford During the Three Years Ended November 30, 1903*, p.33, for Kerr's move to London. For his subsequent career in London, Bentley B. Gilbert, *The Evolution of National Insurance in Britain: The Origins of the Welfare State*, Michael Joseph, 1966, pp.133–43. For Roberts's move, University of Warwick, Modern Records Office, John Trevor Papers, MSS/143/19. Also *Democracy*, 4 May 1901.
80 For Stanton Coit, see I.D. MacKillop, *The British Ethical Societies*, Cambridge University Press, Cambridge, 1986, pp.99–137.
81 For the ethical movement, see Gustave Spiller, *The Ethical Movement in Great Britain: A Documentary History*, printed for the author at the Farleigh Press, 1934, and MacKillop, *The British Ethical Societies*.
82 MacKillop, p.108.
83 Spiller, p.166.
84 Her imminent arrival in London was eagerly awaited. See *Ethics*, 22 November 1902; also *Ethics*, 6 December 1902: One of the most attractive courses of lectures to be given weekly after Christmas . . . will be that of Miss McMillan . . . on "Education through the Imagination".
85 London School of Economics, Francis Johnson Collection, 1899/130, Stanton Coit to John Keir Hardie, 20 November 1899.
86 MacKillop, pp.110–11.
87 University of Liverpool, Sidney Jones Library, Glasier Papers, I.2, MS Diaries of John Bruce Glasier, entry for 25 November 1902: 'Educational meeting at Essex Hall. A poor affair. Audience hardly fills hall. Speaking with exception of Miss McMillan and Hardie – mostly off the rails. Alack these London speakers . . . '.
88 Margaret McMillan, *Education Through the Imagination*, Swan Sonnenschein, 1904.
89 J.W. Slaughter, 'Labour and Childhood: The Books of Margaret McMillan', *Highway*, December 1908.
90 National Froebel Foundation Archives, Archives of the Froebel Society, Council Minutes, vol. IX, 1904–1907. University of Liverpool, Sidney Jones Library, Glasier Papers, I.2, MS Diaries of John Bruce Glasier, entry for 28 July 1906. ILP, *Report of the Fourteenth Annual Conference of the ILP*, 1906 pp.22–3. Workers' Educational Association Archives, Annual Reports, Sixth Annual Report and Statement of Accounts.
91 GLC Record Office, LCC Records, Education Committee, Minutes of Proceedings, Sept.–Dec. 1904, p.1834. School Board Records (unclassified material), Managers' Yearly Reports for Deptford Park, Trundley's Road and Alveston Park schools.
92 Slaughter, 'Labour and Childhood'.
93 Mary Fels, *Joseph Fels: His Life Work*, Allen & Unwin, 1920; see below for Fels's involvement in McMillan's work.
94 Mansbridge, pp.75–6. Margaret McMillan, 'School Clinics: Their First Fruit', *Labour Leader*, 9 July 1909. Reginald Tribe, 'Results of Treatment at the Poplar School Clinic', *School Hygiene*, May 1911. Clara Grant was the headteacher at Devons Road. See Clara Grant, *From 'Me' to 'We'*

(Forty Years on Bow Common), privately printed, Fern Street Settlement, n.d., pp.44–5. See also her *Farthing Bundles*, privately printed, Fern Street Settlement, n.d.

95 See above, p.30.

96 For a classic account of the campaign, see Gilbert, pp.117–58. I have counted one major article a week on the topic written by McMillan between 1906 and 1908 (though there were probably many more).

97 For McMillan's attentions to Robert Morant, Permanent Under-Secretary at the Board of Education, see Gilbert, pp.117–58.

98 ibid., p.120.

99 Simon, *Education and the Labour Movement*, for the neurologist Sir Victor Horsley's involvement in this campaign.

100 Gilbert, p.117.

101 ibid., p.118.

102 G.A.N. Lowndes, *Margaret McMillan, The Children's Champion*, Museum Press, 1960, p.61.

103 See the McMillan–Morant correspondence, Rachel McMillan College Library, McMillan Collection, A1/8-35.

104 ibid., A1/19, Robert Morant to Margaret McMillan, 19 October 1910; 1/20, Robert Morant to Margaret McMillan, 12 October 1910; A1/35, Robert Morant to Margaret McMillan, 16 November 1913, concerning visits, donations and presents for the Deptford Centre.

105 Gilbert, pp.128–9.

106 McMillan Collection, A1/12, Robert Morant to Margaret McMillan, 22 December 1909.

107 ibid., Robert Morant to Margaret McMillan, 26 June 1907.

108 See Simon, pp.176–246, *passim*.

109 ibid., A1/13, Robert Morant to Margaret McMillan, 12 April 1910. Morant was generous with information, though. Having left the Board of Education for the National Insurance Commission, he wrote to McMillan telling her that 'enemies in the Treasury' had cut down the grant for treatment (possible now under the local Education Authorities [Medical Treatment] Act, 1909). 'I am not sure what you can safely do: but at least some Labour man might buttonhole . . . L.G. [Lloyd George] in the Lobby & ask how it is going, & how much it is going to be. But you must get them to do this *without* telling them that you believe things are going badly . . .; A1/30, Robert Morant to Margaret McMillan, 22 February 1912. The system of Exchequer grants for local authorities undertaking treatment came in this year for the first time. See Gilbert, p.154.

110 See Brian Simon on Morant's 'contempt for the abilities of ordinary people', and his determination to separate a working-class elementary education from a middle-class secondary education: Simon, pp.171, 194–6, and *passim*.

111 Francis Johnson Collection, 1906/189, 22 May 1906, Margaret McMillan to John Keir Hardie.

112 Gilbert, pp.123–4.

113 University of Liverpool, Sidney Jones Library, Glasier Papers, I.2, MS Diaries of John Bruce Glaiser, entry for 28 July 1906.

NOTES

114 ILP, *Report of the Fifteenth Annual Conference of the Independent Labour Party*, 1907, pp. 43, 69–70.
115 Margaret McMillan, 'Schools and Hospitals', *Labour Leader*, 8 January 1909. And see a letter to Morant on this topic, Rachel McMillan College Library, McMillan Collection, A1/25, Margaret McMillan to Robert Morant, 1 November 1911, on the attitude of some doctors: 'There is going to be trouble unless there is change. Mothers go away in tears.'
116 University of Liverpool, Sidney Jones Library, Glasier Papers, I.1, 1917/5, 3–6, John Bruce Glasier to Elizabeth Glasier Foster, 13 June 1917.
117 See McMillan's complaint on this point: London School of Economics, Archives of the British Association for Early Childhood Education, Nursery School Association Records, Box 18, Margaret McMillan to Miss de Lissa, 18 May 1929: 'I am a figurehead. My name wins adherents and seems to sanction all you do and say. But of co-operation on your side, there is none.'
118 Mansbridge, p. 99.
119 London School of Economics, Archives of the British Association for Early Childhood Education, Nursery School Association Records, Box 18, Margaret McMillan to Grace Owen, 29 November 1927.
120 ibid., Box 18, Margaret McMillan to Mrs Eveleigh, 1 May 1929.
121 ibid., Box 18, Margaret McMillan to Miss de Lissa, 8 May 1929.
122 McMillan, *Nursery School*, Dent, 1919, pp. 12–31.
123 Greater London Record Office, LCC Records, Education Office Records, EO/PS/1/43, Rachel McMillan Nursery School, Deptford, General Papers 1921/1922, Miss Faulkner to Miss Boston, 2 September 1921.
124 ibid.
125 Reading University Library, Astor Papers, MS1416/1/74, Nancy Astor to the Duchess of Atholl, 28 July 1927.
126 It should be noted, though, that the Plymouth Constituency Conservative Party did not think this a move beyond party, and was keenly aware of the propagandist value of having 'a great figure in the Labour Party' support Lady Astor. They had reprinted as an election fly-sheet the report of her visit in the *Western Independent*, 19 May 1929. Reading University Library, Astor Collection, MS 1066/1/1536, item marked '1929 Election'.
127 London School of Economics, Archives of the British Association for Early Childhood Education, Nursery School Association Records, Box 18, Katharine Bruce Glasier to Grace Owen, 7 June 1927.
128 London School of Economics, Archives of the British Association for early Childhood Education, Nursery School Association Records, Box 18/1, 'Statement' of Mary Chignell, May 1928, p. 4.
129 ibid., p. 1.
130 Reading University Library, Astor Papers, MS 1416/1/4/68. Katharine Bruce Glasier to Nancy Astor, 30 March 1931.
131 See above, p. 26.
132 Hinton, pp. 75–9.
133 Mansbridge, p. 121.

134 *The Times*, 30 March 1931. *Daily Herald*, 30 March 1931.

3 *Childhood*

1 Viviana A. Zelizer, *Pricing the Priceless Child: The Changing Social Value of Children*, Basic Books, New York, 1985, pp.3–21, 208–28.
2 Lloyd deMause (ed.), *The History of Childhood*, Souvenir Press, New York, 1976, pp.51–4.
3 Margaret Hewitt and Ivy Pinchbeck, *Children in English Society* (2 vols), vol. 2, Routledge & Kegan Paul, 1973, pp.387–513. Marjorie Cruikshank, *Children and Industry: Child Health and Welfare in Northern Textile Towns During the Nineteenth Century*, Manchester University Press, Manchester, 1981, pp.37–45, 75–92, 126–45. B.L. Hutchins and A. Harrison, A *History of Factory Legislation*, Cass., 1966, pp.1–29.
4 For the dark aspect of the poor chimney sweeper/child-to-be-rescued, see Heather Glenn, *Vision and Disenchantment: Blake's Songs and Wordsworth's Lyrical Ballads*, Cambridge University Press, Cambridge, 1983, pp.95–102.
5 Reports from Commissioners Inquiring into Children's Employment, PP 1842, xvii, PP 1843, xiv. Reports of the Commissioners on Employment of Children in Trades and Manufactures Not Already Regulated by Law, PP 1863, xviii, 1864, xxii, 1865, xx, 1866, xxiv, 1867, xvi. Report of the Commission of Inquiry into the Employment of Women and Children in Agriculture, PP 1867–8, xvii.
6 For the represented language of the city, Raymond Williams, *The Country and the City*, Paladin, 1973, pp.259–79. For the child-study movement and attentions paid to child language, Carolyn Steedman, *The Tidy House*, Virago, 1982, pp.85–7; also J.H. Muirhead, 'The Founders of Child Study in England', *Paidologist*, 2:2 (July 1900), pp.114–24; Earl Barnes, 'A Forgotten Student of Child Study', *Paidologist*, 3:3 (November 1901), pp.120–23; Earl Barnes, 'Methods of Studying Children', *Paidologist*, 1 (April 1899), pp.9–17.
7 For Mayhew's sociology of childhood, Steedman, pp.114–23. For an example of the horrified display of poor childhood (with elements of low comedy), see Richard Rowe, *Life in the London Streets*, Nimmo & Bain, 1881.
8 Graham Ovenden and Robert Melville, *Victorian Children*, Academy Editions, 1972. John Thomson and Adolphe Smith, *Street Life in London*, privately printed, 1877.
9 Margaret McMillan, 'The Half-Time System', *Clarion*, 12 September 1896.
10 John Ruskin, 'Fairyland', from 'The Art of England' (1884), *The Library Edition of the Works of John Ruskin*, vol. 33, Allen & Unwin, 1908, pp.338–42, 327–49. See also 'Design in the German School', from 'Ariadne Florentia' (1874), *The Library Edition of the Works of John Ruskin*, vol. 22, Allen & Unwin, 1906, pp.390–421.
11 John Ruskin, 'Humility', from 'Time and Tide' (1867), *The Library Edition of the Works of John Ruskin*, vol. 17, 1906, pp.405–9.
12 ibid., p.406.

13 Katharine Bruce Glasier, *Margaret McMillan and Her Life Work*, Workers' Northern Publishing Co., Manchester, n.d.
14 Ruskin, 'Fairyland', p.341.
15 Margaret McMillan, *Infant Mortality*, Independent Labour Party, 1906.
16 Peter Coveney, *The Image of Childhood, The Individual and Society: A Study of the Theme in English Literature* (first published as *Poor Monkey*, Rockliff, 1957), Penguin, 1967.
17 Robert Pattison, *The Child Figure in English Literature*, University of Georgia Press, Athens, 1978, pp.47–75.
18 See David Armstrong, *The Political Anatomy of the Body*, Cambridge University Press, Cambridge, 1983, pp.54–72, for the development of a psychology of childhood. See Robin Campbell and Roger Wales, 'The Study of Language Acquisition', in John Lyons (ed.), *New Horizons in Linguistics*, Penguin, 1970, pp.242–60, for a brief but thorough mapping of the history of linguistic attention to children's speech.
19 Couze Venn, 'The Subject of Psychology', in Jules Henriques *et al.* (eds), *Changing the Subject*, Methuen, 1984.
20 See Steedman, *The Tidy House*, on this point. See also Deborah Gorham, '"The Maiden Tribute of Modern Babylon" Re-examined: Child Prostitution and the Idea of Childhood in Late Victorian England', *Victorian Studies*, 21:3 (Spring 1978), pp.353–79.
21 See above, pp.24–5, and Notes.
22 Gorham, 'The "Maiden Tribute of Modern Babylon" Re-examined'; Judy Walkowitz, *Prostitution and Victorian Society*, Cambridge University Press, Cambridge, 1980, pp.246–52. Edward J. Bristow, *Vice and Vigilance, Purity Movements in Britain Since 1700*, Gill & Macmillan, 1977, pp.106–11.
23 Bentley B. Gilbert, *The Evolution of National Insurance in Great Britain: The Origins of the Welfare State*, Michael Joseph, 1966, pp.103–13. John Hurt, *Elementary Schooling and the Working Classes, 1860–1918*, Routledge & Kegan Paul, 1977, pp.141–2.
24 B. Seebohm Rowntree, *Poverty: A Study of Town Life*, 1901. Arnold White, *Efficiency and Empire*, Methuen, 1901. For the critique of the city where the perspective of child health is implicit rather than revealed, see Andrew Lees, *Cities Perceived: Urban Society In European and American Thought*, Manchester University Press, Manchester, 1985, pp.105–88; and below, pp.98–9.
25 Hurt, pp.128–52.
26 See above, p.33. Margaret McMillan, 'Zoë', *Clarion*, 9 March 1895.
27 Margaret McMillan, 'Gutterella: A Woman of the Age of Gold', *Weekly Times and Echo*, 28 December 1895.
28 Margaret McMillan, 'In Holy Isle', *Highway*, October 1911.
29 Margaret McMillan, 'Lola', 'Lola: Conclusion', *Clarion*, 21 February, 3 March 1897.
30 I have been unable to trace the source of this quotation. When McMillan used it again, years later, she called it a Russian proverb, and in *Imagination* (1923) attributed it to 'Turgenieff' (p.52).
31 Margaret McMillan, 'A la Salpêtrière', *Clarion*, 29 April 1897.
32 Henri F. Ellenberger, *The Discovery of the Unconscious: The History and*

275

Evolution of Dynamic Psychiatry, Allen Lane, 1970. Lancelot Law Whyte, *The Unconscious Before Freud*, Julian Friedman, 1979.

33 See above, pp.44–5. Margaret McMillan, 'School Board Notes', *Labour Echo*, 18 September 1897.

34 Margaret McMillan, *The Beginnings of Education* (City Branch Pamphlet No. 8), City of London Branch of the ILP, 1902 (1903).

35 Margaret McMillan, 'Children's Corner: Ann: A Tale for Children', *Clarion* 14, 21, 28 April 1898.

36 Margaret McMillan, 'Education in the Primary School', *Labour Leader*, 27 April 1899.

37 ibid.

38 Edith Mary Jewson, 'The Advent Angels in Deptford: Miss Margaret McMillan and Her Work', *Christian Commonwealth*, 6 December 1911.

39 Margaret McMillan, 'How I Became a Socialist', *Labour Leader*, 11 July 1912.

40 Richard N. Coe, *When the Grass Was Taller, Autobiography and the Experience of Childhood*, Yale University Press, New Haven, 1984, pp.1–40.

41 Deafness is mentioned in McMillan, *Life*, pp.9–10, and in 'How I Became a Socialist' (1912), where she wrote, of attending church in Inverness: 'though I was deaf I could hear the wailing Gaelic singing'. It is also mentioned by G.A.N. Lowndes, *Margaret McMillan, The Children's Champion*, Museum Press, 1960, p.29.

42 Margaret McMillan, 'Handel Stumm', *Labour Leader*, weekly between 1 September 1900 and 3 March 1901. Deafness is also a feature of 'The Gifts That Cannot be Stolen, An Allegory for Children of All Ages', *The Two Worlds*, 12 May, 19 May, 26 May, 2 June 1899; and of 'A Fairy Tale by the Fairies', *Young Socialist*, twelve episodes between May 1907 and February 1908. This fiction depicts Mairi, a deaf girl-child of the Islands.

43 McMillan, 'Handel Stumm', 27 October 1900. Here, Handel Stumm's teacher uses a method reminiscent of the course of treatment followed by Jean Itard in his instruction of the Wild Boy of Aveyron. See below, pp.215–16.

44 Julia Dawson, 'Our Woman's Letter', *Clarion*, 26 February 1904.

45 Margaret McMillan, 'At the Foot of the Rainbow', *Christian Commonwealth*, 10 February 1915.

46 Bradford Record Office, Miriam Lord Collection, 22D77/15/24, Copy of letter from Margaret McMillan to Kathleen Hyde, n.d.

47 For Édouard Seguin, see Mabel E. Talbot, *Édouard Seguin: A Study of the Educational Approach to the Treatment of Mentally Defective Children*, Teachers' College, New York, 1964; Henry Holman, *Seguin and His Physiological Method of Education*, Pitman, 1914; and below, pp.194–7.

48 Rachel McMillan College Library, McMillan Collection, Letters, A1/1, Margaret McMillan to Sally Blatchford, 22 February 1895.

49 Henry Drummond, *Lowell Lectures on the Ascent of Man*, Hodder & Stoughton, 1894. Katharine Bruce Glasier, *Socialism and the Home*, ILP Press, 1911, p.7. The Reclus brothers, Michel-Elie (1827–1904) and Jean-Jacques Elisée (1830–1905) published works of ethnology, anthropology

and geography which gave a significant role to the child in the history of human development and culture.

50 Drummond, p.282.
51 ibid., p.288.
52 ibid., pp.346–7.
53 ibid., p.338.
54 'The strong affection for progeny becomes in the hands of nature the agent of a double culture, serving at once to fashion parent and child into the desired form. And beautiful it is to see how the most powerful instinct is made the means of holding men under a discipline to which nothing else perhaps could make them submit.' See Herbert Spencer, 'The Status of Children' in *The Principles of Sociology*, vol. 1, Williams & Norgate, 1877, pp.767–79.
55 Arthur Greenwood, *All Children Are Mine: Inaugural Margaret McMillan Lecture*, University of London Press for the Margaret McMillan Fellowship, 1952, p.16.
56 Franco Moretti, 'Kindergarten', in *Signs Taken for Wonders*, Verso, 1983, pp.157–81.
57 ibid., p.162.
58 McMillan, 'Lola: Conclusion' (1897).
59 Margaret McMillan, 'In a Garden' *Highway*, June 1911; 'In Our Garden', *Highway*, July 1911; 'In Our Garden, Marigold, An English Mignon', *Highway*, September 1911; In Our Garden, I–V', *Highway*, April–September 1912. See a reprint of 'Marigold, An English Mignon', *Christian Commonwealth*, 3 January 1912.
60 Johann Wolfgang von Goethe, *Wilhelm Meister's Years of Apprenticeship* (trans. H.M. Wardson), 6 vols, John Calder, 1977. For the song, vol. 1, Book III, pp.167–8. For the musical arrangement, 'Mignons Gesang', *Schubert-Lieder*, Band III, C.F. Peters, Frankfurt, n.d., pp.221–4.
61 See *The Times*, 22, 28 February, 22 April 1910; *The Times Literary Supplement*, 14 April 1910; *Wilhelm Meisters Theatralische Sedung, Von Goethe*, Rascher, Zurich, 1910; *Wilhelm Meisters Theatralische Sedung*, Stuttgart, 1911; *Wilhelm Meister's Theatrical Mission* (trans. Gregory A. Page), Heinemann, 1913. In reviewing the earlier version, the *TLS* noted that in the first version of Mignon's song the laurel tree stretched high with more ecstasy (*hoch* having later replaced the first choice, *froh*) – in a manner reminiscent of Mignon's bodily movements?
62 Goethe (1977), pp.87, 88–9.
63 ibid., pp.87, 89.
64 ibid., vol. 1, Book III, pp.139–40; vol. 2, Book V, pp.110–11.
65 ibid., vol. 4, Book VIII, pp.89–90.
66 ibid., p.105.
67 William Gilby, 'The Structural Significance of Mignon in *Wilhelm Meisters Lehrjahre*', *Seminar*, 26 (1980), pp.136–50.
68 Goethe (1977), vol. 1, Book II, pp.95, 98.
69 McMillan, 'Marigold' (1911).
70 ibid. For Mignon's impulsiveness, Goethe (1977), vol. 1, Book II, pp.124–5; Book III, pp.167–8.

71 Franco Moretti, *The Way of the World: the Bildungsroman in European Culture*, Verso, 1987, p.47.
72 Goethe (1977), vol.3, Book VIII, pp.130–31.
73 Steve Neale, 'Melodrama and Tears', *Screen*, 27:6 (November/December 1986), pp.6–22.
74 Gilby, p.149.
75 For another writing of this moment, see Margaret McMillan, *The Nursery School*, Dent, 1919, p.182; and for Marigold's fate, Margaret McMillan, *The Camp School*, Allen & Unwin, 1917, pp.82–3: '"Was she saved by the Camp?" some gentle voice may ask. No, she was not. Some were saved . . . [but] Marigold was not among them. She tasted the joy of one new summer. Then her father, the hawker, was killed. Her mother "moved". We saw her long after. Her lovely face had coarsened so as to be almost unrecognisable . . . Why dwell on one tragedy among so many thousands?'

4 Gardens

1 Peter Coveney, *The Image of Childhood, The Individual and Society: A Study of the Theme in English Literature* (first published as *Poor Monkey*, Rockliff, 1957), Penguin, 1967, pp.37–51, 68–90.
2 Robert Pattison, *The Child Figure in English Literature*, University of Georgia Press, Athens, 1978, p.58.
3 Humphrey Carpenter, *Secret Gardens: The Golden Age of Children's Literature*, Allen & Unwin, 1985, p.9.
4 Pattison, *Child Figure*, pp.79–80.
5 ibid., p.80.
6 Coveney, pp.280–81.
7 P. Woodham-Smith, 'History of the Froebel Movement in England', in Evelyn Lawrence (ed.), *Friedrich Froebel and English Education*, Routledge & Kegan Paul, 1969, pp.34–94. Maurice Galton *et al.*, *Inside the Primary Classroom*, Routledge & Kegan Paul, 1980, pp.33–4. Henry Morley, 'Infant Gardens', *Household Words*, 21 July 1855, pp.577–82. Bertha Maria von Marenholtz-Buelow. *Women's Educational Mission, Being an Explanation of Friedrich Froebel's System of Infant Gardens*, Dalton, 1855.
8 Michael Steven Shapiro, *The Child's Garden: The Kindergarten Movement from Froebel to Dewey*, Pennsylvania State University Press, University Park, 1983, pp.20–25.
9 ibid., p.22.
10 ibid., pp.25–7. Ann Taylor Allen, 'Spiritual Motherhood: German Feminists and the Kindergarten Movement, 1848–1911', *History of Education Quarterly*, 22:3 (Fall 1982), pp.319–39. Carolyn Steedman, 'The "Mother Made Conscious": The Historical Development of a Primary School Pedagogy', *History Workshop Journal*, 20 (Autumn 1985), pp.149–63.
11 Marenholtz-Buelow, *Women's Educational Mission*.
12 Woodham-Smith, pp.48–63.
13 E.M.M., 'The Garden of Children', *Labour Prophet*, October 1894,

January 1895. Froebelian ideas were being discussed in ILP circles in the mid 1890s. See Lizzie Glasier's account of the Glasgow Women's Labour Party, and her proposals for instructing children in socialist thought through a Froebelian method: *Labour Leader*, 26 April 1895.

14 *Labour Leader*, 15 April 1899. Bradford Record Office, Bradford School Board Records, School Management Sub-Committee Minute Book, 25D75/II/8/8, Meetings of 24 May, 25 June, 6 July 1898.

15 ibid. *Tenth Triennial Report of the Proceedings of the School Board for Bradford During the Three Years Ended November 30, 1900*, School Board Office, Bradford, p.118. For Florence Kirk (*née* Hewitt), see *Journal of the Sanitary Institute*, 24 (1903), pp.788–91, 822–3. Margaret McMillan, *1901–1926, Anniversary Celebrations*, Bradford Froebel Society and Child Study Association, 1926. 'The "New" Education', *Highway*, June 1913. Mrs Florence Kirk, *Old English Games and Physical Exercises*, Longman Green, 1906.

16 Bradford School Board Records, School Management Sub-Committee Minute Book, 25D75/II/8/8, Meeting of 21 February 1899. 25DII/8/9, Meeting of 11 January 1903.

17 National Froebel Foundation, Archives of the Froebel Society, Council Minutes, vol. ix, 1904–1907.

18 Albert Mansbridge, *Margaret McMillan, Prophet and Pioneer: Her Life and Work*, Dent, 1932, p.90. Annual Reports for the Centre were published in James Kerr's and David Eder's journal *School Hygiene*. McMillan herself wrote very widely about the work of the Clinic; e.g. Margaret McMillan, 'The School Clinic, The Problems of Treatment Today', *Morning Leader*, 24 November 1910; 'The Tooth Clinic and Kindred Matters'. *Christian Commonwealth*, 13 July 1910; 'An Instruction to the Clarion Fellowship: The Deptford Health Centre', *Clarion*, 29 July 1910; 'The Deptford Health Clinic, A Health Centre for School Children', *Child*, 1:8 (May 1911), pp.672–9.

19 McMillan, *Life*, pp.123–4.

20 Margaret McMillan, *The School Clinic Today: Health Centres and What They Mean to the People*, ILP and National Labour Press, 1912.

21 Leonard P. Ayres, *Open-Air Schools*, Russell Sage Foundation, New York, 1912. Malcolm Seaborne and Roy Low, *The English School, Its Architecture and Organisation, Vol.2, 1870–1970*, Routledge & Kegan Paul, 1977. James Kerr, *Fundamentals of School Health*, Allen & Unwin, 1926.

22 Roger Cooter, 'Open-Air Therapy and the Rise of Open-Air Hospitals', *Society for the Social History of Medicine Bulletin*, 35 (December 1984), pp.44–6. Margaret McMillan, 'History and Aims of the Open-Air Nursery School', *Scottish Health Magazine*, 1:1 (April 1929). In *The Foul and the Fragrant: Odor and the French Social Imagination*, Berg, Leamington Spa, 1986, Alain Corbin has plotted out an early-nineteenth-century conceptualisation of air in movement as beneficial, but for the later century it is still unclear what practitioners like McMillan saw as the actual properties of fresh air.

23 Edith Mary Jewson, 'The Advent Angels in Deptford: Miss Margaret McMillan and Her Work', *Christian Commonwealth*, 6 December 1911,

quoting Margaret McMillan writing in *Child Life*, November 1911.

24 See above, pp.52–3, and Notes.

25 See above, pp.25, 33.

26 John Saville, 'Henry George and the British Labour Movement', *Bulletin of the Society for the Study of Labour History*, 5 (1962), pp.18–26. E.P. Lawrence, *Henry George in the British Isles*, Michigan State University Press, East Lansing, 1957. Royden Harrison, 'The Land and Labour League', *International Institute of Social History Bulletin*, 8 (1953), pp.169–95. David Howell, *British Workers and the Independent Labour Party, 1888–1906*, Manchester University Press, Manchester, 1983, pp.135–6.

27 Ursula Vogel, 'The Land Question: A Liberal Theory of Communal Property', *History Workshop Journal*, 27 (Spring 1989), pp.106–35. Henry George, *Progress and Poverty*, Routledge & Kegan Paul, 1881.

28 Mary Fels, *Joseph Fels: His Life Work*, Allen & Unwin, 1920, pp.208–13.

29 ibid., p.213.

30 Workers' Educational Association Archives, WEA Executive and Council Minutes, 1908–1912. Minutes of the Council held on 7 May 1910.

31 Fels, pp.208–13.

32 'We think', minuted the Committee, 'that if Mr Fels would waive the personal character of the instruction and medical care . . . and make the mass character of the instruction more prominent, a scheme might be established which would enable the Council to accept Mr Fels' offer. 'GLC Record Office, LCC Records, Education Committee, Minutes of Proceedings, July–December 1906. Day School Sub-Committee Report, pp.2515–16.

33 See above, pp.52–3. Mansbridge, p.60.

34 Nuffield College, Fabian Society Papers, Correspondence, A/7/2/17, Joseph Fels to Edward Pease, 19 March 1909.

35 Margaret McMillan, 'Marigold, An English Mignon', *Highway*, September 1911.

36 McMillan, *Life*, p.118.

37 See Margaret McMillan, *The Bard at the Braes*, ILP Press, 1909. 'Handel Stumm' opens with a drama of disinheritance among the crofters. See also Margaret McMillan, 'The Land Raiders in Barra', *Labour Leader*, 9 May 1909; 'The Serf and His Son', *Christian Commonwealth*, 13 May 1910.

38 See above, pp.25–6.

39 David Armstrong, *The Political Anatomy of the Body*, Cambridge University Press, Cambridge, 1983, pp.8, 10.

40 McMillan, *Life*, p.93.

41 ibid., p.94.

42 ibid., pp.94–5.

43 Margaret McMillan, *The Camp School*, Allen & Unwin, 1917, pp.78–9.

44 ibid., pp.79–80. See Plates.

45 See above, pp.76–80.

46 McMillan, *Camp School*, pp.84–5.

47 ibid., p.85.

48 Margaret McMillan, 'The Camp School', *Transactions of the National*

Liberal Club Political and Economic Circle, Part 89a (12 December 1914), P.S. King, 1914.

49 Margaret McMillan, 'Camp Schools: The New Grant for the Children', *Clarion*, 17 May 1912.

50 McMillan, *Camp School*, pp.92–116.

51 Mansbridge, p.92.

52 McMillan, *Camp School*, p.96.

53 ibid., pp.100–01.

54 ibid., pp.117–37.

55 ibid., pp.51–77.

56 ibid., pp.54–5.

57 ibid., p.52. Margaret McMillan, *The Nursery School*, Dent, 1919, p.27.

58 ibid., p.33.

59 ibid.

60 ibid., pp.44–9. On children and the naming of things, see Pattison, p.26.

61 McMillan, *Nursery School*, pp.46–8.

62 See McMillan's account of reverie in *Education Through the Imagination*, Dent, 1923, pp.76–7, where she described the way in which 'all the thwarted instincts and impulses, the desires that are not realised . . . are lifted above the subconscious (whence they emerge in dreams), into a middle region of reverie.'

63 McMillan, *Camp School*, p.67. See also *Nursery School*, p.142.

64 McMillan, *Camp School*, pp.63–4.

65 Elizabeth Bradburn, *Margaret McMillan, Framework and Expansion of Nursery Education*, Denholm Press, Redhill, 1976, pp.84–5.

66 McMillan, *Camp School*, pp.63–4.

67 McMillan, *Nursery School*, pp.29–30. *Camp School*, p.52.

68 Margaret McMillan, 'Faith and Fear', *Labour Leader*, 27 January 1911.

69 Emma Stevinson, *The Open-Air Nursery School*, Dent, 1923, pp.1–13.

70 'Interview with Miss McMillan: The Schools of Tomorrow', *Christian Commonwealth*, 21 January 1914.

71 See the stories 'Guy and the Stars' and 'Guy and the Morning', *Nursery School*, pp.154–69.

72 Margaret McMillan, 'The Children's Bread', *Labour Leader*, 31 December 1909.

73 Margaret McMillan, 'Johnny and Me', *Christian Commonwealth*, 2 November 1910.

74 McMillan, *Life*, p.90.

75 Jane Lewis, *The Politics of Motherhood: Child and Maternal Welfare in England, 1900–1939*, Croom Helm, 1980, pp.61–113. Anna Davin, 'Imperialism and Motherhood', *History Workshop Journal*, 5 (Spring 1978), pp.61–113. Peter W.G. Wright, 'Babyhood: The Social Construction of Infant Care as a Medical Problem in England', in M. Lock and D. Gordon (eds), *Biomedicine Examined* (in preparation). Caroline Rowan, 'Child Welfare and the Working Class Family', in Mary Langan and Bill Schwarz (eds), *Crisis in the British State*, Hutchinson in association with the Centre for Contemporary Cultural Studies, 1985, pp.226–39.

76 McMillan, *Camp School*, p.53.

77 Raymond Williams, *The Country and the City*, Paladin, 1973.
78 Pattison, *The Child Figure in English Literature*, Introduction.
79 See Note 8.
80 Shapiro, p.22.
81 Philip McCann and Francis A. Young, *Samuel Wilderspin and the Infant School Movement*, Croom Helm, 1982, pp.164–5.
82 Édouard Seguin, *Report on Education* (1875), Delmar, New York, 1976, pp.132–47.
83 Miles Hadfield, *A History of British Gardening*, Penguin, 1985, pp.360–430. Mrs Hambledon is mentioned in McMillan, *Nursery School*, pp.46, 262, 353.
84 'The lovely Madame Édouard Heriot, which I believed to be fitted only to the highest class order of gardens, has bloomed most freely and kindly'. McMillan, *Camp School*, p.64.
85 For McMillan's involvement in Welwyn, see *Highway*, March 1909. See also Robert Beevers, *The Garden City Utopia: A Critical Biography of Ebenezer Howard*, Macmillan, 1988.
86 Patrick Geddes, *City Development, A Study of Parks, Gardens and Culture Institutes: A Report to the Carnegie Dunfermline Trust*, Edinburgh, 1904, pp.43–4, 64–5, 203. Geddes spoke about the city gardens and parks as 'this whole wealth of concrete educational resources [developing] towards that larger conception of the natural world, that of Lyell, and Darwin, of Humboldt and Reclus . . .'. McMillan knew Geddes's work and was interested in his idea of the enclosed wilderness in which children might play. See Margaret McMillan, 'The Child-World: The Open School Commended', *Co-operative News*, 14 January 1905.
87 Margaret McMillan, 'The Gardens Under the Sea', *Highway*, October 1910.
88 See below, p.209.

5 Cities

1 B. Seebohm Rowntree, *Poverty: A Study of Town Life*, (1901), Nelson, 1904, pp.243–6, 248–56.
2 ibid., pp.443–4.
3 See this literature discussed in Bentley B. Gilbert, *The Evolution of National Insurance in Great Britain: The Origins of the Welfare State*, Michael Joseph, 1966, pp.59–101.
4 Interdepartmental Committee on Physical Deterioration, Report of Commissioners, PP 1904, xxxii.
5 ILP, *Report of the Twelfth Annual Conference of the ILP*, 1904, pp.33–4.
6 James Cantlie, *Degeneration Among Londoners*, Field & Tuer, 1885. Arnold White, *The Problems of a Great City*, Remington, 1886. John Milner Fothergill, *The Town Dweller, His Needs and Wants*, H.K. Lewis, 1889. John Peere Williams-Freeman, *The Effect of Town Life on General Health*, W.H. Allen, 1890.
7 Margaret McMillan, 'Building Up the British Race', *Labour Leader*, 6 July 1906. Margaret McMillan and Mrs Cobden Sanderson, *London's Children:*

How To Feed Them and How Not To Feed Them, ILP, April 1909.

8 David Howell, *British Workers and the Independent Labour Party, 1888–1906*, Manchester University Press, Manchester, 1983, pp.350–1.

9 McMillan, *Life*, p.34.

10 Isabella Ford, *On the Threshold*, Arnold, 1895.

11 McMillan, *Life*, p.34. Endsleigh Gardens, where the hostel was situated, might operate as the biographer's synthesising setting if we had more information about the years Rachel (and possibly Margaret) McMillan spent here, for the Gardens was the birthplace, and in the late 1880s still the home, of David Eder, cousin of Israel Zangwill, Secretary to the Bloomsbury Socialist Society in the late 1880s, much later the first British translator of Freud and school doctor to the McMillans' Bow and Deptford clinics after 1908. (See below, p.209, for David Eder.) We cannot make these earlier connections, though, from the evidence available, neither can we be entirely certain that Margaret McMillan actually lived in the Endsleigh Gardens hostel with her sister. McMillan's first piece of journalism appeared in the *Christian Socialist* in October 1889, and she records moving to London after its publication (though Mansbridge, mysteriously, says that this move took place in 1887). In February 1890 she applied for a ticket to the British Museum Reading Room, not giving her address as 8 Endsleigh Gardens, where there was a Home for Working Girls in London, nor Number 12, where there was a Home for Young Women Employed in Houses of Business, but filling in the ledger with an address at Number 20, where it is possible that she lodged until she moved to Chelsea, probably in 1892.

12 McMillan, *Life*, pp.35–6.

13 Margaret McMillan, 'A Woman of the Age of Gold: Mary Muse', *Clarion*, 8 September 1894.

14 By July 1892 both sisters appear to have been lodging in Chelsea, in Tadema Road, though Rachel apparently kept her job at the hostel for some time to come. McMillan, *Life*, pp.53–4. University of Liverpool, Sidney Jones Library, Glasier Papers, I.1, 1892/27, 28-12, Barbara Fraser to John Bruce Glasier, 28 December 1892.

15 McMillan, *Life*, pp.43–72 for the Lady X episodes. Reading University Library, Astor Papers, MS 1416/1/4/68, Margaret McMillan to Nancy Astor, 5 January 1929, thanking her for the gift of a coat. MS 1416/1/4/68, Nancy Astor to McMillan, disparaging Snowden's socialism; and again, complaining about socialist politicians, in MS 1416/1/4/68, Nancy Astor to Margaret McMillan, 17 September 1930.

16 McMillan, *Life*, pp.50–51. Rachel McMillan College Library, McMillan Collection, A/9, John Ruskin, *The Seven Lamps of Architecture*, George Allen, 1890. Inscribed 'A Present to Rachel McMillan from Lady Meux', 1890. According to this account, Lady Meux paid for McMillan's stage training, sending her to work under Emile Behnke, a theorist of vocal physiology and teacher of voice production. She may also have attended sessions at Henry Neville's drama studio in Oxford Street. See below, pp.216, 232, for McMillan's voice and stage training. See *The Times* 19 September 1892, for Behnke's obituary. The Democratic Club was a

residential and dining club for socialists, instituted to afford 'working men and women the means of social intercourse, mutual helpfulness, mental and moral improvement and rational recreation'. Lecture series were run and it functioned as a social centre. Democratic Club, *Copy of Rules*, 1892. See also *Clarion*, 7 September 1892, for an interview with Keir Hardie when he was staying with his family at the Club.

17 For women and the settlement movement (the establishment of centres of culture in the wastelands of working-class districts, in which the middle-class social worker and teacher actually settled and lived) see Martha Vicinus, *Independent Women, Work and Community for Single Women, 1850–1920*, Virago, 1985, pp.211–46. For Campbell, see above, pp.35, 101.

18 *Labour Prophet*, April 1892. The entirely unexplained educational rescue work that McMillan recalled taking part in in the East End in this period was probably under his aegis. McMillan, *Life*, pp.38–41, and *Labour Prophet*, April 1892, which suggested that Campbell wanted women missionaries for his enterprise.

19 See p.267, Note 10.

20 Hinton, *Labour and Socialism: A History of the British Labour Movement, 1867–1974*, Wheatsheaf, Brighton, 1983, pp.62–3.

21 *Labour Prophet*, June 1892. *Clarion*, 28 May 1893.

22 London School of Economics, Francis Johnson Collection, 1893/187, E.R. Halford to Francis Johnson, n.d. See *Labour Prophet*, August and December 1892, for the founding of the Bradford Labour Church.

23 This was Bruce Glasier's phrase, as he recommended McMillan to his fiancée Katharine Conway. University of Liverpool, Sidney Jones Library, Glasier Papers, I.1, 1893/31, John Bruce Glasier to Katharine Bruce Glasier, 19 April 1893.

24 See below, pp.173–88.

25 Mansbridge, *Margaret McMillan, Prophet and Pioneer*, Dent, 1932, p.23. Nevertheless, there is evidence that McMillan did visit Bradford before 1893. Her Fabian Society Membership card was issued to her in September 1892 at the Labour Church Institute, Bradford. Nuffield College, Fabian Society Papers, Card Index of Members.

26 University of Liverpool, Sidney Jones Library, Glasier Papers, I.1, 1893/35, Katharine Bruce Glasier to Barbara Fraser, 6 June 1893. There are various versions of the move to the North, all conflicting. McMillan herself remembered in 1927 how, after the formation of the Independent Labour Party in January 1893, 'the Socialist group in the wool city sent a formal deputation . . . asking me to make my home in that city.' In this version, it was F.W. Jowett who led the deputation (McMillan, *Life*, p.73). In an earlier autobiographical piece, she recorded being invited to lecture in the city in June 1893 by Harry Smith, and then being asked 'to stop altogether' (McMillan, 'How I Became a Socialist' [1912]).

27 McMillan, *Life*, pp.73–4. See Plate 10.

28 Robert Pattison, *The Child Figure in English Literature*, University of Georgia Press, Athens, 1978, pp.70–74, discusses the political uses to which Shaftesbury put the sentimentalised child-figure, and suggests the uses to which his own biography was put after his death.

29 McMillan, *Life*, pp.73–4. This kind of portentous arrival in Bradford has also been noted by Angela Carter, *Nothing Sacred*, Virago, 1982, p.61. Those who look up at Oastler's statue seem peculiarly unable to *see* it accurately. The two little mill workers may have been soot-blackened, but they are not bowed, as in McMillan's description, and Oastler is not uplifting them (as in Carter's account), merely indicating their piteous condition. See Plate 10.

30 See Pattison, pp.70–74, for the evocation of the figure of Shaftesbury as the archetypal rescuer of childhood.

31 W.D. Ross, 'Bradford Politics, 1880–1906', Ph.D, Bradford University, 1977, pp.180–3, 188, 190–91.

32 McMillan, *Life*, p.125.

33 University of Liverpool, Sidney Jones Library, Glasier Papers, I.3, MS Notebooks of John Bruce Glasier, entry for 24 October 1896. See also entries for 20 November 1895, 30 November 1895, 17 August 1896, 22 October 1896.

34 *Bradford Labour Echo*, 6 April, 25 April, 1 June, 8 June, 15 June, announcing 'Classes for Working Men' on Demeter and Persephone, Ariadne, Pan and Hippolytus. See *Clarion*, 17 August 1895, *Labour Leader*, 24 August 1895, for her series on the French Revolution. See *Labour Leader*, 3 November 1894, for McMillan's election as president of the Bradford Cercle Français.

35 ILP, Series I, 1, Pamphlets and Leaflets, 1901/13. Margaret McMillan, 'Wanted: A Blend of Heroism and Specialism', *Young Oxford*, March 1901. Payments to ILP lecturers are discussed by D.R. Hopkins, 'The Newspapers of the Independent Labour Party, 1893–1906', Ph.D, University College of Wales, 1981, p.127.

36 *Clarion*, 24 March 1894.

37 J.W., 'Miss McMillan's New Book', *Labour Echo*, 7 September 1895.

38 Margaret McMillan, *Samson*, Clarion Press, Manchester, 1895, p.40.

39 ibid., p.129.

40 'Almost a Notable Book', *Labour Leader*, 8 June 1895. The reviewer remarked: 'my deduction is a vague, almost a mystic desire for a deeper faith as a basis for her Socialism. Miss McMillan apparently considers that we have not yet adequately tapped the springs of the human heart . . . perhaps she is not quite certain of it herself.' Robert Blatchford reported to John Bruce Glasier that the book was selling badly: 'It has been boycotted by the Press [*sic*]. Except in the labour press there has never been a single review of it: they do love us, these newspapers.' Manchester Central Library, Blatchford Papers, MS F 920 5B, Robert Blatchford to John Bruce Glasier, 31 July 1895.

41 McMillan, *Life*, p.81.

42 Margaret McMillan, 'Drink in Labour Clubs', *Clarion*, 24 February 1894.

43 Margaret McMillan, 'Music in Labour Clubs', *Clarion*, 3 March 1894. McMillan, 'Drink in Labour Clubs (1894).

44 'How A Duchess Was Taught Socialism', *M.A.P.*, 4 November 1899. Miriam Lord, *Margaret McMillan in Bradford, Fourth Margaret McMillan Lecture*, University of London Press for the Margaret McMillan

Fellowship, 1957, p.8. For the Duchess of Sutherland, see below, p. 140. For Margaret Verney, see R.F. Verney (ed.), *In Memory of Margaret Maria Lady Verney*, Garden City Press, Letchworth, 1930.

45 Ross, p.6.

46 J. Reynolds and K. Laybourn, 'The Emergence of the Independent Labour Party in Bradford', *International Review of Social History*, 20 (1975), pp.313–46.

47 Ross, pp.11–12.

48 ibid., p.7. Reynolds and Laybourn, p.317.

49 Royal Commission on Labour, PP 1892, xxxv, quoted in Reynolds and Laybourn, p.317.

50 Ross, p.38.

51 For the medical view on half-time, see Marjorie Cruikshank, *Children and Industry: Child Health and Welfare in the Northern Textile Towns During the Nineteenth Century*, Manchester University Press, Manchester, 1981, pp.94–101.

52 Barbara Thompson, 'Public Provision and Private Neglect: Public Health', in D.G. Wright and J.A. Jowitt (eds), *Victorian Bradford*, City of Bradford Metropolitan Council, Bradford, 1981, pp.137–64.

53 ibid., pp.144–5.

54 ibid., pp.145–6.

55 ibid., pp.147–9; for some further discussion of housing in Bradford, see Keith Laybourn and Jack Reynolds, *Liberalism and the Rise of Labour, 1890–1918*, Croom Helm, 1984, pp.1–11.

56 McMillan, *Life*, p.75, and above, p.14. For the club scene in Bradford, see Keith Laybourn, '"The Defence of the Bottom Dog": The Independent Labour Party in Local Politics', in Wright and Jowitt (eds), p.224; see also Ross, pp.161–96.

57 Margaret McMillan, 'A Great Social Problem: Feeding the Slum Children of Leeds', *Co-operative News*, 1 October 1904.

58 McMillan, *Life*, pp.87–8.

59 Margaret McMillan, 'My Experiences on the School Board', *Labour Prophet*, November 1895.

60 She used this phrase in 'Save the Children: A Plea for the Social Treatment of Disease', *Labour Leader*, 17 November 1911.

61 See above, pp.39–40.

62 See above, p.37.

63 ibid.; Howell, p.344.

64 See above, p.43.

65 *Bradford Observer*, 24 January 1895.

66 Report of the Bradford School Board Meeting of 23 January 1895 in *Bradford Observer*, 24 January 1895.

67 Margaret McMillan, *Child Labour and the Half-Time System* (Clarion Pamphlet No. 15), Clarion Newspaper Co., 1896.

68 Katharine St John Conway, *The Cry of the Children*, Labour Press, Manchester (2nd edn), 1894.

69 McMillan, *Child Labour*.

70 ibid.

71 See *Journal of the Royal Sanitary Institute*, 25 (1904), pp.943–4, 992. *Clarion*, 6 April 1895; *Bradford Observer*, 1 April 1895; *Tenth Triennial Report of the Proceedings of the School Board for Bradford during the Three Years Ended November 30, 1900*, School Board Office, Bradford, 1900, p.135.

72 Manchester Central Library, Blatchford Papers, MS F 920 5B26, Robert Blatchford to William Palmer, 16 April 1930.

73 Laurence Thompson, *Robert Blatchford: Portrait of an Englishman*, Gollancz, 1953, pp.62–3.

74 Keith Laybourn, 'The Issue of School Feeding in Bradford, 1904–1907', *Journal of Educational Administration and History*, 14:2 (July 1982), pp.30–38.

75 Margaret McMillan, 'The Cost of Mental Effort', *Ethical World*, 21 January 1900.

76 'Miss McMillan on the Fellowship', *Clarion*, 1 April 1901; 'Free Meals', *Labour Leader*, 22 March 1907; McMillan and Cobden Sanderson, *London's Children*.

77 McMillan, 'Cost of Mental Effort'.

78 Margaret McMillan, *The Beginnings of Education* (City Branch Pamphlet No.8), City of London Branch of the ILP, 1903. *Education Through the Imagination*, Swan Sonnenschein, 1904, p.70.

79 Margaret McMillan, 'Penalties of Greatness', *Labour Leader*, 26 April 1907; 'The Claims of the "Practical" in Education', *Highway*, January 1910; 'To Save the Children: Work to be Done Now', *Clarion*, 26 September 1913.

80 McMillan, 'My Experiences'.

81 ibid.; 'Children's Corner: Ann: A Tale for Children', *Clarion*, 14, 21 April 1898.

82 See above, p.67.

83 See above, p.96 and Note 82.

84 Margaret McMillan, 'School Board Notes', *Bradford Labour Echo*, 18, 25 September, 22 October 1897. The following articles were also a contribution of the series: 'Rest', 21 January 1899; 'Baths', 13 April 1899.

85 McMillan, 'School Board Notes', 18 September 1897.

86 ibid., 22 October 1897.

87 Report of the Bradford School Board Meeting of 22 September 1897 in the *Bradford Observer*, 23 September 1897. See also Bradford Record Office, Bradford School Board Records, School Attendance Sub-Committee Minute Book, 52D75/7/4, Meetings of 17 June, 9 December 1896, 20 January, 17 February 1897. See *Bradford Labour Echo*, 1 April 1897: 'Some time ago Miss McMillan made certain references anent the cleanliness – or rather the want of it – among a large number of children attending our board schools, which roused the ire and indignation of a few persons . . . .'.

88 'Clothes – and the Making of Them', *Young Socialist*, July 1912. Also 'Clothes and How To Make Them', *Young Socialist*, August, September, October 1912. See also Margaret McMillan, *The Camp School*, Allen & Unwin, 1917, pp.89–91.

89 McMillan, 'Clothes', July 1912.
90 McMillan, 'School Board Notes', 25 September 1897.
91 Malcolm Hardman, *Ruskin and Bradford: An Experiment in Victorian Cultural History*, Manchester University Press, Manchester, 1986, pp.94–5.
92 McMillan, 'Clothes', July 1912. See also Margaret McMillan, 'In Our Garden', *Highway*, August 1912; and Mrs L. Glasier Forster, *The New Needlecraft*, with a Preface by Margaret McMillan, P.S. King, 1919.
93 Arthur Greenwood, *'All Children Are Mine': Inaugural Margaret McMillan Lecture*, University of London Press for the Margaret McMillan Fellowship, 1952, p.11.
94 University of Liverpool, Sidney Jones Library, Glasier Papers, I.1, 1902/9, 27–11, John Bruce Glasier to Elizabeth Glasier Foster, 22 November 1902.
95 McMillan, *Life*, p.99.
96 See above, pp.86–7.
97 For the background to McMillan's isolation in these years, see Paul Thompson, *Socialists, Liberals and Labour*, Routledge & Kegan Paul, 1967. See the *Clarion*, 7 June 1907, for a report of the ILP committee chaired by McMillan; also 'School Clinics: Their First Fruit', *Labour Leader*, 9 September 1909; and Mansbridge, pp.75–6.
98 McMillan, *Life*, p.121.
99 ibid., pp.103, 101.
100 ibid., pp.103–4.
101 GLC Record Office, School Board Records (unclassified material), Alverton Street School, Managers' Yearly School Report, School Year Ended February 1903; Trundley's Road, Managers' Yearly School Report, School Year Ended February 1903; Deptford Park School, Managers' Yearly School Report, School Year Ended February 1903.
102 Alverton Street, Managers' Report, School Year Ended February 1905.
103 ibid.
104 Margaret McMillan, *Infant Mortality*, Independent Labour Party, 1906.
105 For expressions of this relationship, see Margaret McMillan, 'Ethics for Mothers', *Ethics*, 23 April 1904; 'A New Epoch for Children', *Labour Leader*, 22 November 1907.
106 McMillan, *Child Labour*.
107 McMillan, 'Save the Children'. See also 'Our Ailing School Children: And Then?', *Wheatsheaf*, January 1912.
108 Winifred Blatchford, 'Twenty Years Ago', *Clarion*, 11 July 1913.
109 Raymond Williams, *The Country and the City*, Paladin, 1975, pp.259–79.
110 McMillan, *Life*, p.105.
111 Margaret McMillan, 'Deptford's Health Clinic: On Patients and Visitors', *Clarion*, 4 November 1910; 'Help the Children'.
112 McMillan, 'In Holy Isle', *Highway*, October 1911.
113 McMillan, *Life*, pp.106–8.
114 Margaret McMillan, 'A Slum Mother', *Woman Worker*, 3 July 1908.
115 Margaret McMillan, 'Clouds and Rain', *Woman Worker*, 17 July 1908.

116 Reading University Library, Astor Papers, MS 1416/4/68, Margaret McMillan to Nancy Astor, 15 December 1926.
117 Williams, pp.271–4. Arthur Morrisson, *Tales of Mean Streets*, Methuen, 1894; *Child of the Jago*, Methuen, 1896.
118 Williams, p.272.
119 Blatchford, 'Twenty Years Ago'. The miles and miles of streets are found too in Morrisson (1894), Introduction: ' . . . there is no other way in the world that can more properly be called a single street, because of its dismal lack of accent, its sordid uniformity, its utter remoteness from delight . . .'.
120 McMillan, 'How I Became a Socialist', *Labour Leader*, 11 July 1912.

6 Women

1 Jane Lewis, *Women in England, 1870–1950: Sexual Divisions and Social Change*, Wheatsheaf, Brighton, 1984, pp.83–5.
2 ibid., pp.88–9.
3 August Bebel, *Woman in the Past, Present and Future*, Modern Press, 1885, p.88.
4 David Eder, *The Endowment of Motherhood*, New Age Press, 1908.
5 Nuffield College Library, Fabian Society Papers, C4 Minute Book, entry dated 12 September 1892.
6 University of Liverpool, Sidney Jones Library, Glasier Papers, I.1, 1892/24, 2-10, Barbara Fraser to John Bruce Glasier, 2 October 1892.
7 Margaret McMillan, 'Louise Michel', *Labour Prophet*, December 1892, January 1893.
8 University of Liverpool, Sidney Jones Library, Glasier Papers, II.3, MS Notebooks of Katharine Bruce Glasier, 'Our Fabian Circle'.
9 University of Liverpool, Sidney Jones Library, Glasier Papers, I.1, 1893/80, 2-1, Margaret McMillan to John Bruce Glasier, 2 January 1893.
10 Diana Burfield, 'Theosophy and Feminism: Some Explorations in Nineteenth Century Biography', in Pat Holden (ed.), *Women's Religious Experience*, Croom Helm, 1983, pp.27–56.
11 University of Liverpool, Sidney Jones Library, Glasier Papers, I.1, 1893/81,4-2, Margaret McMillan to John Bruce Glasier, 2 February 1893.
12 ibid., I.1, 1893/24, John Bruce Glasier to Barbara Fraser, 6 June 1893.
13 ibid., I.1, 1892/37, 2-8, Margaret McMillan to John Bruce Glasier, 2 August 1892.
14 As did Drummond's thesis in *The Ascent of Man*. See above, pp.73–4.
15 University of Liverpool, Sidney Jones Library, Glasier Papers, I.1, 1892/37, 2-8, Margaret McMillan to John Bruce Glasier, 2 August 1892.
16 ibid., I.1, 1893/21, 12-1, Barbara Fraser to John Bruce Glasier, 12 January 1893.
17 ibid., I.1, 1892/37, 2-8, Margaret McMillan to John Bruce Glasier, 2 August 1892.
18 Joseph Edwards, *Labour Annual*, Labour Press, Manchester, 1896, pp.212–13.

19 Edward Carpenter, *Love's Coming of Age*, Labour Press, Manchester, 1896, pp. 43–4, for ladydom.
20 University of Liverpool, Sidney Jones Library, Glasier Papers, II.3, MS Notebooks of Katharine Bruce Glasier, 'Our Fabian Circle', pp. 16, 161.
21 Isabella O. Ford, *On the Threshold*, Arnold, 1895, pp. 28–9. Leeds-based member of the ILP, from a wealthy background. A member of the NAC of the ILP at the same time as McMillan.
22 ibid., pp. 134–5.
23 ibid., p. 201.
24 Rachel McMillan College Library, McMillan Collection, A1/1, Margaret McMillan to Sally Blatchford, 2 February 1895. She also offered comfort over the dead baby in the passage quoted at the opening of this chapter, continuing her observations thus: 'And these great people never . . . see anything but what they have tried to see a long, long time, it was there all the time, but saw it only after long looking. "There are more things in Heaven & Earth than are dreamed of in our philosophies". And Angel had only been looking for Tess, and Huxley for bones, and you dear for your Sweet little Baby. Yes. I do think that he lives yet, and that you will see him again.'
25 Margaret McMillan, 'Women of the ILP', *Clarion*, 10 March 1894. See also Margaret McMillan, 'Women in Relation to the Labour Movement', in Edwards, pp. 138–9.
26 McMillan, 'Women of the ILP' (1894).
27 Margaret McMillan, 'Shop Life', *Labour Prophet*, June 1893. 'Silk Workers', *Labour Prophet*, September 1893. 'R.M.' (Rachel McMillan), 'Female Labour', *Liverpool Labour Chronicle*, 2 September 1895.
28 Margaret McMillan, 'Women of the Age of Gold: Lady Featherpoll – A Woman in Society', *Labour Prophet*, February 1893.
29 Christine Collette, 'Socialism and Scandal', *History Workshop Journal*, 23 (Spring 1987), pp. 102–11.
30 ibid., p. 105.
31 For Montefiore, see Dora B. Montefiore, *From a Victorian to a Modern*, E. Archer, 1927; and Collette, p. 110.
32 For George Belt, see Collette, p. 111.
33 London School of Economics, Francis Johnson Collection, 1899/22, Margaret MacDonald to John Keir Hardie, 19 April 1899.
34 Collette, p. 104.
35 For a fiction of women falling and fallen women, see Margaret McMillan, 'The Clarion Round Table: A Reed Shaken in the Wind', *Clarion*, 8 December 1900.
36 Francis Johnson Collection, 1899/13, Dora Montefiore to John Keir Hardie, 3 April 1899. She wrote from 49 Hanover Square, Bradford.
37 Francis Johnson Collection, 1899/27, Margaret McMillan to John Keir Hardie, 11 November 1899.
38 Margaret McMillan, 'Shop Life', 'Silk Workers', *Labour Prophet*, June 1893, September 1893.
39 For Louise Michel, see Irma Boyer, *Louise Michel, d'après des documents inédits*, Paris, 1927 (by which publication McMillan may have been

prompted into memory for her writing of the *Life*); Anne Zévaès, *Louise Michel*, Paris, 1936; Edith Thomas, *Louise Michel*, Gallimard, Paris, 1971. See also Louise Michel, 'Why We Are Anarchists', *Commonweal*, 26 September 1891.

40 McMillan, *Life*, pp.59–60.
41 ibid., pp.65–70.
42 ibid., pp.71–2.
43 ibid., p.72.
44 Margaret McMillan, 'Louise Michel', *Labour Prophet*, December 1892, January 1893.
45 All accounts seem to agree that 'Lily Bell' was really Mrs Bream Pearce, the wife of one of Hardie's backers for the *Labour Leader*; but I harbour some suspicion that on occasion Hardie wrote this column, in transmogrification from his 'Daddy Time' children's column, and Kenneth O. Morgan (*Labour People*, Oxford University Press, Oxford, 1987, p.26) thinks so too. For the electrifying Glasgow performance, see 'Lily Bell', 'The Apotheosis of Woman', *Labour Leader*, 26 December 1896.
46 Edwards, *Labour Annual*, pp.212–13.
47 'J.E.', 'Caroline E.D. Martin' [*sic*], *Liverpool Labour Chronicle*, 1 August 1895.
48 See above, p.39 and Note 27.
49 Jill Liddington and Jill Norris, *One Hand Tied Behind Us: The Rise of the Women's Suffrage Movement*, Virago, 1978, p.127.
50 McMillan, *Life*, p.37.
51 Bradford Record Office, Miriam Lord Collection, 22D77/14/19, Miriam Senior to Miriam Lord, 22 February 1956. See also Collette, p.105.
52 Liddington and Norris, pp.168–9 and *passim*.
53 ibid., p.125.
54 ibid., pp.184–5. ILP, *Report of the Thirteenth Annual Conference of the ILP*, 1905.
55 Martin Pugh, 'Labour and Women's Suffrage', in K.D. Brown (ed.), *The First Labour Party, 1906–1914*, Croom Helm, 1985, pp.233–53.
56 Isabella Ford was elected to the NAC in 1903, McMillan in 1906.
57 Liddington and Norris, p.127.
58 ibid., pp.167–92.
59 McMillan, *Life*, p.85.
60 Margaret McMillan, 'Women in Relation to the Labour Movement', in Edwards, pp.138–9.
61 Enid Stacey, 'A Century of Women's Rights', in Edward Carpenter (ed.), *Forecasts of the Coming Century*, Labour Press, Manchester, 1897.
62 Enid Stacey, 'Women's Work and the ILP', in Edwards, pp.116–18.
63 Margaret McMillan, 'Women of the ILP', *Clarion*, 10 March 1894.
64 Margaret McMillan, 'Are Women Awake?', *Labour Leader*, 9 January 1913.
65 Lewis, pp.92–7; especially p.94.
66 *Journal of the Royal Sanitary Institute*, 18 (1897), pp.50–6; 19 (1898), pp.126–7; Women's Sanitary Inspectors' Association, *Reports*, 1905–1907/8.
67 For Mary Gregory, see Malcolm Ross, 'Bradford Politics, 1880–1906', Ph.D,

Bradford University, 1977, p.365. See above, p.42. See also Patricia Hollis, *Ladies Elect: Women in English Local Government, 1865–1914*, Clarendon Press, 1987, pp.1–68, for a discussion of the relationship between philanthropy and work in local politics.

68 Liddington and Norris, pp.205–6. Margaret McMillan, 'The Women in Prison', *Clarion*, 2 November 1906.

69 Liddington and Norris, p.205.

70 For the girl-heroine, see above, pp.24–5. See also Margaret McMillan, 'Where Women Fight and Die', *Clarion*, 17 August 1906.

71 McMillan, 'Women in Prison'.

72 Rebecca West, 'A Quiet Day With the Constitutionals', *Clarion*, 1 August 1913; see also her 'Miss McMillan and the Police', *Christian Commonwealth*, 30 July 1913. This incident also produced one of the few surviving letters from Rachel McMillan: Rachel McMillan College Library, McMillan Collection, A1/.

73 For the idea of McMillan's 'special work', see 'Miss McMillan's Breakdown', *Christian Commonwealth*, 18 February 1914.

74 Liddington and Norris, p.207.

75 London School of Economics, Francis Johnson Collection, 1906/366, Isabella Ford and Margaret McMillan to Francis Johnson, 28 October 1906.

76 ILP, *Report of the Fifteenth Annual Conference of the ILP*, 1907, pp.47–8. See also E.S. Pankhurst, *The Suffrage Movement* (1931), Virago, 1977, pp.249–50.

77 ILP, *Report*, 1907, p.33.

78 ibid., pp.22, 31, 43.

79 Margaret McMillan, 'Women and the Franchise', *Clarion*, 21 September 1906.

80 Margaret McMillan, 'The Case for the Industrial Woman', *Men's League on Women's Suffrage Handbook*, 1912.

81 Margaret McMillan, 'The Franchise for Working-Class Women', pamphlet issued by the People's Suffrage Federation, n.d., in Rachel McMillan College Library, McMillan Collection, A11/misc. For the People's Suffrage Federation, see Liddington and Norris, p.247.

82 Margaret McMillan, 'A Message of Spring', *Woman Worker*, April 1908.

83 See above, pp.22, 33, 129–30.

84 See the *Clarion*, 11 November 1899.

85 Duke of Sutherland, *Looking Back*, Odhams Press, 1957. Dennis Stuart, *Dear Duchess: Millicent Duchess of Sutherland, 1867–1955*, Gollancz, 1982, pp.93–6, 104–13. The Duchess dramatised the ideological conflicts of this new world in Millicent Sutherland, *One Hour and the Next*, Methuen, 1899.

86 Julia Dawson, 'Our Woman's Letter', *Clarion*, 16 April 1898. University of Liverpool, Sidney Jones Library, Glasier Papers, I.1, 1899/34, 17-11, Katharine Bruce Glasier to John Bruce Glasier, 17 November 1899.

7 *Journalism*

1 Amy Bulley and Margaret Whiteley, *Women's Work*, Methuen, 1894, pp.4–5. The Duchess of Sutherland was another source of advice on

journalism as a job for the girls; see a notice in the *Labour Leader*, 24 June 1899, and her forthcoming presidency of a session on this topic at the Women's International Congress of 1899.

2 A.J. Lee, *The Origins of the Popular Press in England, 1855–1914*, Croom Helm, 1976, pp.111–20. R.L. Schults, *Crusader in Babylon: W.T. Stead and the Pall Mall Gazette*, University of Nebraska Press, Lincoln, 1972, pp.29–65. Raymond Williams, *The Long Revolution*, Chatto & Windus, 1961, pp.173–213.

3 Bulley and Whiteley, p.4. See Lee, p.129.

4 Bulley and Whiteley, p.5.

5 Raymond Williams, *Marxism and Literature*, Oxford University Press, Oxford, 1977, pp.145–98, for the instability of these categories. See also a discussion of them in the journalism of George Orwell: Raymond Williams, *Orwell*, Fontana, 1984, pp.41–2, 50–52.

6 For Blatchford's fictional productions, see Laurence Thompson, *Robert Blatchford, Portrait of an Englishman*, Gollancz, 1951, pp.122, 123, 125, 127–8; for a description of a piece of Hardie's extended fiction, see Fred Reid, *Keir Hardie: The Making of a Socialist*, Croom Helm, 1978, pp.186–92.

7 Williams (1961), p.178.

8 Logie Barrow, 'The Socialism of Robert Blatchford and the *Clarion*', Ph.D, University of London, 1975, pp.53–8, 65.

9 For personal journalism of this kind, see D.R. Hopkins, 'The Newspapers of the Independent Labour Party, 1893–1906', Ph.D, University College of Wales, Aberystwyth, 1981, pp.96–7, 103. See also Deian Hopkins, 'The Labour Party Press', in K.D. Brown (ed.), *The First Labour Party, 1906–1914*, Croom Helm, 1985, pp.106–28; also Deian Hopkins, 'The Socialist Press in Britain, 1890–1910', in George Boyce *et al.* (eds), *Newspaper History from the Seventeenth Century to the Present*, Constable, 1978, pp.294–306.

10 She called herself a 'social worker' for her entry in the *Englishwoman's Year Book and Directory* (ed. G.E. Mitton), Adam & Charles Black, 1914.

11 Hopkins (1981), pp.119–20.

12 See above, pp.34–5.

13 Margaret McMillan, 'Louise Michel', *Labour Prophet*, January 1893. For the development of the interview, see Schults, pp.61–5 and *passim*.

14 Margaret McMillan, 'Silk Workers', *Labour Prophet*, September 1893.

15 Margaret McMillan, 'A True Capitalist', *Labour Prophet*, December 1893.

16 Margaret McMillan, 'A Halt on the Hill', *Clarion*, 14 April 1894.

17 Margaret McMillan, 'Two Friends', *Clarion*, 24 November 1894.

18 Margaret McMillan, 'Women of the Age of Gold: Lady Featherpoll – A Woman in Society', *Labour Prophet*, February 1893.

19 See above, pp.46–7, and below.

20 'Ethel' was one of these. See above, p.139.

21 These stories were used as teaching material in the Socialist Sunday Schools, and like all writers for children, McMillan wrote them with two audiences in mind: the children listening and the adult reading aloud.

22 Thompson, pp.113–31.
23 ibid., pp.96–113, 114.
24 Provincial weeklies often had a higher circulation than this, of between 30,000 and 40,000. Lee, p.179.
25 Thompson, p.114.
26 Lee, p.71.
27 Thompson, p.114.
28 Quoted ibid., p.82.
29 Williams (1961), pp.173–5.
30 See Williams (1961), pp.192–206.
31 See above, pp.24, 67.
32 Schults, p.136.
33 Lee, p.118. Schults, pp.193–211.
34 Thompson, p.114; and see Barrow, p.230.
35 *Clarion*, 24 March 1894.
36 David Howell, *British Workers and the Independent Labour Party, 1888–1906*, Manchester University Press, Manchester, 1983, p.380.
37 Barrow, pp.53–8. Thompson, p.230.
38 McMillan, *Life*, p.82.
39 For women's columns, Chris Waters, '"Masculine Socialism" and the Development of Women's Columns in the British Socialist Press, 1884–1914', unpublished paper, November 1986.
40 Barrow, pp.56–7; Thompson, p.130.
41 Lee, p.189.
42 Barrow, pp.62–3, for the 'educationalist' project of the *Clarion*.
43 Quoted by Thompson, p.114.
44 University of Liverpool, Sidney Jones Library, Glasier Papers, I.1, 1908/79, 18-1, Margaret McMillan to John Bruce Glasier, 13 January 1908.
45 Margaret McMillan, 'On the Embankment', *Labour Leader*, 17 January 1908.
46 Margaret McMillan, 'The Two Conquerors', *Clarion*, 6 May 1895. Was 'Hope' Tom Maguire? See Margaret McMillan, 'Tom Maguire: A Remembrance', *Labour Leader*, 25 October 1895: 'he lived long enough and produced enough to let us know that in the movement another child of Hope was born and a strong son given.' See E.P. Thompson, 'Homage to Tom Maguire', in Asa Briggs and John Saville (eds). *Essays in Labour History*, Macmillan, 1960, pp.276–316.
47 Waters, '"Masculine Socialism . . ."'.
48 For social motherhood, see above, pp.121–2.
49 Waters, pp.34–5.
50 'A Woman's Point of View', the women's column of the SDF paper *Justice*, also promoted Margaret McMillan. See *Justice*, 24 October, 7 November 1908.
51 Robert Blatchford, 'Socialism Made Easy', *Woman Worker*, 5 June 1908. Blatchford quoted in Thompson, p.125.
52 For domestic child-study, see Carolyn Steedman, *The Tidy House*, Virago, 1982, pp.61–88. As practised in the Blatchford household, see Thompson, pp.23, 49, 64, 218–36.

53 Raymond Williams, *Writing in Society*, Verso, n.d. (1981), p.71.
54 ibid., p.73.

8 *Socialism*

1 Rachel McMillan College Library, McMillan Collection, A1/80, Ethel Snowden to Margaret McMillan, 16 November 1929. The money was the paying off of McMillan's debts, incurred in the building of the Rachel McMillan Training College.
2 David Howell, *British Workers and the Independent Labour Party, 1888–1906*, Manchester University Press, Manchester, 1983, p.2.
3 ibid., pp.2–5. Kenneth O. Morgan, *Labour People*, Oxford University Press, Oxford, 1987, p.26.
4 ibid., pp.1–2.
5 For very brief biographies of these women, see Stephen Yeo, 'A New Life: The Religion of Socialism in Britain, 1888–1896', *History Workshop Journal*, 4 (Autumn 1977), pp.5–56.
6 Percy Redfern, 'People and Books: Margaret McMillan', *Wheatsheaf*, May 1932.
7 Karl Pierson, *Marxism and the Origins of British Socialism*, Cornell University Press, Ithaca, 1973, pp.160–61.
8 Redfern, 'People and Books'. See also Percy Redfern, *Journey to Understanding*, Allen & Unwin, 1946, pp.18–19, for another description of the same incident.
9 Laurence Thompson, *Robert Blatchford, Portrait of an Englishman*, Gollancz, 1951, pp.113–31. Howell, p.381.
10 Howell, pp.353–5.
11 James Hinton, *Labour and Socialism: A History of the British Labour Movement, 1867–1974*, Wheatsheaf, Brighton, 1983, pp.58–63.
12 Howell, pp.354, 361.
13 ibid., p.362.
14 Katharine Bruce Glasier, 'Miss M'Millan's Book', *ILP News*, June 1900.
15 See Laurence Thompson, *The Enthusiasts: A Biography of John and Katharine Bruce Glasier*, Gollancz, 1971, pp.88–91.
16 See above, pp.33–5; also Margaret McMillan, 'Socialism in a Highland Kirk', *Clarion*, 19 May 1894.
17 Margaret McMillan, 'Liberty', *Christian Socialist*, April 1890.
18 ibid.; see also 'Help', *Christian Socialist*, April 1891.
19 ibid.
20 'Almost a Notable Book', *Labour Leader*, 8 June 1895.
21 *Justice*, 25 March 1911.
22 University of Liverpool, Sidney Jones Library, Glasier Papers, I.1, 1905/14, 1–9, John Bruce Glasier to Elizabeth Glasier Foster, 1 September 1905.
23 Howell, p.352; Hinton, p.42.
24 What mattered *is* discussed by Pierson, pp.27–37; and by Raymond Williams, *Culture and Society* (1958), Hogarth Press, 1987, pp.133–48.
25 See above, pp.46–7 and below, pp.194–7.

26 William Jolly, *Ruskin on Education, Some Needed But Neglected Elements*, Allen & Unwin, 1894, pp.37, 38, 118. John Ruskin, 'Fors Clavigera', Letters 37–72 (1874), *The Library Edition of the Works of John Ruskin*, vol. 28, George Allen, 1907, p.655.

27 Pierson, p.90.

28 See below, pp.209–10. Evidence of her understanding of the work of Charcot in the 1890s is found in Margaret McMillan, 'A la Salpêtrière', *Clarion*, 29 April 1897; 'The Subconscious: the Lorelei', *Clarion*, 12 June 1897; 'In the Pantheon', *Clarion*, 20 November 1897.

29 Margaret McMillan, 'Growth', *Clarion*, 20 February 1897.

30 Douglas Guthrie, *A History of Medicine*, Nelson, 1958. G. Zilboorg and G.W. Henry, *A History of Medical Psychology*, Norton, New York, 1941.

31 See above, p.130.

32 Which she kept up with. Much of her journalism involved conveying ideas from European social policy to British labour and socialist audiences. See, for example, 'Germany and Its Children', *Clarion*, 22 June 1906; 'Shower Baths', *Labour Leader*, 7 September 1906; 'Municipalisation of Hospitals', *Labour Leader*, 28 September 1906; 'A "Special" School Day', *Labour Leader*, 28 February 1908; 'A Day at Askov', *Highway*, October 1910; 'Why Are the Germans Clean?', *Clarion*, 17 June 1910; 'Vive la France', *Highway*, August 1910; *A Children's Day*, Women's Printing Society, 1910.

33 For Saint-Simonianism, see below, p.194. See also Pierson, p.41. I am grateful to Joan Simon for making this connection plain to me.

34 Hinton, p.41. Ian Bullock, 'Socialists and Democratic Form in Britain, 1880–1914', Ph.D, University of Sussex, 1981, pp.80–81.

35 Howell, p.359.

36 See above, pp.39–40.

37 Hinton, p.59.

38 ibid., pp.62, 74, 76.

39 ibid., p.62.

40 Katharine Conway, *The Cry of the Children*, Labour Press, Manchester, 2nd edn, 1894.

41 Katharine Bruce Glasier, *Socialism and the Home*, ILP Press, 1909.

42 ILP, *Report of the Sixteenth Annual Conference of the Independent Labour Party*, 1908. NAC Report: 'At the last annual Conference, the Party voted solid in favour of a Medical Board at Whitehall . . . This unanimous vote had an important effect on the deliberations of Government, and no report would be faithful which ignores the splendid work done by our Comrade Miss Margaret McMillan and the influence of our Conference.'

43 See above, p.54.

44 See summaries of Margaret McMillan's and Keir Hardie's contributions to the conference in 'Nurture versus Education', *The Needs of Little Children, Report of a Conference on the Care of Babies and Young Children*, Women's Labour League, London, 1912, pp.6–7. See also Caroline Rowan, 'Women in the Labour Party, 1906–1920', *Feminist Review*, 12 (October 1982), pp.74–91.

45 For the SDF position on medical inspection, see Brian Simon, *Education*

and the Labour Movement, 1870–1920, Lawrence & Wishart, 1965, pp. 285–92.

46 Howell, pp. 347–8.

47 Simon, pp. 20–23.

48 Albert Mansbridge, *Margaret McMillan, Prophet and Pioneer: Her Life and Work*, Dent, 1932, pp. 145–7. Mansbridge dates this letter 1899.

49 On this point, see below, pp. 215–25, *passim*.

50 Rodney Barker, 'The Labour Party and Education for Socialism', *International Review of Social History*, 15 (1969), pp. 22–53. See also Clive Griggs, 'Labour and Education', in K. D. Brown (ed.), *The First Labour Party, 1906–1914*, Croom Helm, 1985, pp. 158–82.

51 *Labour Leader*, 20 April 1906, quoted by Brian Simon, p. 285.

52 See Simon, pp. 285–92. See also a letter from Will Thorne supporting McMillan and condemning Ramsay MacDonald's position on medical treatment, *Labour Leader*, 20 August 1908. See also *Report of the Ninth Annual Conference of the Labour Party*, Labour Party, 1909.

53 See above, pp. 49–51; and Simon, pp. 208–46.

54 ibid., pp. 218–35.

55 Howell, p. 348.

56 Hinton, pp. 73, 74.

57 ILP, *Commercialism and Child Labour* (City of London Branch Pamphlets No. 4), City Branch of the ILP, 1900, p. 3. McMillan probably wrote this pamphlet.

58 ILP, *Report of the Fourteenth Annual Conference of the Independent Labour Party*, 1906, Resolutions.

59 Simon, pp. 284–5. See ILP, *Report of the Seventeenth Annual Conference of the Labour Party*, Labour Party, 1909. See also David Eder, 'The Treatment of School Children', *New Age*, 5 August 1908, for an account of MacDonald's attitude towards medical inspection.

60 Simon, p. 281. See also Clive Griggs, *The Trades Union Congress and the Struggle for Education, 1868–1925*, Falmer Press, Lewes, 1983, pp. 109–58.

61 Simon, pp. 282–3.

62 ibid., pp. 286–7. *Justice*, 11 May 1907.

63 Margaret McMillan, 'The Trades Union Congress and School Clinics', *Labour Leader*, 3 September 1909, for this remark. See also a report of the 1909 ILP Conference by McMillan in the *Christian Commonwealth*, 14 April 1909.

64 ILP, *Report of the Seventeenth Annual Conference of the Independent Labour Party*, 1909. See also *Labour Leader*, 20 August 1909.

65 Howell, p. 358.

66 See above, pp. 73–4.

67 *Clarion*, 18 August 1894 (McMillan's emphasis). See also *Clarion*, 30 June, 14 July 1894. See Bullock, pp. 78–83.

9   Education

1 For a brief account of the historiography of educational history, see Harold Silver, *Education as History*, Methuen, 1983, pp. 17–24.

2 Stephen Yeo, 'A New Life: The Religion of Socialism in Britain, 1888–1896', *History Workshop Journal*, 4 (Autumn 1977), pp.5–56.
3 McMillan, *Life*, p.30.
4 William Morris, quoted in Asa Briggs (ed.), *William Morris, Selected Writing and Designs*, Penguin, 1962, p.143.
5 Fred Reid, 'Socialist Sunday Schools in Britain, 1892–1939', *International Review of Social History*, 2 (1966), pp.18–47.
6 *Labour Leader*, 26 May 1895.
7 Reid, pp.33–4.
8 ibid., pp.35–8.
9 Margaret McMillan, 'Clothes – And the Making of Them', *Young Socialist*, July 1912.
10 Margaret McMillan, 'School Mates', *Young Socialist*, November 1903.
11 Margaret McMillan, 'Mazzini', *Young Socialist*, June 1909.
12 Margaret McMillan, 'Arithmetic', *Young Socialist*, July, August, September 1904. For the failed primer, see Reid, p.23.
13 Margaret McMillan, 'The Swifts', *Young Socialist*, March 1904.
14 For the fairy-tale debate, see *Young Socialist*, September 1907, February 1908.
15 Reid, pp.26–7.
16 Margaret McMillan, 'A Letter from Margaret McMillan', *Young Socialist*, February 1908.
17 The editor commented, of the above: 'We are honoured this month with a special article by Miss M'Millan. Teachers are urged to get hold of the Boole books'; McMillan had discussed Mary Everest Boole's *Introduction to Science* (by which McMillan probably meant *The Preparation of the Child for Science*) (1904), *The Logic of Arithmetic* (1903), and *Logic Taught by Love* (1890).
18 See reports in the *Young Socialist*, October 1902, September, November 1903.
19 *Young Socialist*, July 1904.
20 *Young Socialist*, May 1909.
21 ibid., pp.4–6.
22 *ILP News*, November 1899.
23 *Bradford Labour Echo*, 25 May, 1, 8, 15 June 1895. *Clarion*, 17 August 1895. *Labour Leader*, 24 August 1895. *Clarion*, 11, 18, 25 January; 1, 8 February 1896.
24 *Bradford Labour Echo*, 28 March 1896. *Clarion*, 28 March, 4, 11 April 1896.
25 *Bradford Labour Echo*, 4 April 1896.
26 *Bradford Labour Echo*, 19 April 1896. *Labour Leader*, 18 April 1896.
27 *Clarion*, 6, 20, 27 March, 24 April 1897.
28 *Labour Prophet*, May 1896.
29 Margaret McMillan, *The Child and the State*, Socialist Library IX, National Labour Press, Manchester, 1911, p.166.
30 McMillan, *Life*, pp.83, 84.
31 Margaret McMillan, 'The Door of the North', *Highway*, September 1909.
32 McMillan, *The Child and the State*, p.134.

33 Brian Simon, *Education and the Labour Movement, 1870–1920*, Lawrence & Wishart, 1965.

34 J. Ramsay MacDonald, 'Socialism and Society', in B. Barker (ed.), *Ramsay MacDonald's Political Writings*, Allen Lane, 1972.

35 Albert Mansbridge, *An Adventure in Working Class Education*, Longman, Green, 1920. Simon, pp.303–11. For Morant and the WEA, see also B.M. Allen, *Sir Robert Morant*, Macmillan, 1934, p.251.

36 Albert Mansbridge, 'Educational Causerie', *Co-operative News*, 8 January 1910. Simon, p.307.

37 Editorial, *Highway*, October 1908.

38 Workers' Educational Association Council Minutes, Minutes of an Executive meeting on 30 April 1910. WEA Annual Reports, 1903–11, *Seventh Annual Report*, 1 July 1910, p.13. McMillan, 'Door of the North' (1909), Margaret McMillan, 'A Day at Askov', *Highway*, October 1909; 'A Visit to a Danish High School', *Highway*, December 1912. See also *Highway*, June 1910.

39 McMillan, *Child and State*, (1911), pp.95–124.

40 See Jonathan Rée, *Proletarian Philosophers, Problems in Socialist Culture in Britain, 1900–1940*, Clarendon Press, Oxford, 1984.

41 Margaret McMillan, 'Worker and Student', *Highway*, July 1909. Pierre Loti was the author of the classic 'childhood', *Le roman d'un enfant*, Paris, 1890.

42 Albert Mansbridge, *Margaret McMillan, Prophet and Pioneer: Her Life and Work*, Dent, 1932, p.54.

43 Margaret McMillan, 'Flower in a Slum', *Christian Commonwealth*, 14 September 1910.

44 McMillan, *Life*, pp.85–6.

45 Mansbridge (1932), p.149. 'There shall be no more sea': The Revelation of St John the Divine, 21:1: 'for the first heaven and the first earth were passed away; and there was no more sea'? What did McMillan mean by using this text? It provided the epigraph for her novel *Samson* as well. Does it simply evoke the completely new world, the old one swept convulsively away? If so, then the new world is evoked negatively, in terms of great loss and sadness.

46 Margaret McMillan, 'How I Became a Socialist', *Labour Leader*, 11 July 1912.

47 Denison Deasey, *Education Under Six*, Croom Helm, 1978, pp.130–35.

48 Elizabeth Bradburn, *Margaret McMillan, Framework and Expansion of Nursery Education*, Denholm Press, Redhill, 1976, pp.77–91, 135–59, and *passim*. Margaret McMillan, *The Nursery School*, Dent, 1919, pp.21–31, 317–46. Margaret McMillan, *What the Open-Air Nursery School Is*, Labour Party, 1929. Margaret McMillan, *The Nursery School*, Dent, 1930, pp.31–42.

49 Margaret McMillan, 'Discipline', *Clarion*, 24 October 1913: 'I sometimes (but not often), take a class in my own camp school, and it is not a very big one, and yet though we are out in the open air, and the boys are clean and healthy and intelligent, and though we are good friends, and keen and so on, yet I have called these boys names and at times they have got a certain

amount of joy out of tormenting me.' Early in the 1890s, undertaking educational rescue work with girl factory workers in the East End, she had experienced something similar. See McMillan, *Life*, pp.38–41.

50 McMillan, *Nursery School* (1919), pp.19–20.

51 Miles Franklin Papers, in the Mitchell Library of Macquarie University, MS 364, vol.13, pp.19–25, Margaret McMillan to Stella Franklin, 21 November 1915. I am very grateful to Jill Roe of the School of History, Macquarie University, for telling me about Franklin's Deptford interlude.

52 Schlesinger Library, Radcliffe University, Cambridge, Mass.; Abigail Adams, Papers, 1885–1979, general preamble. My thanks to Hetty Startup for giving me this reference.

53 McMillan, *Nursery School* (1919), pp.15–16.

54 ibid., pp. 176–80.

55 ibid.

56 See, for example, material in Bradford Record Office, Miriam Lord Collection, 22D77/15/24, Kathleen Wicks to Miriam Lord, n.d. (1956). Bradburn, pp.116–59, *passim*. G.A.N. Lowndes, *Margaret McMillan, The Children's Champion*, Museum Press, 1960, pp.78–82.

57 Reading University Library, Astor Papers, MS 1416/1/4/68, Margaret McMillan to Nancy Astor, 10, 20 November 1926.

58 ibid., MS 1416/1/74, Nancy Astor to Julius Rosenwald, 30 December 1927. There is a voluminous correspondence on the building of the College.

59 ibid., MS 1416/1/1/71, Nancy Astor to Julius Rosenwald, 16 November 1928.

60 ibid., MS 1416/1/1/68, Henrietta Brown Smith to Nancy Astor, 14 November 1929.

61 'Miss McMillan's Speech at the Opening of the College, May 8th, 1930', quoted in Lowndes, pp.107–9.

62 Anna Freud, 'The Role of the Teacher', *Harvard Education Review*, 22:4 (Fall 1952).

63 For a development of this argument, see Carolyn Steedman, 'Prisonhouses', *Feminist Review*, 20 (Summer 1985), pp.3–21.

64 Lowndes, p.78.

65 McMillan, *Nursery School* (1919), p.182. Alain Corbin, *The Foul and the Fragrant*, Berg, Leamington Spa, 1986, pp.151–7; pp.152–3: ' . . . the premises of the poor. The only means of entry was through low, narrow, dark alleys . . . Gaining access to the poor man's stinking dwelling almost amounted to an underground expedition . . . inside the dwelling . . . the cage rather than the den was the dominant image . . . In particular, writings focused on the aspect of narrowness . . . .'.

66 Mansbridge (1932), pp.140–41.

10 *Bodies*

1 London School of Economics, Francis Johnson Collection, 1899/16, John Keir Hardie to David Lane, 6 April 1899.

2 J.W. Slaughter, 'Labour and Childhood: The Books of Margaret McMillan', *Highway*, December 1908, January 1909.

3 Garland E. Allen, *Life Sciences in the Twentieth Century*, Cambridge University Press, Cambridge, 1978, pp.xi–xxiii, 18–19.

4 ibid., pp.xxi–xxii.

5 She rarely evoked these names in her journalism. The most extensive use of their research is to be found in the book under discussion, and in *Education Through the Imagination* (1904 edn).

6 She probably read the work of Karl Groos (1861–1946) and Wilhelm Wundt (1832–1920) in the original.

7 For the work of Pinel, Esquirol and Itard, see Lancelot Law Whyte, *The Unconscious Before Freud*, Friedmann, 1979; and for accounts of Jean Itard's work, which was of particular importance to McMillan as transmitted by Édouard Seguin, see Harlan Lane, *The Wild Boy of Aveyron*, Paladin, 1979, pp.73–95, 133–60, 257–86.

8 Margaret McMillan, *Early Childhood*, Swan Sonnenschein, 1900, p.11.

9 ibid., pp.11–12.

10 The neurologist who appeared most frequently in McMillan's writing was William Carpenter (1813–85), probably (though McMillan never gave references) in an account of his *Principles of Mental Physiology* (1874), in which he discussed 'unconscious cerebration' and the means by which thought and feeling could be regarded as 'an expression of brain-change'. His *Nature and Man: Essays Scientific and Philosophical* (1888) discussed 'ideomotor action' – the way in which ideas might become the sources of muscular action, quite independently of volition or emotion.

11 McMillan, *Early Childhood*, pp.12–13.

12 ibid., pp.31–2.

13 She made unacknowledged reference to what is probably Paul Broca's (1824–80) work on pp.39, 157–8 of *Early Childhood*. She made explicit reference to his work on accumulation in Margaret McMillan, 'Forecast of Civilisation', *Ethical World*, 21, 28 October 1899. See also Note 10.

14 McMillan, *Early Childhood*, p.156.

15 ibid., pp.55–6.

16 ibid., pp.169–70.

17 David Armstrong, *The Political Anatomy of the Body*, Cambridge University Press, Cambridge, 1983, pp.1–6.

18 McMillan, *Early Childhood*, p.49.

19 Armstrong, pp.8–10.

20 ibid., p.114.

21 On the body as an interiority, see Michel Foucault, *Birth of the Clinic: An Archaeology of Medical Perception*, Tavistock, 1973, pp.124–73.

22 McMillan, *Early Childhood*, p.35.

23 ILP, *Report of the Eleventh Annual Conference of the Labour Party*, Labour Party, 1911, p.86.

24 McMillan, *Early Childhood*, pp.35, 90.

25 ibid., p.90.

26 For Seguin, see Mabel E. Talbot, *Édouard Seguin*, Bureau of Publications, Teachers' College, New York, 1964, and the important account in Lane, pp.261–78. There is some account of the Itard/Seguin/Montessori route in Shelley Phillips, 'Maria Montessori and Contemporary Cognitive

Psychology', *British Journal of Teacher Education*, 3:1 (January 1977), pp.55–68.

27 See Lane, *passim*.

28 For Itard's and Seguin's work with the deaf, see Lane, pp.185–254. Édouard Seguin, *Traitement moral, hygiène, et éducation des idiots*, Ballière, Paris, 1846. For Jacob Pereire, see also Harlan Lane, *When the Mind Hears: A History of the Deaf*, Penguin, 1988, pp.67–71.

29 For Saint-Simonianism, see Ghita Ionescu, *The Political Thought of Saint-Simon*, Oxford University Press, Oxford, 1976, pp.1–13, 29–57, 204–18. Georg G. Iggers, *The Doctrine of Saint-Simon*, Schocken, New York, 1972, pp.ix–xlvii. G.D.H. Cole, *Socialist Thought: The Forerunners, 1789–1850*, Macmillan, 1953, pp.37–61. Keith Taylor, *The Political Ideas of the Utopian Socialists*, Frank Cass, 1982, pp.132–59.

30 Édouard Seguin, *Idiocy and Its Treatment By the Physiological Method* (1866), Augustus M. Kelly, New York, 1971, p.29.

31 ibid., p.28.

32 Édouard Seguin, *Report on Education*, (1875), Delmar, New York, 1976.

33 Édouard Seguin, *Rapport et mémoire sur l'éducation des enfants normaux et anormaux*, Bibliothèque d'Éducation Spéciale III, Alcan, Paris, 1895.

34 Margaret McMillan, *Education Through the Imagination* (1924 edn), Dent, 1924, p.90.

35 Margaret McMillan, 'The "New" Education', *Highway*, June 1913. See Phillips, and Lane, pp.281–6, for Montessori's use of Seguin's ideas. See also Margaret McMillan, 'The Montessori System', *Christian Commonwealth*, 26 June 1912; and 'Backward Children: A New Method of Teaching', *Christian Commonwealth*, 29 January 1913.

36 Seguin (1866), pp.104–18.

37 ibid., pp.137 f.

38 Talbot, p.44.

39 McMillan, 'Backward Children'.

40 Seguin (1966), pp.116–18.

41 McMillan, *Early Childhood*, pp.34–46. See also Margaret McMillan, *Labour and Childhood*, Swan Sonnenschein, 1907, for her promotion of Kropotkin's work.

42 Édouard Seguin (1875), pp.10, 14, 26.

43 Seguin (1866), pp.110–11.

44 McMillan, 'Forecast of Civilisation' (1899). See also Margaret McMillan, 'One of the Trespassers', *Clarion*, 5 November 1895; 'Economic Aspects of Child Labour and Education', *Transactions of the National Liberal Club, Political and Economic Circle*, 5:9 (18 December 1905).

45 McMillan, *Early Childhood*, p.34.

46 Brian Evans and Bernard Waites, *IQ and Mental Testing*, Macmillan, 1981. Leon J. Kamin, *The Science and Politics of IQ*, Penguin, Harmondsworth, 1977. L.S. Hearnshaw, *Cyril Burt, Psychologist*, Random House, New York, 1981. Brian Simon, *Intelligence, Psychology and Education*, Lawrence & Wishart, 1971.

47 Couze Venn, 'The Subject of Psychology', in Jules Henriques *et al.* (eds), *Changing the Subject*, Methuen, 1984, pp.119–52.

48 *Bradford Observer*, 13 November 1900.
49 Margaret McMillan, 'The Claims of the "Practical" in Education', *Highway*, January 1910.
50 McMillan, 'Backward Children'.
51 McMillan, 'Claims of the "Practical"'.
52 Margaret McMillan, 'My Experiences on the School Board', *Labour Prophet*, November 1895.
53 Margaret McMillan, 'School Board Notes', *Bradford Labour Echo*, 18 September 1897.
54 Rachel McMillan College Library, McMillan Collection, A1/6, Margaret McMillan to Fred Jowett, 11 December 1905.
55 McMillan, *Early Childhood*, pp.84–5.
56 Margaret McMillan, *The Beginnings of Education* (City Branch Pamphlet No.8), City of London Branch of the ILP, 1903.
57 Margaret McMillan, *The Camp School*, Allen & Unwin, 1917, pp.56–7.
58 ibid., p.118.
59 This scene has been noted before. See above, p.30.
60 Albert Mansbridge, *Margaret McMillan, Prophet and Pioneer: Her Life and Work*, Dent, 1932, pp.137, 138.
61 ibid., pp.159–60.
62 See above, p.262, Note 28.
63 Mansbridge, pp.145–7.
64 J.S. Hurt, *Elementary Schooling and the Working Classes, 1860–1918*, Routledge & Kegan Paul, 1979, pp.131–2, 170.
65 Alain Corbin, *The Foul and the Fragrant*, Berg, Leamington Spa, 1986, pp.142–60; and see Armstrong, pp.10–13.
66 Corbin, pp.1–8.
67 ibid., pp.231–2.
68 ibid., p.231.
69 See below, pp.215–25, *passim*.
70 Mansbridge, p.160.
71 Margaret McMillan, 'Clothes – And the Making of Them', *Young Socialist*, July 1912.
72 Margaret McMillan, 'Miss McMillan on the Fellowship', *Clarion*, 5 January 1901.

11 Minds

1 Lancelot Law Whyte, *The Unconscious Before Freud*, Friedmann, 1979, pp.169–70.
2 See above, pp.190–91.
3 Whyte, pp.153–76. See also Henri F. Ellenberger, *The Discovery of the Unconscious: The History and Evolution of Dynamic Psychiatry*, Allen Lane, 1970.
4 Whyte, p.161.
5 Her accounts of the 1890s, which conveyed the work of Charcot at the Salpêtrière hospital in Paris to the readers of the *Clarion*, were framed by the understanding that the work she described was neurological.

6 Henry Head, *Studies in Neurology*, 2 vols, Oxford University Press/ Hodder & Stoughton, 1920. Hughlings Jackson, *Neurological Fragments*, Oxford University Press, 1925. Both these works were the summary of decades of research, findings of which had been widely published. Hughlings Jackson, 'On Some Implications of the Dissolution of the Nervous System', *Medical Press and Circular*, 1882 (2), pp.411, 433; 1883 (2), pp.64, 84; 'Croonian Lectures on Evolution and Dissolution of the Nervous System', *British Medical Journal*, 1884 (1), pp.591, 660, 703; 'Evolution and Dissolution of the Nervous System', *Popular Science Monthly*, 25 (1886), pp.171–80; 'Remarks on the Evolution and Dissolution of the Nervous System', *Medical Press and Circular*, 1887 (2), pp.461, 491, 511, 586, 617; 'Remarks on the Relations of Different Divisions of the Central Nervous System to One Another, and to Parts of the Body', *Lancet*, 1898 (1), and in the *British Medical Journal*, 1898 (1), p.65.
7 James Kerr, 'Physical Inspection', *Journal of the Royal Sanitary Institute*, 26 (1905), pp.59–63.
8 James Kerr, 'Physical Standards for Teachers', Medical Officers of Schools Association, *Annual Proceedings and Report*, 1935, pp.24–40.
9 See Head, vol.1, pp.324–9, for an account of these two sets of nervous impressions, the protopatic and the epicritic; and vol. 2, pp.333–5, 805–8, for a discussion of the development of mind through a series of accumulations and discharges of energy in the peripheral nerves.
10 *School Hygiene* articles were diverse: Ernest Jones, 'Psycho-Analysis and Education', February, March 1911; Cyril Burt, 'Psychology and the Emotions', May 1916; Margaret McMillan, 'Speech Defects and Speech Training', August 1910; Oscar Pfistes, 'Psychoanalysis and Child Study', July, August 1911; Reginald Tribe, 'Results of Treatment at the Poplar School Clinic', May 1911.
11 Though of course Kerr's colleague, David Eder, made the widest and most innovative use of Freudian theory. See below, p.209.
12 Margaret McMillan, *Education Through the Imagination*, Swan Sonnenschein, 1904, Introduction.
13 ibid.
14 Shelley Phillips, 'Maria Montessori and Contemporary Cognitive Psychology', *British Journal of Teacher Education*, 3:1 (January 1977), pp.55–6.
15 See below, pp.252–4.
16 McMillan, *Imagination* (1904), pp.8, 28.
17 ibid., pp.33–4.
18 See Note 6.
19 See Head, vol. 2, p.801, where the fate of Jackson's work is discussed, and an account is given of the way in which his innovative theories of the unconscious got lost as the highly experimental and empirical British physiological school became 'obsessed with the study of anatomical and topographical detail'.
20 Margaret McMillan, *Early Childhood*, Swan Sonnenschein, 1900, p.23.
21 ibid., p.103.
22 ibid., p.70.
23 ibid., p.71.

NOTES

24 Margaret McMillan, 'School Board Notes', *Bradford Labour Echo*, 22 October 1898.
25 McMillan, *Imagination* (1904), pp.4–12, 28.
26 ibid., p.12.
27 ibid., p.70.
28 ibid., p.41.
29 See Margaret McMillan, *The Beginnings of Education* (City Branch Pamphlet No. 8), City of London Branch of the ILP, 1903; also her 'School Board Notes', *Bradford Labour Echo*, 18 September 1897.
30 McMillan, *Imagination* (1904), p.9.
31 J.B. Hobman (ed.), *David Eder: Memoirs of a Modern Pioneer*, Gollancz, 1945, p.14.
32 See 'Child Life and Sex Teaching', *Yorkshire Observer*, 1 January 1914.
33 Hobman, p.77.
34 Eder later delivered the same paper to the Child Life Society, and a longer version of it appeared as M.D. Eder and Mrs Eder, 'The Conflicts of the Unconscious in the Child', *Child Study*, 9:6 (October 1916), pp.79–83; 9:7/8 (November/December 1916), pp.105–8.
35 'What Reforms Are Most Needed', *Christian Commonwealth*, 5 January 1910.
36 David Eder, *The Endowment of Motherhood*, New Age Press, 1908, p.2. Hobman's memoriam volume called Eder a devotee of 'Socialism, Zionism, Psychoanalysis, and all humane causes' [jacket copy].
37 Margaret McMillan, *Education Through the Imagination*, Dent, 1923, p.44.
38 ibid., pp.97–8.
39 Margaret McMillan, *The Camp School*, Allen & Unwin, 1917, pp.125–6.
40 For Carpenter's advice on sex education, see Edward Carpenter, *Love's Coming of Age*, Labour Press, Manchester, 1896, pp.8–10, 177–9.
41 Margaret McMillan, *The Child and the State*, Socialist Library IX, National Labour Press, Manchester, 1911, p.177.
42 McMillan, *Camp School* (1917), p.126.
43 McMillan, *Early Childhood* (1900), p.55.
44 ibid., pp.56–7.
45 McMillan, *Imagination* (1904), p.6. For accounts of developmental linguistics available in this period, see Aaron Bar-Adon and Werner F. Leopold, *Child Language: A Book of Readings*, Prentice-Hall, New Jersey, 1971.
46 Henry Holman, *Seguin and His Physiological Method of Education*, Pitman, 1914, pp.197–8, 65–8.
47 Margaret McMillan, *The Nursery School*, Dent, 1919, p.110. Édouard Seguin (1866), pp.177–84; Holmes, pp.163–70.
48 McMillan, *Nursery School* (1919), p.111. For methods of teaching reading in this period, see Ronald Morris, *Success and Failure in Learning to Read*, Penguin, 1973.
49 McMillan, *Nursery School* (1919), p.113.
50 Greg Brooks and A.K. Pugh, *Studies in the History of Reading*, Centre for the Teaching of Reading, University of Reading School of Education, Reading, 1984.

51 Maria Montessori, *The Montessori Method*, Heinemann, 1914, pp.246–325.

52 Harlan Lane, *The Wild Boy of Aveyron*, Paladin, 1979, pp.133–60. Itard was not teaching Victor to read by this method so much as teaching him speech by breaking language down into its component parts.

53 McMillan, *Nursery School* (1919), pp.114–15.

54 ibid., p.116.

55 ibid., pp.116–21.

56 ibid., pp.122–3.

57 McMillan, *Life*, p.190.

58 Margaret McMillan, 'New Ends and Purposes', *Highway*, November 1909.

59 Margaret McMillan, 'The Child at School: Speech Training', *Co-operative News*, 7 January 1905.

60 Margaret McMillan, 'A New Epoch for Children', *Labour Leader*, 22 November 1907.

61 McMillan, 'Child at School' (1905). The Turgenev short story she is referring to is 'Mu-Mu' (1852).

12 Voices

1 Harlan Lane, *The Wild Boy of Aveyron*, Paladin, 1979, pp.185–254.

2 Édouard Seguin, *Idiocy and Its Treatment By the Physiological Method* (1866), Augustus M. Kelley, New York, 1971, p.34.

3 See above, p.72 and Note 41.

4 Margaret McMillan, 'The Gifts That Cannot Be Stolen: An Allegory for Children of All Ages', *The Two Worlds*, 12, 19, 26 May 1899. See also 'Three Leaves from a Deaf Man's Diary', *Two Worlds*, 10 July 1898.

5 Margaret McMillan, 'A Fairy Tale by the Fairies', *Young Socialist*, monthly between May 1907 and April 1908.

6 Margaret McMillan, 'Handel Stumm', *Labour Leader*, weekly between 1 September 1900 and 3 March 1901. Édouard Seguin (1866), pp.23–5. For Pereire, see also Lane, pp.150–52.

7 McMillan, *Life*, pp.52–3.

8 Lennox Browne and Emil Behnke, *Voice, Song and Speech, A Practical Guide for Singers and Speakers from the combined view of a vocal surgeon and voice trainer*, Samson, Low, Marston, Searle and Livington, 1883.

9 *The Times*, 19, 20 September 1892.

10 McMillan, *Life*, pp.52–3.

11 Louise Jopling, *Twenty Years of My Life, 1867–1887*, John Lane, 1925, p.286.

12 Mrs Emil Behnke, *The Speaking Voice: Its Development and Preservation*, J. Curwen, 1879. 'School Teachers and Voice Production', *Bradford Observer*, 3 March 1896. Bradford Record Office, Bradford School Board Records, Education Sub-Committee Minute Book, 52D75/II/2/12, Meetings of 14, 26 February 1896.

13 Bradford Record Office, Miriam Lord Collection, unclassified papers, communication from Miss Kate Emil Behnke, n.d.

14 Margaret McMillan, *Early Childhood*, Swan Sonnenschein, 1900, pp.59–60.

15 Margaret McMillan, *Schools of Tomorrow*, J.P. Steele Shenton, Stoke-on-Trent, 1908, pp.15–16.

16 McMillan, *Early Childhood*, p.24.

17 James Kerr, 'Physical Standards for Teachers', Medical Officers of Schools Association, *Annual Proceedings and Report*, 1935, pp.24–40.

18 McMillan, *Early Childhood*, p.58.

19 Margaret McMillan, 'On Pleasant Speech', *Woman Worker*, 11 September 1908.

20 ibid.; McMillan, *Early Childhood*, p.58.

21 Margaret McMillan, *The Child and the State*, Socialist Library IX, National Labour Press, Manchester, 1911, p.154.

22 McMillan, *Early Childhood*, p.58.

23 Margaret McMillan, *Education Through the Imagination*, Dent, 1923, pp.82–3.

24 McMillan, *Early Childhood*, p.58.

25 ibid., p.63.

26 For a very clear account of this twentieth-century development, see John R. Edwards, *Language and Disadvantage*, Arnold, 1979.

27 Margaret McMillan, *Early Childhood*, pp.49–50.

28 Reading University Library, Astor Papers, MS 1416/1/1/71, 'A College for Training Students for Nursery Schools', n.d.

29 McMillan, *Imagination* (1923), p.78.

30 ibid., p.78.

31 ibid., p.82.

32 Margaret McMillan, 'Voice Production in Board Schools', *Clarion*, 28 November 1896.

33 McMillan, *Imagination* (1923), p.93.

34 ibid., p.86.

35 See Logie Barrow's comment in *Independent Spirits: Spiritualism and British Plebeians, 1850–1910*, Routledge & Kegan Paul, 1986, p.118.

36 See *Lyceum Banner*, August 1900. She had visited a Spiritualist Sunday School and had approved the gym displays, and 'her pleasure and surprise at the mode of tuition and training of children . . . she felt, although she was not a Spiritualist, that they were building wider than they at present realised'.

37 Bradford Record Office, Miriam Lord Collection, 22D77/3/5, Copy of letter from Margaret McMillan to Margaret Sutcliffe, 12 December 1923.

38 On Hardie's spiritualism, see Kenneth O. Morgan, *Labour People*, Oxford University Press, Oxford, pp.23–38. University of Liverpool, Sidney Jones Library, Glasier Papers, I.1, MS Diaries of John Bruce Glasier, entry for Tuesday 21 November 1893. John and Katharine Bruce Glasier were sharing a diary at this point.

39 University of Reading Library, Astor Papers, MS 1416/1/1/80, Margaret McMillan to Nancy Astor, 2 June 1930.

40 Raymond Williams, *The Country and the City*, Paladin, 1973, p.272.

41 See above, pp.144–5.

42 'J.W.', 'Miss McMillan's New Book', *Labour Echo*, 7 September 1895. For work on the West Yorkshire dialect, see Yorkshire Dialect Society, *Transactions*, Bradford, 1898– , and the many editions of *Specimens of the Yorkshire Dialect*; T. Holderness, Driffield.

43 Margaret McMillan, 'An Old Chartist', *Ethics*, December 1903.

44 Williams, p.272. As McMillan had actually got wrong the history that this old man represented, she might have been expected to have some difficulty in expressing his political import. She seems to have thought that Peterloo was a scene of Chartist struggle – or that those events in Manchester took place twenty years later than they actually did.

45 Aaron Bar-Adon and Werner F. Leopold, *Child Language: A Book of Readings*, Prentice Hall, New Jersey, 1971, pp.1–13.

46 Mark Baldwin's work was a likely source for her understanding. She mentioned him in 'Ambidexterity in Schools', *Ethics*, 9 April 1904. Mark J. Baldwin, *The Story of the Mind*, Newnes, 1902, pp.64–117.

47 Margaret McMillan, 'On Reports and Other Things', *Common Cause*, 25 April 1913.

48 Margaret McMillan, *Education Through the Imagination*, Swan Sonnenschein, 1904, p.196.

49 See above, p.77.

50 Margaret McMillan, 'Bob's Christmas Day', *Christian Commonwealth*, 6 December 1911.

51 Margaret McMillan, 'At the Foot of the Rainbow', *Christian Commonwealth*, 10 February 1915.

13 *Legends*

1 Albert Mansbridge, *Margaret McMillan, Prophet and Pioneer: Her Life and Work*, Dent, 1932, p.157.

2 ibid., pp.157–8.

3 Bernard Crick, *George Orwell, A Life*, Penguin, 1980, p.30.

4 British Museum Additional Manuscripts, Mansbridge Papers, C (i), I. (Cameron) Jeaffreson to Albert Mansbridge, n.d.

5 See above, p.195.

6 London School of Economics, British Association for Early Childhood Education Records, Nursery School Association Records, Box 18/1, 'Statement' signed Mary Chignell, May 1928.

7 ibid., letter from Mary Chignell to Miss Owen, 14 June 1928.

8 University of Liverpool, Sidney Jones Library, Glasier Papers, I.1, 1907–12, John Bruce Glasier to Elizabeth Glasier Foster, 17 May 1907. At the first meeting of the NAC that McMillan attended he noted that she was 'full of complaints about MacDonald and Hardie', and that the next day she spoke rudely to them – 'she is fearfully hurt that they did not do as she wanted in the House': ibid., I.2, Manuscript Diaries of John Bruce Glasier, entries for 28 and 29 July 1906.

9 Bradford Record Office, Miriam Lord Collection, 22D77/4/21, '"The Legend of Margaret McMillan, A Play in Three Acts", by Margaret Sutcliffe'.

10 G.A.N. Lowndes, *Margaret McMillan: The Children's Champion*, Museum Press, 1960, p.18.
11 Rachel McMillan College Library, McMillan Collection, A 5/18, *c*.1930, Copy of John Mansbridge's portrait of Margaret McMillan, from a photograph taken in 1930. See Plate 16.
12 Mansbridge, p.139.
13 ibid., p.167.
14 Marina Warner, *Joan of Arc, The Image of Female Heroism*, Weidenfeld & Nicolson, 1981, pp.242–3; 253.
15 Thomas de Quincey, *Joan of Arc and Other Selections from Thomas de Quincey*, ed. Henry Belfield, Leach, Sherwell and Sandborn, Boston, 1892. John Ruskin, 'Proserpina', vol. 1 (1879), *The Library Edition of the Works of John Ruskin*, vol.35, Allen & Unwin, 1909, p.350; 'Sesame and Lilies' (1865), *The Library Edition of the Works of John Ruskin*, vol.18, Allen & Unwin, 1905, pp.133–6. See also William Jolly, *Ruskin on Education, Some Needed But Neglected Elements*, Allen & Unwin, 1894, p.37.
16 Warner, pp.237–54.
17 Mansbridge, pp.108–11.
18 *The Times*, 30 March 1931; *Daily Herald*, 30 March 1931.
19 G.F. McCleary, *The Maternity and Child Welfare Movement*, P.S. King, 1935, pp.111–15.
20 Bentley B. Gilbert, *The Evolution of National Insurance in Great Britain: The Origins of the Welfare State*, Michael Joseph, 1966, pp.117–58. See above, pp.53–4.
21 Joseph Edwards (ed.), *Labour Annual*, Labour Press, Manchester, 1895, pp.12–13.
22 University of Liverpool, Sidney Jones Library, Glasier Papers, I.1, 1892/23, 1–8, Barbara Fraser to John Bruce Glasier, 1 August 1892.
23 Glasier Papers I.1, 1892/23, 1-8, Barbara Fraser to John Bruce Glasier, 1 August 1892; 1892/24, 2-10, Barbara Fraser to John Bruce Glasier, 2 October 1892; 1893/21, 12-1, Barbara Fraser to John Bruce Glasier, 12 January 1893.
24 Barbara Fraser to John Bruce Glasier, 12 January 1893.
25 See above, pp.103–4. For this talent of McMillan, see also Bradford Record Office, Miriam Lord Collection, 22D77/10/11, extract from letter from F.G. Foster, Esq. to Mary Davis, 8 February 1952.
26 Glasier Papers, I.1, 1893/31, John Bruce Glasier to Katharine Bruce Glasier, 19 May 1893.
27 ibid., I.1, 1893/21, 12-1, Barbara Fraser to John Bruce Glasier, 12 January 1893.
28 'Lily Bell', 'Apotheosis of Woman', *Labour Leader*, 26 December 1896.
29 Margaret McMillan, 'A Woman of the Age of Gold: Mary Muse', *Clarion*, 8 September 1894.
30 Hugh Campbell, Robert Frederick Brewer and Henry G. Neville, *Voice, Speech and Gesture*, Charles William Decon, 1895.
31 ibid., p.110.
32 ibid., p.105.

33 Julia Dawson, 'Our Woman's Letter', *Clarion*, 26 February 1904.

34 Winifred Blatchford, 'Twenty Years Ago and Today: Working for the Children', *Clarion*, 11 July 1913.

35 Rachel McMillan College Library, McMillan Collection, A1/99, Robert Blatchford to Albert Mansbridge, 18 June 1931.

36 Margaret McMillan, 'Zoë', *Clarion*, 9 March 1895.

37 J.F. Mallon, 'The Portrait Gallery, Miss Margaret McMillan', *Woman Worker*, 5 June 1908.

38 Mansbridge, p.119.

39 'The Conference Concert', *Labour Leader*, 8 April 1899.

40 On the presence on the platform speaking louder than words, see Paul A. Pickering, 'Class Without Words: Symbolic Communication in the Chartist Movement', *Past and Present*, 112 (August 1986), pp.144–62.

41 David Howell, *British Workers and the Independent Labour Party, 1888–1906*, Manchester University Press, Manchester, 1983, p.339.

42 'How A Duchess Was Taught Socialism', *M.A.P. [More About People]*, 4 November 1899.

43 See above, Note 13.

44 See above, pp.121–2.

45 Edward Carpenter, *Love's Coming of Age*, Labour Press, Manchester, 1896, pp.66–7.

46 Rachel McMillan College Library, McMillan Collection, A1/99, Robert Blatchford to Albert Mansbridge, 18 June 1931.

47 ibid., A1/100, Robert Blatchford to Albert Mansbridge, 20 June 1931. Henry de Vere Stacpoole, *The Beach of Dreams, a Romance*, John Lane, New York, 1919.

48 Margaret McMillan to Julia Dawson, 'Our Woman's Column', *Clarion*, 22 April 1904.

49 Mallon, 'The Portrait Gallery'.

50 Bradford Record Office, Miriam Lord Collection, 22D77/98, lecture notes, dated 16 January 1946.

51 William Leech, 'A Frankly Biased View of It', *Bradford Pioneer*, 9 January 1914.

52 Blatchford, 'Twenty Years Ago'.

53 Franco Moretti, 'Kindergarten', in *Signs Taken for Wonders*, Verso, 1983, pp.157–81. Steve Neale, 'Melodrama and Tears', *Screen*, 27:6 (November/December 1986), pp.6–22.

54 See above, pp.79–80.

55 Warner, p.266.

PART THREE

Biographical Questions

1 For a recent account of the excitements of autobiography, see Laura Marcus, '"Enough about you, let's talk about me": Recent Autobiographical Writing', *New Formations*, 1 (Spring 1987), pp.77–94. For the theoretical dullness of biography, in a book that belies its title, see Eric Homberger and John Charmley, *The Troubled Face of Biography*, Macmillan, 1988.

2 Raymond Williams, *Marxism and Literature*, Oxford University Press, Oxford, 1977, p.148.

3 On this historiographical point, see Carolyn Steedman, 'Prisonhouses', *Feminist Review*, 20 (Summer 1985), pp.7–21.

4 Paul Ricoeur, *Time and Narrative*, University of Chicago Press, Chicago, 1984, pp.91–174. Roland Barthes, 'History as Discourse', in Michael Lane, *Structuralism: A Reader*, Cape, 1970, pp.145–55.

5 Lewis O. Mink, 'Everyman His or Her Own Annalist', *Critical Inquiry*, 7:4 (1981), pp.777–83.

6 For the Puritan tradition of autobiography, see D.A. Stauffer, *English Biography before 1700*, Russell & Russell, 1964; G.A. Starr, *Defoe and Spiritual Autobiography*, Gordion Press, New York, 1971; Linda H. Peterson, *Victorian Autobiography*, Yale University Press, New Haven, 1986, pp.1–28.

7 Roy Pascal, *Design and Truth in Autobiography*, Routledge & Kegan Paul, 1960. John Morris, *Versions of the Self: Studies in English Biography from John Bunyan to John Stuart Mill*, Basic Books, New York, 1966. David Vincent, *Bread, Knowledge and Freedom: A Study of Nineteenth Century Working Class Autobiography*, Methuen, 1982.

8 Karl J. Weintraub, 'Autobiography and Historical Consciousness', *Critical Inquiry*, 1 (1975), pp.821–48.

9 Peterson, pp.7–22.

10 In *The Troubled Face of Biography*, the editors make what I think is essentially the same point in the following way: 'The broad appeal of biography is reassuring. It suggests that in our interest in the lives of others there is at least the possibility, the hint of a surviving common culture.' Homberger and Charmley (eds), Introduction.

11 For a development of this argument, see Carolyn Steedman, 'True Romances', in Raphael Samuel (ed.), *Patriotism: The Making and Unmaking of British National Identity*, vol.1, Routledge, 1989, pp.26–35.

12 Robert Skidelsky, 'Only Connect: Biography and Truth', in Homberger and Charmley (eds), p.1.

13 Robert M. Young, 'Biography: The Basic Discipline for Human Science', *Free Associations*, 11 (1988), pp.108–30.

14 A point indicated by Elizabeth Fox Genovese, 'Placing Women's History in History', *New Left Review*, 133 (1982), but not argued through there. A particularly effective example of the sadness of this absence is to be found in Leonore Davidoff and Catherine Hall, *Family Fortunes: Men and Women of the English Middle Class, 1780–1850*, Hutchinson, 1987, 'Prologue' and 'Epilogue'.

15 Ruth Oldenziel, 'Gender, Self and the Writing of Biography', paper presented to the International Conference on Women's History, 1986. Estelle C. Jelinek (ed.), *Women's Autobiography: Essays in Criticism*, Indiana University Press, Bloomington, 1980. For a brief comment on claims like these, Natalie Zemon Davies, 'What Is Women's History?', in Juliet Gardiner (ed.), *What Is History Today?*, Macmillan, 1988, pp.85–7.

16 Percy Redfern, *Journey to Understanding*, Allen & Unwin, 1946, pp.18–19.

17 Mikhail Bakhtin, *The Dialogic Imagination: Four Essays*, ed. Michael Holquist, University of Texas Press, Austin, 1981, pp. 130–46.
18 The work that deals most directly with this usage concerns literature for children, particularly the fairy-tale. See Bruno Bettelheim, *The Uses of Enchantment: The Meaning and Importance of Fairy Tales*, Penguin, 1978.
19 Though as has been noted, we know very little indeed about the popular lecture itself.
20 Reading University Library, Astor Papers, MS 1416/1/4/68, Margaret McMillan to Nancy Astor, 13 December 1930.
21 Albert Mansbridge, *Margaret McMillan, Prophet and Pioneer: Her Life and Work*, Dent, 1932, p. 136.
22 Rachel McMillan College Library, McMillan Collection, A1/1, Margaret McMillan to Sally Blatchford, 2 February 1895.
23 See above, p. 124, and Note 16.
24 Mansbridge, p. 166.
25 Margaret McMillan, 'The Faith I Live By', *Christian Commonwealth*, 10 December 1913.
26 Margaret McMillan, *Education Through the Imagination*, Dent, 1923, p. 185. Richard Maurice Bucke, *Cosmic Consciousness, A Study in the Evolution of the Human Mind*, Innes, Philadelphia, 1905, pp. 51–68.
27 Rachel McMillan College Library, McMillan Collection, A1/53, Margaret McMillan to Margaret Sutcliffe, 29 April 1922.
28 McMillan, *Life*, p. 25.
29 Mansbridge, p. 167.
30 See Plates.
31 Margaret McMillan, 'A Woman of the Age of Gold: Mary Muse', *Clarion*, 8 September 1894.
32 See above, p. 100.
33 Margaret McMillan, 'Mary's Lover', *Clarion*, 15 February 1896.
34 See above, p. 77; and for Franco Moretti's charge of vulgarity against Goethe, p. 78, Note 71.
35 For an excellent summary of the psychological and political import of a huge range of literature, see John Edwards, *Language and Disadvantage*, Arnold, 1979.
36 For the decline of the school medical service, and the connection of that decline to the National Health Service reorganisation of 1974, see Department of Education and Science, *The School Health Service, 1908–1974*, HMSO, 1975; Medical Officers of School Association, *Handbook of School Health*, MTP Press, Lancaster, 1984; Kingsley Whitmore, *Health Services in Schools – A New Look*, Spastics International Medical Publications, 1985. For the abandonment of the principle of school meals, and the end of the practice of feeding children, see The Lancashire School Meals Campaign, *Now You See Them, Now You Don't*, LSMC, 1981; *Provision of School Meals – Autumn 1984 (Results of the School Meals Census in England in October 1984)*, Chartered Institute of Public Finance and Accountancy, 1984; Family Policy Studies Centre, *School Meals and Social Security*, FPSC, 1986; National Union of Public

Employees, *Save Our School Meals Service*, NUPE/CPAG n.d.; Geraldine Hackett, 'Cheap and Choosy', *The Times Educational Supplement*, 19 June 1987; Sarah Bayliss, 'No Such Thing As A Free Lunch', *The Times Educational Supplement*, 8 April 1988.

37 For an elaboration of this argument, see Carolyn Steedman. 'Prisonhouses', *Feminist Review*, 20 (Summer 1985), pp.7–21.

38 Margaret McMillan, *Education Through the Imagination*, Swan Sonnenschein, 1904, pp.196, 194.

39 Margaret McMillan, 'Discipline', *Clarion*, 24 October 1913.

Sources and Bibliography

(The place of publication is London, unless otherwise indicated.)

I Record Offices and Other Archive Material

Astor Papers, in the Library of the University of Reading.

Blatchford Papers, in the Manchester Central Library.

Bradford School Board Records, Minute Books, 52D75/I/9 10, 11; School Attendance Sub-Committee Minute Books, 52D75/II/9/ 7, 8; Education Sub-Committee Minute Book, 52D75/II/2/ 2, 3, 4, 5; Sites and Buildings Sub-Committee Minute Book, 52D75/11/1/4; in the Bradford Record Office.

Fabian Society Papers, in the Library of Nuffield College, Oxford.

Francis Johnson Collection, in the Library of the London School of Economics.

Froebel Society Council Minutes, Froebel Society Lecture, Conference and Propaganda Committee Minutes, the Archives of the National Froebel Foundation, at the Froebel Institute, Roehampton Institute of Higher Education, Roehampton.

Glasier Papers, in the Sidney Jones Library of the University of Liverpool.

John Trevor Papers, Modern Records Office, University of Warwick.

Kent County Council Technical Education Committee Minute Books, Kent Archives Office, Maidstone.

London County Council Education Committee Records, Greater London Council Records, in the Library of the Greater London Council.

McMillan Collection, at the Rachel McMillan College Library, Goldsmiths' College, University of London.

Mansbridge Collection, in the Additional Manuscript Collection of the British Museum.

Miles Franklin Papers, Mitchell Library, Macquarie University, New South Wales, Australia.

Miriam Lord Collection, in the Bradford Record Office.

Nursery School Association Papers, in the British Association for Early Childhood Education Collection, in the Library of the London School of Economics.

Women Sanitary Inspectors' Association, Annual Reports, 1905–, and Minutes, 1902–1906, Health Visitors' Association Records in the Library of the Health Visitors' Association, London.

II Books, Pamphlets and Articles by Margaret McMillan

'A Sign of the Times', *Christian Socialist*, October 1889. 'The Church and Socialism', *Christian Socialist*, December 1889. 'Liberty', *Christian Socialist*, April 1890. 'Labour, the Mother of Capital', *Christian Socialist*, June

1890. 'Evolution and Revolution', *Christian Socialist*, August 1890. 'Help', *Christian Socialist*, April 1891. 'Louise Michel', *Labour Prophet*, December 1892, January 1893. 'Shop Life', *Labour Prophet*, June 1893. 'Women of the Age of Gold: Lady Featherpoll – A Woman in Society'. *Labour Prophet*, February 1893. 'Silk Workers', *Labour Prophet*, September 1893. 'Coal and Colliers', *Labour Prophet*, October 1893. 'A True Capitalist', *Labour Prophet*, December 1893. 'Drink in Labour Clubs', *Clarion*, 24 February 1894. 'Music in Labour Clubs', *Clarion*, 3 March 1894. 'The Women of the ILP', *Clarion*, 10 March 1894. 'A Halt on the Hill', *Clarion*, 14 May 1894. 'Socialism in a Highland Kirk', *Clarion*, 21 May 1894. 'A Woman of the Age of Gold: Mary Muse', *Clarion*, 8 September 1894. 'To All Overworked Mothers', *Clarion*, 29 September 1894. 'To All Overworked Men', *Clarion*, 27 October 1894. 'Two Friends', *Clarion*, 11 November 1894. 'Silicon, Maid of Much Work', *Clarion*, 16 March 1895. 'The Two Conquerors', *Clarion*, 6 April 1895. 'One of the Trespassers', *Clarion*, 11 May 1895. 'The Bacchanals', *Labour Echo*, 11 May 1895. 'Demeter and Persephone', *Labour Echo*, 25 May 1895. 'Ariadne', *Labour Echo*, 1 June 1895. 'Pan', *Labour Echo*, 8 June 1895. 'Hippolytus', *Labour Echo*, 15 June 1895. 'The Beginning: According to the Greeks', *Labour Echo*, 6 July 1895. 'Zoë', *Clarion*, 9 March 1895. 'Gutterella: A Woman of the Age of Gold', *Weekly Times and Echo*, 28 December 1895. 'Mistress and Maid', *Clarion*, 1 June 1895. 'Women in Relation to the Labour Movement', in *The Labour Annual* (ed. Joseph Edward), Labour Press, Manchester, 1895, pp.138–9. *Samson*, Clarion Newspaper Company, 1895. 'To the Electors', *Labour Echo*, 9 July 1895. 'A Living Wage', *Labour Echo*, 9 July 1895. 'To the Electors', *Labour Echo*, 11 July 1895. 'Tom Maguire: A Remembrance', *Labour Leader*, 26 October 1895. 'My Experiences on the School Board', *Labour Prophet*, November 1895. 'Women in the New Party', in *The New Party* (ed. Andrew Reid), Hodder, 1895, pp.70–76. *Child Labour and the Half Time System* (Clarion Pamphlet No.15), Clarion Newspaper Company, 1896. 'The Half-Time System', *Clarion*, 12 September 1896. 'The Half-Time System: Part II', *Clarion*, 19 September 1896. 'A Woman of the Age of Gold: Mrs Heavytop', *Labour Leader*, 8 August 1896. 'Mary's Lover', *Clarion*, 15 February 1896. 'Voice Production in Board Schools', *Clarion*, 28 November 1896. 'The Education of Children: A Half Hour in the Assembly Room of a Board School', *Clarion*, 14 November 1896. 'Growth', *Clarion*, 20 February 1897. 'Lola', *Clarion*, 27 February 1897. 'Lola: Conclusion', *Clarion*, 6 March 1897. 'The Ventilation of Schools', *Bradford Labour Echo*, 15 May 1897. 'A la Salpêtrière', *Clarion*, 29 May 1897. 'The Subconscious: the Lorelei', *Clarion*, 12 June 1897. 'Marie Bashkirsteff's Grave', *Clarion*, 26 June 1897. 'Levana', *Clarion*, 14 August 1897. 'School Board Notes', *Bradford Labour Echo*, 18 September 1897. 'School Board Notes', *Bradford Labour Echo*, 25 September 1897. 'School Board Notes', *Bradford Labour Echo*, 22 October 1897. 'In the Pantheon', *Clarion*, 11 November 1897. 'The Inn Keeper's Daughter', *Clarion*, 18 December 1897. 'Children's Corner: Ann: A Tale for Children', *Clarion*, 14, 21, 28 May 1898. 'Three Leaves from a Deaf Man's Diary', *The Two Worlds*, 7 October 1898. 'Physical Training', *Bradford Labour Echo*, 12 November

1898. 'Art Training in Board Infant Schools', *Bradford Labour Echo*, 19 November 1898. 'Mona's Sister: A Christmas Tale for Little Folks', *Two Worlds*, 10 December 1898. 'Children's Corner: Tale of a Pearl Button', *Clarion*, 7 January 1899. 'Rest', *Bradford Labour Echo*, 21 January 1899. 'An English Kindergarten', *Bradford Labour Echo*, 25 March 1899. 'An English Kindergarten', *Labour Leader*, 15 April 1899. 'The Gifts That Cannot Be Stolen: An Allegory for Children of All Ages', *The Two Worlds*, 12, 19, 26 May, 2 June 1899. 'Baths', *Bradford Labour Echo*, 13 May 1899. 'Education in the Primary School', *Labour Leader*, 27 May, 10, 24 June, 1, 8, 15, 22, 29 July 1899. 'The Silence of the Humble', *The Two Worlds*, 9, 16, 23, 30 June 1899. 'Musical Training', *Labour Leader*, 12 August 1899. 'Fatigue: Normal and Abnormal', *Ethical World*, 16 September 1899. 'A Forecast of Civilization', *Ethical World*, 21, 28 October 1899. 'Tale of an Old Yew Tree: for Little People', *Clarion*, 21 October 1899. 'Literature and Children', *Ethical World*, 16 December 1899. 'The Literature of Children', *Ethical World*, 30 December 1899. *Early Childhood*, Swan Sonnenschein, 1900. 'The Ethical End in Education', in *Ethical Democracy: Essays in Social Dynamics* (ed. Stanton Coit), Grant Richards, 1900. 'The Cost of Mental Effort', *Ethical World*, 21 January 1900. 'Four Ideals in Education. I – The Military', *Labour Leader*, 5 May 1900. 'Four Ideals in Education. II – The Aesthetic', *Labour Leader*, 12 May 1900. 'Four Ideals in Education. III – The Monastic', *Labour Leader*, 19 May 1900. 'Four Ideals in Education. IV – The Medical Ideal', *Labour Leader*, 26 May 1900. 'Suppliant and Worshipper', *Ethical World*, 1 September 1900. 'Handel Stumm', *Labour Leader*, 1, 15, 23, 29 September, 6, 13, 20, 27 October, 3, 10, 17, 24 November, 1, 8, 15, 23 December 1900; 12, 19, 26 January, 2, 9, 16, 23 February, 2, 16, 23, 30 March 1901. 'The Two Spectres', *Co-operative News*, 22 September 1900. 'The Government and the People's Schools', *Ethical World*, 29 September 1900. 'Monasteries Old and New', *Ethical World*, 17 November 1900. 'The Clarion Round Table: A Reed Shaken in the Wind', *Clarion*, 8 December 1900. 'Schools and School Boards', *Co-operative News*, 20 December 1900. 'Miss McMillan on the Fellowship', *Clarion*, 5 January 1901. 'Wanted, A Blend of Heroism and Specialism', *Young Oxford*, March 1901. 'Schools and School Boards', *Clarion*, 20 July 1901. 'Higher Grade Schools', *Clarion*, 10 October 1901. 'Child Labour', in *Dangerous Trades: Historical, Social and Legal Aspects . . .* (ed. Thomas Oliver), John Murray, 1902. *The Beginnings of Education (City Branch Pamphlet No.8)*, ILP, City of London Branch, 1903. 'The Stranger from Wonderland: A Fairy Tale', *Clarion*, 7, 14 March 1902. 'The Gifts That Cannot Be Stolen: A Child's Story', *Clarion*, 11 July 1902. *The Mission of Children, (Ethical Essay No.8)*, Ethical Society, 1903. 'In the Islands of the Sea', *Ethics*, February 1903. 'Toys', *Young Socialist*, March 1903. 'A la Salpêtrière', *Ethics*, 4 April 1903. 'A Salvation Meeting', *Ethics*, 11 April 1903. 'A Wesleyan Missionary Meeting', *Ethics*, 25 April 1903. 'Topsy', *Ethics*, 30 May 1903. 'The Office of a Teacher', *Ethics*, 25 July 1903. 'Vivisection', *Ethics*, 1 August 1903. 'The New Commission on Physical Culture', *Ethics*, 8 August 1903. 'Infancy and Physique', *Ethics*, 15 August 1903. 'Psychology of the Tramp', *Ethics*, 22 August 1903. 'A School in the Western Isles', *Ethics*, 5 September 1903. 'A Maid of the Isles', *Ethics*, 19 September 1903. 'Ethical Teaching in a Yorkshire School', *Ethics*, 26 September, 10 October 1903. 'The Schoolmates', *Young Socialist*, November 1903. 'Neptune: A Dog', *Young Socialist*, December 1903. 'The Slums', *Ethics*, 12 December 1903. 'An Old Chartist', *Ethics*, 19 December 1903. *Education Through the Imagination*, Swan Sonnenschein, 1904. 'Internationalism in Education', *Ethics*, 13 February 1904. 'The Pottery School for Cripples', *Ethics*, 20 February 1904. 'The Swifts', *Young Socialist*, March 1904. 'Ambidexterity in Schools', *Ethics*, 9 April 1904. 'Ethics for Mothers', *Ethics*, 23 April 1904. 'The Flower and the Rock', *Young Socialist*, June 1904. 'The Feeding of the Bairns: Jewish and English Children Compared', *Co-operative News*, 6 November 1904. 'Arithmetic', *Young Socialist*, July 1904. 'Child-Study – Fatigue', *Child Life*, July 1904. 'Arithmetic', *Young Socialist*, August, September 1904. 'A Great Social Problem: Feeding the Slum Children of Leeds', *Co-operative News*, 1 October 1904. 'The Child Under Five: Suggestions . . .', *Child Life*, January 1905. 'Dear Julia', *Clarion*, 6 January 1905. 'The Child at School: Speech Training', *Co-operative News*, 7 January 1905. 'The Child World: The Open School Commended', *Co-operative News*, 14 January 1905. 'Sorcha's Dream', *Weekly Times and Echo*, 5 March 1905. 'True and False Applications of Froebel's Principles . . .', *Child Life*, July 1905. 'Mending the Lives of the Little Ones: A Work Worth Peeping Into', *Labour Leader*, 1 September 1905. *Economic Aspects of Child Labour and Education*, National Liberal Club, 18 December 1905. *Infant Mortality*, ILP, 1906. *New Life in Our Schools: The Clinic, What It Is and What It Is Not*, Women's Co-operative Guild, Manchester, 1906. 'The Higher Senses: Hearing', *Labour Leader*, 4 April 1906. 'The Five Year Old at School', *Labour Leader*, 6 April 1906. 'The Higher Senses: Seeing', *Labour Leader*, 11 April 1906. 'The Education Bill', *Labour Leader*, 18 April 1906. 'What To Do Now', *Clarion*, 25 April 1906. 'The Labour Party and the Children', *Labour Leader*, 1 June 1906. 'The Great Clause of the Education Bill', *Clarion*, 8 June 1906. 'In Horse Yard', *Labour Leader*, 15 June 1906. 'The Beginning of the End', *Labour Leader*, 22 June 1906. 'Germany and Its Children', *Clarion*, 22 June 1906. 'Building Up the British Race', *Labour Leader*, 6 July 1906. 'The School Doctor: How to Find Him', *Clarion*, 13 July 1906. 'The Triumph for Childhood', *Clarion*, 20 July 1906. 'A Fairy Tale by the Fairies', *Young Socialist*, August 1906. 'Where Women Fight and Die', *Clarion*, 17 August 1906. 'Shower Baths', *Labour Leader*, 7 September 1906. 'The Robber: A Tale of the Hebrides', *Weekly Times and Echo*, 16 September 1906. 'Women and the Franchise', *Clarion*, 21 September 1906. 'Ishbel's Return', *Weekly Times and Echo*, 23 September 1906. 'Municipalisation of Hospitals', *Labour Leader*, 28 September 1906. 'The Women in Prison', *Clarion*, 2 November 1906. *Labour and Childhood*, Swan Sonnenschein, 1907. 'Jewels', *Young Socialist*, February 1907. 'The Hope of Spring', *Young Socialist*, March 1907. 'Free Meals', *Labour Leader*, 22 March 1907. 'Penalties of Greatness', *Labour Leader*, 26 April 1907. 'A Fairy Tale by the Fairies', *Young Socialist*, May 1907. 'The Beginning That May Have to Halt', *Labour Leader*, 17 May 1907. 'The

Alien', *Weekly Times and Echo*, 26 May 1907. 'A Coming Conference', *Labour Leader*, 26 July 1907. 'The Scholarship Child', *Labour Leader*, 23 August 1907. 'After Echoes of the Congress on School Hygiene', *Labour Leader*, 30 August 1907. 'A Fairy Tale by the Fairies', *Young Socialist*, June, July, September, October, November, December 1907; January, February, March, April 1908. 'The Star of Beauty', *Labour Leader*, 18 October 1907. 'A New Epoch for Children', *Labour Leader*, 22 November 1907. 'School Dinners Today', *Labour Leader*, 29 November 1907. 'The Way of the River', *Weekly Times and Echo*, 29 December 1907. 'Woman in the Past and the Future', in *The Case for Woman's Suffrage* (ed. Brougham Villiers), Fisher Unwin, 1908. *Schools of Tomorrow*, J.P. Steel Shelton, Stoke on Trent, 1908. 'Democracy and Higher Education', *Socialist Review*, 1 (1908). *The Child and the State*, Metropolitan District Council of the ILP, n.d. (1908). 'New Report of the Education Board', *Labour Leader*, 1 January 1908. 'On the Embankment', *Labour Leader*, 17 January 1908. 'The Socialist Sunday Schools', *Young Socialist*, February 1908. 'Bradford Leads Again', *Labour Leader*, 7 February 1908. 'From School to Embankment', *Labour Leader*, 14 February 1908. 'A "Special" School Day', *Labour Leader*, 28 February 1908. 'A Message of Spring', *Woman Worker*, May 1908. 'Apostles from Bradford', *Labour Leader*, 17 May 1908. 'The New Act and How It Works', *Labour Leader*, 26 June 1908. 'A Story for Lilley', *Young Socialist*, July 1908. 'A Slum Mother', *Woman Worker*, 3 July 1908. 'Mr Leech's Reform', *Labour Leader*, 10 July 1908. 'Clouds and the Rain', *Woman Worker*, 17 July 1908. 'The Coming Conference', *Labour Leader*, 31 July 1908. 'The Crow', *Young Socialist*, August 1908. 'On Pleasant Speech', *Woman Worker*, 11 September 1908. 'A British School Clinic and Other Matters', *Labour Leader*, 25 September 1908. 'A Bard at the Braes', *Woman Worker*, 25 September, 2, 9, 16, 23 October, 2, 9, 16, 30 December 1908. 'Child Labour', *Child Life*, October 1908. 'A London School Treatment Centre', *Labour Leader*, 11 December 1908. 'The Care of Schoolchildren: London Moves at Last', *Labour Leader*, 15 December 1908. *The Bard at the Braes*, ILP 1909. 'Medical Inspection of Schoolchildren', *Woman Worker*, 6 January 1909. 'Schools and Hospitals', *Labour Leader*, 8 January 1909. 'The School Clinic and Land Values', *Labour Leader*, 15 January 1909. 'The Little White Gull: A Story for Ishbel', *Young Socialist*, February 1909. 'As the Echoes Die', *Labour Leader*, 2 December 1909. 'In a School of Today', *Christian Commonwealth*, 24 February 1909. 'The Garden Under the Water', *Young Socialist*, March 1909. 'Near the Flame and in the Shadow', *Christian Commonwealth*, 10 March 1909. 'Ten Hundred Thousand Philips', *Christian Commonwealth*, 24 March 1909. 'The Tree That Waited: A Story for Charlie', *Young Socialist*, April 1909. 'Homes of England', *Christian Commonwealth*, 7 April 1909. 'What Women Are Thinking: The Child Slaves of England: Miss McMillan's Statement', *Woman Worker*, 28 April 1909. (With Mrs Cobden Sanderson) *London's Children: How to Feed Them and How Not to Feed Them*, ILP, April 1909. 'All Around the Problem', *Christian Commonwealth*, 12 April 1909. 'Diary of a Dayschool Scholar', *Christian Commonwealth*, 5 May 1909. 'The Land-Raiders in Barra', *Labour Leader*, 9 May 1909. 'A

Calendar of Socialist Saints: Biographies in Brief: Mazzini', *Young Socialist*, June 1909. 'The Problem of Child Life', *Christian Commonwealth*, 9 June 1909. 'Worker and Student', *Highway*, July 1909. 'Things That Talk', *Young Socialist*, July 1909. 'Secrets of the Child Soul', *Christian Commonwealth*, 7 July 1909. 'School Clinics: Their First Fruit', *Labour Leader*, 9 July 1909. 'Lifeboat on the Ocean of Suffering', *Christian Commonwealth*, 21 July 1909. 'Socialism and Health', *Christian Commonwealth*, 18 August 1909. 'The Door of the North', *Highway*, September 1909. 'The Trades Union Congress and School Clinics', *Labour Leader*, 3 September 1909. 'The School Clinic: What It Is and What It Is Not', *Co-operative News*, 25 September 1909. 'A Danish Festival', *Christian Commonwealth*, 29 September 1909. 'A Day at Askov', *Highway*, October 1909. 'The School Clinic: What It Is and What It Is Not', *Co-operative News*, 2 October 1909. 'New Ends and Purposes', *Highway*, November 1909. 'The Great Awakening', *Christian Commonwealth*, 3 November 1909. 'A New Kitchen', *Labour Leader*, 12 November 1909. 'Adolescence', *Highway*, December 1909. 'The Christmas Rose', *Christian Commonwealth*, 8 December 1909. 'Philip's Christmas Day', *Christian Commonwealth*, 8 December 1909. 'A Visit to a Danish High School', *Christian Commonwealth*, 29 December 1909. 'The Children's Bread', *Labour Leader*, 31 December 1909. *A Children's Day*, Women's Printing Society, 1910. 'To A Little Friend Who Is Ill', *Young Socialist*, January 1910. 'The Claims of the "Practical" in Education', *Highway*, January 1910. 'On the Threshold', *School Hygiene*, January 1910. 'Waiting', *Child Life*, January 1910. 'Physical Education', *Christian Commonwealth*, 5 January 1910. 'The First Medical Report from Whitehall', *Christian Commonwealth*, 19 January 1910. 'One of the New Army', *Christian Commonwealth*, 26 January 1910. 'The First Medical Report from Whitehall', *Highway*, February 1910. 'Mary Jane', *Christian Commonwealth*, 2 February 1910. 'Education and the Labour Conference', *Labour Leader*, 4 February 1910. 'The London County Council Election: What We Should Demand', *Christian Commonwealth*, 23 February 1910. 'About Some Who Have Taken the Plunge', *Christian Commonwealth*, 9 March 1910. 'The Serf and His Son', *Christian Commonwealth*, 13 May 1910. 'Dress in Elementary Schools', *Child Life*, June 1910. 'Why Are the Germans Clean?', *Clarion*, 17 June 1910. 'Medical Treatment in London', *Labour Leader*, 17 June 1910. 'The Bradford School Clinic', *Clarion*, 24 June 1910. 'The Tooth Clinic and Kindred Matters', *Christian Commonwealth*, 13 July 1910. 'An Instruction to the Clarion Fellowship: The Deptford Health Centre', *Clarion*, 29 July 1910. 'Vive la France', *Highway*, August 1910. 'Speech Defects and Speech Training', *School Hygiene*, August 1910. 'The Fairway: Some East End Holiday Makers', *Morning Leader*, 25 August 1910. 'Notes on a Closed Door', *Highway*, September 1910. 'A Flower in a Slum', *Christian Commonwealth*, 14 September 1910. 'The Gardens Under the Sea', *Highway*, October 1910. 'At Deptford Again', *Christian Commonwealth*, 19 October 1910. 'The People That Are Above Us', *Highway*, November 1910. 'Johnny and Me', *Christian Commonwealth*, 2 November 1910. 'Deptford's Health Clinic: On Patients and Visitors', *Clarion*, 4 November 1910. 'The School Clinic: The Problems of Treatment Today', *Morning Leader*, 24 November 1910. 'Higher

319

Education and the Working Woman', *Highway*, December 1910. *The Child and the State*, National Labour Press, Manchester, 1911. 'Education in America: Miss Margaret McMillan's Impressions', *Christian Commonwealth*, 18 January 1911. 'Faith and Fear', *Labour Leader*, 27 January 1911. 'The Second Medical Report from Whitehall', *Highway*, February 1911. 'In the Middle West', *Highway*, March 1911. 'Nurseries for All Children', *Sheffield Guardian*, March 1911. 'The Child Coal Heaver', *Christian Commonwealth*, 15 March 1911. 'Children of the Plain and the Forest', *Highway*, April 1911. 'The Deptford Health Clinic, or Health Centre for Schoolchildren', *Child*, May 1911. 'Joseph and Arnold Toynbee', *Highway*, May 1911. 'The Healers: April Night and May Morning', *Labour Leader*, 25 May 1911. 'In a Garden', *Highway*, June 1911. (Anon.) 'With Arms Akimbo', *Highway*, June 1911. 'In Our Garden – Chapterette II', *Highway*, July 1911. 'Means and Ends in Education Today', *Christian Commonwealth*, 9 August 1911. 'Marigold – An English Mignon (Kenst du das Land?)', *Highway*, September 1911. 'In Holy Isle', *Highway*, October 1911. 'Save the Children: A Plea for the Social Treatment of Disease', *Labour Leader*, 17 November 1911. 'Bob's Christmas Day', *Christian Commonwealth*, 6 December 1911. *The School Clinic Today: Health Centres and What They Mean to the People*, ILP and National Labour Press, 1912. 'Nurture versus Education', *The Needs of Little Children, Report of a Conference on the Care of Babies and Children*, Women's Labour League, 1912. 'The Case for the Industrial Woman', *Men's League on Women's Suffrage Handbook*, 1912. 'Our Ailing Schoolchildren; and Then?' *Wheatsheaf*, January 1912. 'Marigold: An English Mignon', *Christian Commonwealth*, 3 January 1912. 'Travellers' Joy', *Highway*, February 1912. 'In Our Garden', *Highway*, May 1912. 'Camp Schools: The New Grant for the Children', *Clarion*, 17 May 1912. 'In Our Garden', *Highway*, June 1912. 'The Montessori System', *Christian Commonwealth*, 26 June 1912. 'Clothes – And the Making of Them', *Young Socialist*, July 1912. 'In Our Garden – IV', *Highway*, July 1912. 'How I Became a Socialist', *Labour Leader*, 11 July 1912. 'In Our Garden – V', *Highway*, August 1912. 'Clothes and How To Make Them', *Young Socialist*, August 1912. 'Clothes and How To Make Them', *Young Socialist*, September 1912. 'In Our Garden – VI', *Highway*, September 1912. 'A Pioneer', *Labour Leader*, 5 September 1912. 'Clothes and How To Make Them', *Young Socialist*, October 1912. 'In an Indian School', *Christian Commonwealth*, 14 December 1912. 'The Child of the Future: When the Stains Are Washed Away', *Labour Leader*, 26 December 1912. 'In an Open-Air Camp-School', *Daily Herald*, 3 January 1913. 'Are Women Awake?' *Labour Leader*, 9 January 1913. 'Backward Children: A New Method of Teaching', *Christian Commonwealth*, 29 January 1913. 'The New Programme in Education', *Christian Commonwealth*, 26 February 1913. 'In Our Garden: an Experiment with Teddy', *Christian World*, 27 March 1913. 'On Reports and Other Things', *Common Cause*, 25 April 1913. 'The "New" Education', *Highway*, June 1913. 'Our Educational System: The Education of Children Under Seven', *Highway*, July 1913. 'Our Educational System: Medical Treatment – and What It Leads To', *Highway*, August, September 1913. 'To Save the Children: Work to be Done Now', *Clarion*, 26 September 1913. 'Discipline', *Clarion*, 24 October 1913. 'Children of

Deptford: Findings of the Fourth Report of the Deptford Health Centre', *Christian Commonwealth*, 29 October 1913. 'In the City of Sorrow', *Clarion*, 28 November 1913. 'The Faith I Live By', *Christian Commonwealth*, 10 December 1913. 'Religious Controversy and Education', *Clarion*, 19 December 1913. 'The Power Stations of the World', *Clarion*, 9 January 1914. 'Interview with Miss Margaret McMillan: "The Schools of Tomorrow"', *Christian Commonwealth*, 21 January 1914. 'The School Camp in December', *Clarion*, 3 July 1914. 'The Camp School', *Transactions of the National Liberal Club Political & Economic Circle*, Part 89a (12 December 1914), P.S. King, 1914. 'At the Foot of the Rainbow', *Christian Commonwealth*, 10 February 1915. 'The Romance of the Slums', *Christian Commonwealth*, 7 April 1915. 'The Romance of the Slums', *Christian Commonwealth*, 14 April 1915. 'The Vision of the Heroes', *Clarion*, 28 May 1915. 'Jimmy', *Highway*, June 1915. *The Camp School*, Allen & Unwin, 1917. 'Baby Week', *Christian Commonwealth*, 4 July 1917. '"The Labour Programme": In Our Garden', *Christian Commonwealth*, 13 February 1918. 'The Fate of Lennie', *Christian Commonwealth*, 16 October 1918. *The Nursery School*, Dent, 1919. *Education Through the Imagination*, Dent, 1923. *What the Nursery School Is*, Labour Party, 1923, 1928. *1901–1926, Twenty-fifth Anniversary Celebrations*, Bradford Froebel Society, Bradford, 1926. *The Life of Rachel McMillan*, Dent, 1927. 'Laying the Foundation of Good Health: What Nursery Schools Can Achieve', *Labour Woman*, 1 March 1928. 'History and Aims of the Open-Air Nursery School', *Scottish Health Magazine*, April 1929.

III Books, Pamphlets and Articles

Allen, B.M., *Sir Robert Morant*, Macmillan, 1934.

Allen, Garland E., *Life Sciences in the Twentieth Century*, Cambridge University Press, Cambridge, 1978.

Allen, Ann Taylor, 'Spiritual Motherhood: German Feminists and the Kindergarten Movement, 1848–1911', *History of Education Quarterly*, 22:3 (Fall 1982), pp.319–39.

Anderson, Robert, 'In Search of the "Lad of Parts": the Mythical History of Scottish Education', *History Workshop Journal*, 19 (Spring 1985), pp.82–104.

Armstrong, David, *Political Anatomy of the Body*, Cambridge University Press, Cambridge, 1983.

Arnot, R. Page, *William Morris: The Man and the Myth*, Lawrence & Wishart, 1964.

Ayres, Leonard P., *Open-Air Schools*, Russell Sage Foundation, New York, 1912.

Bakhtin, Mikhail, *The Dialogic Imagination: Four Essays*, ed. Michael Holquist, University of Texas Press, Austin, 1981.

Baldwin, Mark J., *The Story of the Mind*, Newnes, 1902.

Bar-Adon, Aaron and Leopold, Werner F., *Child Language: A Book of Readings*, Prentice-Hall, New Jersey, 1971.

Barker, Rodney, 'The Labour Party and Education for Socialism', *International*

Review of Social History, 15 (1969), pp.22–53.

Barnes, Earl, 'Methods of Studying Children', *Paidologist*, 1 (April 1899).

Barnes, Earl, 'A Forgotten Student of Child Study', *Paidologist*, 3:3 (November 1901).

Barrow, Logie, 'Socialism in Eternity: the Ideology of Plebeian Spiritualists, 1853–1913', *History Workshop Journal*, 9 (Spring 1980), pp.37–69.

Barrow, Logie, *Independent Spirits: Spiritualism and British Plebeians, 1850–1910*, Routledge & Kegan Paul, 1986.

Barthes, Roland, 'Historical Discourse', in Michael Lane (ed.), *Structuralism, A Reader*, Cape, 1970.

Bebel, August, *Woman in the Past, Present and Future*, The Modern Press, 1885.

Beevers, Robert, *The Garden City Utopia: A Critical Biography of Ebenezer Howard*, Macmillan, 1988.

Behnke, Mrs Emil, *The Speaking Voice: Its Development and Preservation* (8th edn), J. Curwen, 1897.

Bernstein, Basil, *Class Codes and Control*, vol.3, *Towards a Theory of Educational Transmissions*, Routledge & Kegan Paul, 1977.

Bettelheim, Bruno, *The Uses of Enchantment: the Meaning and Importance of Fairy Tales*, Penguin, 1978.

Binyon, G.C. *The Christian Socialist Movement in England*, SPCK, 1931.

Blackie, John Stuart, *Gaelic Societies, Highland Depopulation and Land Law Reform*, David Douglas, Edinburgh, 1880.

Blackie, John Stuart, 'The Philosophy of Education', in *Essays on Social Subjects*, David Douglas, 1890.

Blatchford, Robert, 'Socialism Made Easy', *Woman Worker*, 5 June 1908.

Blatchford, Winifred, 'Twenty Years Ago and Today: Working for the Children, *Clarion*, 11 July 1913.

Blatchford, Winifred, 'Work for Us to Do: Save the Children', *Clarion*, 14 August 1914.

Bledstein, Burton, J., *The Culture of Professionalism: the Middle Class and the Development of Higher Education in America*, W.W. Norton, New York, 1976.

Boyce, George *et al*. (eds), *Newspaper History from the Seventeenth Century to the Present*, Constable, 1978.

Boyer, Irma, *Louise Michel, d'après des documents inédits*, Paris, 1927.

Bradburn, Elizabeth, *Margaret McMillan, Framework and Expansion of Nursery Education*, Denholm Press, Redhill, 1976.

Bradford Corporation, *Education in Bradford Since 1870*, Bradford Corporation, Bradford, 1970.

Bristow, J., *Vice and Vigilance, Purity Movements in Britain Since 1700*, Gill & Macmillan, 1977.

Browne, Lennox and Behnke, Emil, *Voice, Song and Speech, A Practical Guide for Singers and Speakers from the combined view of a vocal surgeon and voice trainer*, Samson, Low, Marston, Searle, Rivington, 1883.

Bucke, Richard Maurice, *Cosmic Consciousness, A Study in the Evolution of the Human Mind*, Innes & Sons, Philadelphia, 1905.

Bulley, Amy and Whiteley, Margaret, *Women's Work*, Methuen, 1894.

Burfield, Diana, 'Theosophy and Feminism: Some Explorations in Nineteenth Century Biography', in Holden, Pat (ed.), *Women's Religious Experience*, Croom Helm, 1983.

Burt, Cyril, 'Psychology and the Emotions', *School Hygiene*, 7:2 (May 1916), pp.57–69.

Campbell, Hugh, Brewer, Robert Frederick, and Neville, Henry, *Voice, Speech and Gesture*, Charles William Decon, 1895.

Campbell, Robin and Wales, Roger, 'The Study of Language Acquisition', in Lyons, John (ed.), *New Horizons in Linguistics*, Penguin, 1970.

Campbell, William H. Paul, *The Robbery of the Poor*, Modern Press, 1884.

Campbell, William H. Paul, 'Notes on the Great Strike', *Christian Socialist*, September 1889.

Cantlie, James, *Degeneration Among Londoners*, Field & Tuer, 1885.

Carlyle, Thomas, *Past and Present* (1843), Chapman & Hall, 1893.

Carpenter, Edward, *Love's Coming of Age*, Labour Press, Manchester, 1896.

Carpenter, Humphrey, *Secret Gardens: The Golden Age of Children's Literature*, Allen & Unwin, 1985.

Coe, Richard N., *When the Grass Was Taller, Autobiography and the Experience of Childhood*, Yale University Press, New Haven, 1984.

Coit, Stanton (ed.), *Ethical Democracy: Essays in Social Dynamics*, Grant Richards, 1900.

Cole, G.D.H., *Socialist Thought: The Forerunners, 1789–1850*, Macmillan, 1953.

Collette, Christine, 'Socialism and Scandal', *History Workshop Journal*, 23 (Spring 1987), pp.102–11.

Conway, Katharine St John, *The Cry of the Children* (2nd edn), Labour Press, Manchester, 1894.

Conway, Katharine St John, and Glasier, John Bruce, *The Religion of Socialism: Two Aspects*, Labour Press, Manchester, 1895.

Cooter, Roger, 'Open-Air Therapy and the Rise of Open-Air Hospitals', *Society for the Social History of Medicine Bulletin*, 35 (December 1984), pp.44–6.

Corbin, Alain, *The Foul and the Fragrant: Odor and the French Social Imagination*, Berg, Leamington Spa, 1986.

Coveney, Peter, *The Image of Childhood, The Individual and Society: A Study of the Theme in English Literature* (first published as *Poor Monkey*, Rockliffe, 1958), Penguin, 1967.

Cresswell, D'Arcy, *Margaret McMillan, A Memoir*, Hutchinson, 1948.

Crick, Bernard, *George Orwell, A Life*, Penguin, 1980.

Cruikshank, Marjorie, *Children and Industry: Child Health and Welfare in Northern Textile Towns During the Nineteenth Century*, Manchester University Press, Manchester, 1981.

Cusden, P., *The English Nursery School*, Kegan Paul, 1938.

Davidoff, Leonore and Hall, Catherine, *Family Fortunes: Men and Women of the English Middle Classes*, Hutchinson, 1987.

Davies, Natalie Zemon, 'What is Women's History?', in Juliet Gardiner (ed.), *What Is History Today?*, Macmillan, 1988.

Davin, Anna, 'Imperialism and Motherhood', *History Workshop Journal*, 5 (Spring 1978), pp.61–113.

Deasey, Denison, *Education Under Six*, Croom Helm, 1978.

deMause, Lloyd, *The History of Childhood*, Souvenir Press, New York, 1976.

de Quincey, Thomas, *Joan of Arc and Other Selections from Thomas de Quincey*, ed. Henry Belfield, Leach, Sherwell & Sandborn, Boston, Mass., 1892.

Dingwall, Robert W.J., 'Collectivism, Regionalism and Feminism: Health Visiting and British Social Policy', *Journal of Social Policy*, 6:3 (July 1977), pp.291–315.

Donald, A.K., 'Socialism in Scotland', *Commonweal*, 24 February 1887.

Drummond, Henry, *Lowell Lectures on the Ascent of Man*, Hodder & Stoughton, 1894.

Eder, M.D. and Mrs Eder, 'The Conflicts of the Unconscious in the Child', *Child Study*, 9:6 (October 1916), pp.79–83; 9:7/8 (November 1916), pp.105–8.

Eder, M.D., *The Endowment of Motherhood*, New Age Press, 1908.

Edwards, John R., *Language and Disadvantage*, Arnold, 1979.

Edwards, Joseph (ed.), *Labour Annual*, Labour Press, Manchester, 1895, 1896.

Ellenberger, Henri F., *The Discovery of the Unconscious: The History and Evolution of Dynamic Psychiatry*, Allen Lane, 1970.

'E.M.M.', 'The Garden of Children', *Labour Prophet*, October 1894, January 1895.

Evans, Brian and Waites, Bernard, *IQ and Mental Testing*, Macmillan, 1981.

'Eye Witness', 'How Militants Are Made: the Treatment of a Women's Deputation', *Christian Commonwealth*, 30 July 1913.

Fels, Mary, *Joseph Fels: His Life Work*, George Allen & Unwin, 1920.

Ford, Isabella O., *On the Threshold*, Edward Arnold, 1895.

Forster, Mrs L. Glasier, *The New Needlecraft, with a Preface by Margaret McMillan*, P.S. King, 1919.

Fothergill, John Milner, *The Town Dweller, His Needs and Wants*, H.K. Lewes, 1889.

Foucault, Michel, *Birth of the Clinic: An Archaeology of Medical Perception*, Tavistock, 1973.

Fraser, B.M., 'Idealism', *Christian Socialist*, June 1890.

Frazer, W.M., *A History of English Public Health, 1834–1939*, Baillière, Tindall & Cox, 1950.

Freud, Anna, 'The Role of the Teacher', *Harvard Educational Review*, 22:4 (Fall 1952).

Freud, Sigmund, *On Dreams* (trans. M.D. Eder), Heinemann, 1914.

Galton, Maurice *et al.*, *Inside the Primary Classroom*, Routledge & Kegan Paul, 1980.

Geddes, Patrick, *City Development: Study of Parks, Gardens and Culture Institutes*, A Report to the Carnegie Dunfermline Trust, Edinburgh, 1904.

Genovese, Elizabeth Fox, 'Placing Women's History in History', *New Left Review*, 133 (1982).

George Henry, *Progress and Poverty*, Routledge & Kegan Paul, 1881.

Gilbert, Bentley, B., *The Evolution of National Insurance in Britain: The Origins of the Welfare State*, Michael Joseph, 1966.

Gilby, William, 'The Structural Significance of Mignon in *Wilhelm Meisters Lehrjahre*', *Seminar*, 26 (1980), pp. 136–50.

Gilray, John, 'Centres of Influence VI: Modern Athens', *Christian Socialist*, January 1891.

Glasier, Katharine Bruce (Katharine Conway), 'Miss M'Millan's Book', ILP *News*, June 1900.

Glasier, Katharine Bruce (Katharine Conway), *Socialism for Children: City of London Branch Pamphlets, No.6*, City of London Branch of the ILP, 1906.

Glasier, Katharine Bruce (Katharine Conway), *Socialism and the Home*, ILP Press, 1911.

Glasier, Katharine Bruce (Katharine Conway), 'The Part Women Played in Founding the ILP', *Labour Leader*, 9 April 1914.

Glasier, Katharine Bruce (Katharine Conway), *Margaret McMillan, and Her Life Work*, Workers' Northern Publishing Co., Manchester, n.d.

Glasier, Katharine Bruce (Katharine Conway), 'The Hope of Socialism – East and West: Some Holiday Harvestings', *Northern Voice*, September 1930.

Glasier, Lizzie and Russell, Alfred, *Socialist Sunday Schools and Their Methods*, Glasgow, 1908.

Glasse, John, *Modern Christian Socialism*, Co-operative Wholesale Society, Manchester, 1897.

Glasse, John, *The Relation of the Church to Socialism*, ILP, Edinburgh, 1900.

Glenn, Heather, *Vision and Disenchantment: Blake's Songs and Wordsworth's Lyrical Ballads*, Cambridge University Press, Cambridge, 1983.

Goethe, Johann Wolfgang von, *Wilhelm Meisters Theatralische Sedung*, Rascher, Zurich, 1910.

Goethe, Johann Wolfgang von, *Wilhelm Meisters Theatralische Sedung* Stuttgart, 1911.

Goethe, Johann Wolfgang von, *Wilhelm Meisters Theatralische Sedung* (trans. Gregory A. Page), Heinemann, 1913.

Goethe, Johann Wolfgang von, *Wilhelm Meister's Years of Apprenticeship* (trans. H.M. Wardson), 6 vols, John Calder, 1977.

Gorham, Deborah, 'The "Maiden Tribute of Modern Babylon" Re-examined: Child Prostitution and the Idea of Childhood in Late Victorian England', *Victorian Studies*, 21:3 (Spring 1978), pp. 353–79.

Grant, Clara E., *From 'Me' to 'We' (Forty Years on Bow Common)*, privately printed at the Fern Street Settlement, n.d.

Grant, Clara E., 'Then and Now in the Infants' School: Some Reminiscences', *Child Life*, 15 September, 15 October 1910.

Greaves, C. Desmond, *The Life and Times of James Connolly*, Lawrence & Wishart, 1961.

Greenwood, Arthur, *'All Children Are Mine': Inaugural Margaret McMillan Lecture*, University of London Press for the Margaret McMillan Fellowship, 1952.

Griggs, Clive, *The Trades Union Congress and the Struggle for Education, 1868–1925*, Falmer Press, Lewes, 1983.

Griggs, Clive, 'Labour and Education', in Brown, K.D. (ed.), *The First Labour Party, 1906–1913*, Croom Helm, 1985.

Guthrie, Douglas, *A History of Medicine*, Nelson, 1958.

Haddow, William Martin, *My Seventy Years*, Robert Gibson, Glasgow, 1943.

Hadfield, Miles, *A History of British Gardening*, Penguin, 1985.

Hardman, Malcolm, *Ruskin and Bradford: An Experiment in Victorian Cultural History*, Manchester University Press, Manchester, 1986.

Harrison, Royden, 'The Land and Labour League', *International Institute of Social History Bulletin*, 8 (1953), pp. 169–95.

Head, Henry, *Studies in Neurology* (2 vols), Oxford University Press/Hodder & Stoughton, 1920.

Hearnshaw, L.S., *Cyril Burt, Psychologist*, Random House, New York, 1981.

Hewitt, Margaret and Pinchbeck, Ivy, *Children in English Society*, vol.2, Routledge & Kegan Paul, 1973.

Hinton, James, *Labour and Socialism: A History of the British Labour Movement, 1867–1974*, Wheatsheaf, Brighton.

Hobman, J.B., *David Eder, Memoirs of a Modern Pioneer*, Gollancz, 1945.

Hobsbawm, Eric, *The Age of Empire, 1895–1914*, Weidenfeld & Nicolson, 1987.

Hollis, Patricia, *Ladies Elect: Women in English Local Government, 1865–1914*, Clarendon Press, Oxford, 1987.

Holman, Henry, *Seguin and His Physiological Method of Education*, Pitman, 1914.

Homberger, Eric and Charmley, John, *The Troubled Face of Biography*, Macmillan, 1988.

Hopkins, Deian, 'The Socialist Press in Britain, 1890–1910', in George Boyce *et al*. (eds), *Newspaper History from the Seventeenth Century to the Present*, Constable, 1978, pp. 294–306.

Hopkins, Deian, 'The Labour Party Press', in Brown, K.D. (ed.), *The First Labour Party, 1906–1914*, Croom Helm, 1985.

Hopkins, Mary Alden, 'Psychoanalysis and Education', *Child Study*, April 1916.

Howell, David, *British Workers and the Independent Labour Party, 1886–1906*, Manchester University Press, Manchester, 1983.

Hurt, John, *Elementary Schooling and the Working Classes, 1860–1918*, Routledge & Kegan Paul, 1979.

Hutchins, B.L., and Harrison, A., *A History of Factory Legislation*, Cass, 1966.

Iggers, Georg G., *The Doctrine of Saint-Simon*, Schocken, New York, 1972.

Independent Labour Party, *Commercialism and Child Labour: City of London Branch Pamphlets No. 4*, City Branch of the ILP, London, 1900.

Independent Labour Party, *The Platform No. 19: Child Labour*, ILP, 1901.

Independent Labour Party, *The Platform No. 58: The Slaughter of the Innocents*, ILP, 1902.

Independent Labour Party, *The Platform No. 24: Education: A Socialist's Idea*, ILP, 1907.

Independent Labour Party, *Commonsense Politics, No. 9: A Socialist View of Education*, ILP, 1909.

Ionescu, Ghita, *The Political Thought of Saint-Simon*, Oxford University Press, Oxford, 1976.

Jackson, Hughlings, *Neurological Fragments*, Oxford University Press, 1925.

Jeffreys, Sheila, *The Spinster and Her Enemies: Feminism and Sexuality, 1880–1930*, Pandora, 1985.

Jelinek, Estelle C. (ed.), *Women's Autobiography: Essays in Criticism*, Indiana University Press, Bloomington, 1980.

Jewson, Edith Mary, 'The Advent Angels in Deptford: Miss Margaret McMillan and Her Work', *Christian Commonwealth*, 6 December 1911.

Jolly, William, *Ruskin on Education, Some Needed But Neglected Elements*, George Allen, 1894.

Jones, Ernest, 'Psycho-Analysis and Education', *School Hygiene*, February 1911.

Jones, Ernest, 'The Unconscious Mental Life of the Child', *Child Study*, April, May 1916.

Jones, Peter, d'A., *The Christian Socialist Revival, 1877–1914*, Princeton University Press, Princeton, 1968.

Jopling, Louise, *Twenty Years of My Life, 1867–1887*, John Lane, 1925.

Jordan, Thomas E., *Victorian Childhood, Themes and Variations*, State University of New York Press, Albany, 1987.

Kamin, Leon J., *The Science and Politics of IQ*, Penguin, 1977.

Kerr, James, 'Physical Inspection', *Journal of the Royal Sanitary Institute*, 26 (1905).

Kerr, James, *Fundamentals of School Health*, Allen & Unwin, 1926.

Kerr, James, 'Physical Standards for Teachers', in Medical Officers of Schools Association, *Annual Proceedings and Report*, 1935.

Kirk, Mrs Florence, *Old English Games and Physical Exercises*, Longmans, Green, 1906.

Kropotkin, Peter, *An Appeal to the Young* (trans. H.M. Hyndman), The Modern Press, 1885.

Lane, Harlan, *The Wild Boy of Aveyron*, Paladin, 1979.

Lawrence, E.P., *Henry George in the British Isles*, Michigan State University Press, East Lansing, 1957.

Laybourn, Keith, '"The Defence of the Bottom Dog": The Independent Labour Party in Local Politics', in Wright, D.G. and Jowett, J.A., *Victorian Bradford, Essays in Honour of Jack Reynolds*, City of Bradford Metropolitan Council, Bradford, 1981.

Laybourn, Keith, 'The Issue of School Feeding in Bradford, 1904–1907', *Journal of Educational Administration and History*, 14:2 (July 1982), pp.30–39.

Laybourn, Keith and Reynolds, Jack, *Liberalism and the Rise of Labour, 1890–1918*, Croom Helm, 1984.

Lee, A.J., *The Origins of the Popular Press in England, 1855–1914*, Croom Helm, 1976.

Lees, Andrew, *Cities Perceived: Urban Society in European and American Thought*, Manchester University Press, Manchester, 1985.

Lewis, Jane, *The Politics of Motherhood: Child and Maternal Welfare in England, 1900–1939*, Croom Helm, 1980.

Lewis, Jane, *Women in England, 1870–1950: Sexual Divisions and Social Change*, Wheatsheaf, Brighton, 1984.

Liddington, Jill and Norris, Jill, *One Hand Tied Behind Us: The Rise of the Women's Suffrage Movement*, Virago, 1978.

'Lily Bell', 'The Apotheosis of Woman', *Labour Leader*, 26 December 1896.

Lord, Miriam, *Margaret McMillan in Bradford: Fourth Margaret McMillan Lecture*, University of London Press for the Margaret McMillan Fellowship, 1957.

Lowndes, George, *Margaret McMillan, The Children's Champion*, Museum Press, 1960.

McCann, Philip and Young, Francis A., *Samuel Wilderspin and the Infant School Movement*, Croom Helm, 1982.

McCleary, G.F., *The Maternity and Child Welfare Movement*, P.S. King, 1935.

McCleary, G.F., *The Early History of the Infant Welfare Movement*, H.K. Lewis, 1933.

MacDonald, Ramsay, 'Socialism and Society', in Barker, B. (ed.), *Ramsay MacDonald's Political Writings*, Allen Lane, 1972.

MacKillop, I.D., *The British Ethical Societies*, Cambridge University Press, Cambridge, 1986.

Maguire, Tom, *Tom Maguire: A Remembrance*, *Labour Leader* Office, Glasgow, 1895.

Mallon, J.F., 'The Portrait Gallery: Miss Margaret McMillan', *Woman Worker*, 5 June 1908.

Mannin, Ethel, *Confessions and Impressions*, Jarrolds, 1930.

Mansbridge, Albert, 'Educational Causerie', *Co-operative News*, 8 January 1910.

Mansbridge, Albert, *An Adventure in Working Class Education*, Longmans, Green, 1920.

Mansbridge, Albert, *Margaret McMillan, Prophet and Pioneer: Her Life and Work*, Dent, 1932.

Mansbridge, Albert, *The Trodden Road*, Dent, 1940.

Marcus, Laura, '"Enough about you, let's talk about me": Recent Autobiographical Writing', *New Formations*, 1 (Spring 1987), pp. 77–94.

Marenholtz-Buelow, Bertha Maria von, *Women's Educational Mission, Being an Exploration of Friedrich Froebel's System of Infant Gardens*, Dalton, 1855.

Martyn, Caroline, 'Politeness', *Labour Leader*, 14 September 1895.

Mavor, James, *My Window on the Street of the World* (2 vols), Dent, 1923.

Meredith, Sheila, 'Margaret McMillan and Her Work in Deptford, 1910–1931', *Transactions of the Lewisham Local History Society*, 1980.

Michel, Louise, 'Why We Are Anarchists', *Commonweal*, 26 September 1891.

Mink, Lewis, O., 'Everyman His or Her Own Annalist', *Critical Inquiry*, 7:4 (1981), pp. 777–83.

Mitton, G.E. (ed.), *Englishwoman's Year Book and Directory*, Adam & Charles Black, 1914.

Montefiore, Dora B., *From a Victorian to a Modern*, E. Archer, 1927.

Montessori, Maria, *The Montessori Method*, Heinemann, 1914.

Moretti, Franco, 'Kindergarten', in *Signs Taken for Wonders*, Verso, 1983.

Moretti, Franco, *The Way of the World: The Bildungsroman in European Culture*, Verso, 1987.

Morgan, Kenneth O., *Labour People*, Oxford University Press, Oxford, 1987.

Morley, Henry, 'Infant Gardens', *Household Words*, 21 July 1855.

Morris, John, *Versions of the Self: Studies in English Biography from John Bunyan to John Stuart Mill*, Basic Books, New York, 1966.

Morris, Ronald, *Success and Failure in Learning to Read*, Penguin, 1973.

Morrisson, Arthur, *Tales of Mean Streets*, Methuen, 1894.

Morrisson, Arthur, *Child of the Jago*, Methuen, 1896.

Muirhead, J.H., 'The Founders of Child Study in England', *Paidologist*, 2:2 (July 1900).

Neale, Steve, 'Melodrama and Tears', *Screen*, 27:6 (November/December 1986).

Newman, Sir George, *The Health of the Young Child on Admission to School*, reprinted by HMSO for the Nursery School Association, 1928.

Nursery School Association of Great Britain, *Historical Record of the Nursery School Association of Great Britain from 1923–1944*, 1944.

Oppenheim, Janet, *The Other World: Spiritualism and Psychical Research in England, 1850–1914*, Cambridge University Press, Cambridge, 1985.

Ovenden, Graham and Melville, Robert, *Victorian Children*, Academy Editions, 1972.

Owen, Grace (ed.), *Nursery School Education*, Methuen, 1920.

Paget, Stephen, *Sir Victor Horsley, A Study of His Life and Work*, Constable, 1919.

Palin, J.H., *Bradford and Its Children: How They Are Fed*, ILP, n.d.

Palin, J.H., 'Our Educational System: Medical Inspection and Treatment', *Highway*, August 1913.

Pankhurst, E.S., *The Suffragette Movement*, (1931), Virago, 1977.

Pascal, Roy, *Design and Truth in Autobiography*, Routledge & Kegan Paul, 1960.

Pattison, Robert, *The Child Figure in English Literature*, University of Georgia Press, Athens, 1978.

Peterson, Jeanne M., 'The Victorian Governess: Status Incongruence in Family and Society', *Victorian Studies*, 14:1 (1970), pp. 7–26.

Peterson, Linda H., *Victorian Autobiography*, Yale University Press, New Haven, 1986.

Pfistes, Oscar, 'Psychoanalysis and Child-Study', *School Hygiene*, July 1911.

Phillips, Shelley, 'Maria Montessori and Cognitive Psychology', *British Journal of Teacher Education*, 3:1 (January 1977), pp. 55–68.

Pickering, Paul A., 'Class Without Words: Symbolic Communication in the Chartist Movement', *Past and Present*, 112 (August 1986), pp. 144–62.

Pierson, Stanley, 'John Trevor and the Labour Church Movement in England, 1891–1900', *Church History*, 29:4 (December 1960), pp. 463–78.

Pierson, Stanley, *Marxism and the Origins of British Socialism*, Cornell University Press, New York, 1973.

Potts, Patricia, 'Medicine, Morals and Mental Deficiency: the contribution of doctors to the development of special education in England', *Oxford Review of Education*, 9:3 (1983), pp. 181–96.

'P.R.', 'At the Deptford Health Centre', *Wheatsheaf*, September 1913.

Pugh, Martin, 'Labour and Women's Suffrage', in Brown, K.D. (ed.), *The First Labour Party, 1906–1914*, Croom Helm, 1985.

Redfern, Percy, 'People and Books: Margaret McMillan', *Wheatsheaf*, May 1932.

Redfern, Percy, *Journey to Understanding*, George Allen & Unwin, 1946.

Rée, Jonathan, *Proletarian Philosophers, Problems in Socialist Culture in Britain, 1900–1940*, Clarendon Press, Oxford, 1984.

Reid, Fred, *Keir Hardie, The Making of a Socialist*, Croom Helm, 1978.

Reid, Andrew (ed.), *The New Party*, Hodder, 1895.

Reid, F., 'Socialist Sunday Schools in Britain, 1892–1939', *International Review of Social History*, 11 (1966), pp. 18–47.

Reynolds, J. and Laybourn, K., 'The Emergence of the Independent Labour Party in Bradford', *International Review of Social History*, 20 (1975), pp. 313–46.

Ricoeur, Paul, *Time and Narrative*, University of Chicago Press, Chicago, 1984.

Roberts, Robert, 'Board Schools and Ethical Education', *Ethical World*, 25 August 1900.

Roberts, Robert, 'The People's Schools', *Labour Leader*, 5 January 1901.

Robinson, Jane, *An Evaluation of Health Visiting*, Council for the Education and Training of Health Visitors, 1982.

Rowan, Caroline, 'Women in the Labour Party, 1906–1920', *Feminist Review*, 12 (October 1982).

Rowan, Caroline, 'Child Welfare and the Working Class Family', in Langan, Mary and Schwarz, Bill (eds), *Crisis in the British State*, Hutchinson in Association with the Centre for Contemporary Cultural Studies, 1985.

Rowe, Richard, *Life in the London Streets*, Nimmo & Bain, 1881.

Rowntree, B. Seebohm, *Poverty, A Study of Town Life*, (1901), Nelson, 1904.

Ruskin, John, 'Sesame and Lilies', (1865), vol. 18 of *The Library Edition of the Works of John Ruskin*, Allen & Unwin, 1905.

Ruskin, John, 'Humility', from 'Time and Tide' (1867), vol. 22 of *The Library Edition of the Works of John Ruskin*, Allen & Unwin, 1906.

Ruskin, John, 'Design in the German Schools,' from 'Ariadne Florentia' (1874), vol. 22 of *The Library Edition of the Works of John Ruskin*, Allen & Unwin, 1906.

Ruskin, John, 'Fors Clavigera', Letters 37–72, vol. 28 of *The Library Edition of the Works of John Ruskin*, Allen & Unwin, 1907.

Ruskin, John, 'Fairyland', from 'The Art of England' (1884), vol. 33 of *The Library Edition of the Works of John Ruskin*, Allen & Unwin, 1908.

Ruskin, John, 'Proserpina', vol. 1 (1879), vol. 35 of *The Library Edition of the Works of John Ruskin*, Allen & Unwin, 1909.

Sanitary Institute, *Examinations in Sanitary Science for Local Surveyors and Inspectors of Nuisances*, Sanitary Institute, 1892.

Saville, John, 'Henry George and the British Labour Movement', *Bulletin of the Society for the Study of Labour History*, 5 (1962), pp. 18–26.

Schults, R.L., *Crusader in Babylon: W.T. Stead and the Pall Mall Gazette*, University of Nebraska Press, Lincoln, 1972.

Seaborne, Malcolm and Low, Roy, *The English School, Its Architecture and Organisation, vol. 2, 1870–1970*, Routledge & Kegan Paul, 1977.

Seguin, Édouard, *Traitement moral, hygiène, et éducation des idiots*, Baillière, Paris, 1846.

Seguin, Édouard, *Idiocy and Its Treatment by the Physiological Method* (1866), Augustus M. Kelly, New York, 1971.

Seguin, Édouard, *Rapport et mémoire sur l'éducation des enfants normaux et anormaux*, Bibliothèque d'Éducation Spéciale III, Alcan, Paris, 1895.

Seguin, Édouard, *Report on Education* (1875), Scholars' Facsimiles & Reprints, Delmar, New York, 1976.

Shapiro, Michael Steven, *The Child's Garden: The Kindergarten Movement from Froebel to Dewey*, Pennsylvania State University Press, University Park, 1983.

Silver, Harold, *Education as History*, Methuen, 1983.

Simon, Brian, *Education and the Labour Movement, 1870–1920*, Lawrence & Wishart, 1965.

Simon, Brian, *Intelligence, Psychology and Education*, Lawrence & Wishart, 1971.

Slaughter, J.W., 'Labour and Childhood: The Books of Margaret McMillan', *Highway*, December 1908, January 1909.

Spiller, G., *The Ethical Movement in Great Britain: A Documentary History*, printed for the author at the Farleigh Press, 1934.

Stacey, Enid, 'Women's Work and the ILP', *Labour Annual* (ed. Joseph Edwards), Labour Press, Manchester, 1895.

Stacey, Enid, 'A Century of Women's Rights', in Carpenter, Edward (ed.), *Forecasts of the Coming Century*, Labour Press, Manchester, 1897.

Stacpoole, V., *The Beach of Dreams, A Romance*, John Lane, New York, 1919.

Starr, G.A., *Defoe and Spiritual Autobiography*, Gordion Press, New York, 1971.

Stauffer, D.A., *English Biography Before 1700*, Russell & Russell, 1964.

Stedman Jones, Gareth, 'Rethinking Chartism', in *Languages of Class, Studies in English Working Class History, 1932–1982*, Cambridge University Press, Cambridge, 1983.

Steedman, Carolyn, *The Tidy House*, Virago, 1982.

Steedman, Carolyn, 'Prisonhouses', *Feminist Review*, 20 (Summer 1985), pp. 7–21.

Steedman, Carolyn, 'The "Mother Made Conscious": The Historical Development of a Primary School Project', *History Workshop Journal*, 20 (Autumn 1985), pp. 149–63.

Stevinson, Emma, *The Open-Air Nursery School*, Dent, 1923.

Stevinson, Emma, *Margaret McMillan, Prophet and Pioneer: Second Margaret McMillan Lecture*, University of London Press for the Margaret McMillan Fellowship, 1954.

Strachey, Ray, *The Cause* (1928), Virago, 1988.

Stuart, Dennis, *Dear Duchess: Millicent Duchess of Sutherland, 1867–1955*, Gollancz, 1982.

Sutherland, Millicent, *One Hour and the Next*, Methuen, 1899.

Sutherland, Duke of, *Looking Back*, Odhams, 1957.

Talbot, Mabel E., *Édouard Seguin: A Study of an Educational Approach to the Treatment of Mentally Defective Children, Bureau of Publications, Teachers' College, New York, 1964.

Taylor, Ann, *Laurence Oliphant, 1829–1888*, Oxford University Press, Oxford, 1982.

Taylor, Keith, *The Political Ideas of the Utopian Socialists*, Cass, 1982.

Thomas, Edith, *Louise Michel*, Gallimard, Paris, 1971.

Thomson, John and Smith, Adolphe, *Street Life in London*, privately printed, 1877.

Thompson, Barbara, 'Public Provision and Private Neglect: Public Health in Bradford', in Wright, D.G. and Jowitt, J.A. (eds), *Victorian Bradford*, City of Bradford Metropolitan Council, Bradford, 1981.

Thompson, E.P., 'Homage to Tom Maguire', in Briggs, Asa and Saville, John (eds), *Essays in Labour History*, Macmillan, 1960.

Thompson, Laurence, *Robert Blatchford, Portrait of an Englishman*, Gollancz, 1951.

Thompson, Laurence, *The Enthusiasts: A Biography of John and Katharine Bruce Glasier*, Gollancz, 1971.

Thompson, Paul, *Socialists, Liberals and Labour: The Struggle for London, 1885–1914*, Routledge & Kegan Paul, 1967.

Thwaite, Ann, *Waiting for the Party, The Life of Frances Hodgson Burnett*, Secker & Warburg, 1974.

Trevor, John, *My Quest for God*, Labour Prophet Office, 1897.

Tribe, Reginald, 'An East End Clinic', *Child Life*, December 1910.

Tribe, Reginald, 'Results of Treatment at the Popular School Clinic', *School Hygiene*, May 1911.

Tribe, Reginald, 'The Banner of Science', *Labour Leader: May Day Special*, 29 April 1910.

Tribe, Reginald, *The Christian Social Tradition*, SPCK, 1935.

Venn, Couze, 'The Subject of Psychology', in Henriques, Jules *et al.* (eds), *Changing the Subject*, Methuen, 1984.

Verney, R.F. (ed.), *In Memory of Margaret Maria, Lady Verney*, Garden City Press, Letchworth, 1930.

Villiers, Brougham (ed.), *The Case for Woman's Suffrage*, Fisher Unwin, 1908.

Vincent, David, *Bread, Knowledge and Freedom, A Study of Nineteenth Century Working Class Autobiography*, Methuen, 1982.

Vicinus, Martha, *Independent Women: Work and Community for Single Women, 1850–1920*, Virago, 1985.

Vogel, Ursula, 'The Land-Question: A Liberal Theory of Communal Property', *History Workshop Journal*, 27 (Spring 1989), pp.106–35.

Walkowitz, Judy, *Prostitution and Victorian Society*, Cambridge University Press, 1980.

Warner, Marina, *Joan of Arc, The Image of Female Heroism*, Weidenfeld & Nicolson, 1981.

Weintraub, Karl J., 'Autobiography and Historical Consciousness', *Critical Inquiry*, 1 (1975), pp.821–48.

West, Rebecca, 'A Quiet Day with the Constitutionals', *Clarion*, 1 August 1913.

White, Arnold, *Problems of a Great City*, Remington, 1886.

White, Arnold, *Industry and Empire*, Methuen, 1901.
Whitbread, Nanette, *The Evolution of the Nursery-Infant School: A History of Infant and Nursery Education in Britain, 1800–1970*, Routledge & Kegan Paul, 1972.
Whyte, Lancelot Law, *The Unconscious Before Freud*, Friedmann, 1979.
Williams-Freeman, John Pearce, *The Effect of Town Life on General Health*, W.H. Allen, 1890.
Williams, Raymond, *The Long Revolution*, Chatto & Windus, 1961.
Williams, Raymond, *The Country and the City*, Paladin, 1973.
Williams, Raymond, *Marxism and Literature*, Oxford University Press, Oxford, 1977.
Williams, Raymond, *Problems in Materialism and Culture*, Verso, 1980.
Williams, Raymond, *Writing in Society*, Verso, n.d. (1981).
Williams, Raymond, *Orwell*, Fontana, 1984.
Williams, Raymond, *Culture and Society*, (1958), Hogarth Press, 1987.
Women Sanitary Inspectors' Association, *Women's Place in Sanitary Administration: A Paper Read on November 25, 1904, by T. Orme, M.D.*, Adlard & Son, 1904.
Women's Labour League, *The Needs of Little Children: Report of a Conference on the Care of Babies and Children*, WLL, (Central London Branch), 1912.
Woodham-Smith, P., 'History of the Froebel Movement in England', in Lawrence, Evelyn (ed.), *Friedrich Froebel and English Education*, Routledge & Kegan Paul, 1969.
Wright, Peter W.G., 'Babyhood: the Social Construction of Infant Care as a Medical Problem in England', in Lock, M. and Gordon, D. (eds), *Biomedicine Examined* (forthcoming).
Yeo, Stephen, 'A New Life: The Religion of Socialism in Britain, 1883–1896', *History Workshop Journal*, 4 (Autumn 1977), pp.5–56.
Young, Robert M., 'Biography: The Basic Discipline for Human Science', *Free Associations*, 11 (1988), pp.108–30.
Zévaès, Anne, *Louise Michel*, Paris, 1936.
Zelizer, Viviana A., *Pricing the Priceless Child: The Changing Social Value of Children*, Basic Books, New York, 1985.
Zusne, Leonard, *Biographical Dictionary of Psychology*, Aldwych Press, 1984.

IV   Journals and Periodicals

Child Life: A Kindergarten Journal, 1891–2, continued as *Child Life Quarterly*, 1899–1934.
Journal of the Sanitary Institute, 1894–1904.
Journal of the Royal Sanitary Institute, 1904–54.
The Highway: A Monthly Journal of Education for the People, August 1908– .
The Lyceum Banner: A Monthly Journal for Conductors, Leaders and Members of the Children's Progressive Lyceum Throughout the World, 1890– .

New Age: A Weekly Record of Christian Culture, Social Service & Literary Life, 1894– .

School Hygiene: A Monthly Review for Educationalists and Doctors, 1910– .

The Two Worlds, November 1887– .

The Woman Worker, 1908–10. This became *Women Folk* (ed. Winifred Blatchford) until 1911, when a new series of the *Woman Worker* was edited by Mary MacArthur and Susan Lawrence.

V   Theses and Other Unpublished Material

Barrow, Logie, 'The Socialism of Robert Blatchford and the *Clarion*', Ph.D, University of London, 1975.

Bullock, Ian, 'Socialists and Democratic Form in Britain, 1880–1914', Ph.D, University of Sussex, 1981.

Cunningham, Hugh, 'Slaves or Savages? Some Attitudes to Labouring Children, 1750–1870', unpublished paper, 1987.

Dodd, Kathryn, 'Historians, The Evidence of Texts, and Ray Strachey's *The Cause*', unpublished paper, 1987.

Gilray, John, 'Early Days of the Socialist Movement in Edinburgh, by John Gilray', National Library of Scotland, Acc. 4965.

Hopkins, D.R., 'The Newspapers of the Independent Labour Party, 1893–1906', Ph.D, University College of Wales, 1981.

Oldenziel, Ruth, 'Gender, Self and the Writing of Biography', a paper presented to the International Conference of Women's History, Amsterdam, 1986.

Ransom, Bernard Campbell, 'James Connolly and the Scottish Left, 1890–1916', Ph.D, University of Edinburgh, 1975.

Ross, W.D., 'Bradford Politics, 1880–1906', Ph.D, Bradford University, 1977.

Smith, Donald C., 'The Failure and Recovery of Social Criticism in the Scottish Churches, 1830–1850', Ph.D, University of Edinburgh, 1963.

Waters, Chris, '"Masculine Socialism" and the Development of Women's Columns in the British Socialist Press, 1884–1914', unpublished paper, 1986.

VI   Official and Other Published Reports
(The abbreviation PP here indicates the Parliamentary Paper Series.)

Reports from Commissioners Inquiring into Children's Employment, PP 1842, xvii; 1843, xiv.

Reports of the Commissioners on Employment of Children in Trades and Manufactures Not Already Regulated by Law, PP 1863, xviii; 1864, xxii; 1865, xx; 1866, xxiv; 1867, xvi.

Report of the Commission of Inquiry into the Employment of Women and Children in Agriculture (1867), PP 1867–8, xvii.

Report of the Commissioners, Interdepartmental Commission on Physical Deterioration, PP 1904, xxxii.

Reports of the Conference of the Independent Labour Party, annually from 1893.

Reports of the Conference of the Labour Party, annually from 1906.

Index

childhood in Westchester County, 17–18; education, 20; friendship with the Duchess of Sutherland, 140; friendship with Nancy Astor, 7, 59; ill-health, 50–51; in Inverness, 18–21; interest in theosophy, 122–3; life in Bradford, 27, 35, 40–51, 53–4, 102–4, 120; life in London, 33, 51, 99–101, 114–20; personality and reputation, 226–39; reaction to Rachel's death, 31; sexuality, 123–5, 236; spiritual occurrence, 21–2, 253–4; stage training, 216, 232, 251; studies music in Frankfurt, 21, 126; death, 61

work with children: Bow Clinic, 52, 53; Deptford camp school, 83–97; Deptford Clinic, 30–31, 53; as a finishing governess, 21, 27; improvement of children's bodies, 198–202; interest in child feeding, 110–12; interest in language development, 211–14; medical inspection of children, 53–7, 138; Seguin's influence on, 193–4, 195–8; theories of child development, 189–93, 195–8; theory of the voice, 215–25; theory of working-class childhood, 108; and transformation of meaning of childhood, 62–8; understanding of children's minds, 203–14

work in education: adult education, 177–84; on Bradford School Board, 28, 38–9, 41–51, 134–5; education policy, 166–70; expertise on nursery education, 57–61; on Froebel Society executive, 52; and the Socialist Sunday Schools, 175–7; as a teacher, 183–4; teacher training, 184–7; on WEA Executive Committee, 52

politics: and the Belt/Montefiore scandal, 128; contact with working class, 164–5; role in the ILP, 4, 47, 156, 161; origins of her political thought, 162–3; political lectures, 35; skill as an orator, 47–8, 124, 158, 216, 228–9, 233–5; socialism, 35, 156–7, 158–70; and the suffrage movement, 135–8; supposed loss of political faith, 161; work for London Ethical Society, 51–2

writings: fiction about children, 68–80, 105; novel, 104–5; reworking of her childhood in, 10, 71–3; sensuality in, 112, 113; sentimental child-figures, 153–5; use of allegory, 142, 144–7; use of dialect, 119–20, 222–3; journalism, 33–5, 43–4, 47, 142–7, 150–53; lectures, 104; the *Life* as her autobiography, 6, 30–31, 32, 139, 243; *see also individual articles and books*

McMillan, Rachel (McMillan's sister), 4, 114; birth, 17; conversion to socialism, 23–6, 29, 173; death, 31, 57, 221; and the

Deptford Clinic, 30–31; health visiting, 28, 29, 88, 135; and the *Life of Rachel McMillan*, 6, 21–32, 202, 229, 254; in London, 125; nurses her grandmother, 21, 23; teaching career, 20, 21; trains as sanitary inspector, 27–8; work in London, 27

McMillan Collection, 226
magazines, 149–50
Mallon, J.F., 238
Manchester, 35, 101, 110, 132, 137, 153, 174
Mann, Tom, 228
Manningham Mills, 35, 36, 41
Mansbridge, Albert, 58, 233; biography of McMillan, 5, 6–7, 17, 19–20, 21, 30, 158, 181, 188, 200, 202, 226–8, 236, 252; on McMillan's voices, 225; and the WEA, 52, 173, 180, 181
Marlowe, Christopher, 89
Martyn, Caroline, 39, 131, 152, 158, 233
Marx, Karl, 178, 179; *Das Kapital*, 26, 160
Marxism, 179
Mary, Queen, 61
'Mary Muse', 33, 68, 100, 144, 202, 254–5
'Mary's Lover', 255–6
materialism, 190
Mayhew, Henry, 65
Mazzini, Giuseppe, 175
medical inspection of schoolchildren, 53–7, 138, 170–71
memoirs, 247
memory, 208
mental testing, 197
Meux, Lady, 101, 129–30, 140, 216
Michel, Louise, 122, 123, 129–30, 140, 143, 210
middle class, 136, 180
'Mignon of the slums', 76, 77–80, 89, 223
Mill, J.S., 178
mind, unconscious, 70, 97, 162, 191, 203–11, 217
'The Miner', 222
Mink, Louis O., 246
Mrs Humphrey Ward Settlement, 101
Montefiore, Dora, 128
Montessori, Maria, 194, 195, 197, 206, 212, 227
Morant, Sir Robert, 7, 55–6, 57, 165, 180, 229
Moretti, Franco, 74–5, 78, 239
Morgan, Kenneth, 157
Morris, William, 25, 113, 124, 173–4
Morrison, Arthur, 119
mothers: class differences, 122; and the Deptford camp school, 94–5; employment, and infant mortality rates, 107; in McMillan's writing, 119–20; maternal and child welfare movement, 94; politicisation of motherhood, 119; social motherhood, 134–5, 138; *see also* women

At the end of the nineteenth century, childhood acquired a new significance. Children – especially working-class children – became symbols of social hope, of a better and healthier future, of individuality and selfhood. Margaret McMillan, charismatic member of the Independent Labour Party and socialist propagandist, played a key role in this development through her writing, her political activism, and her work for the children of Bradford and Deptford. Taking her life and work as a starting point, *Childhood, Culture and Class in Britain* explores a profound transformation in Western sensibility, and looks at the psychological and political fate of this woman who gave up her life 'for the children'.

Carolyn Steedman was born in 1947 and grew up in South London. She studied history at Sussex and Newnham College Cambridge, and for eight years she was a primary-school teacher; she now works as a social historian and lecturer. She is the author of *The Tidy House* (Virago, 1982), winner of the Fawcett Society Book Award; *The Radical Soldier's Tale* (1988); *Landscape for a Good Woman* (Rutgers University Press, 1986); and *Policing the Victorian Community* (1984); and contributed to *Truth, Dare or Promise* (Virago, 1985). Carolyn Steedman is Senior Lecturer in Arts Education at the University of Warwick, and lives in Leamington Spa.